DRAWING ANIMAL PORTRAITS in COLOURED PENCIL

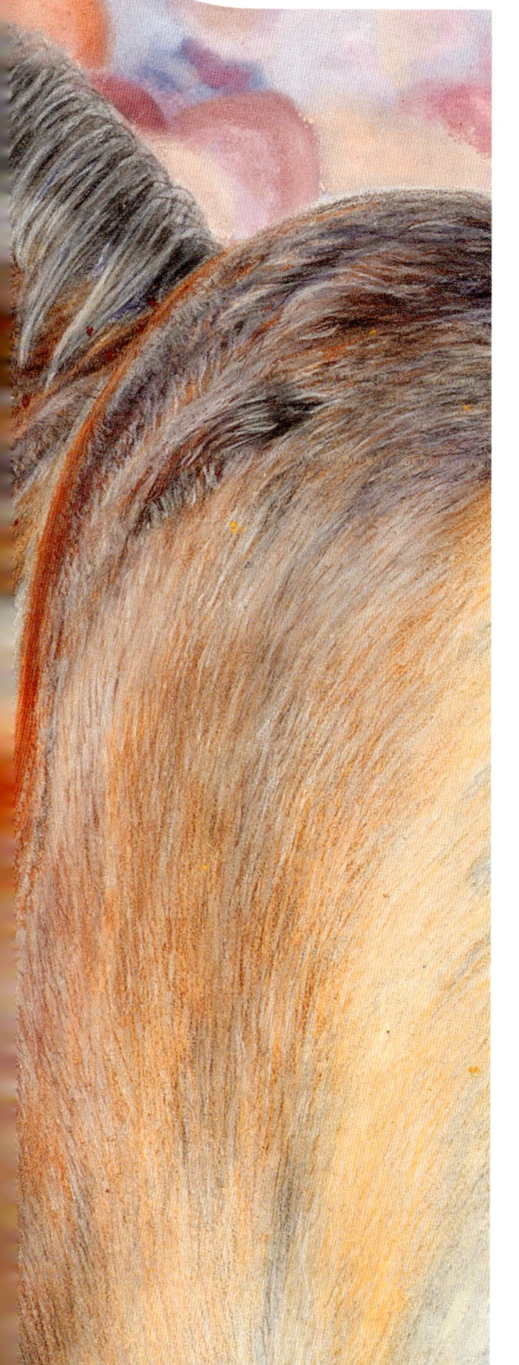

LISA ANN WATKINS

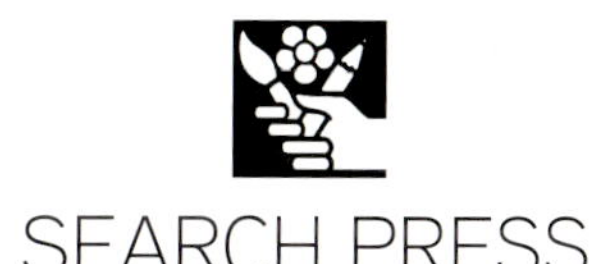

SEARCH PRESS

DRAWING ANIMAL PORTRAITS in COLOURED PENCIL

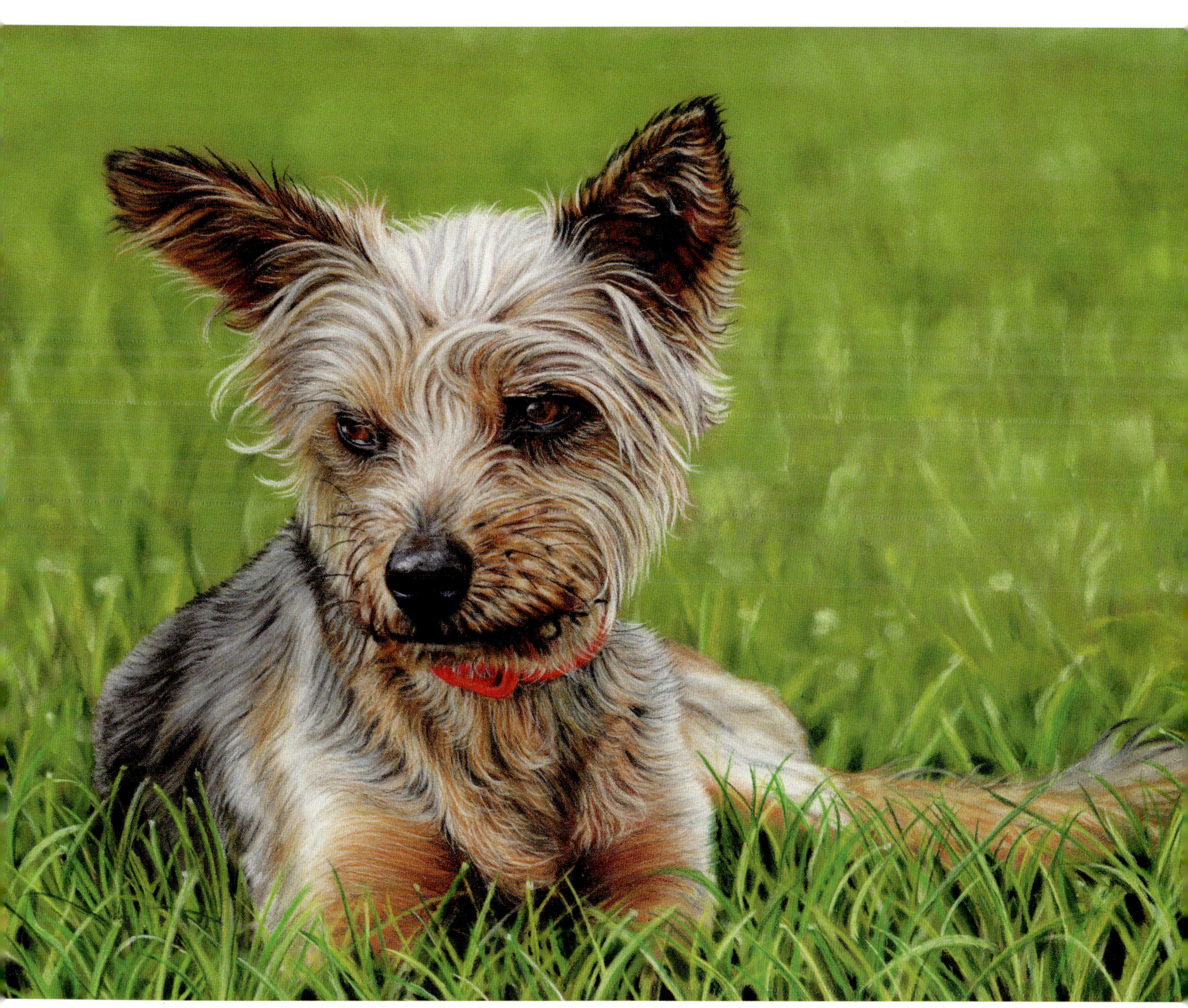

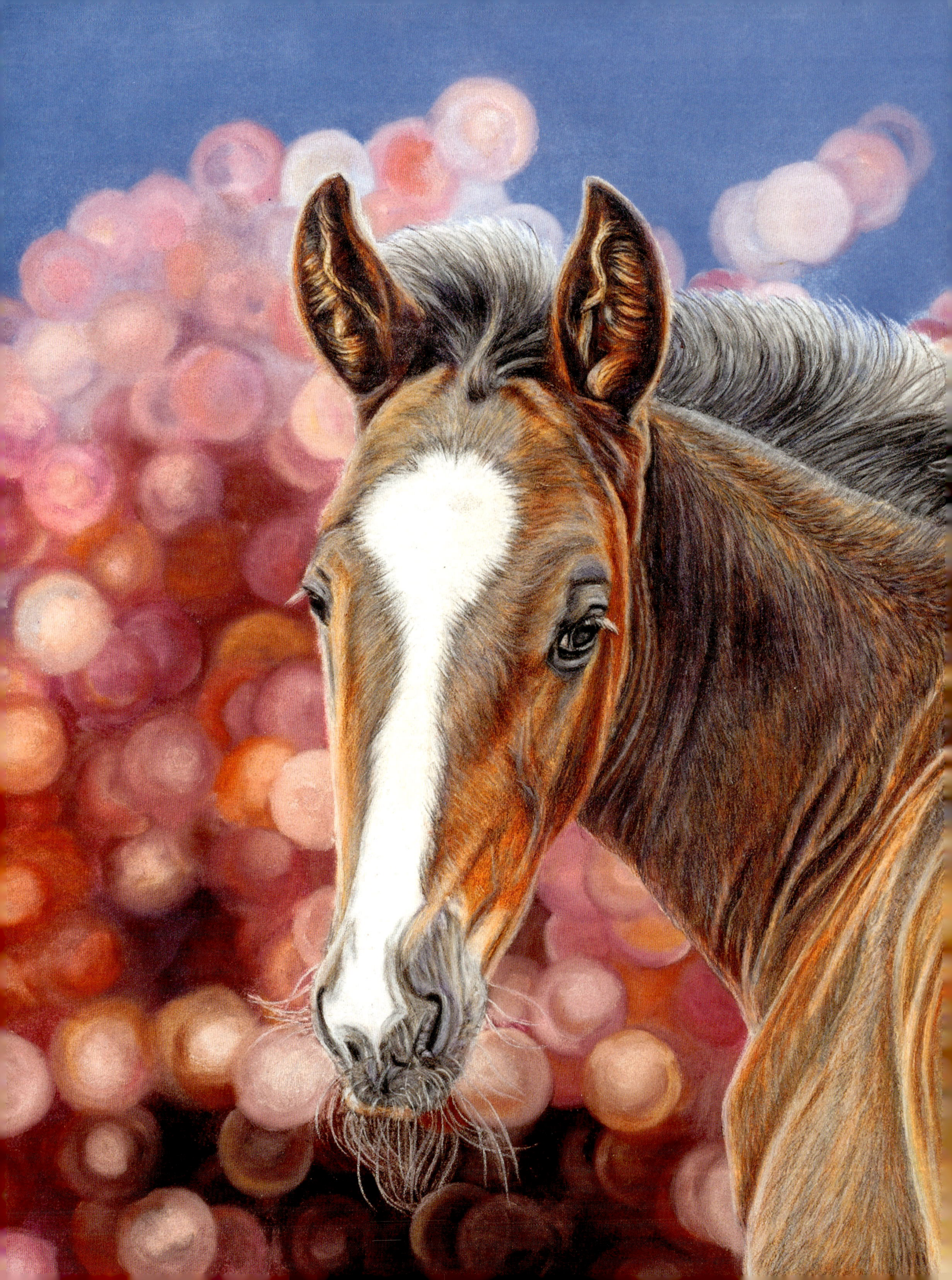

First published in 2022

Search Press Limited
Wellwood, North Farm Road,
Tunbridge Wells, Kent TN2 3DR

5 6 7 8 9 10

Bookmarked Hub
For further ideas and inspiration, and to join our free
online community, visit www.bookmarkedhub.com

Publishers' notes
The Publishers and author can accept no
responsibility for any consequences arising from
the information, advice or instructions given in
this publication.

For errata, please visit our website
(www.searchpress.com) or the Bookmarked Hub
(www.bookmarkedhub.com).

GPSR information can be found at
www.searchpress.com
Printed in China, AP102025

You are invited to visit the author's website:
www.animalartbylaw.co.uk

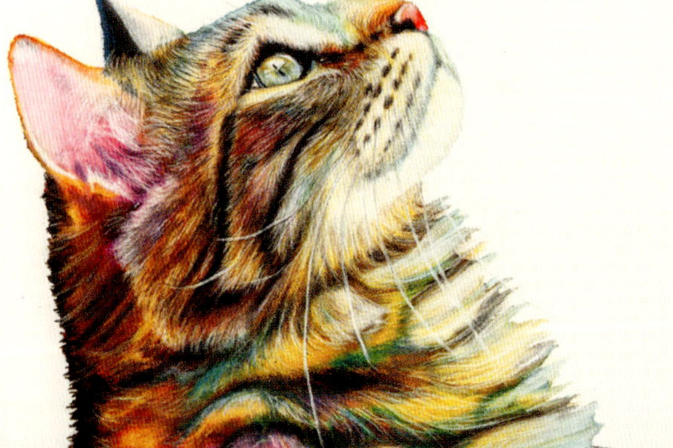

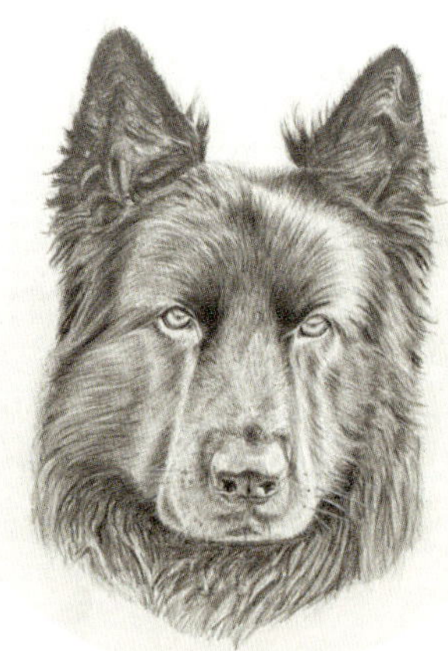

Dedication

I would like to dedicate this book to my husband Rob, who has not only been my rock throughout this process but is also the one who encouraged me to take that leap from hobby to career artist all those years ago.

I also could not have done this without the inspiration of all the animals that have allowed me to be part of their lives. This is for you too.

Acknowledgements

This book could never have come together without the magical touch of my editor, Edward Ralph, who guided me through this process. I am also so grateful to the team at Search Press for having faith in my work and my story to enable this book to become a reality.

My heartfelt thanks go to some very special friends who supported me along the way and helped me to stay on track behind the scenes.
Thank you Alan, Frank, Molly, Ceri,
Sue, Jill, Deb and Susan.

And, of course, I could not have done any of this without the wonderful support of all my patrons, students and followers. I hope that you enjoy what you see on the pages that follow.

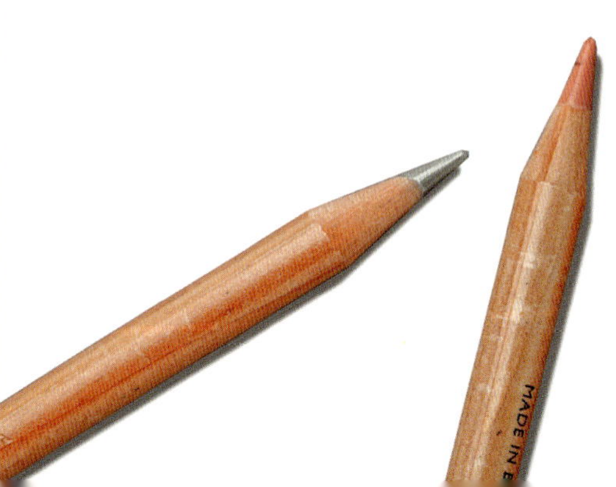

CONTENTS

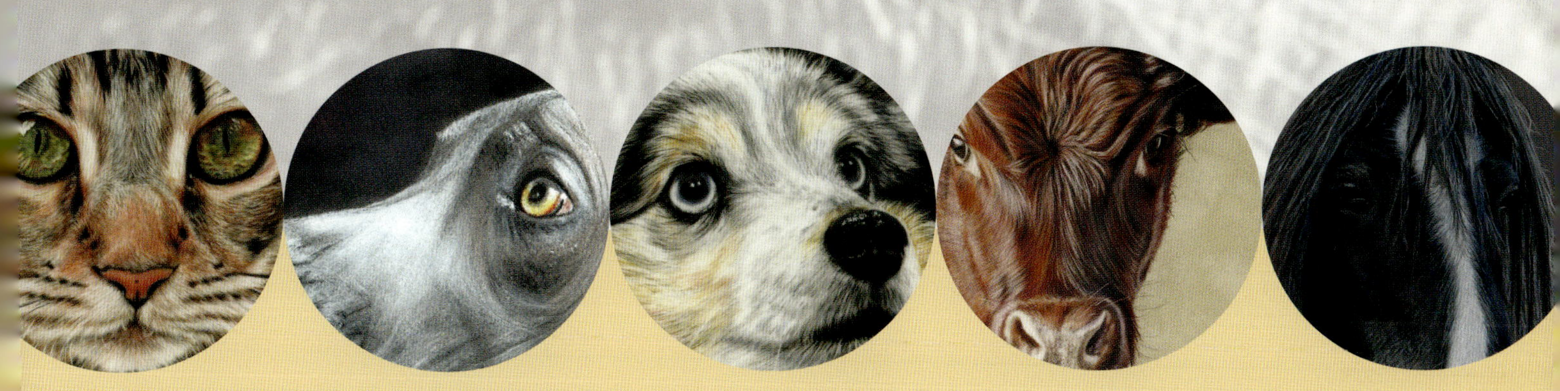

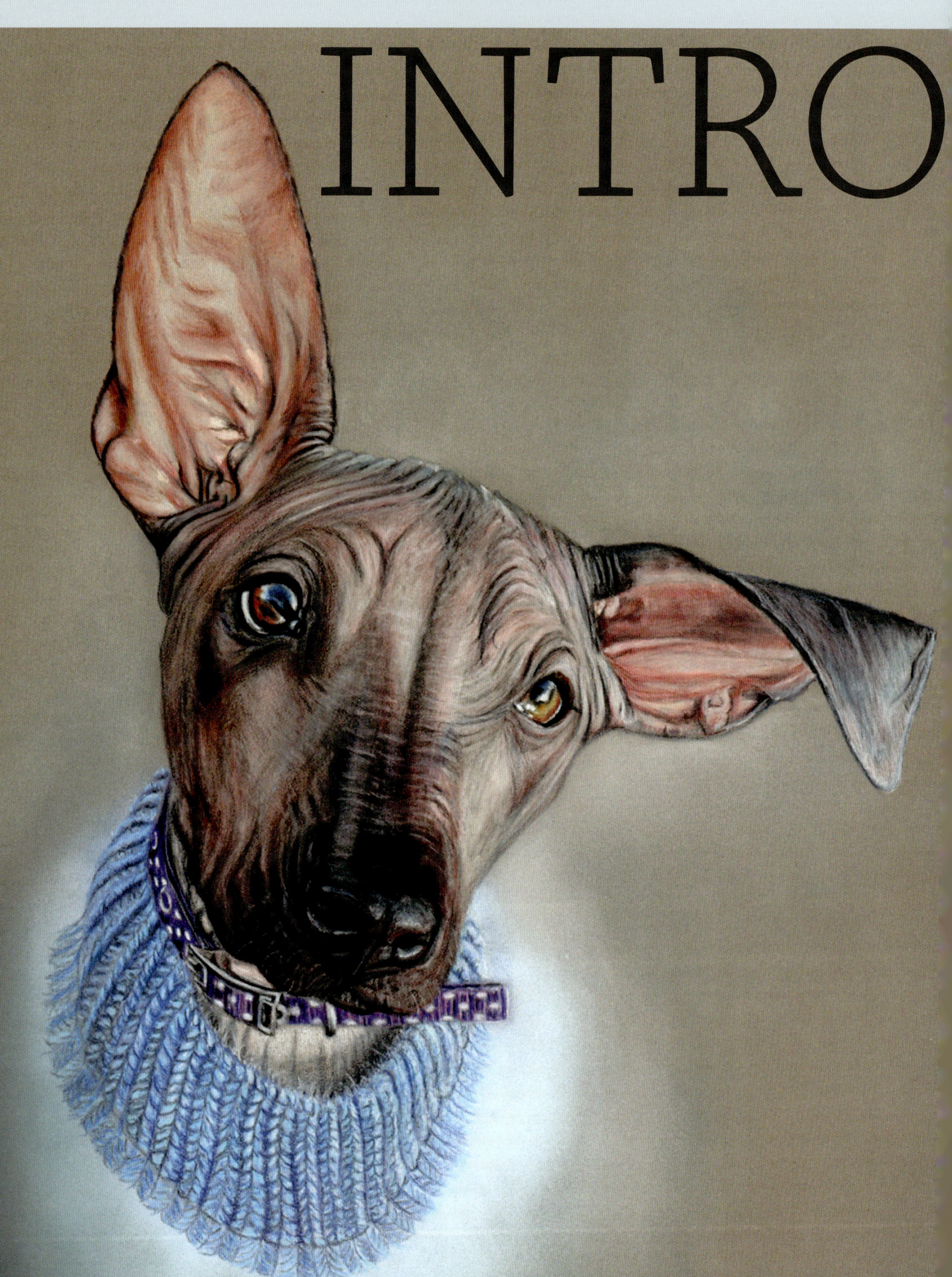

INTRO

DUCTION

Writing this book has allowed me to stop and take a moment to look back on my art journey. Before we begin, I would like to thank you for this opportunity to share my knowledge, my art and my techniques – and also to tell you my own story of art, in the hope that it helps you with your animal portraiture, and your artistic journey in general. I feel it is important to share where and why my story began. Parts of it will resonate with you, and I hope that it kindles a spark of creativity within you.

My creativity and passion for helping animals have been with me since childhood. Growing up in a village in Cornwall, UK, I remember drawing pictures of cats, dogs and horses and then knocking on doors to sell them for a few pennies, which I popped into my plastic flowerpot. This is my earliest memory of using my art to donate monies to help animals.

My education led me on a path towards becoming a maths teacher but then I rebelled and went with my passion of embracing my inner creative. Art college started out as an exciting adventure; but being told that I could 'neither see colour nor could I draw' meant that any joy quickly faded. I turned to flat textile and fashion design, but by the time I graduated, my creativity had been beaten into submission.

This was my first struggle with my mental health. For the next twenty years it was a repetitive spiral of giving my all to a new job – many exciting and interesting   but with my creativity under wraps, I would walk away from each in turn after a couple of years, then start the cycle over.

In 2011 the cycle culminated in a major breakdown. My boss at the time recognized that I needed help and sent me for counselling. I have always been a logical person and need to understand the 'whys' and the 'hows' – something that I believe comes across in my own teachings – and counselling changed my life. There I learned that there are three sides to our support triangle: family, work and creative. At the time, my mum had just had a heart attack; I had also lost my father when I was a teen. I had been throwing all my energy into work but there was no reward, so it had literally exhausted me. My support triangle had fallen over. The only thing left was to rediscover my creative. This was when I bought my first set of coloured pencils – a tin of 120 Faber-Castell Albrecht Dürers, in case you were wondering. The rest, as they say, is history.

LIFE-CHANGING ART

I jumped straight in and threw myself into this amazing world of creating – I felt that I had so much time to make up for. The discovery that I *could* draw and that my work *was* full of colour initially made me angry at those that had told me otherwise so many years before. The biggest and most life-changing part of it all, however, was the realization that my portrayal of the animals I loved were actually pretty darn good. I finally had a way of embracing my creative side, to the benefit of my own mental health and well-being. Not only this, but my art now gave me an opportunity to help the animal rescues that I supported behind the scenes. It not only allowed me to raise funds but it also gave those animals a voice. This will always be one of the core passions behind why I create art.

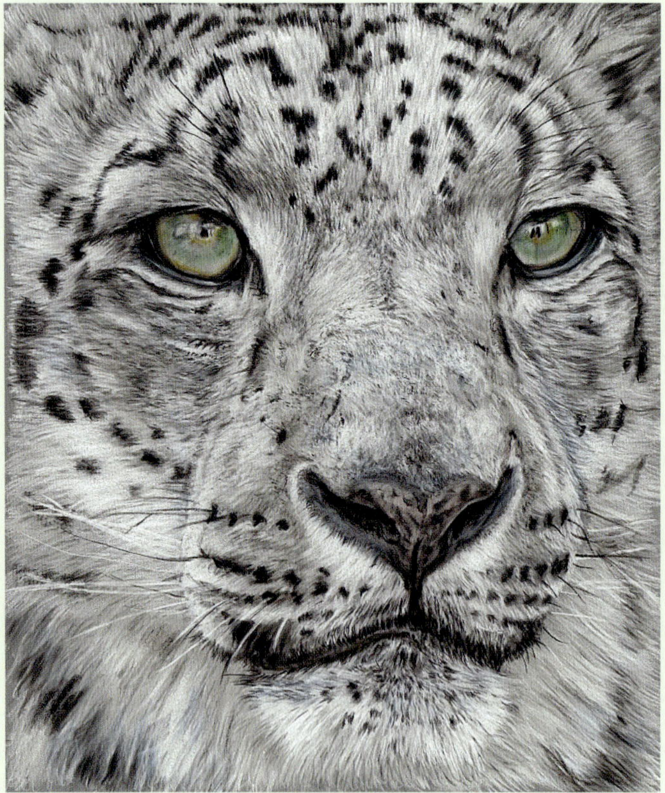

Snow Leopard
Coloured pencils on drafting film. My first animal portrait in coloured pencil and the one that changed my life! This won the beginner section in the *Colored Pencil Magazine* monthly challenge and its popularity led to me becoming an artist full time.

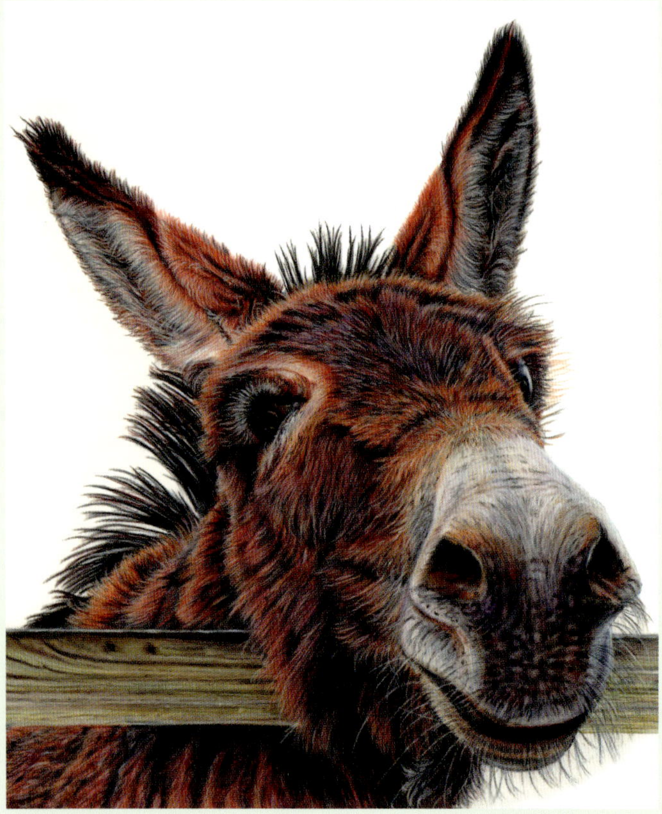

Hee Haw 2
Watercolour pencils on Pastelmat. For a while I found myself with the nickname 'the donkey lady' for the characterful renditions of these animals! This one was created as a tutorial to teach students how to use watercolour pencils wet and dry.

The purchase of that first set of pencils changed my future. Stepping outside of my comfort zone, I pushed hard to develop my skills with this new medium and entered a competition in the *Colored Pencil Magazine*. Both stunned and delighted to win the Beginners' category, a couple of months later I submitted another piece. This was *Snow Leopard*, shown to the left, which was my first attempt at portraying an animal using coloured pencils. When she also won, I gained a huge amount of exposure – and also a ton of self-confidence.

With the support of my husband, and a growing demand from others to create animal art for them, I took the plunge and gave in my notice at my very well-paid job in a paper mill. This was the start of my pet portrait commission business: Animal Art by LAW was born. The years that followed saw me grow in both confidence and skill as I joined societies, entered exhibitions, won many awards and, of course, had my work published around the world. I continue my fundraising work today with some of the world's leading wildlife rescues through exhibitions, donations of artwork and other means.

THIS BOOK

The invitation to create a couple of tutorials for leading art magazines led to people wanting more, and so the physical workshops began. Everything seemed to click into place, like the last piece in a jigsaw. I didn't know until it happened, but I guess I was destined to become a teacher after all.

With some regrets, I had to walk away from my pet portrait business to allow me to focus solely on my teaching – but the joy of enabling others to discover their own creativity, develop their skills and grow their confidence is a reward like no other.

Today I create tutorials, run online classes and travel the globe teaching physical workshops. In the pages that follow, I share with you all the tools, techniques and knowledge that I have built over the years. I hope that my story, along with the knowledge that you will gain from this book, will enable you to embrace your own creative side, and set off on your own journey of animals in art.

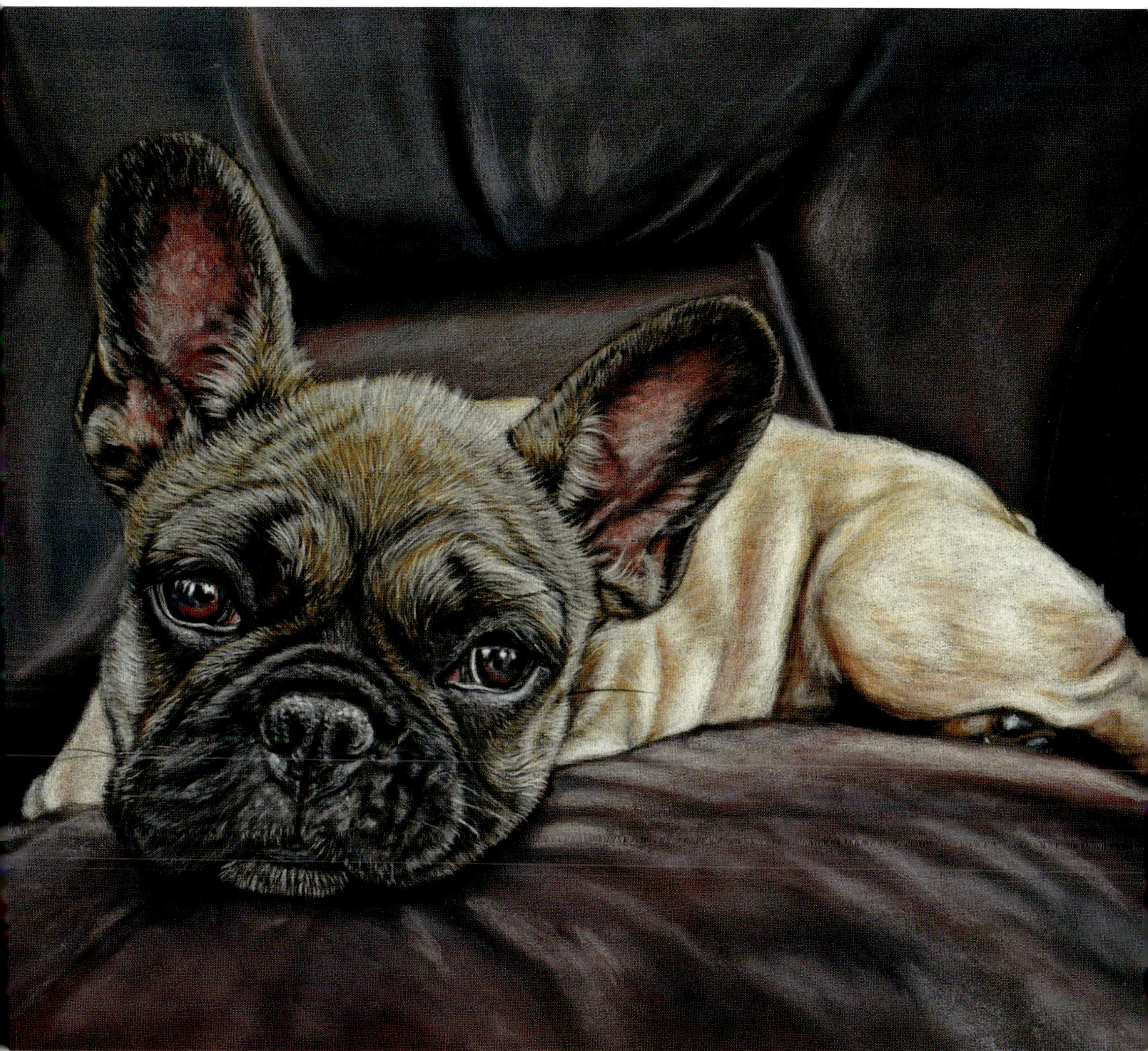

It's All About Stella

Watercolour pencils on Pastelmat. The reference photograph for this one was taken at an opportune moment at a client's house – which makes it a perfect example of always being ready with your phone or camera to get the perfect snap.

I submitted Stella's portrait to the UK Coloured Pencil Society Open Exhibition in London in 2016 when I attended the open evening. I was immediately in tears when she won Best Domestic Animal – and she also picked up the Artist's award and also Reserve Best in Show. She went on to win a few other awards too.

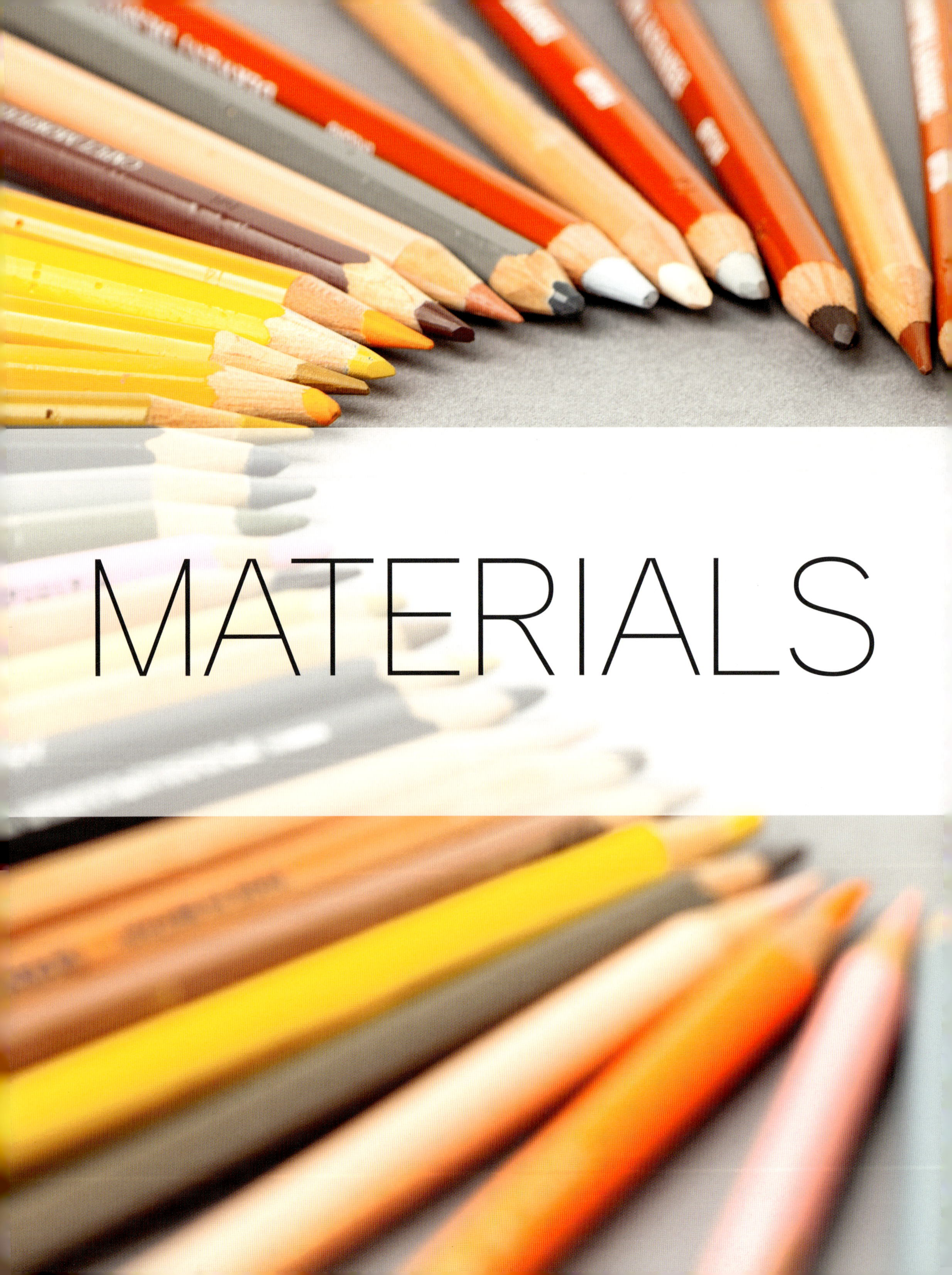

MATERIALS

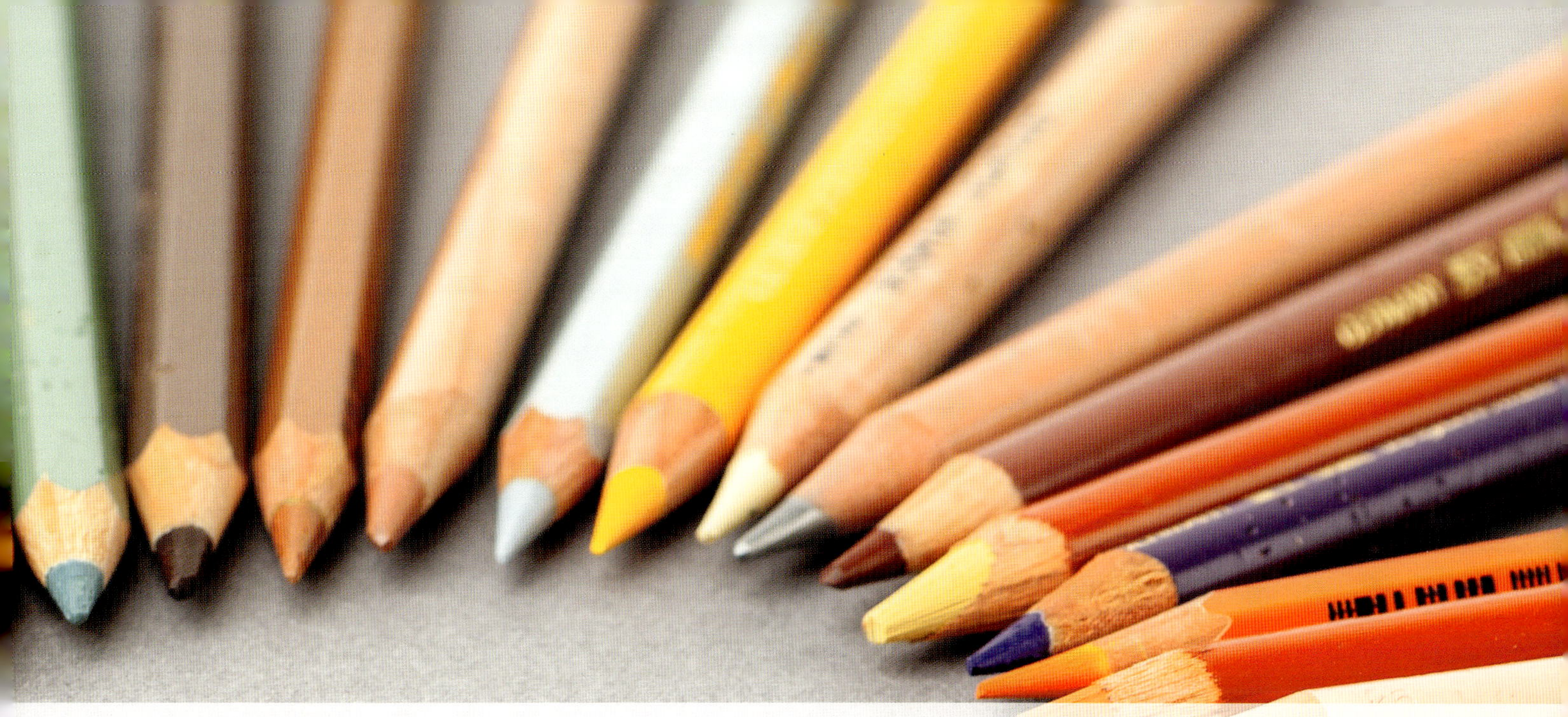

It can be overwhelming when you take a look at the plethora of pencils, supports and other materials out there. The sheer variety of options can put many off before they have even got going. To help to keep things simple, here we look at the pencils, surfaces, materials and tools that I use in my own artwork, and those that you will see in the main projects later in the book.

There are many ways to achieve a finished portrait, but by varying your tools, your application process and your materials, you can also change the look and feel of a piece.

All of the supplies I recommend are fully archival. This means that they will not degrade or fade over time. This is particularly important for supports, but applies to everything. Using archival quality materials will ensure your hard work remains ready for display for a lifetime.

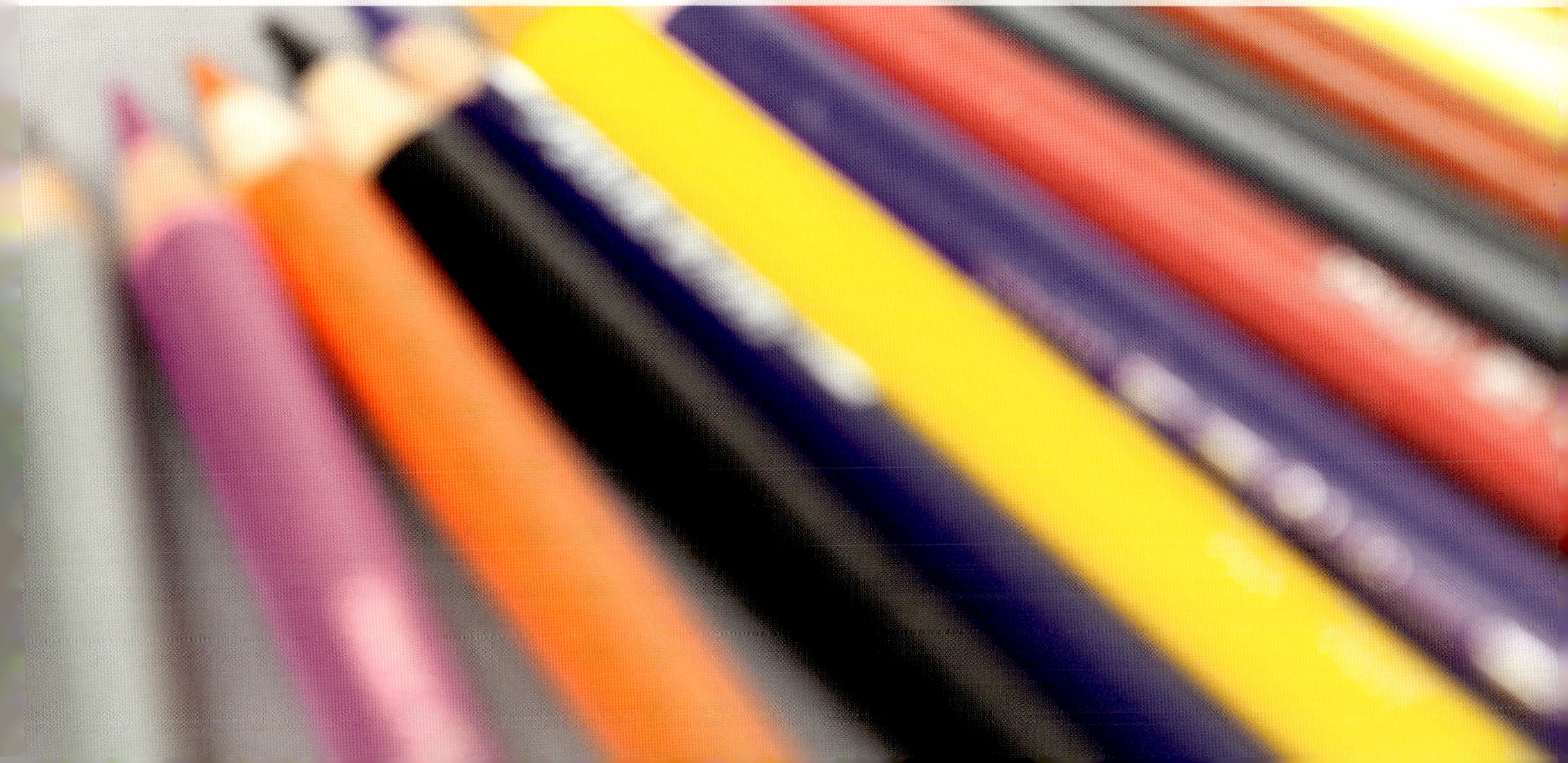

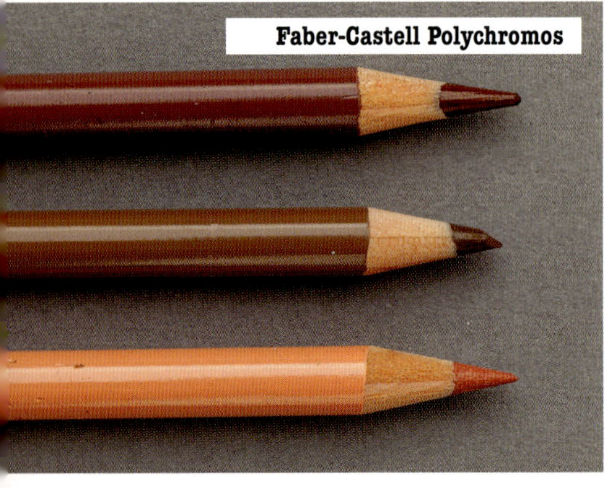

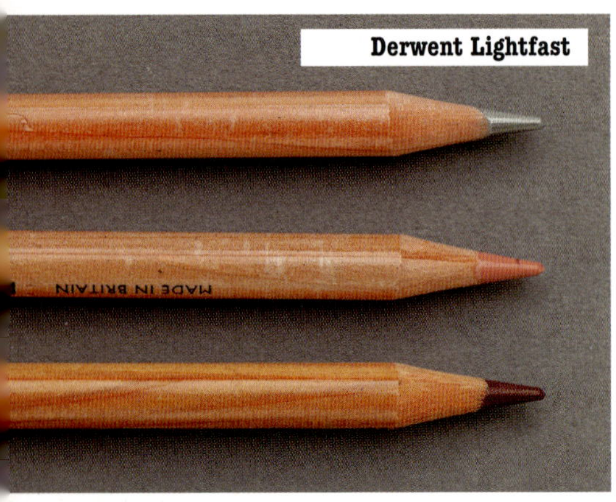

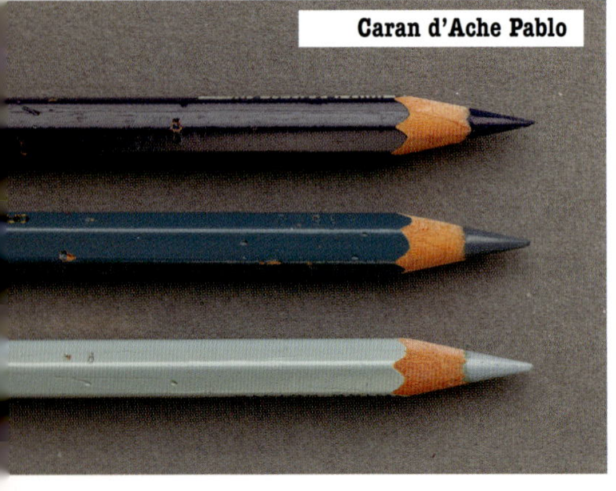

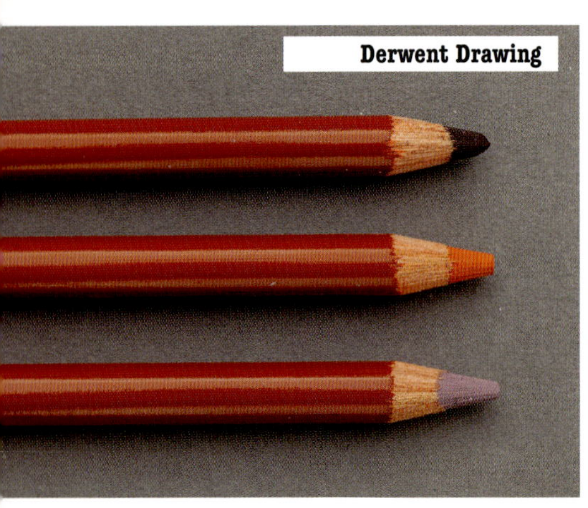

PENCILS

Let's talk coloured pencils! Coloured pencils are made up of a core (the 'lead' of the pencil) which is made of pigment and binder to hold it together; and a wooden case, or shaft, which surrounds the core. They are available in two main types: traditional coloured pencils and watercolour pencils. They differ in that traditional pencil cores are held together with a wax and/or oil binder, and so require solvent to dissolve (see page 19), whereas the core of watercolour pencils includes an emulsifier that dissolves when water is added. In addition to these common types, there are some more unusual ranges, like Derwent Inktense, which are watercolour pencils that produce permanent marks, allowing you to work more wet layers over the top of the the first, once it has dried.

Listed here are my main pencil ranges of choice, but I often pull in the odd pencil from another range, such as Prismacolor, Luminance and Verithin. As with all materials, each artist will have their own preference, so I encourage you to buy a few examples from each range and try them yourself.

Of great importance is the grade, or quality, of pencils. You will achieve a much better laydown of pigment using an artists' grade of pencil. Artists' pencils offer lightfast and archival advantages over cheaper ranges which can often fade rapidly. You will be putting a lot of time and effort into the creation of a piece, so you don't want it to fade.

Traditional coloured pencils

Faber-Castell Polychromos If I were stranded on a desert island and could only take one set of pencils with me, then it would be these. Referred to as oil-based pencils (though see 'Coloured pencil myths', opposite), they have a fantastic range of colours. These pencils lay down beautifully and, being firm, they maintain a sharp point for detail work. They are a little more translucent than other ranges, but this allows for more layering and blending.

Derwent Lightfast These are also referred to as being oil-based but they are much smoother and creamier than the Polychromos. They mix and blend beautifully and, as the name suggests, they have been created for artists who care about the longevity of their works. I often combine these with my Polychromos.

Caran d'Ache Pablo Another range that I love to mix with my Polychromos, Pablos have a wonderful range of colours suited to creating animal portraits. They use a mix of wax and oil in their binder, so they have a lovely soft laydown but can also hold a firm point for details. They are not quite as firm as the Polychromos range.

Derwent Drawing A much smaller range of just twenty-four pencils, these are the most opaque and the creamiest of the ranges that I use, and have their own unique place in my work. Those new to working with coloured pencil often ask if there is a way to speed things up. Using these Drawing pencils allows you to lay down pigment using the same light pressure as the other brands, but their thickness and opacity means that you can fill your initial tooth much more quickly. It doesn't save a huge amount of time but it will help you to get there a little faster.

Watercolour pencils

Using watercolour pencils allows you to create controlled watercolour effect pieces or you can use them as an underpainting to your other pencil brands. You can of course just use them dry if you prefer, so they make for a really versatile pencil to start out with.

The ranges that I use are **Faber-Castell Albrecht Dürer** and **Caran d'Ache Museum Aquarelle** pencils. The former are the pencils that I started out with many years ago. I was scared to add water to them for a long time, but when I did, I was so excited at the possibilities they opened up for me.

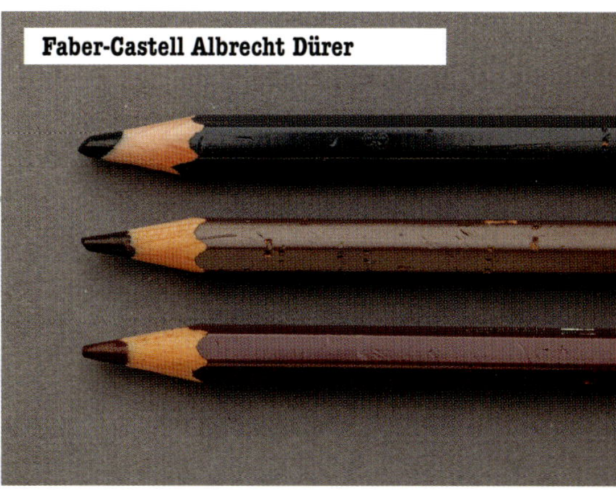

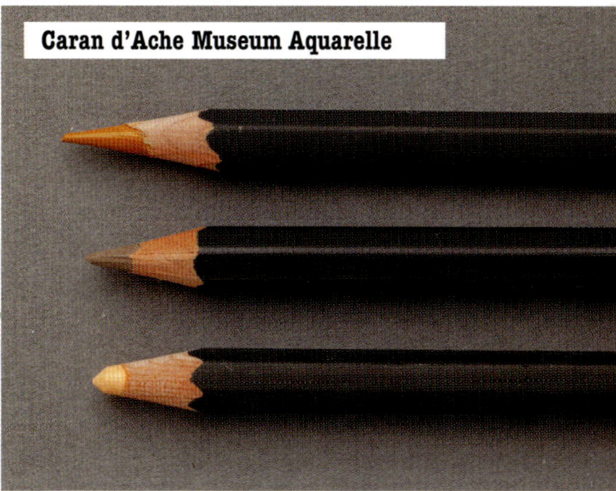

Sharp, rounded and blunt tips

Here are examples of three levels of sharpness on the tips of pencils. Different situations call for the use of each of these different tips and all are equally important.

Sharp tips Perfect for fine details, sharp tips can also be laid on one side for faster application of pigment.

Rounded and blunt tips Great for underpainting or for laying down soft loose strokes where there is less detail.

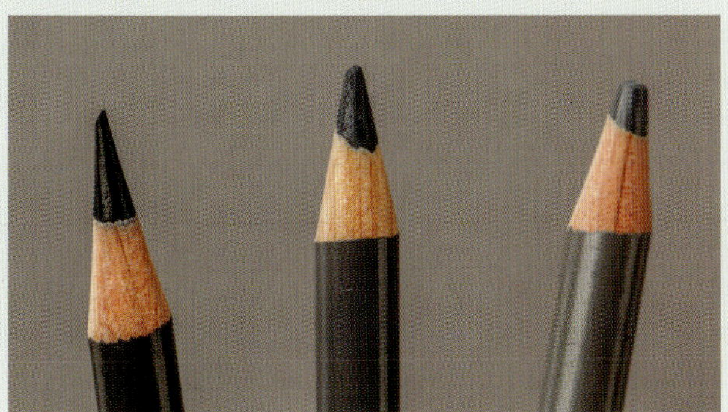

Left to right: sharp, rounded and blunt tips.

Coloured pencil myths

Before moving on, I want to address a couple of myths about coloured pencils. Firstly, coloured pencils are often categorized into either oil or wax, with oil pencils being harder and wax softer. The truth is not so simple. In fact, all coloured pencil ranges have their own unique binder recipe and almost always have a mix of multiple ingredients in them, including both wax and oil in different proportions. Other ingredients besides are also added to the pigment before the oil and wax binder is used to hold the mix together to create the core. These additional ingredients affect the overall performance of the pencil.

Secondly, it's commonly thought that you cannot mix brands when working on a piece, but in reality you can layer and blend any coloured pencil with another. You may get different effects, and some will work together better than others, but there are ways of utilizing the benefits of each range and using each to your advantage.

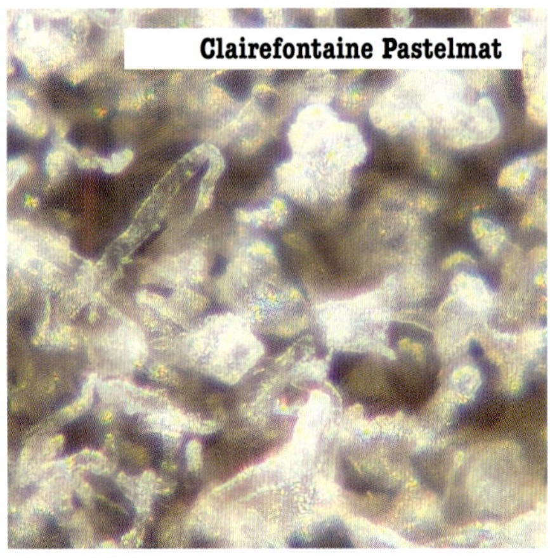

Clairefontaine Pastelmat

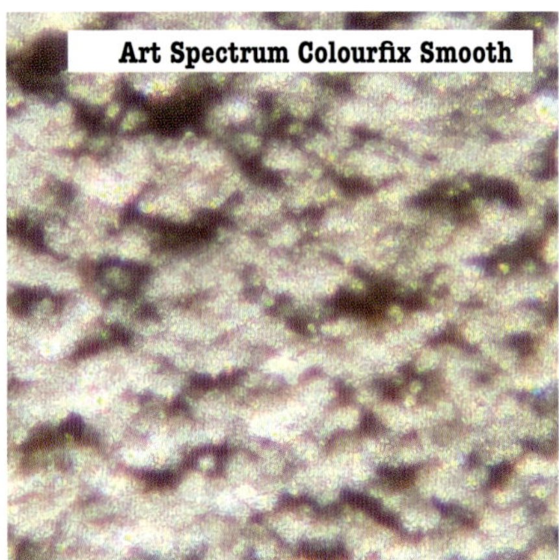

Art Spectrum Colourfix Smooth

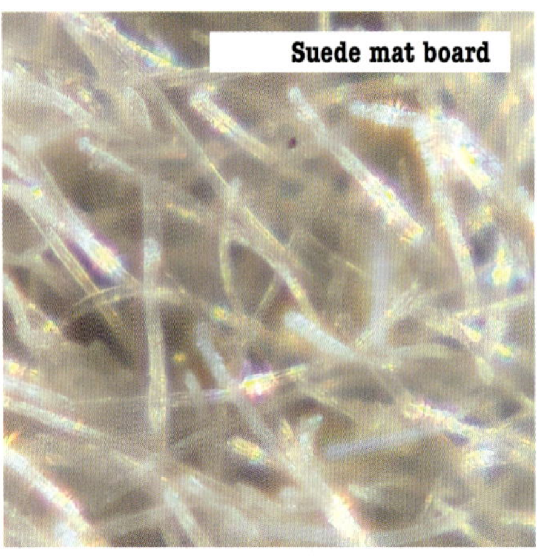

Suede mat board

Drafting film

SUPPORTS

You can create art on pretty much any surface. We refer to this as your 'support'. To this support you apply your materials or pigments and then you can use various tools to manipulate the pigments to create different effects. Here I outline four options that offer different effects. The images to the left show each of the surfaces through a microscope at 90× magnification, to show the underlying differences between the textures.

Coloured pencils work on a surprising nunber of surfaces – and there are even fantastic primers or grounds that allow you to work with coloured pencil on wood, metals and even glass. Trial and error is the best way to find what suits you and your style best – you should never be afraid to step outside of your comfort zone and try something new.

Clairefontaine Pastelmat Originally designed for pastel artists, this is a unique surface that is coarser than velvety velour but softer than sandpapers. It feels smooth to the touch but as soon as you lay your pencil on it the 'tooth', or texture, of the paper is revealed (see page 24 for more on tooth). Pastelmat comes in a wide variety of colours and is very versatile, as it allows wet media to be added with no distortion of the surface.

Art Spectrum Colourfix Smooth Another textured paper that comes in a lovely palette of colours and that allows for many layers. This is my preferred support when working with PanPastels (see page 16) as it allows for clean and easy erasing whereas Pastelmat does not. It does not allow quite so many layers as Pastelmat or sanded papers, but it does allow the method of dark to light (see 'What support to choose', opposite).

Alternative options to the above are the **LuxArchival** and **Uart**. These two supports (not pictured) are true sanded papers. Both allow for working with wet media, multiple layering and the dark to light method, but I find they create a little too much excess dust when working. These come in a natural colour and the Uart also has a dark range.

Suede mat board The surface that gives the softest effect to a piece is actually a mount board typically used for framing finished pieces. Suede mat board is something with which I have a love–hate relationship. It helps to create soft fluffy fur with a single stroke of a pencil, but it can soak up the pigment in between sessions, which dulls the result. This means a lot of repetition of the same layers until the surface is saturated. The soft mottled results, however, can be quite breathtaking, so it is worth persevering.

Drafting film A translucent surface that resembles tracing paper, drafting film is made of pure polyester. Traditionally used by architects and draftsmen for creating plans, it comes in varying thicknesses and qualities, so try to ensure that you use a double matt version to allow you to work on both sides. With little tooth, the film allows for very few layers, so you have to be more selective in your pencil application – but you can achieve super sharp details with very little effort. The vibrancy of pigment can also be very bright. Using tools to lift off pigment to create textures like fur means that this surface allows for a quicker process with very realistic results. I favour the Grafix brand of film.

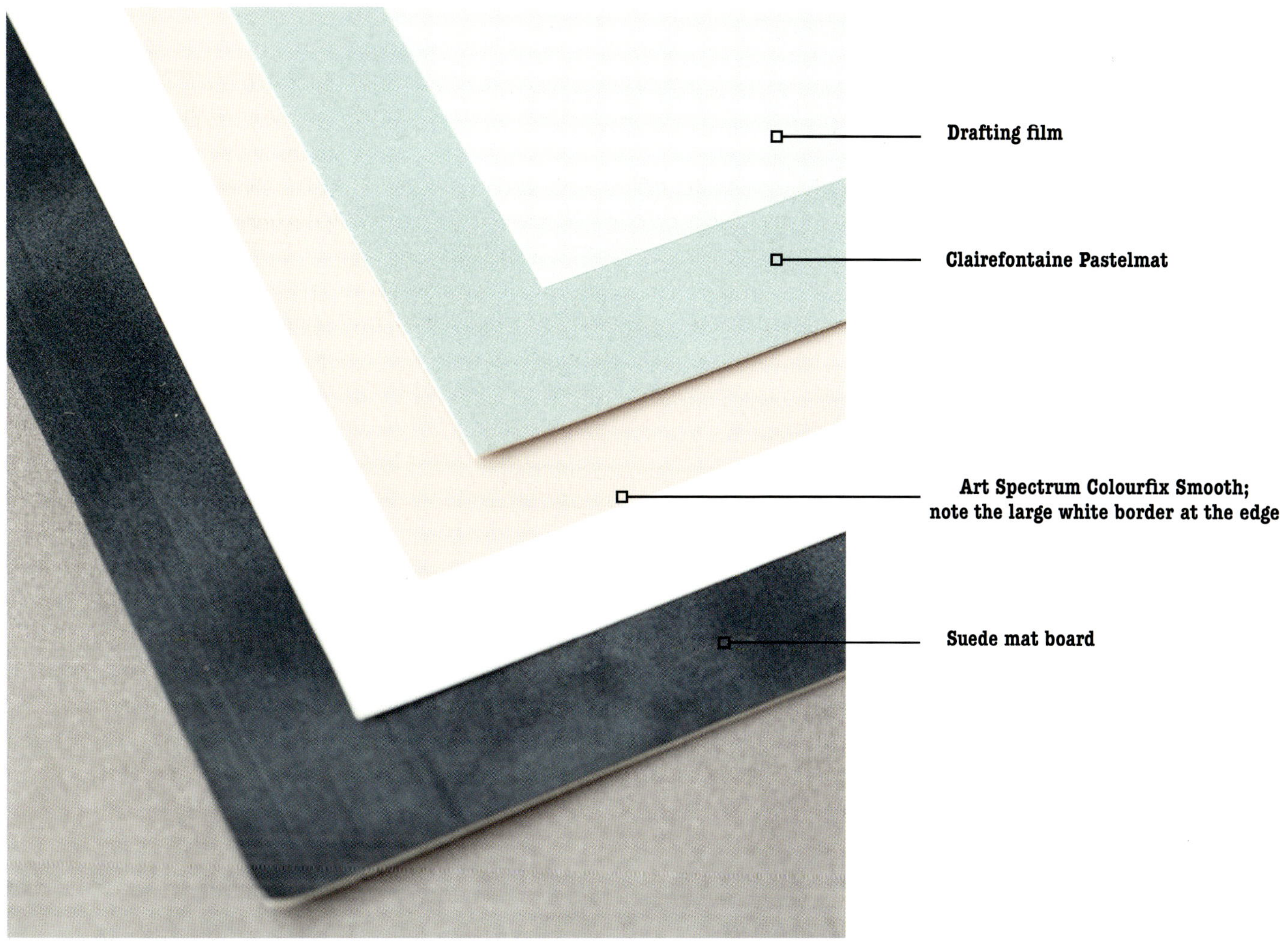

What support to choose

I am mainly known for working on textured papers and films, and also tend to work on coloured supports. This is simply a personal choice and has become part of my own style.

The main advantage of using a textured support is that it allows you to work light over dark. Working on smooth paper means that you have to preserve your lights like a watercolourist would (that is, by avoiding the areas), whereas the deeper tooth of textured and sanded supports allows you to add light pigment over dark. This means you can use your pencils to add fine white hairs over black fur, for example, at the end, rather than preserving them from the outset.

As part of your preparation process you will get a feel for your subject and their character. This can influence how you want your piece to look or feel – and hence what support to use. For a portrait of a long-haired cat that you want to look soft, for example, you might choose a support like a suede mat board to give you that instant effect, or perhaps a coloured support to give some extra drama.

You might instead vary the materials and application techniques to create that softness, rather than relying on the support – there are many roads to Rome and no right nor wrong methods when creating art.

OTHER PAINTING MEDIA

PanPastels

Another method for speeding up the process of coloured pencil work up is to incorporate PanPastels into the process. PanPastels are a unique formula of pastel pressed into pans; you use painting knives and sponge tools to mix and apply them like paint. I tend to use these on a portrait where I want to create softness to the fur, most often as an underpainting but sometimes as a softener on my top layers. They are great for fluffy fur or the soft curls of breeds like labradoodles.

I started using PanPastels to create quick effective backgrounds, but then started to pull them into my main subjects. I use them to create underpaintings, over which I subsequently work with pencils for the detail work. You can see this in the horse project on pages 126–135.

A common belief is that you cannot use PanPastels over coloured pencils. In fact, you can indeed do this, so long as you are using the correct paper to allow it, such as a textured or sanded paper. Doing so will help to blend your coloured pencil pigment, creating a super soft effect.

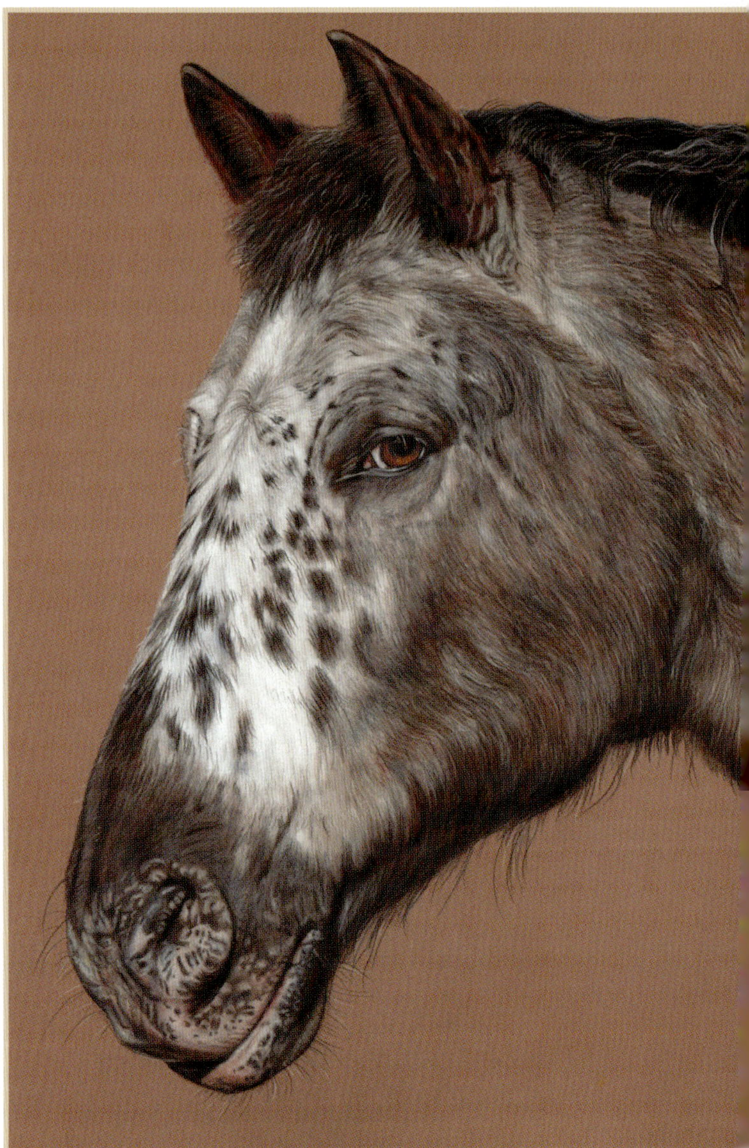

Ziggy
Watercolour pencils, coloured pencils and PanPastel on Pastelmat. This portrait is the perfect example of using PanPastel over and between layers of coloured pencil. The medium not only helps to create a softness to the texture but also adds extra saturation to the lightest highlights.

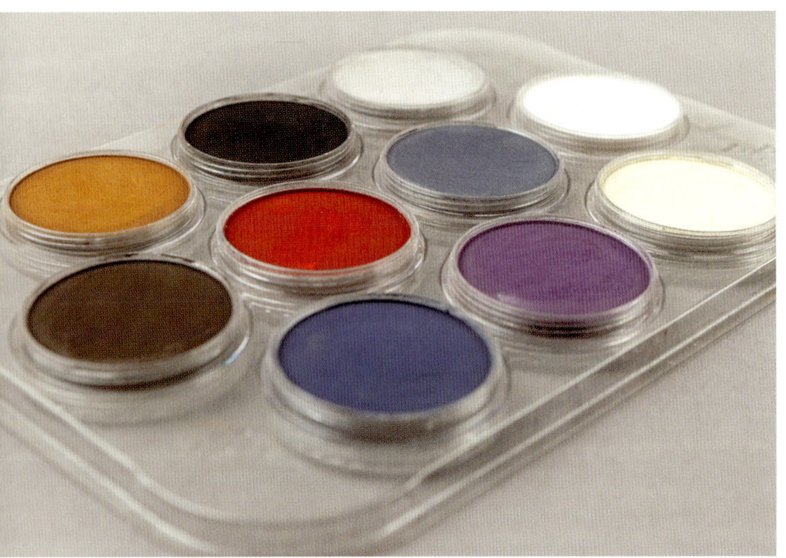

PanPastels: my signature collection
I love working with these so much that I created a special signature collection with PanPastel for those wanting to create animal portraits. This includes the following colours: raw umber extra dark 780.1; ultramarine blue extra dark 520.1; red iron oxide shade 380.3; orange extra dark 280.1; violet shade 470.3; Payne's grey 840.3; black 800.5; hansa yellow tint 220.8; titanium white 100.5; and neutral grey tint 820.7.

The set also includes a palette tray and cover; sizes 1 and 3 painting knives and covers; a sponge bar and an angle slice sponge to apply the PanPastels.

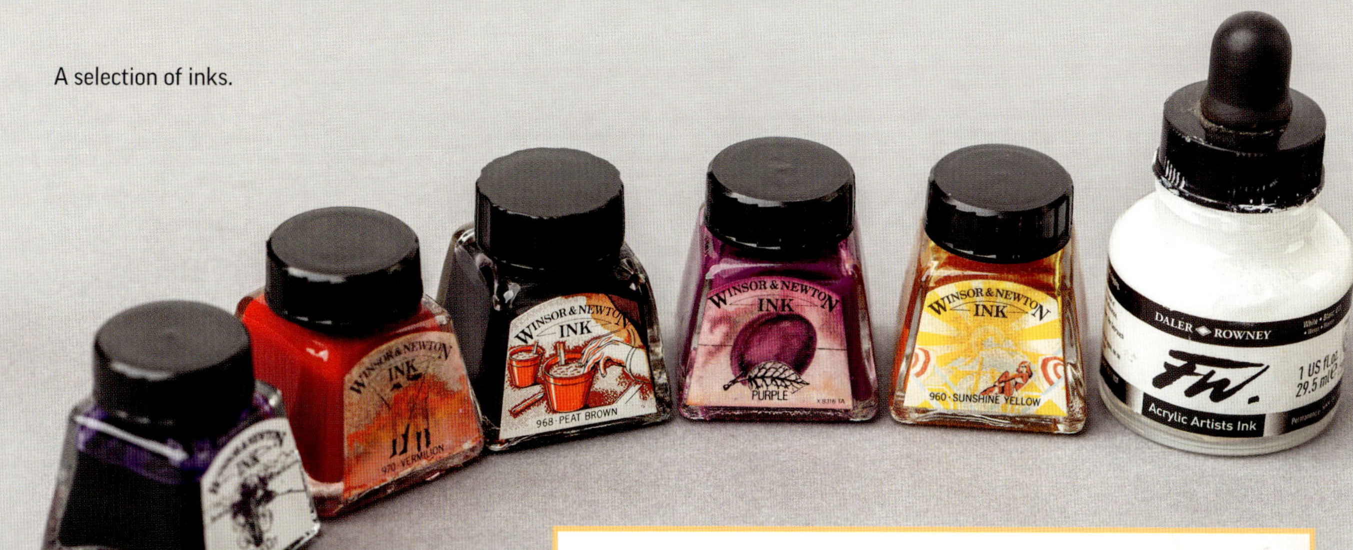

A selection of inks.

Inks

Coloured pencil works are often very precise and detailed pieces. I like to try to loosen up to experiment and have fun, and one of the media I bring into play for this is ink. You can add detail with pencils over an inky underpainting, and this method will allow you to create a piece in a relatively short space of time compared with pure pencil work. The secret is knowing just when to stop in order to ensure that you keep that loose bleed effect of the inks rather than cover it all with detailed pencil strokes.

You can use a brush to apply inks, and also to dilute them with water. My preferred inks are Winsor & Newton drawing inks which are soluble dye-based inks. If you want to push the colour around, use a thicker, more opaque, ink such as Daler-Rowney FW acrylic ink. My favoured support for this method is once again Pastelmat, as the bleed is more intense than on regular watercolour papers.

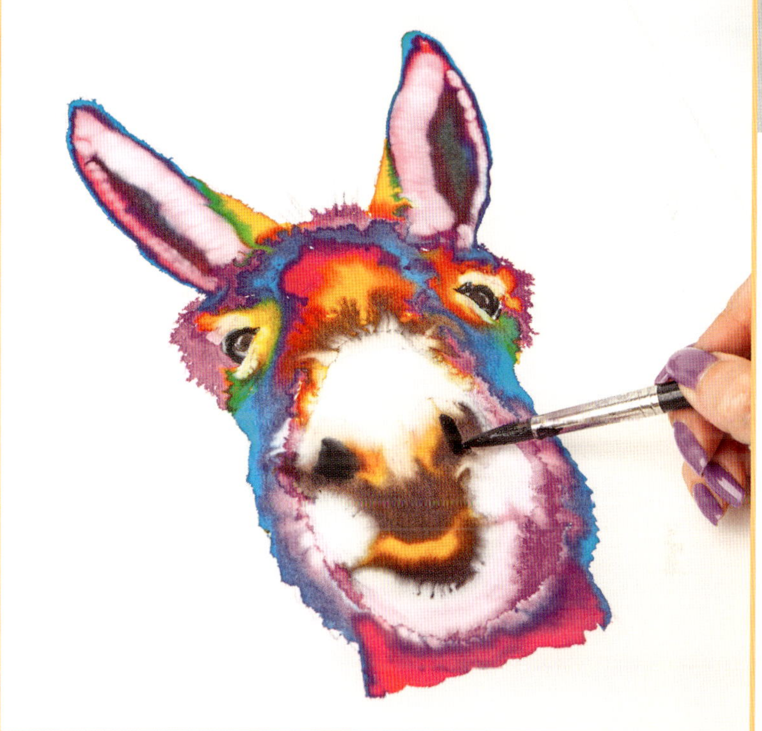

I love that the inks are a little out of my control when they mix in front of my eyes. Applying ink to a support that bleeds the colour is liberating but also quite a scary thing to do. With experience you will be able to aim for a specific outcome, but there will always be an element of the unknown.

Inktense blocks

While not strictly inks, Derwent Inktense pencils are an alternative that will create a very similar effect to inks. Inktense blocks are also available. These are watersoluble ink blocks that can be used like pastels or pencils, allowing you to build large areas of pigment quite quickly. You can use a brush or a water spray to activate the colour – once dry, the marks are fixed and permanent.

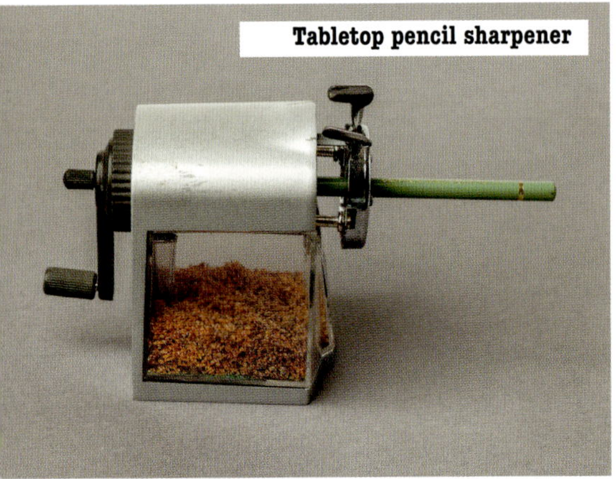

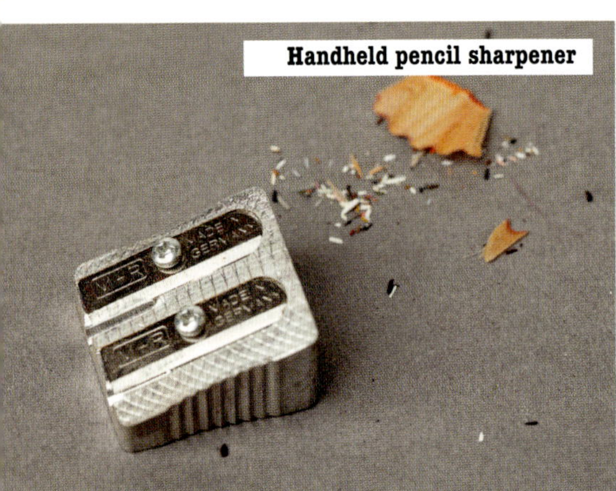

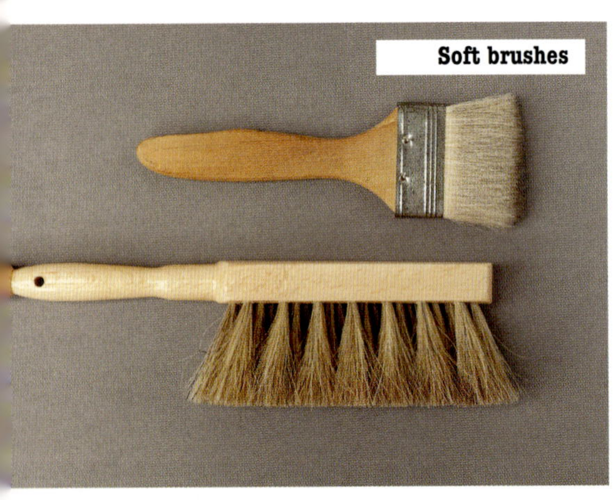

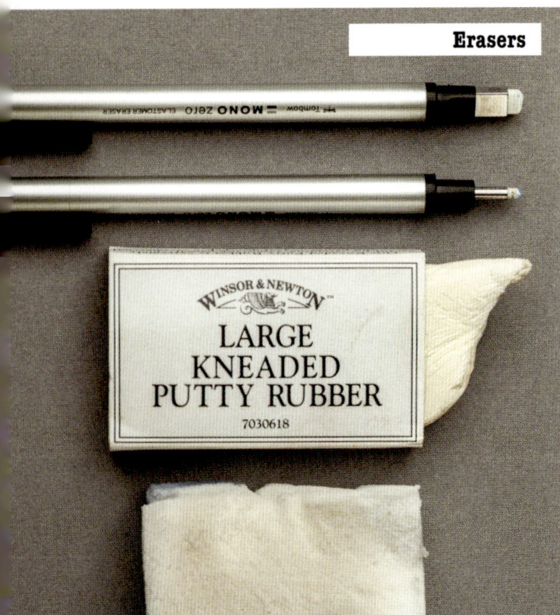

OTHER MATERIALS

My pencils are my pigment, and they create colour, tone and some of the textures in my work. There are, however, other tools that I use which are of equal value. Over time, you will pick up many other tools and bits of equipment but these are my key pieces that I use in almost all of my work. Each of the tools here can be used in different ways to support your pencil work, or to create different textures and effects in their own right.

Pencil sharpener I usually start off my works using rounded or blunt pencils (see page 13) but when it comes to working on a small scale, such as the eyes of a portrait, or for the final details, then I need a super sharp point on my nibs. I have two favoured sharpeners that never let me down. My workhorse is the Jakar 5160, which is a tabletop helical sharpener with no blade. I also use a Möbius and Ruppert handheld sharpener when I am out and about and need something more compact.

Soft brushes A soft brush is invaluable for keeping your work area and artwork free of pencil finings, dust and the like.

Erasers When working on textured papers, I tend not to use an eraser in my work as I can self-correct on the following layers using my pencils. When working on other supports, such as drafting film, I use erasers as part of my process for creating texture. A putty eraser allows a lifting-off of pigment, much as a knife does (see page 33). Erasers can be moulded to lift off different shapes or employed to remove pigment if too much has been laid down in an area. Mounting or sticky putty can be used, but these are not designed for use within art and can leave a greasy residue.

One of my favourite tools is a Tombow Mono eraser. It is multifunctional depending on the pressure that you use. Think of this one as being another pencil but one that removes pigment instead of adding it. You can vary your pressure, with the lightest amount allowing you to mix and blend pigment. You can also cut the eraser nib into a fine point, which allows you to cut into your pigment to create the initial fur texture.

I am also going to mention the Mr Clean Magic Eraser here. A sponge household cleaning product, it is a great tool for cleaning up your support at the end of a drawing. Not many things clean up Pastelmat but this one works brilliantly!

Styluses I use a nail art dotting tool as a stylus for debossing or indenting lines on my support. This works especially well for preserving white whisker lines. I use a dart – the type you throw into a dartboard – to create super fine lines using the same method.

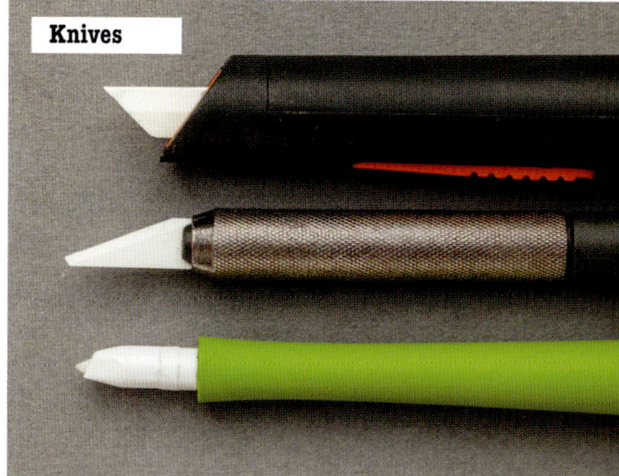

Knives Knives can be thought of as extensions to our sets of pencils: they can be used with varying pressure and strokes to create a myriad of effects. In fact, the blades that I use in my work often create more of the texture than my pencils, especially when working on drafting film, where I would estimate that I create around ninety per cent of the fur texture with my knives.

   When starting out, I used a metal-bladed craft knife but a few years ago one of my students handed me something called a Slice knife. Designed for safety within the packaging industry, these tools have ceramic blades. I find them ideal.

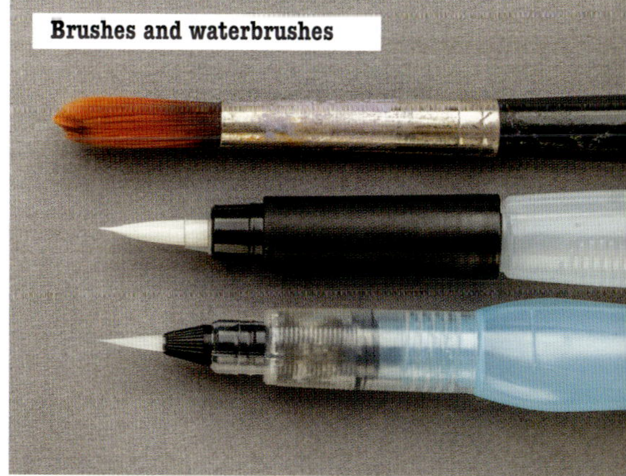

Brushes, powder and solvent You can use any small brush to dissolve the pigment in pencils, whether this is using water on watercolour pencils or solvent to dissolve the wax and oil binders in regular coloured pencils. For solvent, you can use any odourless mineral spirit designed for use with art, as this will ensure its archival quality. For applying water, I prefer to use Pentel Aquash waterbrushes over traditional brushes. These have a brush tip and a plastic body that you fill with water, after which you can use them like a pen. They allow me control of the flow of water and also mean that I do not risk having a pot of water anywhere near my piece of work.

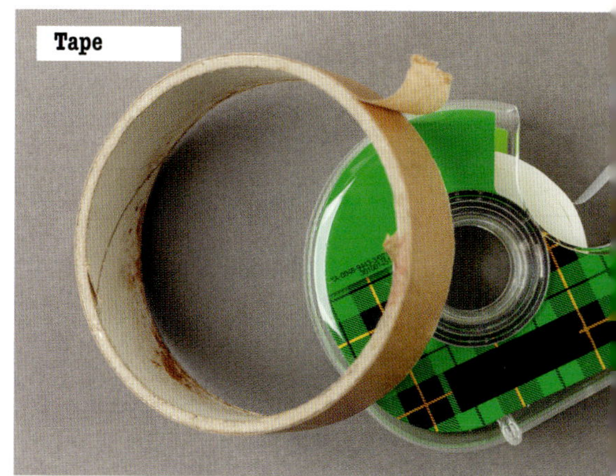

Tape Another method of lifting off pigment is to use a low-tack tape. Scotch Magic tape is fantastic for this. Use to lift off excess pigment, tidy up edges or in combination with the stylus to create textures in the pigment.

Glassine paper (not pictured) This is a wax-free paper that looks like tracing paper. Keep it under your hand as you work to prevent any grease being transferred onto the working surface.

GETTING STARTED

Before we get going on the studies and the bigger projects there are a few fundamentals that we need to look at which are key to your success. I urge you not to omit these short steps. A few minutes spent here on some foundational work will save you hours of frustration further down the line. Even once you have built up some experience, it is good to refresh yourself with these basics on a regular basis.

Here we learn about how much pressure to apply, the different techniques that you will use to lay down your pencil pigment – as well as those needed to lift pigment away again – and how you mix, layer and blend your pencils. These fundamentals can be seen as tools to create realistic work of which you will be proud. Once you have worked through them all, your understanding will have grown so much that you will feel confident to tackle the studies that follow.

SETTING UP

It is important to ensure that you are set up with a good workstation before you get your pencils and paper out. This applies whether you are working in a purpose-built studio with a drafting table and a full lighting system, or on the sofa with a drawing board on your knee. Nowadays I have a wonderful custom set-up, but when I started out I had just a small area at our dining room table, and a piece of wood with clips to hold my paper on – and I had to clear away my pencils and paper whenever it was time to eat!

Ensure you are comfortable to ensure good work. Make sure that you have access to natural light or a daylight lamp, and a good board to support your work.

A Magnetic angled drawing board

B Soft brush

C Pencil holder

D Pencils

E Pencil sharpener

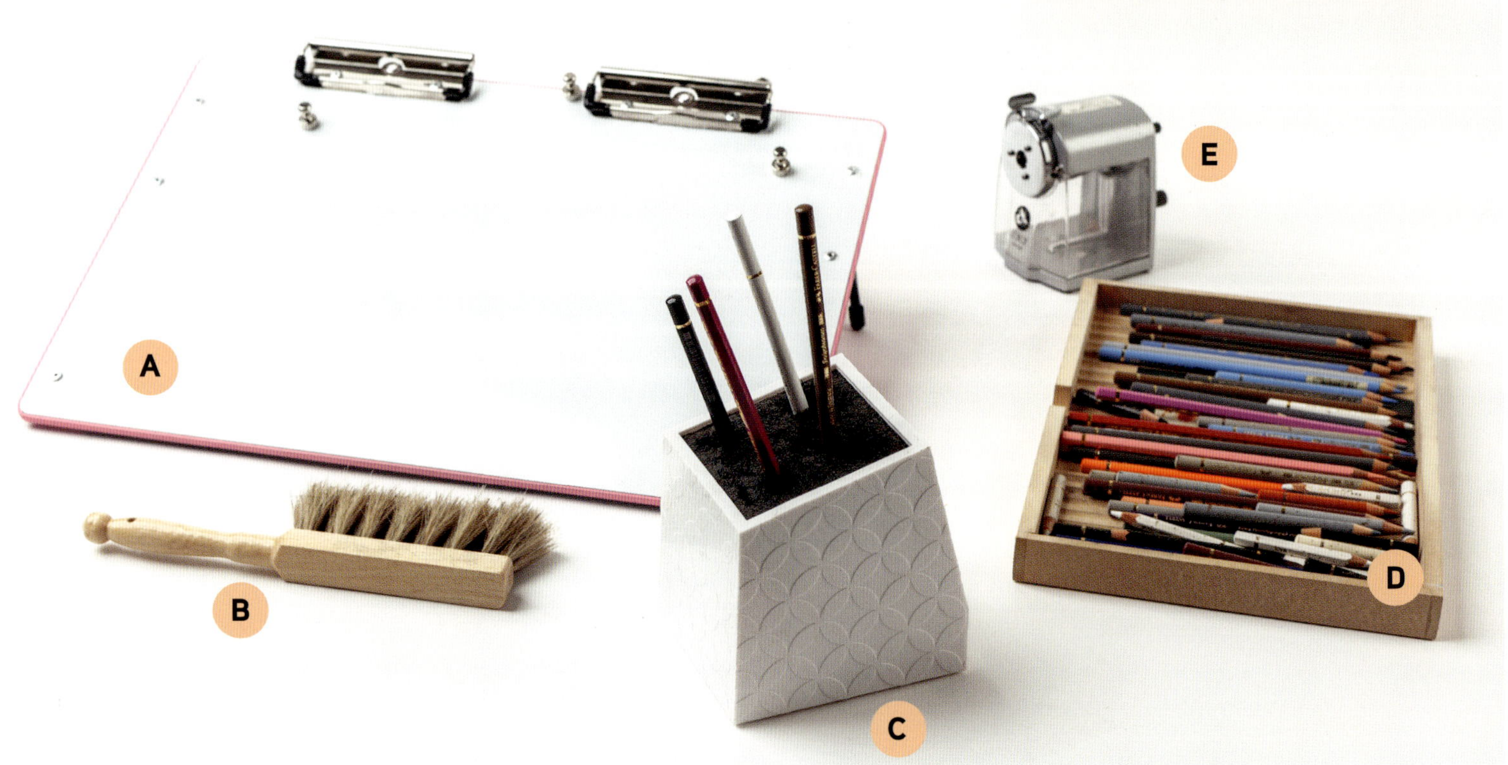

PRESSURE TEST

You do a pressure test for two reasons: firstly, to understand the correct amount of pressure to apply; secondly, to get familiar with your support. A textured support will allow you to apply up to seventy layers – but only if you use the correct pressure right from the start.

One of the main lessons of this exercise is that you can likely create the colour you want with a single heavy sweep of colour – but in so doing, you will likely damage the surface. Better to build up with multiple layers of colour, and keep the surface intact.

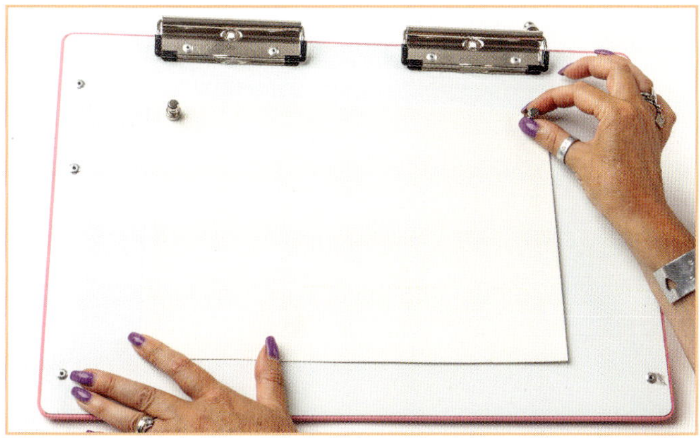

1 Affix your support to your board. I favour a magnetic board, but you can use clips or masking tape – the important thing is that the support doesn't move around.

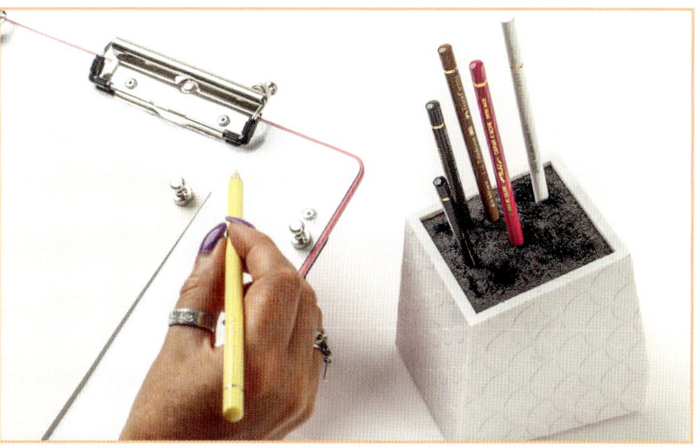

2 From the selection you plan to use in your project, select two light tints, two midtones and two darks. This will give you a good overview of your pencils without having to test all of them – but of course you should feel free to do so if you wish.

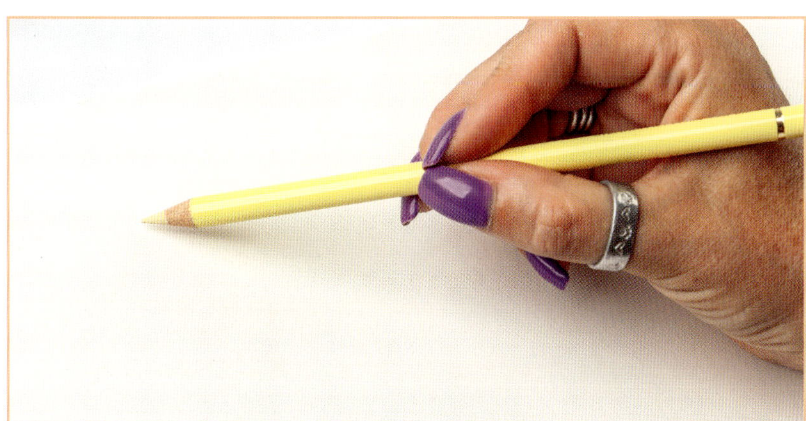

3 Holding the pencil halfway up the shaft (this prevents you applying too much pressure), touch the tip to the surface. A light tint like this can be hard to see when you apply it lightly – that's why you need to become attuned to the touch and feel of your pencils. Trust your materials and the process.

4 Using a very light, feather-touch pressure, begin to create a solid bar of colour by moving the pencil back and forth as you work to the right (or left, if you're left-handed).

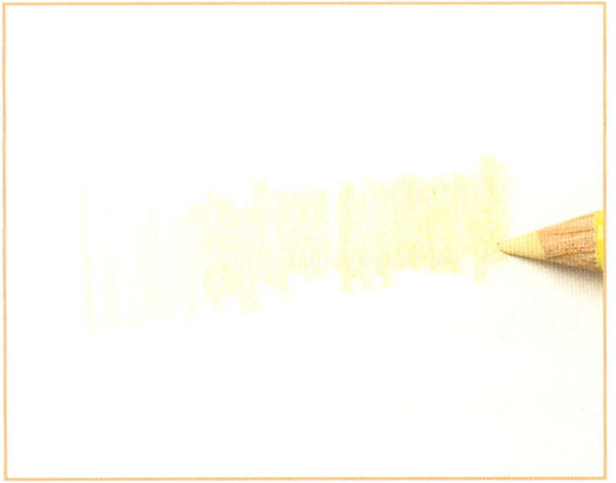

5 As you continue to work across, gradually increase the pressure to apply more pigment. This will naturally increase the saturation.

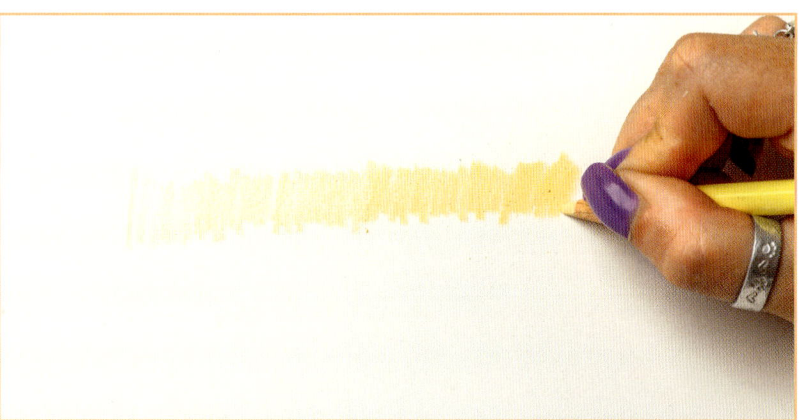

6 Increase the pressure still further, pressing the tip into the surface. You may find shifting your fingers nearer the tip of the pencil helps you to apply more pressure. Get used to the sensation – and contrast it with the feather touch you used at the start of the bar. The surface is designed to grab and hold the pigment, so there's no need to apply it as hard as this when working. What you are doing with this pressure is crushing the fibres and damaging the paper.

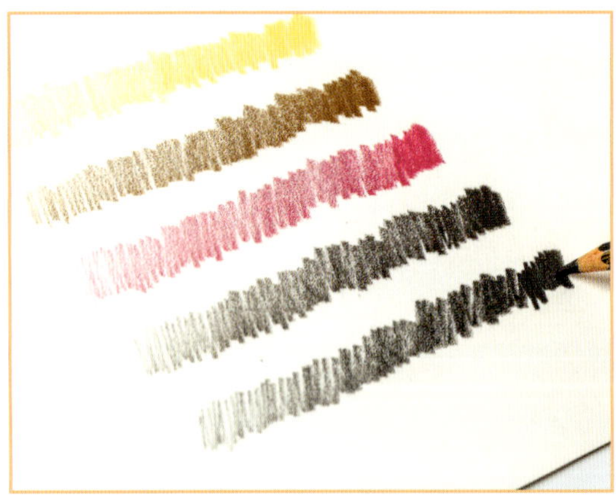

7 Repeat with each of the other pencils; again aiming to work from the lightest to darkest tone the pencil can create.

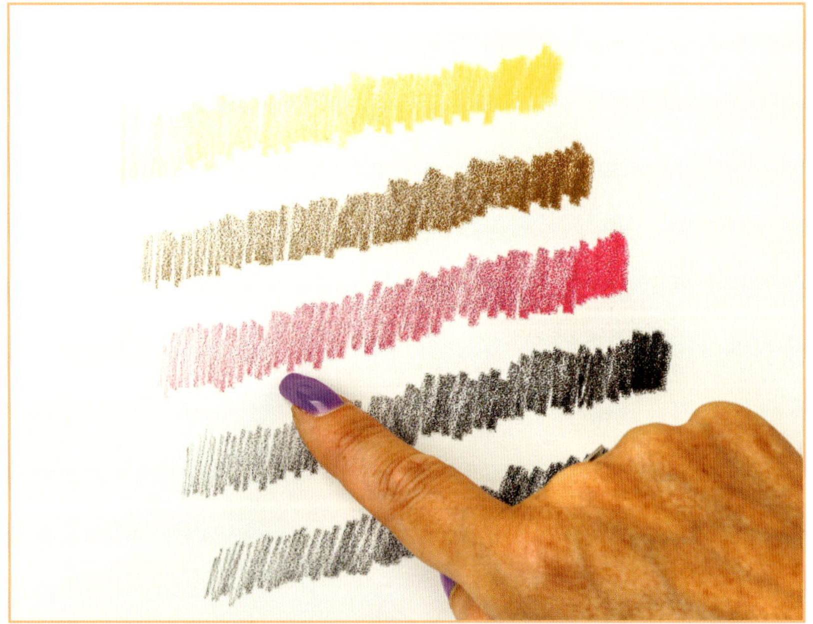

8 The pressure we'll be using throughout the book – with minor exception for particular techniques – is roughly a third of the way along. We refer to this throughout the book as standard pressure (see opposite).

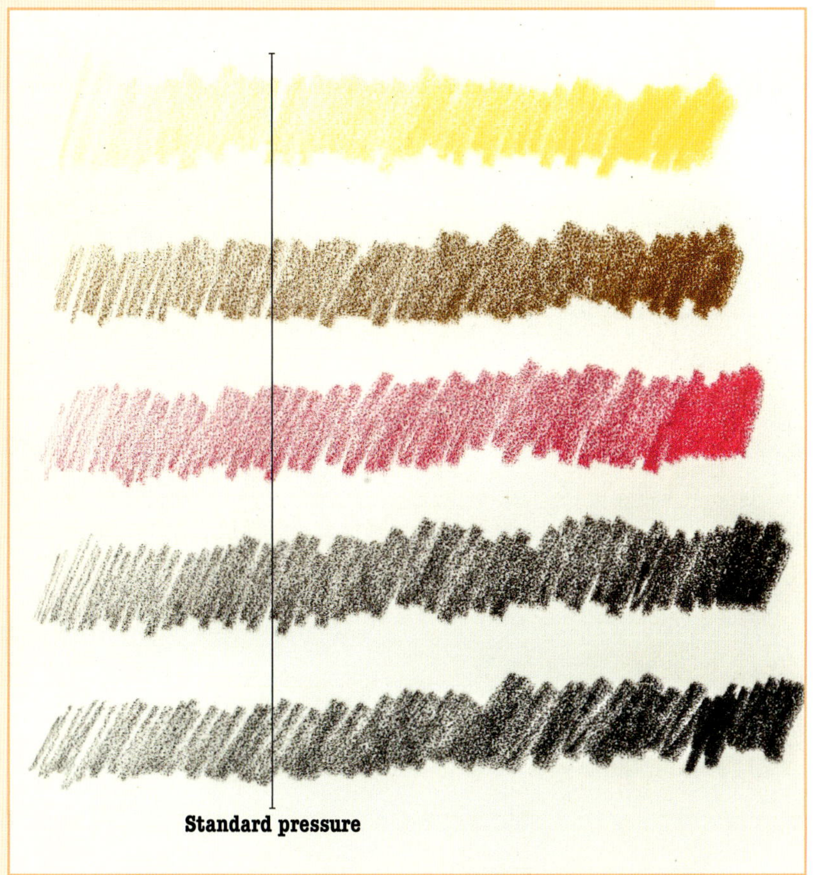

A successful pressure test

The aim is to create a smooth, even gradient from barely-there colour (left) to the deepest, strongest mark of which the pencil is capable (right) – you are taking your pencils from a whisper to a shout as you work across the paper.

Standard pressure

This pressure is as dark as you can create without damaging the paper; and will allow you to create multiple layers for depth, mixing and blending. Standard pressure is marked here by the line. Practise achieving this pressure before you move on.

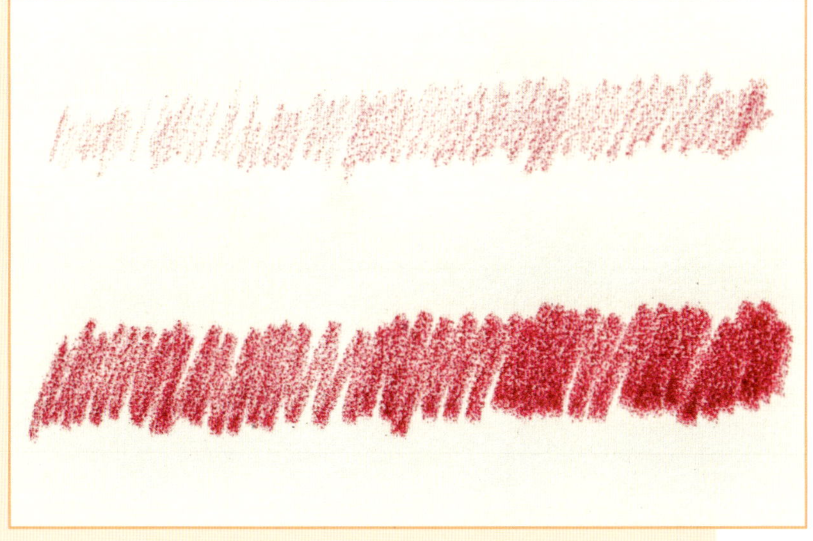

Light and heavy hands

The pressure test is very heavily dependent on how light- or heavy-handed you are naturally; this is why you're aiming to create a smooth gradient. If the tone doesn't change evenly, you're either pressing too heavily or too lightly.

The examples here show too light a touch (top), and too heavy a touch (bottom). Neither shows much variation in pressure. Keep practising and adjusting your pressure until you end up with smooth gradients of tone in your bars, and can work at standard pressure.

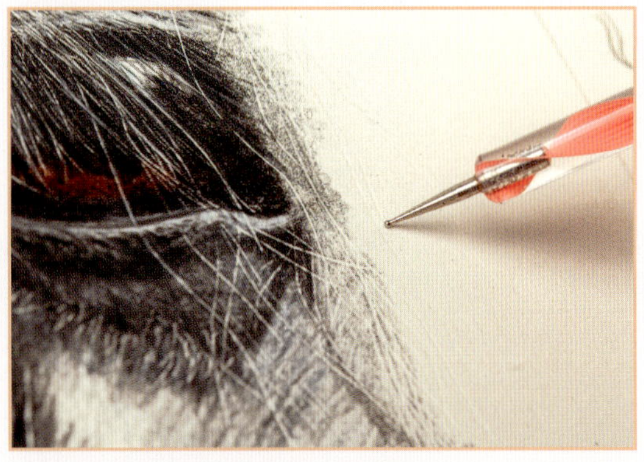

Taking advantage of the tooth
Generally, you want to avoid using too much pressure
as this can damage the surface, crushing the
mountains and leaving you with a smooth, unusable
surface. However, certain techniques do call for
this – using a stylus (above) will allow you to draw
indentations. As long as you glaze over them carefully,
they will remain clean – perfect for depicting fine light
hairs, as in the horse's eye, below.

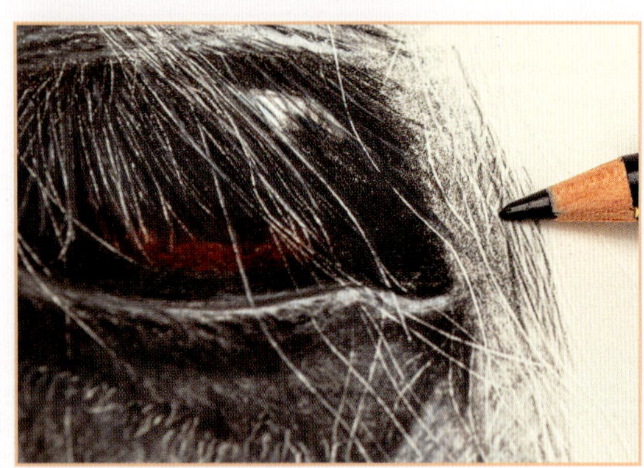

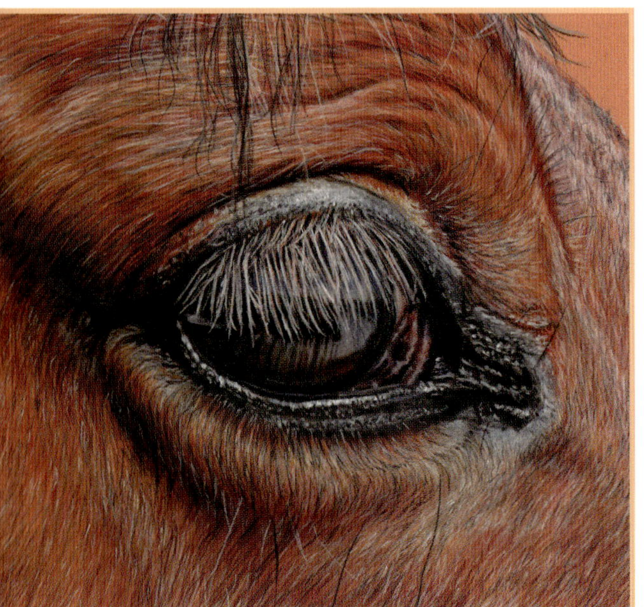

Horse eye study
The eyelashes here were achieved using the
indentation technique.

SURFACE TEXTURE AND PRESSURE

The main difference between a smooth and a textured support is the tooth,
or surface texture. Think of your support as having mountains and valleys.
A smooth paper has very low hills and shallow valleys, while a high-grit
Pastelmat surface will have tall mountains and deep valleys.

When applying the pencil, pigment will be gently ground off the pencil
by the mountains, and will gradually fill the valleys. Until enough layers
have been applied, however, the surface will look quite speckled or grainy,
as you can see opposite.

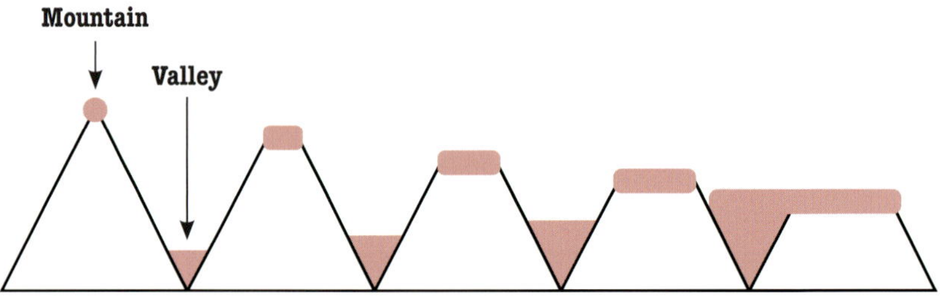

Grainy surface
When applying the
initial layers, pencil
pigment sits on top of
the mountain and also
falls into the valleys.

Halfway surface
As the pigment
builds, the tops of the
mountains smooth out
and the valleys fill more.

Buttery surface
Eventually the valleys
will be filled and the
mountains smoothed
out, giving an even
application of pigment.

Your surface and its tooth

Though trial and error, each artist will learn their own personal choice of
surface texture for their support, and how many layers of each type of
pencil are necessary.

For example, the Pastelmat surface allows you to use multiple layers (it's
a favourite of mine for this reason, as it suits my technique). After applying
around twenty-five layers of coloured pencil at standard pressure to this
surface, enough pigment will have fallen into the valleys of a Pastelmat
surface to create a smooth grit. This will in turn allow you to use a sharp
pencil to create details in clean, sharp lines.

Whatever surface you choose, feel for the 'buttery' resistance on the
surface. The paper will start to feel slick and this is a sign that the tooth is
almost filled.

How much pressure should I use?

Using too much pressure will crush the mountains, damaging the surface
and giving you less depth to work with. It is better to apply multiple layers
using a light or a standard pressure (see page 23), as this ensures the tooth
remains undamaged, leaving 'grip' for the pencils even after the graininess
has disappeared from the eye.

How much pencil do I need to apply?

Each layer you add fills the tooth a little more, brings another level of refinement to your work and, of course, allows for more detail. Think of it as a photograph: the initial colour blocking is an out-of-focus version of the subject. As you add more layers, the refinement, or focus, gets sharper. The more you work your piece, the more in-focus it becomes.

The amount of pigment that you apply comes down to your own personal choice and the result you hope to achieve. Having said that, when you think you are finished, I suggest you add another couple of layers (especially when working on Pastelmat). In general, we want to aim for a 'buttery' surface, with the valleys nearly filled and only the very peaks of the mountains showing.

Virgin surface No pigment has been applied; and the mountains and valleys of the surface are completely untouched. Keep it untouched! You don't want to contaminate it with oils from your fingers.

Grainy surface By using an even pressure, the pigment has fallen evenly into the surface. Of course, the surface itself has natural variation; so as a result, applying the pencil will reveal the grain specific to that support. At the grainy stage, the pencil is catching on the mountains and falling into the valleys, but there's still a big gap between pigment on the mountaintops and in the valley bottoms. As result, some of the surface colour can still be seen.

Halfway surface At this stage, the valleys are halfway full. The action of the pencil will have begun to abrade the sharp edges of the mountaintops, but the surface is still too gritty for some techniques to work to full effect. Some small areas of the surface are still visible.

Buttery surface This is the ideal quality for most of the techniques. Here, the valleys are full enough that only the very tips of the mountains peek out from the layers of applied pigment, which are showing great depth of tone. Tiny hints of the underlying support are visible on close examination.

Smooth surface Too much pigment has been applied; the valleys are completely filled with pigment to the height of the mountains. The pencil will start to skate over the surface, making unwanted marks, as shown. You'll find it harder to control the application of further pigment. The only way to get pigment to stay at this point is to increase the pressure; but this will start to muddy or remove the pigment already applied.

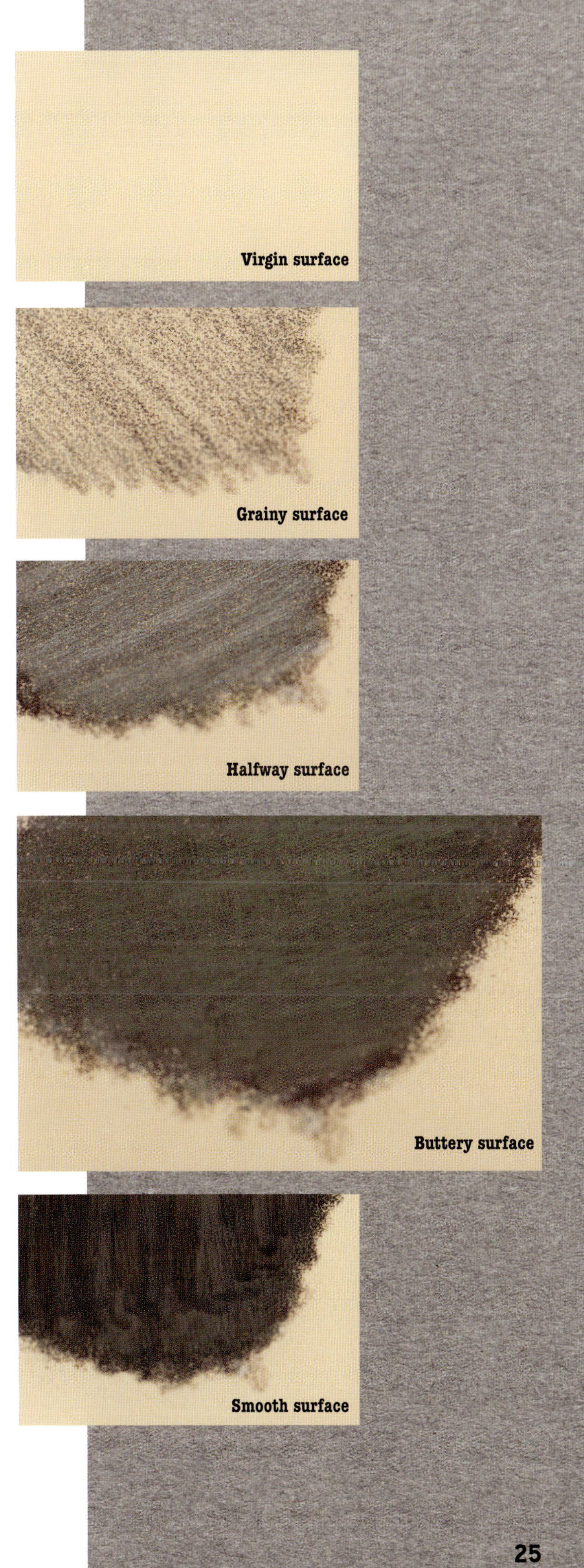

"

MARKMAKING

When creating animal fur, a common mistake is to use the same textural stroke to apply the pigment throughout a piece. This can give a lovely look to the final portrait but it shows no variation in fur texture and therefore becomes more stylized and less realistic. These pages show you how to produce marks and strokes that will give you varying types of texture within a piece.

Using different strokes and varying the pressure of application can create many different textures. You may not use them all, but it is a good idea to understand the options available and the results that they can each achieve. I break these marks down into three categories: dots, lines and circles. In addition, markmaking involves subtraction and layering techniques to allow for further variety in texture, tone and colour. These techniques are also included in this part of the book, which teaches you all the fundamentals you need for portaits of animals.

Pug
A variety of the techniques in this chapter were used for this soulful pug. By the end of the book, I hope that you will feel confident enough to tackle something similar.

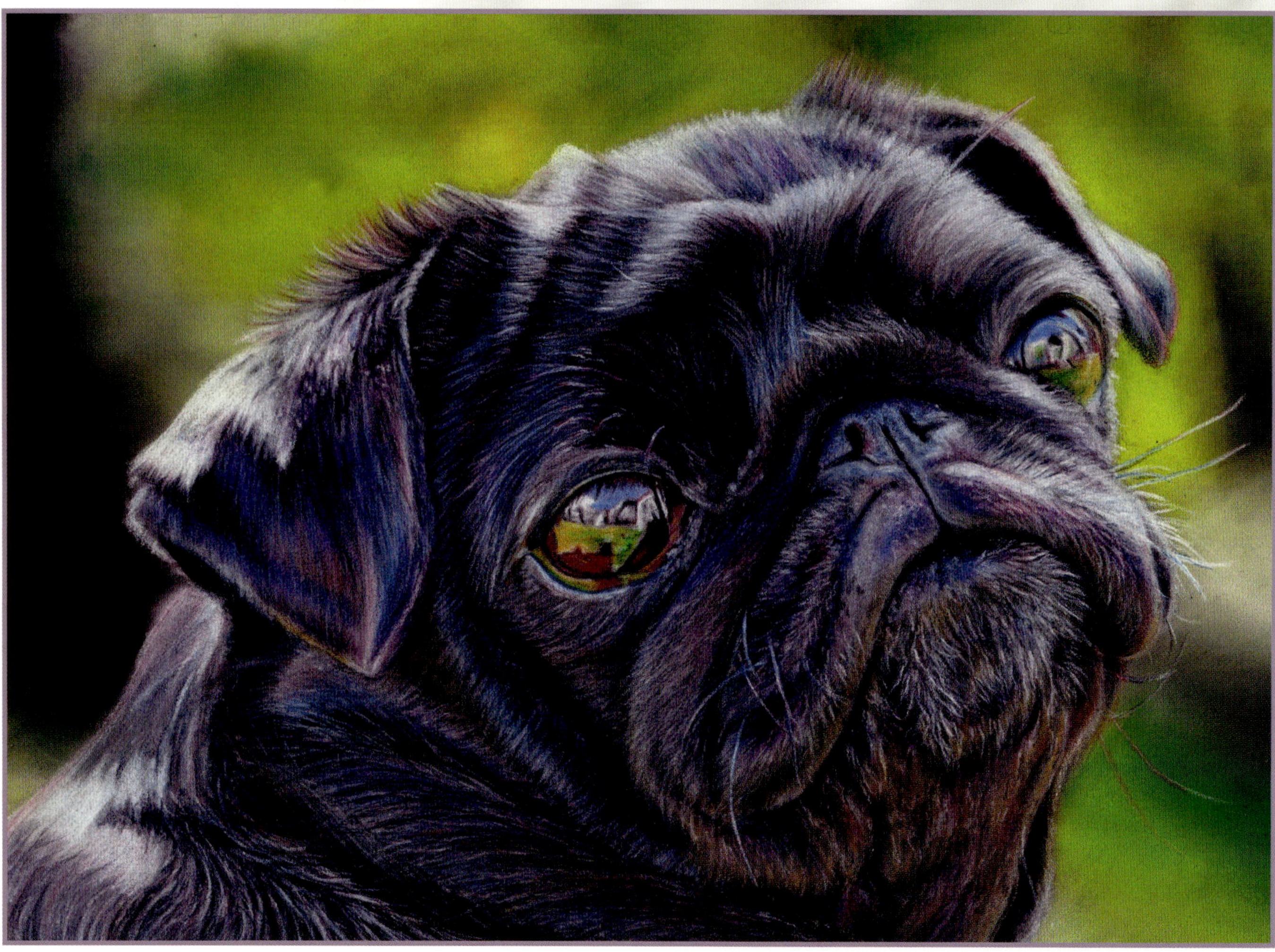

DOT TECHNIQUES

Stippling

This involves holding the pencil in an upright position and repeatedly tapping the tip onto your support to build up an area of tone. You can use a blunt or a sharp pencil to achieve different results. The more stipples that you create, the less the support will show through.

I often use this technique in areas like muzzles where the fur or hair is super short and stubbly. By stippling several colours and tones over each other in an area, you can soon build up a wonderful texture that is completely different to anything else in your piece.

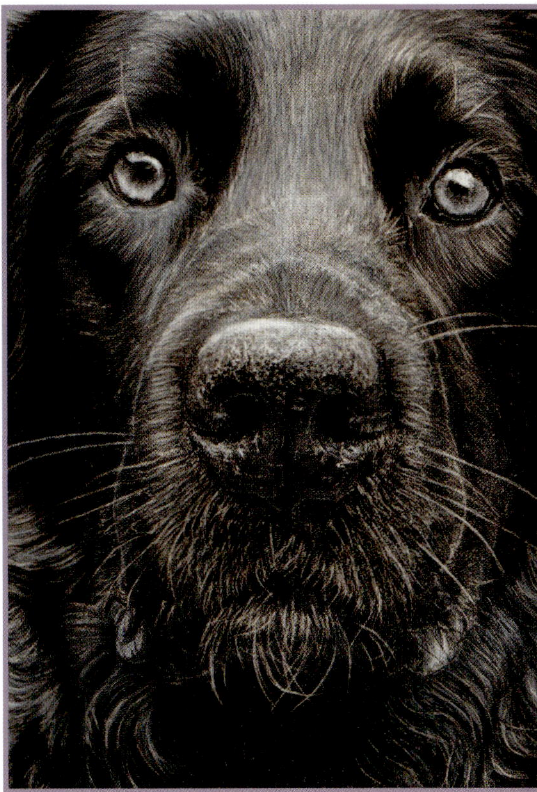

Max
Stippling is used here for the texture on the nose.

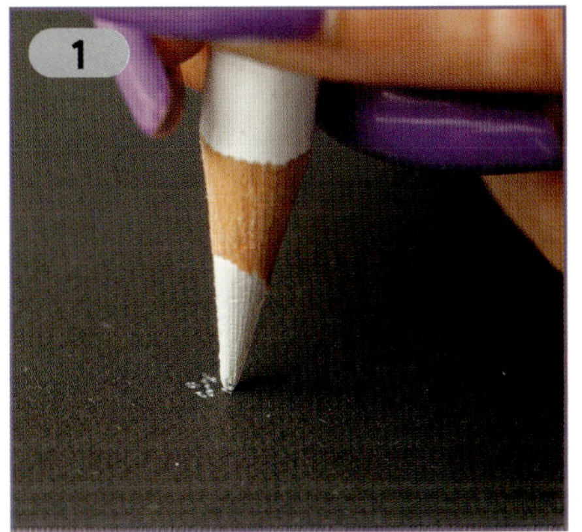

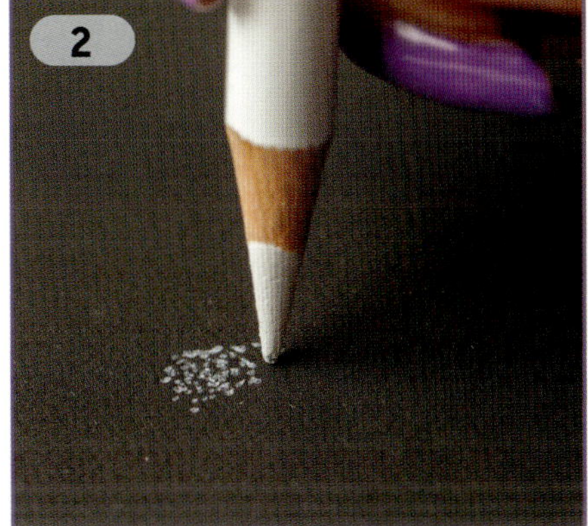

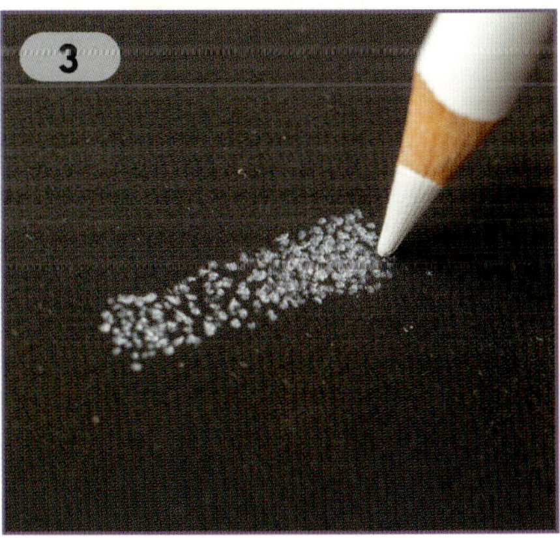

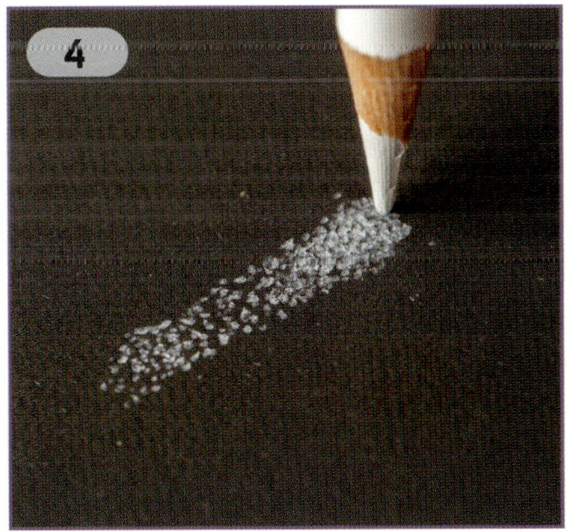

Tip

Blunt or rounded pencils will make bigger dots than sharp ones – this is useful to bear in mind.

1 Holding the pencil almost upright and near the tip, tap it to the surface repeatedly to create fine dots. The pressure is important. These dots need to be visible to the eye: typically this means you need to press slightly harder than standard pressure.

2 Repeat to fill up the shape, keeping the pencil upright throughout.

3 Overlapping areas of stippling will build up the tone; so you can create both stronger and more subtle tones within an area.

4 You can vary the tone within an area by stippling more densely for a stronger effect, and more sparingly for a lighter result.

Back-and-forth stroke

Another stroke useful for smooth texture areas is a back-and-forth stroke. The pencil is kept on the paper and moved back and forth using an even light to medium pressure. The aim is to move the pencil in straight lines as close to each other as possible so that there is a consistent application.

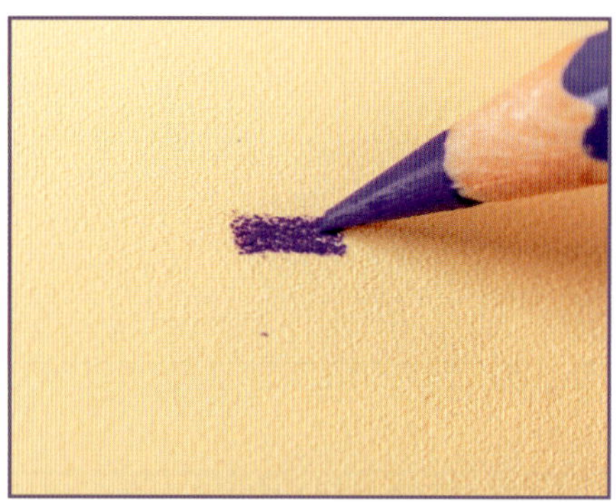

1 Using standard pressure, move the tip of the pencil in a tight back and forth motion. Overlap the previous strokes as you work.

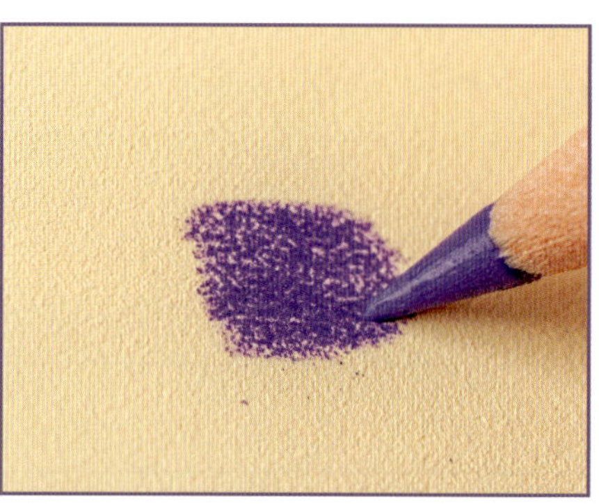

2 The smaller the mark you make, the easier the pencil will be to control. Avoid going too large with the motion, or you will lose control and gaps will appear. Work steadily to cover the surface evenly.

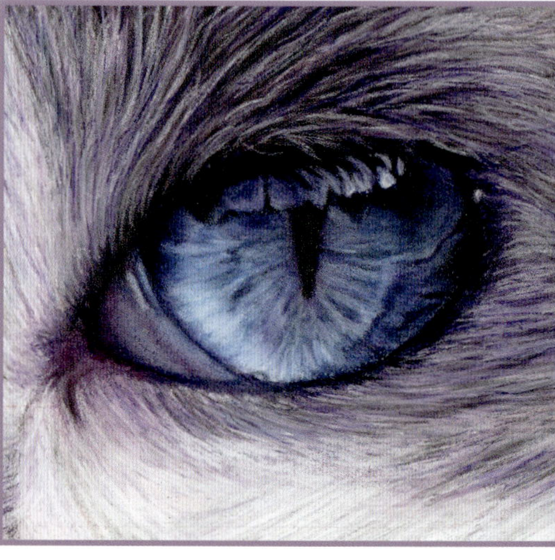

Blue cat eye
This technique is especially useful when creating eyes as you use the back-and-forth motion in the direction of the pupil to the outer rim area of the iris. The eye above had a lot of markings in the iris. While I used a mix of different strokes, the back-and-forth technique was key, as it gives consistent results.

Hatching and crosshatching

Hatching involves drawing straight lines parallel to one another. It is a good method for adding a loose feel to a piece. The closer the lines are together, the more intense the depth of the saturation in an area as you are laying down more pigment and allowing less of the support to show through.

Crosshatching is when another layer of parallel lines are added over the top of the initial hatch lines at a different angle. You can do this using a single hue/colour or you can combine different colours.

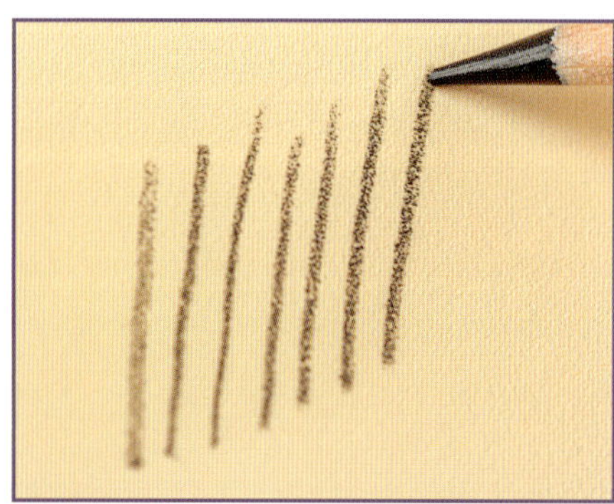

1 Using standard pressure, make a series of parallel lines, with evenly-sized gaps between each. For hatching, you can stop here.

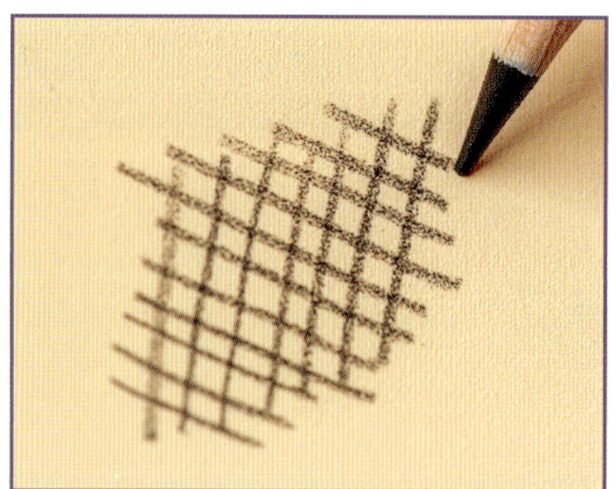

2 For crosshatching, make a second series of parallel lines that cross over the first set at a consistent angle.

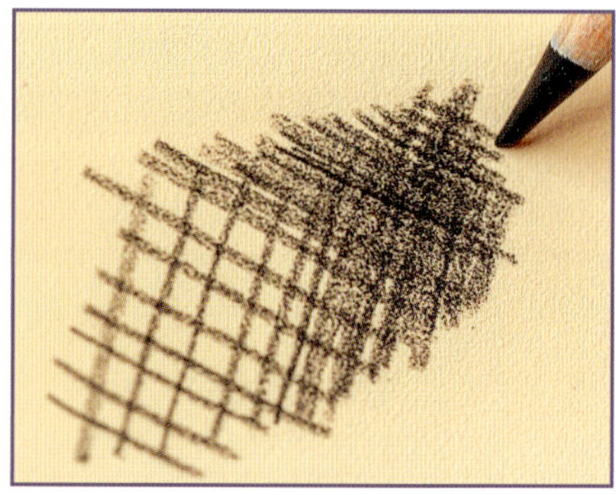

3 Evenly-spaced lines will create an even tone. By reducing the gap between lines, you can create darker tones. The converse is also true.

Striking or tapered marks

This is one of the most common strokes used to create fur texture. I tend to refer to it as the 'press, flick and lift' to describe the motion involved.

Using a sharp pencil you press down on the support with a firm pressure, then flick away, lifting up as you go. The faster that you do this, the looser and more natural the result. The slower the movement of the stroke, the more controlled and consistent the finish of the fur.

These marks can be made straight away on a surface like drafting paper, but on Pastelmat or similar toothed surfaces, they are best added onto a surface previously worked up to a buttery finish (see page 25) as shown here.

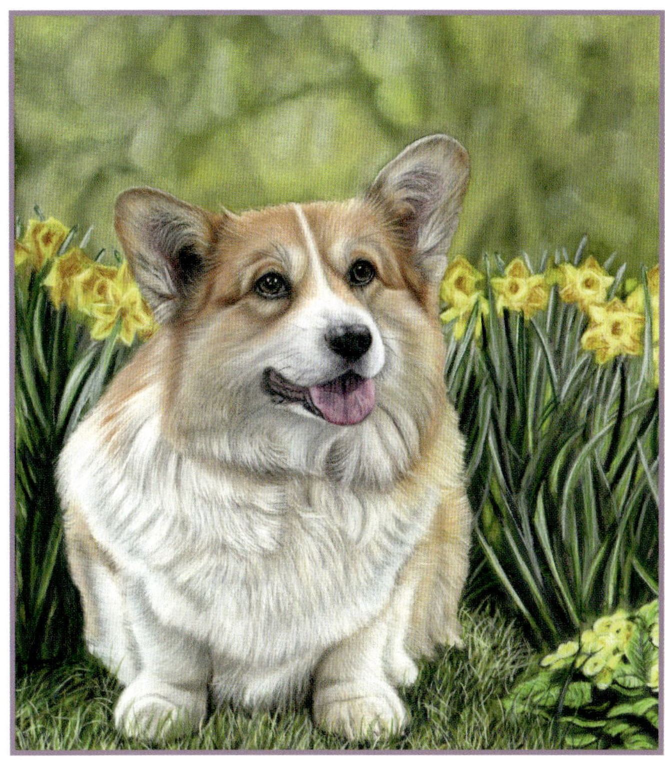

Corgi
This technique was invaluable here for the finer, longer hairs of this corgi's coat.

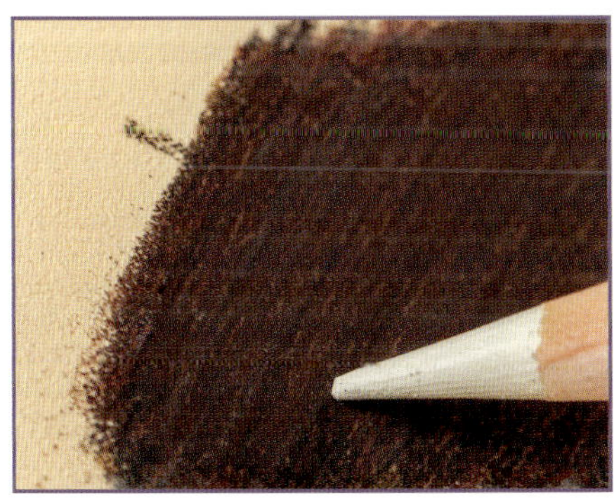

1 Using a sharp pencil, press the tip to the surface with a firm pressure.

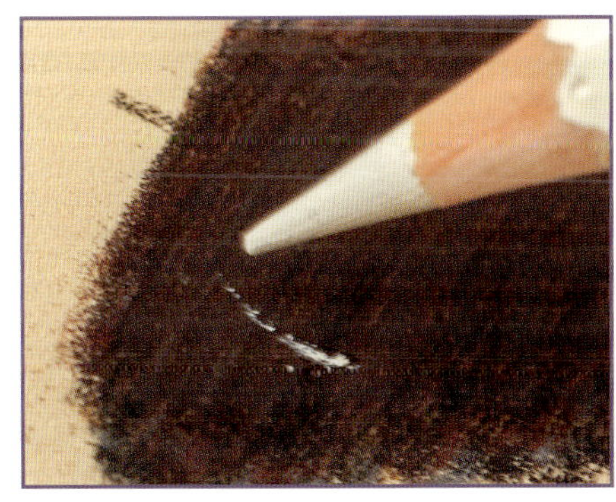

2 Flick the tip away from you, allowing the tip to lift away at the end of the stroke.

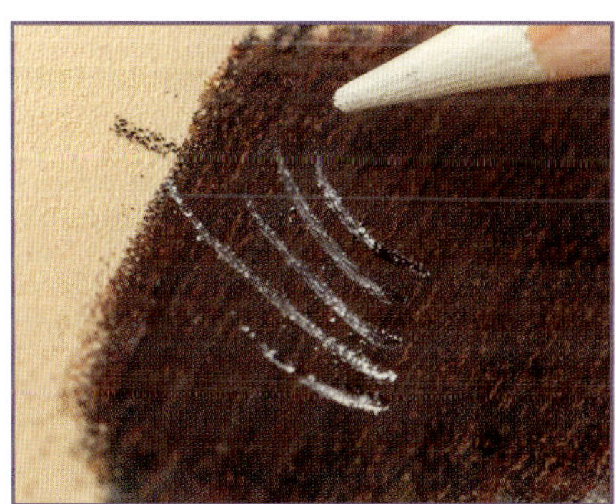

3 You can vary the length of the stroke as you work.

Tip

You may find resting your wrist on the table and moving just your fingers allows you more control over this technique. If making longer, larger struck marks, you'll need to move your whole hand.

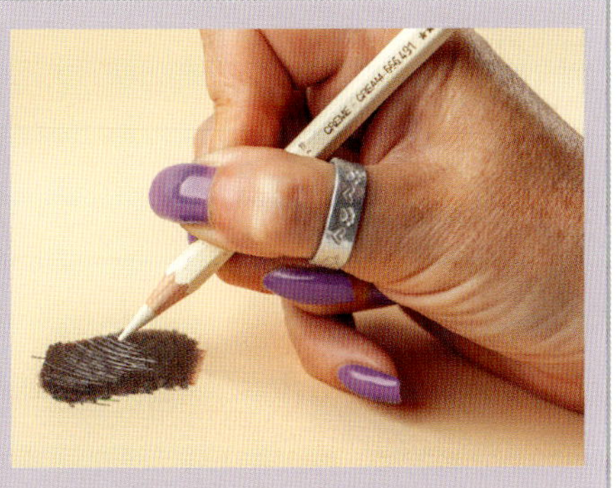

CIRCLE TECHNIQUES

Scumbling

When I want to achieve a smooth finish suitable for skin, or a glossy eye, I lay down my pigment using this technique. Similar to the back-and-forth stroke on page 28, scumbling is a process of applying pigment using a light, consistent, even pressure. Scumbling uses a small, tight circular motion rather than back-and-forth lines.

When working on a textured paper like Pastelmat, make the circular marks both clockwise and anti-clockwise to ensure a nice even application into the tooth from both directions. You can hold the pencil in an upright position to the paper for a more even effect.

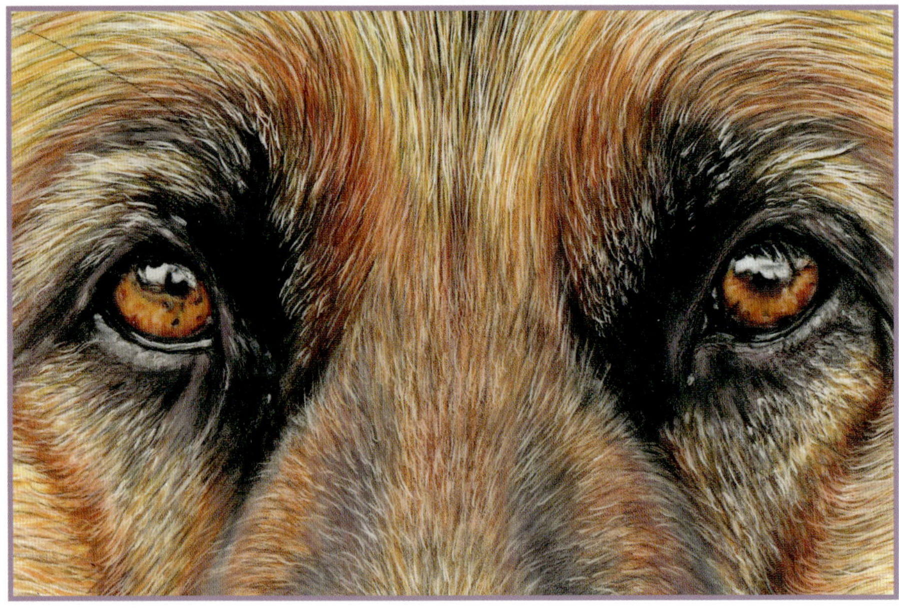

German Shepherd (detail)
Scumbling allowed me to build up the eyes here. It's a subtle effect, but the difference in texture between the glossy eyes and textural fur adds realism.

1 Using standard pressure (see page 23), start to make tight, consistent circles that overlap.

2 Build outwards from the starting point, aiming to leave no gaps and giving a clean, consistent, even application.

3 Continue until you achieve a clean, even colour.

4 Subsequent layers will mix smoothly, evenly and consistently. This technique is about getting a clean finish.

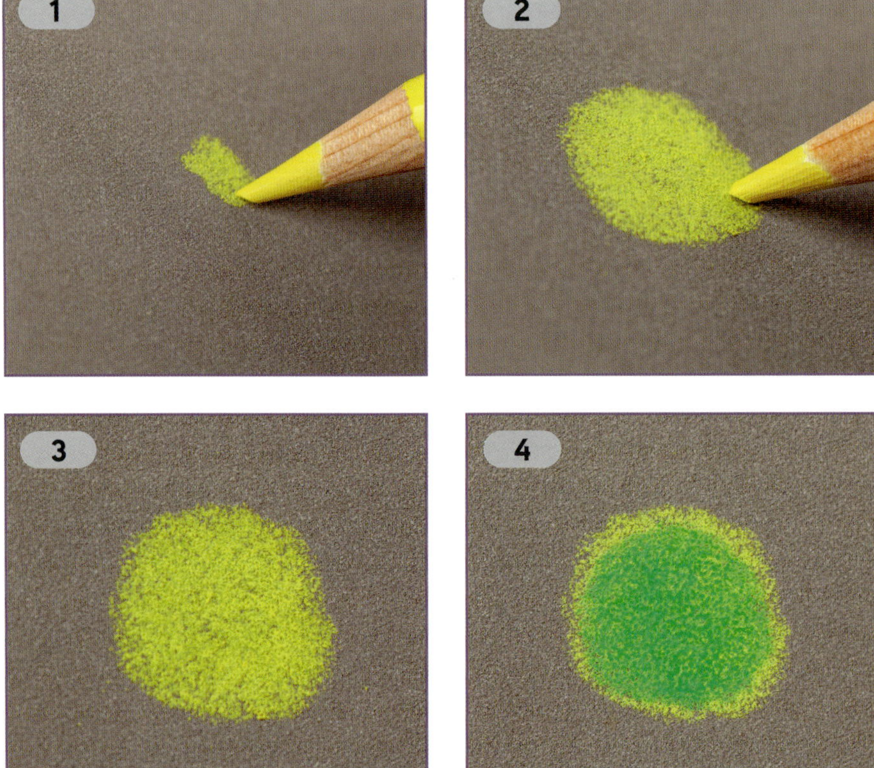

Loose circles

By following the same principle as the scumbling technique opposite, but making your circles wider and more random, you can create a looser texture. This is great for achieving a more sketch-like feel to a piece and to give movement to the fur.

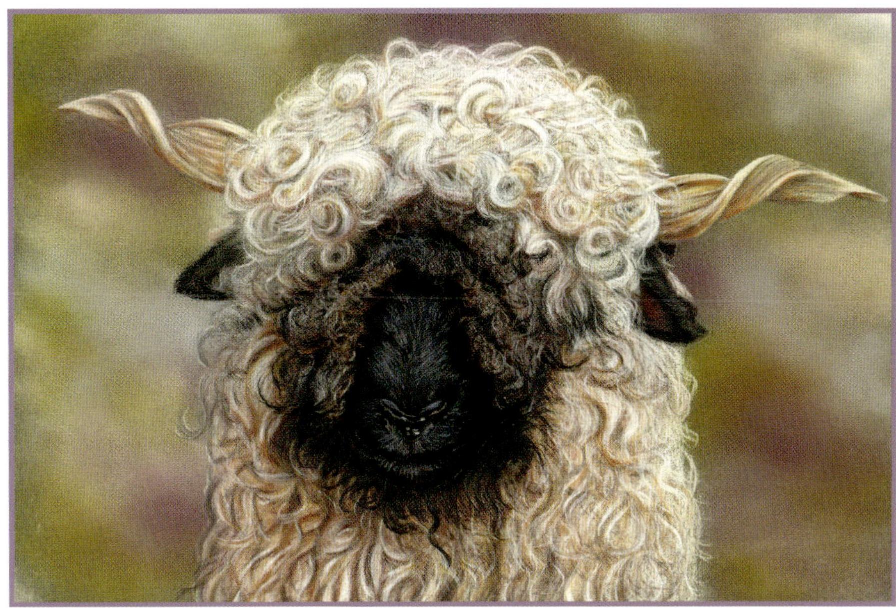

Sheep
Coloured pencils on Pastelmat paper. Here the aim was to create unrefined loose curls, so a random loose circle technique was used. Some of the tooth of the paper was allowed to show through to depict a rough texture. Repetition creates refinement.

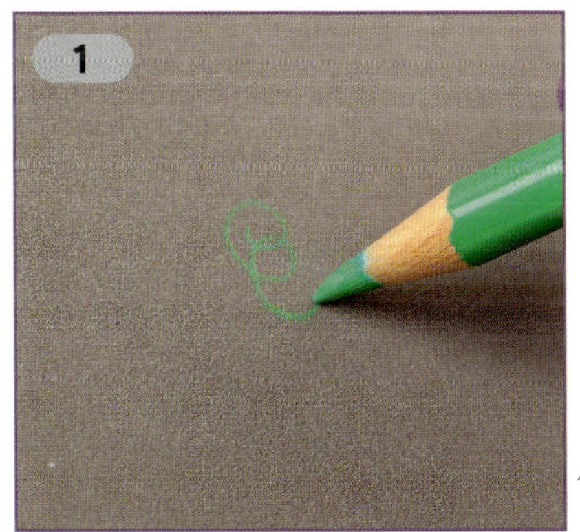

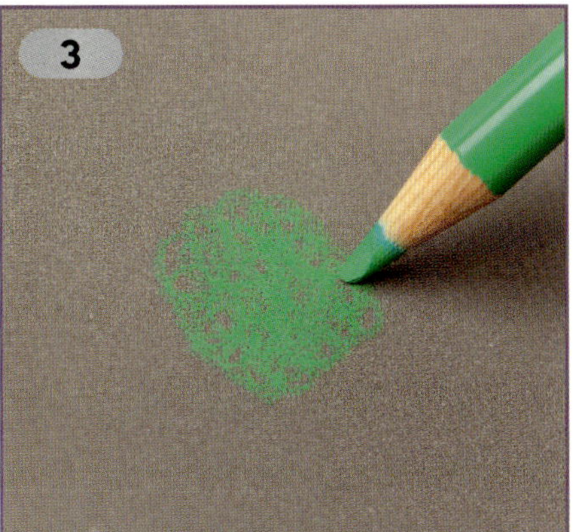

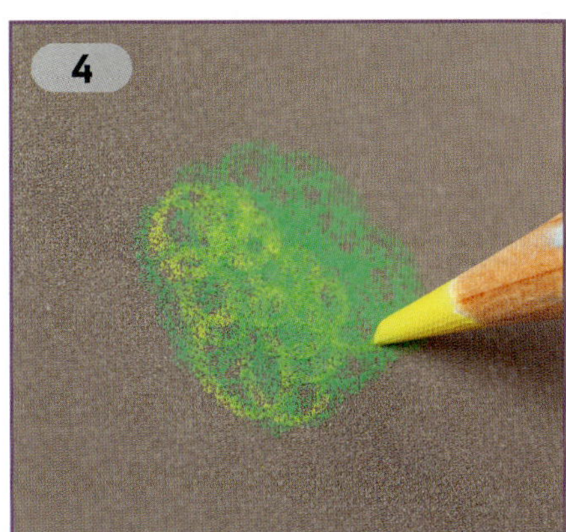

1 Using standard pressure, start to make loose circular marks.

2 Without lifting the pencil tip, overlay and overlap the loose circles. Aim for a random effect; there shouldn't be uniformity in the size of the circles.

3 Continue building up the area. There should be a variety of coverage – some parts might have half a dozen layers, while others are bare paper surface. This creates a loose texture, perfect for fur.

4 You can overlay different colours – as long as you're got the pressure right. This technique makes for good variegated effects with a second or subsequent colour. Some of the new colour will mix with the previous colour, while other parts will touch virgin paper, resulting in a bright, clean effect.

SUBTRACTION TECHNIQUES

These techniques share one thing in common: they leave less pigment on the surface than before. In the case of indentation, we're pressing the tooth of the paper down, so there's nothing for the pigment to grip on to. The other subtraction techniques involve removing pigment already applied.

Using erasers

Handheld erasers come in many forms but my favoured ones are the putty eraser and the Tombow Mono erasers. Putty erasers can be moulded into different shapes and either dabbed on a surface to lift off pigment and texturize, or squeezed into a fine roll shape to create lines and marks.

The Tombow Mono zero erasers are wonderful to use as they come in a casing like a pen, and are retractable. You can trim the nib using a knife to create even finer lines and they are available in both cylindrical or rectangular shapes. I use them mainly on drafting film to create larger chunks of fur texture.

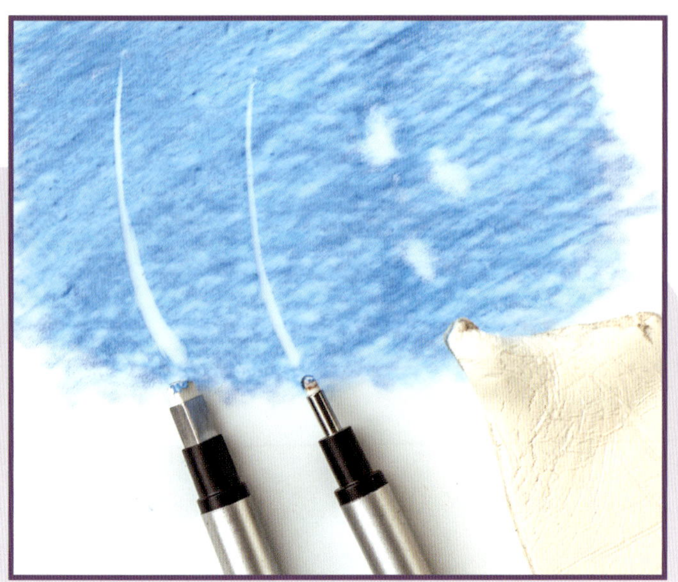

Qualities of marks of different erasers
Rectangular flat Tombow elastomer eraser; Small round Tombow elastomer eraser; and putty eraser formed into a point.

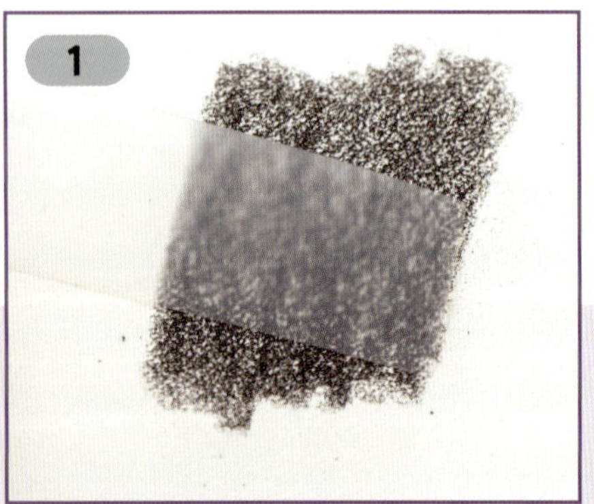

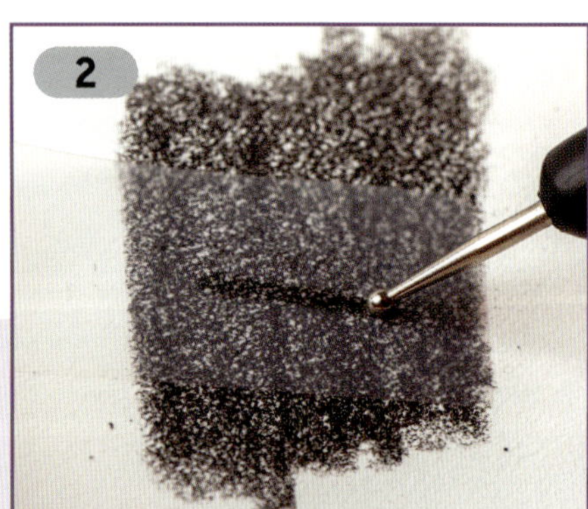

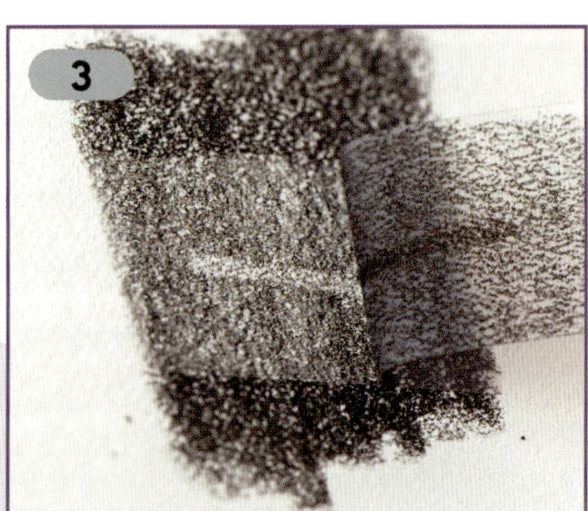

Lifting off with tape

1 Cut a strip of low-tack tape (I use Scotch Magic Tape, as it is clear, allowing you to see the specifics of what you're lifting off) and rest it over the area of colour you want to lift.

2 Use a stylus, with any drawing technique, to press down the tape in any areas from which you want to lift away more pigment.

3 Carefully peel away the tape to reveal the result.

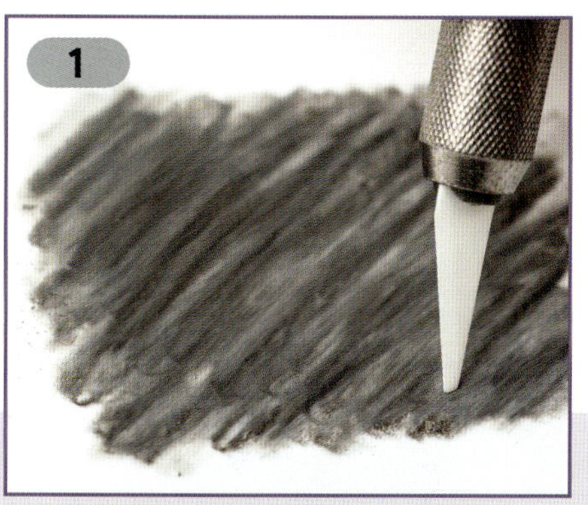
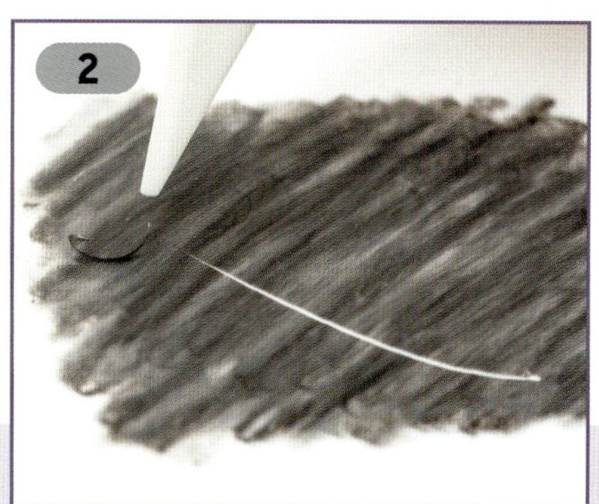
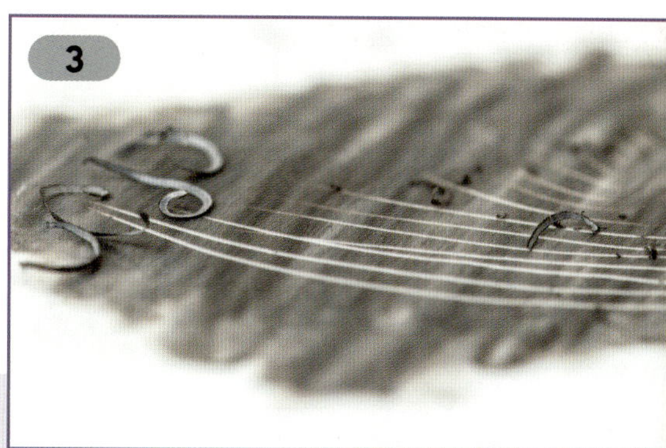

Using a knife

The key things to remember here are, firstly, that you're aiming not to damage the surface – you're not cutting or scraping, so never use the blade towards you in a cutting motion. The best way to avoid this is to turn the blade upside-down and work away from yourself. Secondly, don't think of the knife as something alien, or to be feared. Treat it as you would any other drawing tool, holding and using it exactly like a pencil.

1 Place the back of the blade on the surface.

2 Use it to draw your marks – here I've struck a mark using a tapered stroke.

3 If you have a buttery surface, you can remove just a few layers with a light touch; with a heavy touch, you can take it right back to the bare surface. This technique tends to work best on drafting paper.

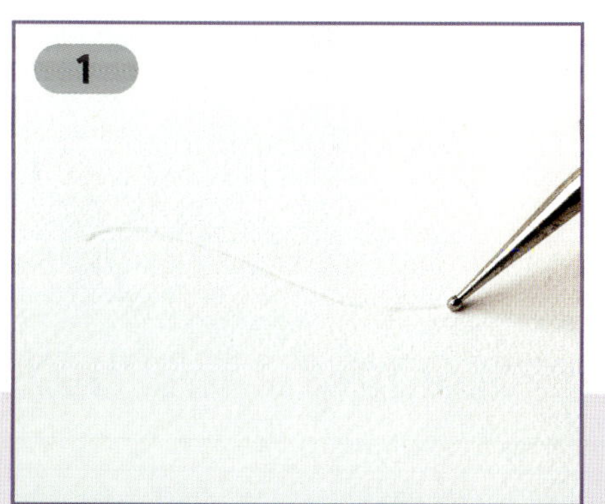
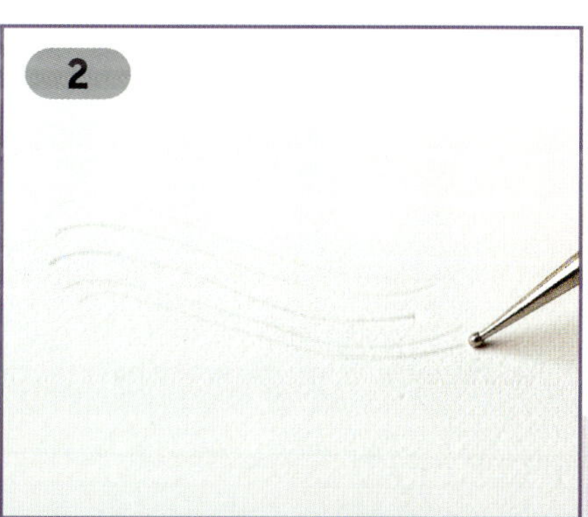
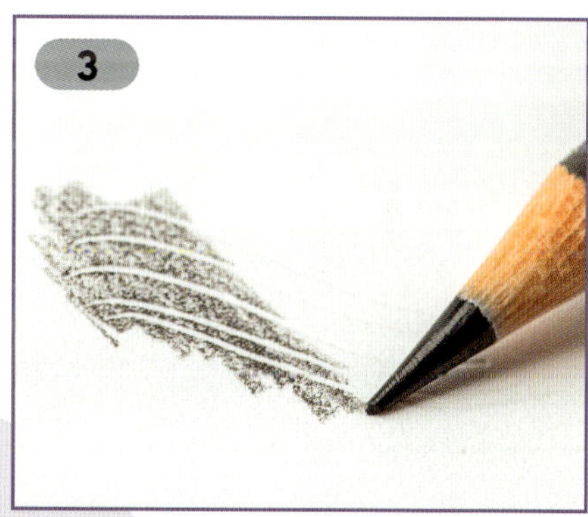

Indenting

1 Using firm pressure (dependent on the mark you want to make, of course) and holding the stylus like a pencil, make your mark. You can use any of the drawing techniques detailed earlier.

2 Make any further marks with the stylus before applying colour. It's possible to indent over colour, but for now let's concentrate on keeping the surface as clean as possible.

3 Now when you work with pencil over the top, the indented areas will remain clean. Be sure to work across the lines at standard pressure to avoid slipping into the line.

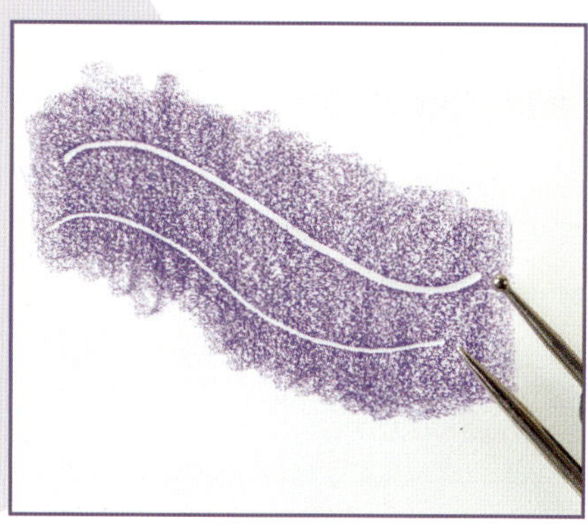

A different stylus size will alter the width of the mark.

COLOUR

CHOOSING YOUR PENCILS

One of the most common problems amongst beginners is that they struggle to see the colours in their reference image. Many take it too literally and reach for their browns to represent a brown dog, when in reality there are myriad hues in that fur. For example, I will often lay a dark indigo and a deep red into my darkest areas to enrich the seemingly black shadows, glaze mauve over a chestnut coat, or add touches of magenta to a black one.

The subject of colour theory could fill a book on its own, and there are lots of resources out there if you want to understand this further. For our purposes here, focus on spending time looking at your reference, and really picking out what's there. In time your brain will begin to pick out the colours automatically and, as you gain knowledge of your pencils, you will instantly be able to colour match. Until then there are other tools that you can use to help you pick out the true colours.

Black and white pencils

It's worth an extra note here on 'black' and 'white' fur or coats. Even what seems the most obvious of black or white fur is never just so, usually incorporating browns, blues or other hues. In fact, pure black and white pencils should only be used as glazes, tints and details.

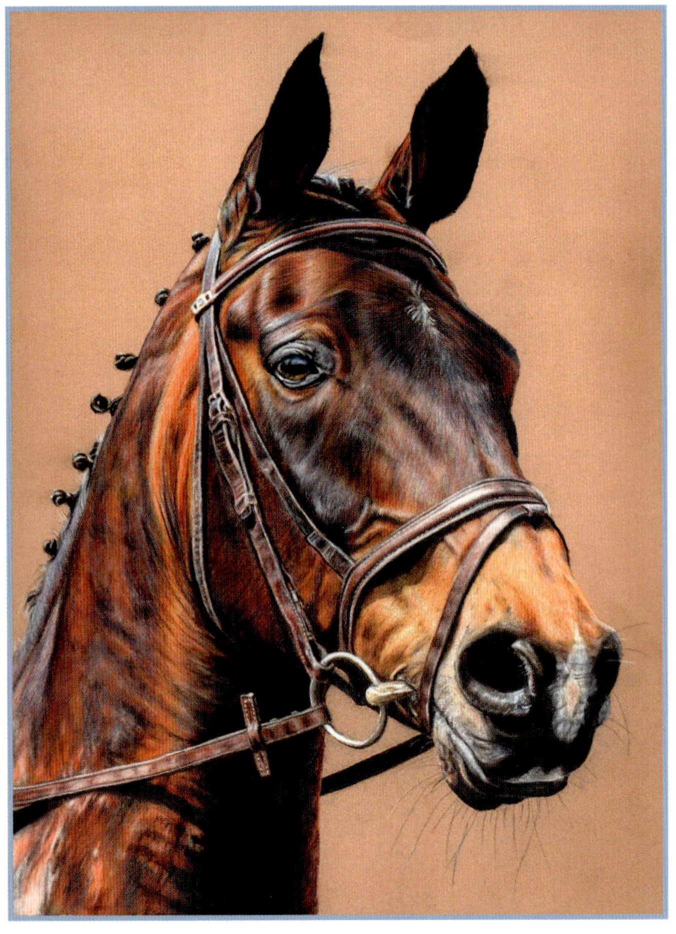

Cowboy
Watercolour pencil base with coloured pencils on Pastelmat. This is an older commission portrait that shows well how a touch of complementary colour added to a piece can really make the coat 'pop'.

Digital help: identifying colour with a colour picker

If you struggle to see colours in your reference, then many apps and programs include colour picker tools to drag those hidden hues out of your photograph, You can then colour match your pencils to those.

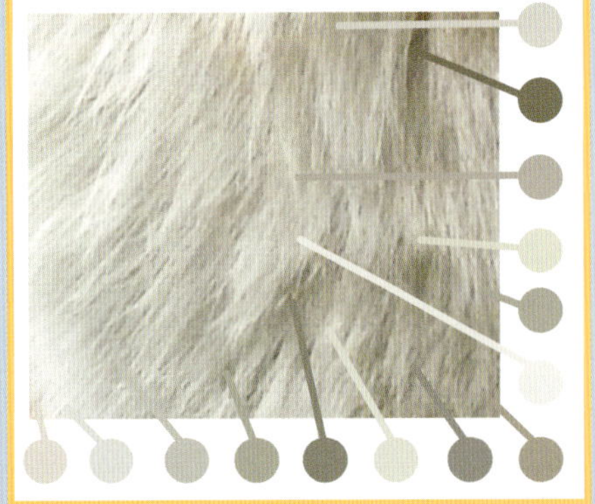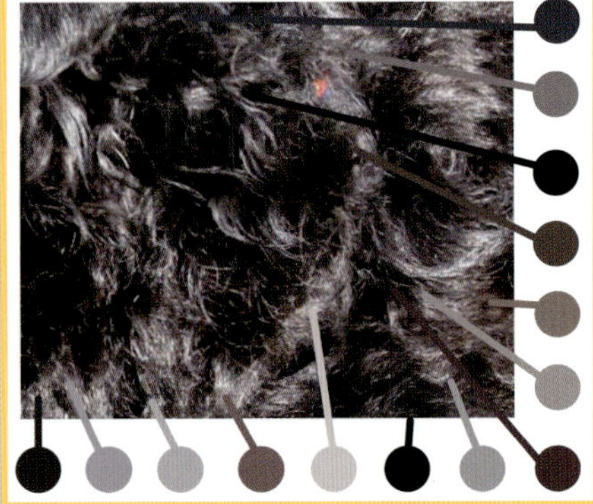

Colour pickers
Just look at the variation of hue and tone in what might first appear simply as white or black.

COLOUR TECHNIQUES

These techniques show you how you can create colours not just by swapping between pencils, but by using multiple thin layers to vary the tone and hue. A basic knowledge of colour theory is beneficial but simple practice with your pencils on a spare sheet of paper will soon develop your understanding.

Mixing colours

It is important to understand how to mix colours using pencils, as it is different from using other media. A painter will squeeze their paints onto a palette and then mix and blend their colours, tones and shades before applying them to their support. With pencils, the colour mixing is done on the support itself.

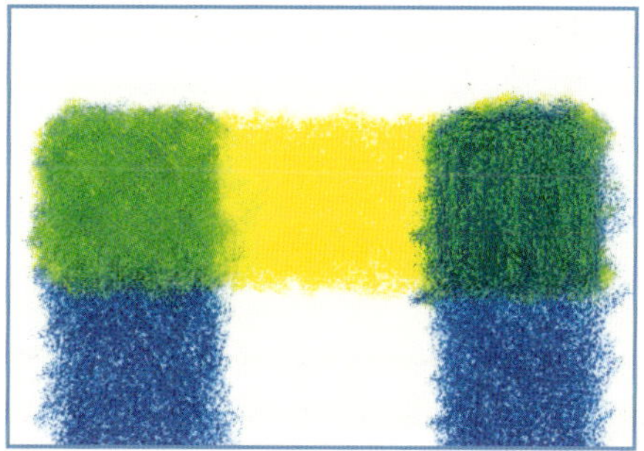

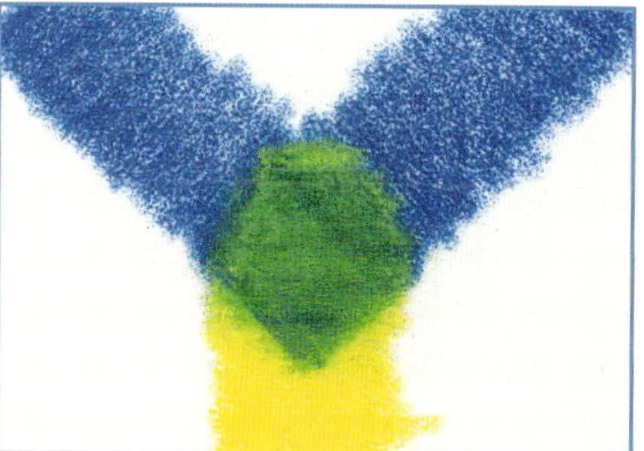

Yellow on blue (top left) and blue on yellow (top right) result in subtly different greens.

Blue on yellow on blue – a stronger bluish-green.

As a result, you don't necessarily need coloured pencils in myriad hues – you can create beautiful, rich realistic works of art just using the primary colours red, yellow, blue, along with a magenta and your black and white; creating the hues you need through layering. The important thing to remember when layering to change the hue is that you need to consider both the ratio and order of the mix. Three layers of yellow over one layer of blue will result in a yellowish-green. If, however, the blue was the last layer added, it will make the green a little more blue.

Adding white will lighten to make a tone. Adding black will darken to create a shade. Knowing the order of application, the amounts and the pressures all come with time and, most importantly, practice.

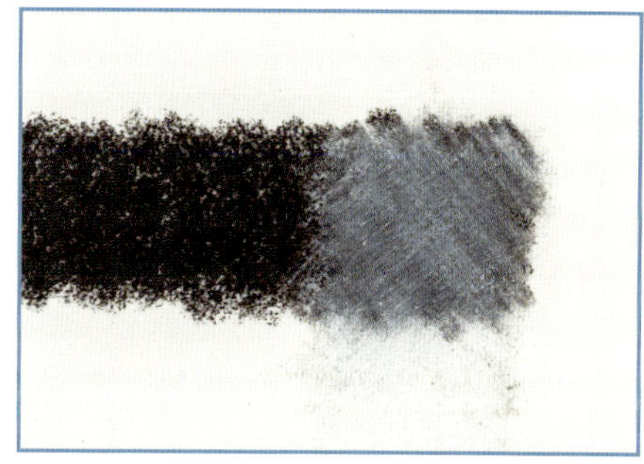

Black and white mix to make a mid-grey.

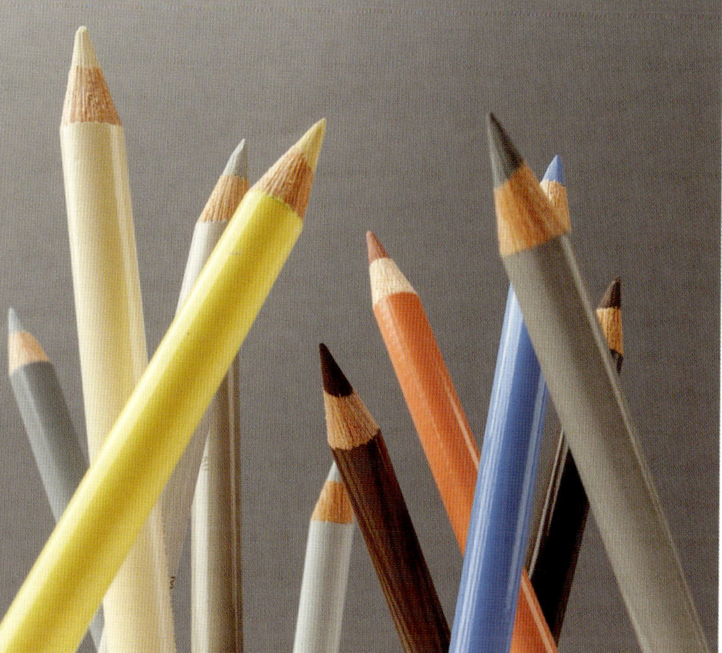

Softening

I refer to some of my pencils as my 'softeners' because when used as part of the layering process they do just that: soften the underlying pigment and give more natural results.

Depending on the underlying colour, I will choose the respective softener to work best. Over a red or orange I might use a cinnamon colour, for example. Over an indigo I would use a sky blue or a cool grey and to soften a brown I might use a nougat, a bistre or even an ivory hue.

A warm grey (such as a Faber-Castell Polychromos Warm grey I) over a darker or brighter hue will soften the pigment down, muting it.

Layering to enrich

The pencils are translucent, so if the same colours are applied with standard pressure, some of the previous layers will remain visible, creating depth and interest.

The pictures here show how single layers of the same pencils can be built up repeatedly with standard pressure. Using the same colour on top will strengthen and enhance the hue. In the centre, you can see the effect of gradually layering a mid-tone, light and dark together. You can see how the three constituent pencils affect and enhance the others, rather than creating a flat result.

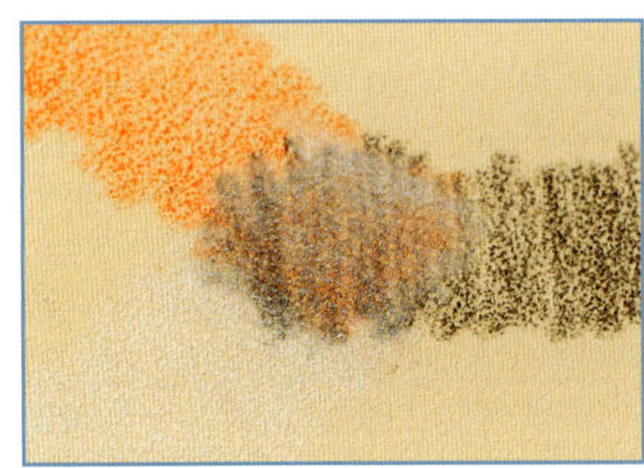

This shows the surface after one layer of each pencil – therefore three in the centre.

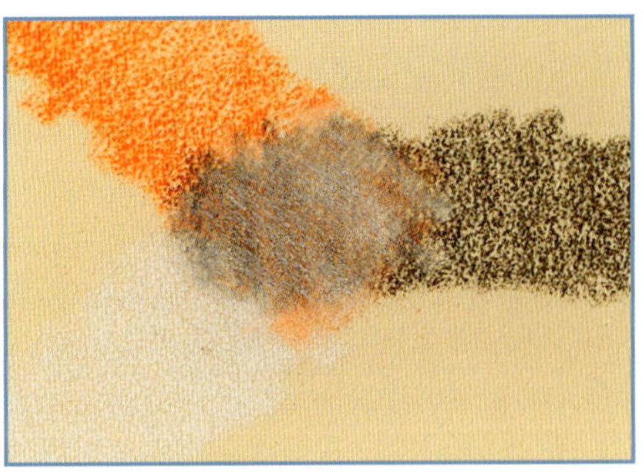

After two layers of each colour, there are six layers in the centre and the colour is beginning to build.

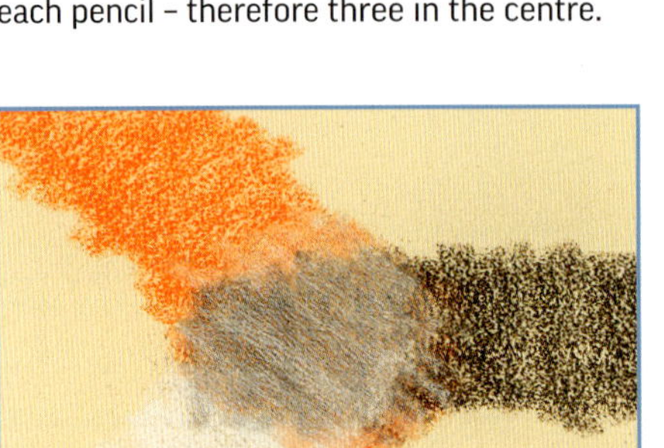

After three layers of each of the midtone, light and dark pencils, there are nine layers in the centre and the colour here is becoming complex and rich.

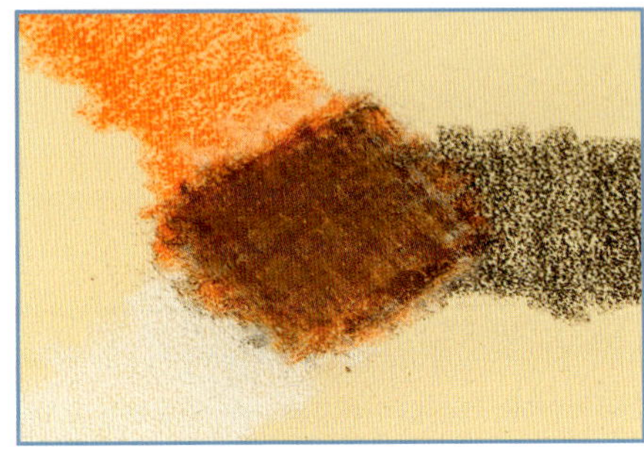

Here, the centre has been worked up to a buttery consistency (see page 25). There are roughly fifty layers or so in total here.

Glazing

Glazing is the application of a translucent layer of colour evenly, smoothly and quickly. It involves using a light pressure, just enough to create a 'glaze' of that colour over the top of the layers of pigment already in place, subtly enriching the hue.

The best way to do this is to adjust your grip on the pencil as shown to the right, almost pinching it, with the whole hand above the pencil. This brings more of the pencil nib's surface area into contact with the surface, and prevents you from applying anything more than the lightest of pressure.

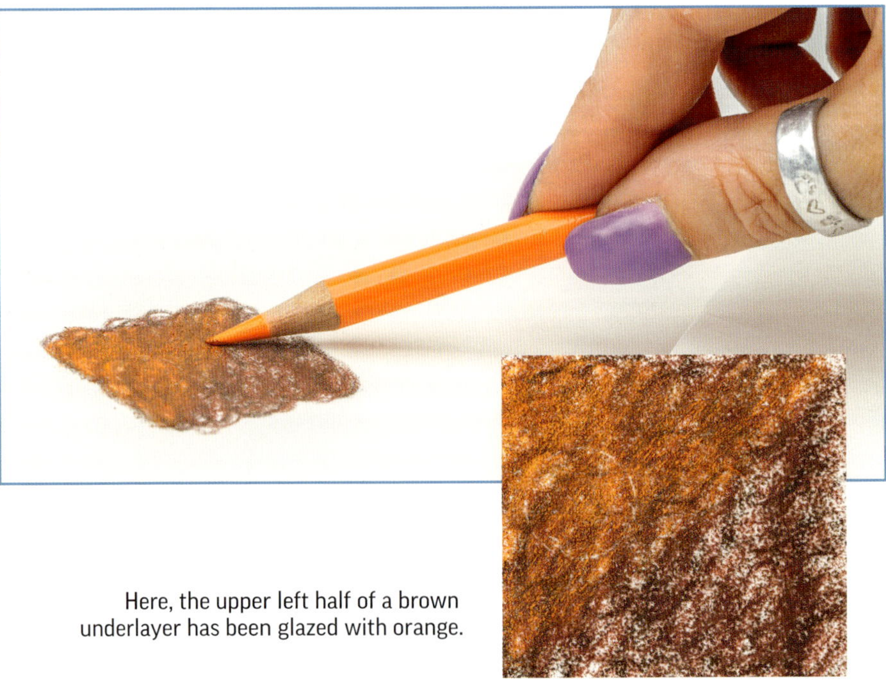

Here, the upper left half of a brown underlayer has been glazed with orange.

Smooshing

This blending technique relies on three things: sufficient pigment already applied; a smooth support such as drafting film; and a soft pencil for the top layer. You can get this technique to work on a textured surface such as Pastelmat, but you need to have more layers in place before you start.

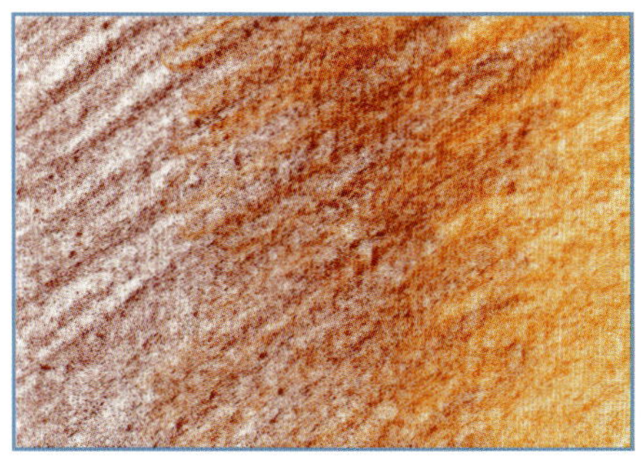

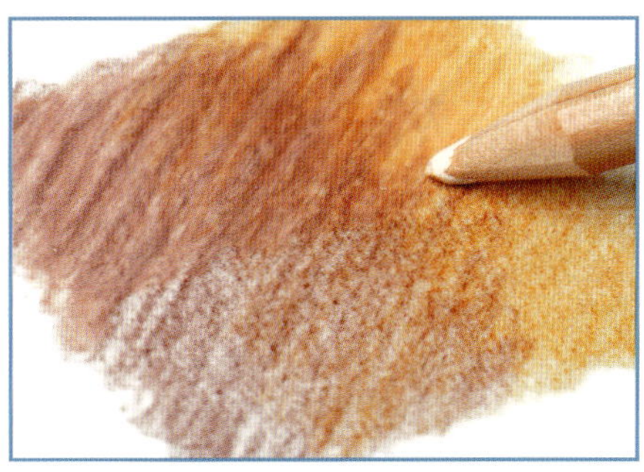

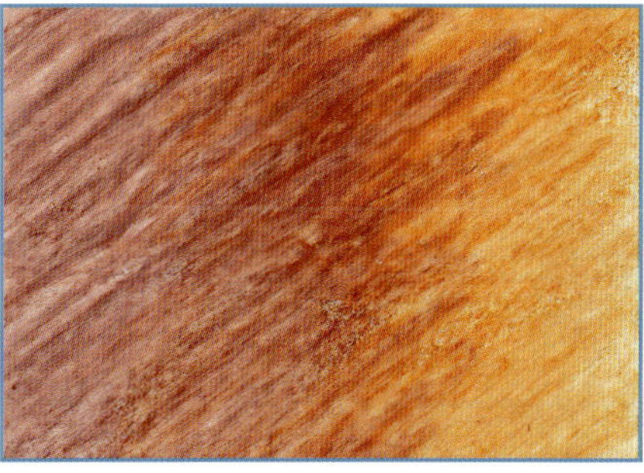

1 Build up to three or four layers of pigment on your drafting film. You can use any sort of pencil for this step.

2 Using your soft pencil, work over the top with a firm pressure. The aim is to drag or press all of the underlying pigment together. Choose a colour that's a lighter variation of one of the base layers. For this warm brown-orange example I'm using a warm pink-white.

Smooshing softens and blends the pencil marks together.

Colour blocking

Identifying blocks of similar tone or hue is a good way to simplify complex fur. Note that blocks of colour can overlap. Don't fill your work in like a jigsaw, bumping edges with no interaction between colours.

1 Squint (or, if you wear spectacles, remove your glasses) to make things blurry. You stop seeing objects, and reduce things to abstracts blocks of colour.

2 Start by identifying the darkest blocks and mark them in. These initial layers shoud be made with a back-and-forth motion at standard pressure. Even at this stage, I'm thinking about the direction in which the fur grows, and blocking in with this in mind.

3 Identify the next large obvious shape and block it in with the closest match of tone and colour – in this case the black fur has a deep blue tinge.

4 Carry on building up the blocks of colour, overlapping where appropriate.

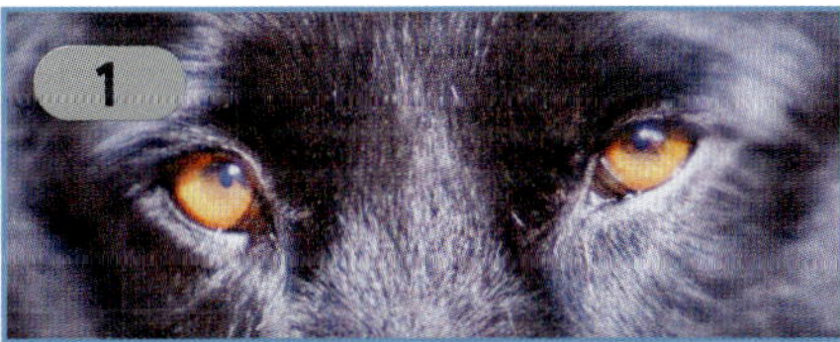

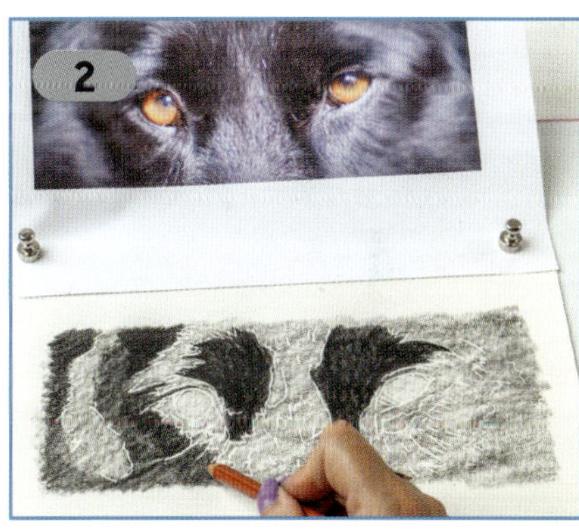

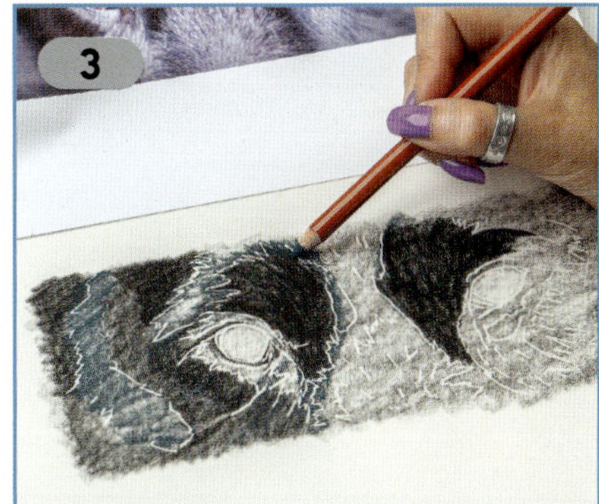

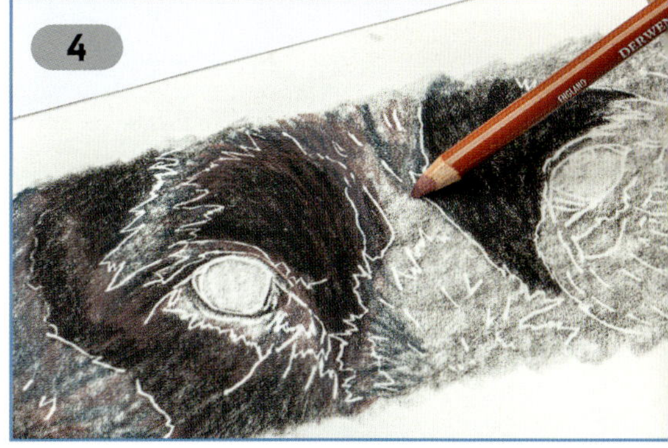

Tip

A variation on this technique is useful when creating line art – see pages 46–47.

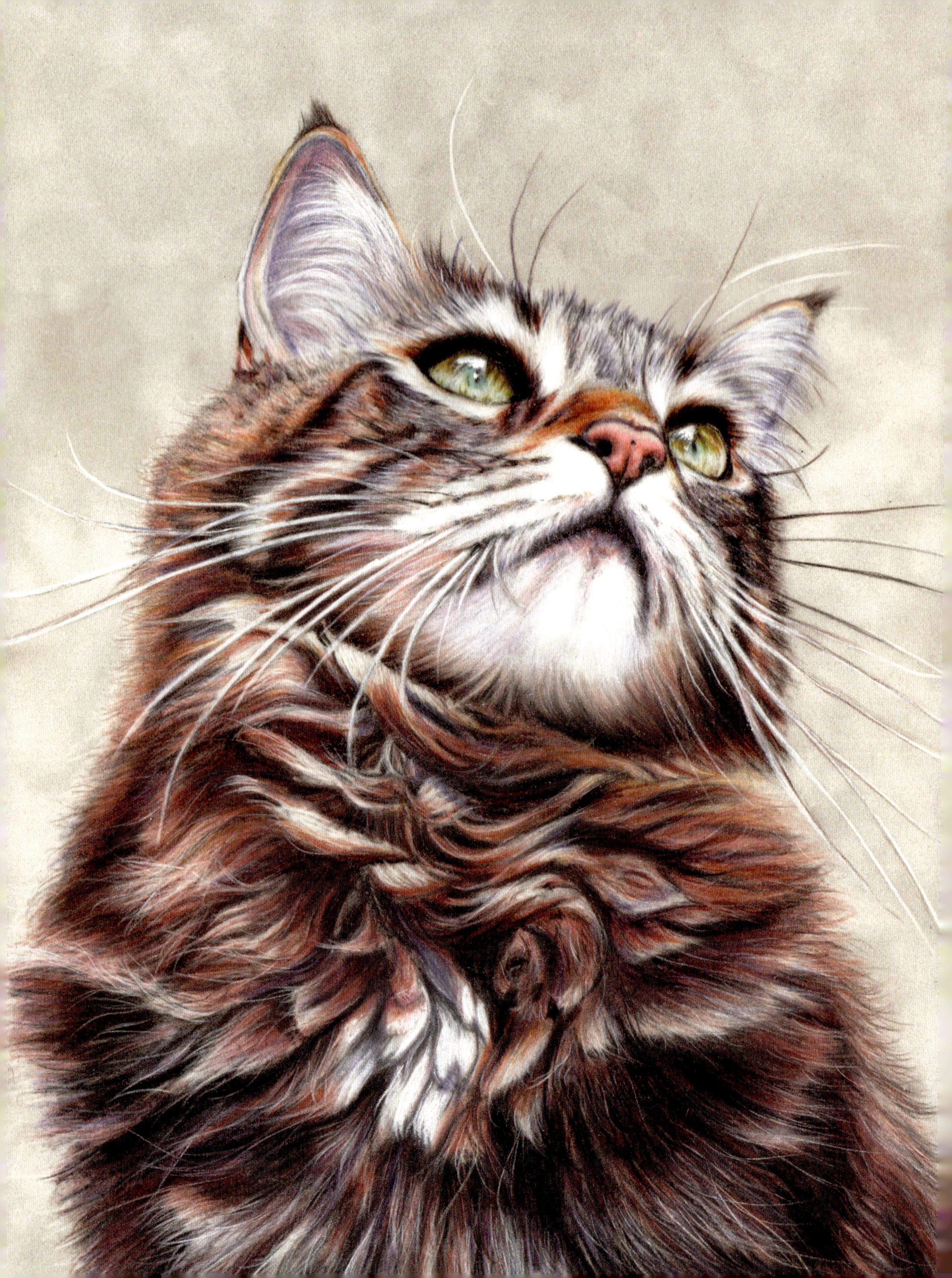

COMPOSING YOUR PORTRAIT

We have looked at the basics regarding different supports, materials and techniques for laying down coloured pencils. It is essential to practise these until you feel that you understand the application processes involved and the way in which your support and your choice of pencil stroke can affect the end result. The studies that are coming up are designed for you to take this knowledge further, building your skills until you feel confident enough to move on to the complete portrait projects that start on page 96.

Before this, however, I want to talk to you about some other key parts of the equation when looking to create an animal portrait – getting good reference photographs, producing a useful drawing and getting that drawing onto your final support.

Having access to a sharp, clear photograph taken at the perfect angle can make all the difference to your finished artwork, so there are also some optional hints and tips on editing and enhancing your reference digitally to get it looking its absolute best.

Knowing how to compose a piece so that it best suits the subject is hugely important to a successful animal portrait. We start this chapter by looking at how to get the best from your model.

Opposite:
Aura
Coloured pencils on suede mat board. A great deal of preparation is required to produce a finished artwork like this – but the more effort you put in early, the more likely you are to be successful.

This has been a hugely popular piece for me, especially at exhibitions. Aura is another example of capturing that perfect reference photograph and combining it with the right choice of materials and support.

REFERENCE PHOTOGRAPHS

When I first picked up my pencils, no one told me that I would also need to be a bit of a whizz with a camera! Don't worry; you don't need an intimate understanding of the camera itself – I largely rely on the standard 'auto' settings – but it is important to know enough about the camera to capture what you need in an image. Rest assured that you don't need an expensive or complex camera. Modern smartphone cameras are often of excellent quality, and for our purposes, can capture as useful an image as a professional set-up.

Wherever I go, I try to have a camera with me – just in case. However, I often envision a piece in my head months or even years ahead of meeting my subject and capturing that perfect photograph of them. When you click the camera and you know that amongst the hundreds of photographs that you take of a subject, there are a handful where you managed to catch the perfect image, you come away with a smile on your face and also in your heart.

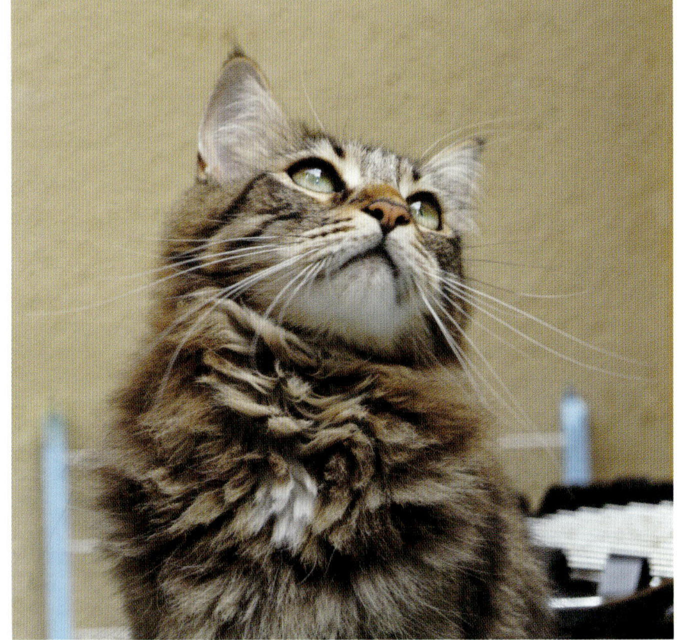

There is a fine balance between how much you try to match your work to the reference image. It isn't just about creating a likeness. It is about capturing a moment, the essence of an emotion that connects with the viewer.

What is the cat above thinking? What is she looking at? What is she about to do next? Considering questions like this adds to the look and feel of your artwork and takes it from being just a reproduction of a photograph to a piece of art that leaves the viewer wanting more.

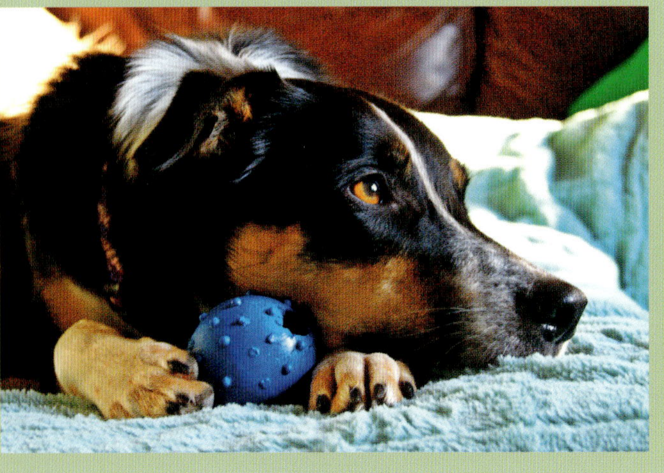

Photography and copyright

Working from my own reference photographs is very important to me, as it is for many artists. It means that I have exclusive rights to my images and any work created from them is unique.

If you choose to work from others' photographs, please always ensure that you have written permission from the photographer. Also, take the time to clarify the copyright laws for your own country.

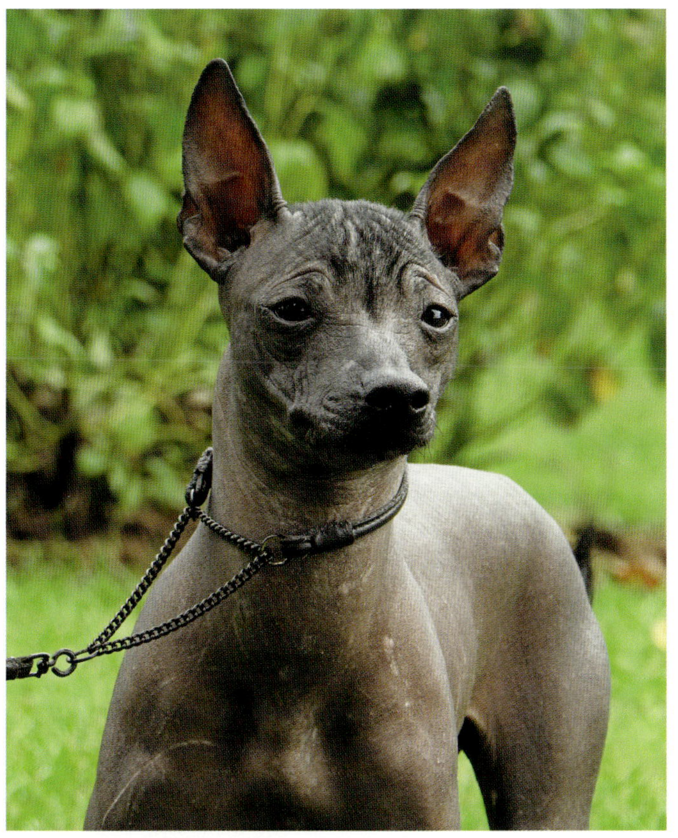

Accuracy and interpretation

I often use elements of several photographs to create one subject. The pose may be perfect in one but the lighting and detail poor. In such cases, I will look for supporting reference photographs that show good lighting, true coloration and also details such as the fur texture and – of course – the eyes, as these are so important to the character of a portrait.

Alongside the reference photograph or photographs you need to understand the character of your subject, as this is the quality of a portrait that allows it to capture more than a photograph. Understanding the character behind the animal will help to take your work from being a simple copy of the reference image to a rendition of 'that' animal – from an anonymous drawing of a typical tabby cat to being a portrait of Bob, the cheeky little tabby who has used up six of his nine lives already and cannot wait until his next playtime with his owner.

When creating a commission piece I always ask for a character description of the animal alongside other reference material. What makes the animal tick? What is the connection between the owner and the animal? What is it about their animal that makes the owner laugh out loud or cry with despair? Asking yourself these or similar questions is useful when preparing any portrait.

It is often a balance or combination of several photographs that will be used to complete a portrait. Let's take these two photographs as an example. The top image is perfect for the pose of a portrait of this dog. However, this breed (a xoloitzcuintle, or Mexican hairless dog), is known for being darker in the summer than in the winter; the second image, and possibly more, are necessary to help you represent the true coloration. If this is a commission piece, you will need to speak to your client to find out which version is truest to how they want the dog rendered. You could use the digital tools mentioned on pages 34, 44 and 45 to edit your images and also to help pick out the colours.

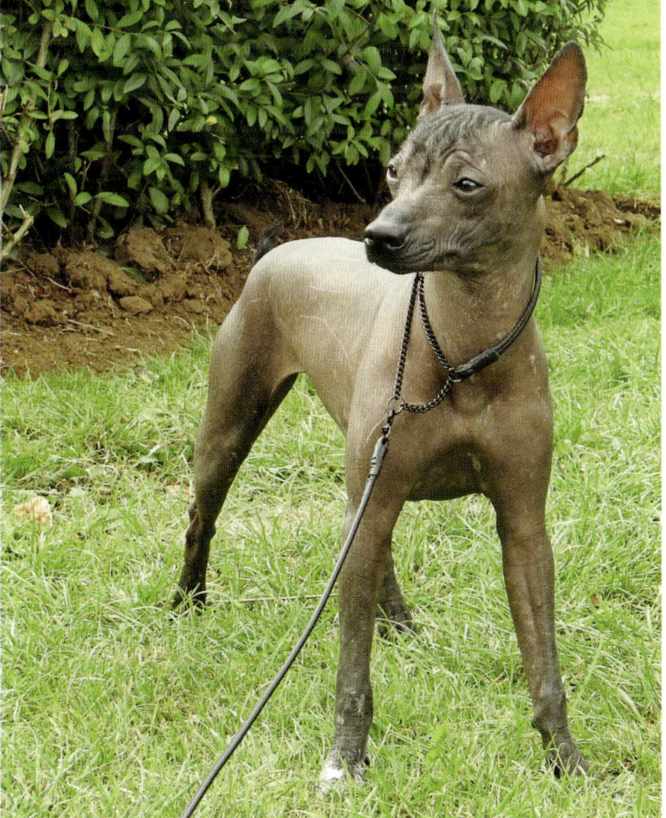

GETTING PERFECT PHOTOGRAPHS

'Never work with children or animals' goes the old saying – but while there is a certain amount of unpredictability to photographing animals, patience and guidance for your subject (and their owner) will always help you to get the results you need. Here are some of my top tips to help you capture the perfect reference photographs.

- Be prepared to sit quietly if your subject is nervous. This gives the animal time to calm down and get used to you, and also allows you to study its character and behaviour.

- Where possible, try to arrange a photoshoot on neutral ground, not at the owner's home. Not only will this help to alleviate the animal's stress that you are intruding on their space, it also provides lots of novel sights and scents to engage and interest the subject.

- Bear in mind that you do not have to capture the perfect pose, perfect light, perfect coloration and detail in one single photograph.

- Multiple reference images of the same subject are invaluable. Take plenty of pictures, so in amongst them you have everything that you need.

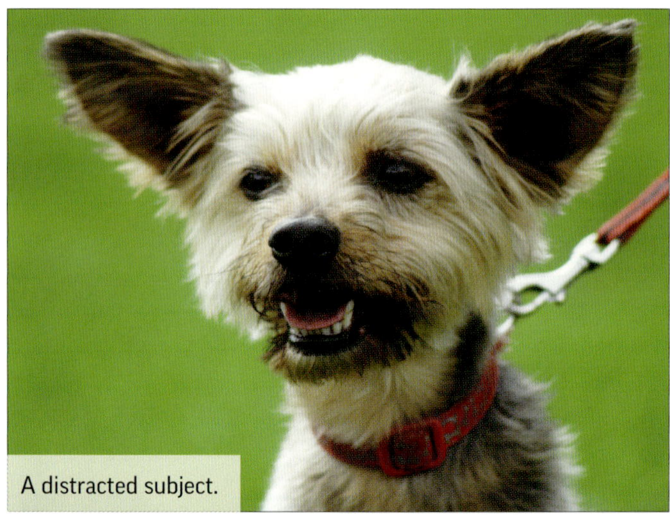
A distracted subject.

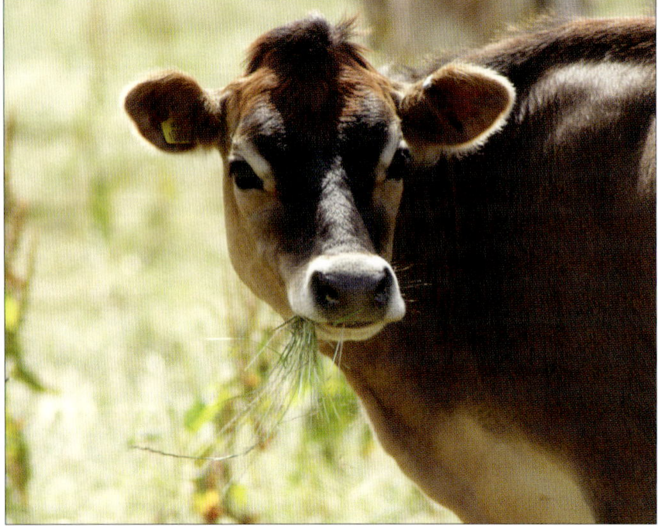

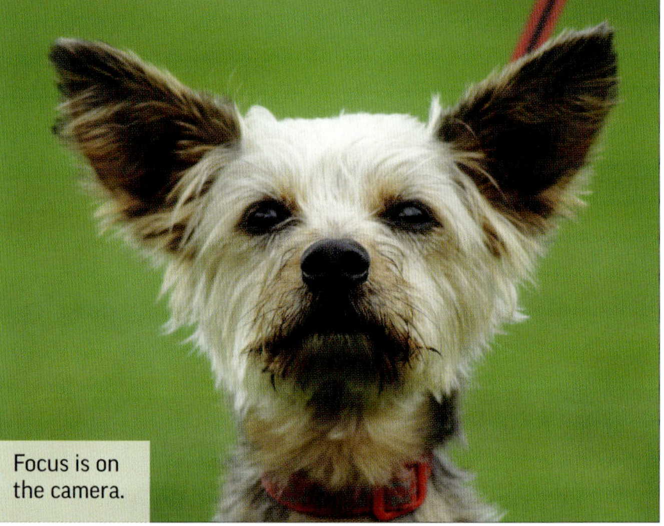
Focus is on the camera.

Sit at a distance

Having a good zoom on your camera will allow you to position yourself further away from your subject, and the owner or handler can then interact naturally with their animal. This allows all parties to relax and you are more likely to capture 'that moment' between a pet and its owner, which is priceless.

This advice is also very useful for getting photographs of farm, zoo or wild animals, as in the example shown above.

Get the subject's attention

An extra pair of hands is always helpful. Try to always have at least the owner plus another person to hand to help focus your subject. If the subject is food-driven, arrange the photography shoot before a meal. This will ensure that tasty treats can be used as bribes during the session itself. Similarly, If the animal is toy-focused, then ask for them not to have been walked or played with until the session for the same reason.

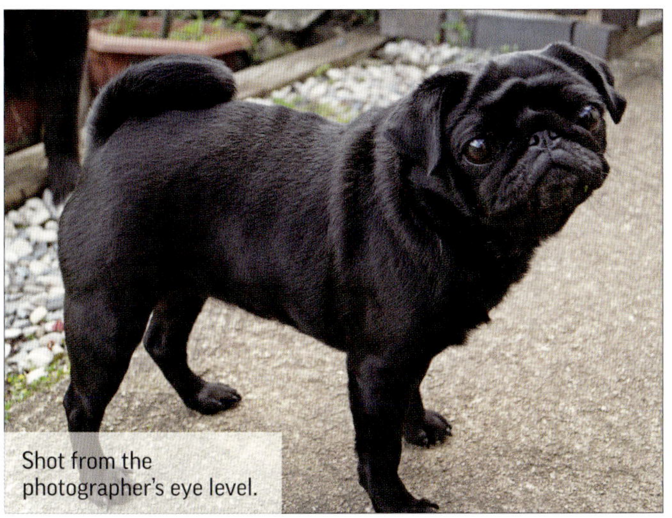

Shot from the photographer's eye level.

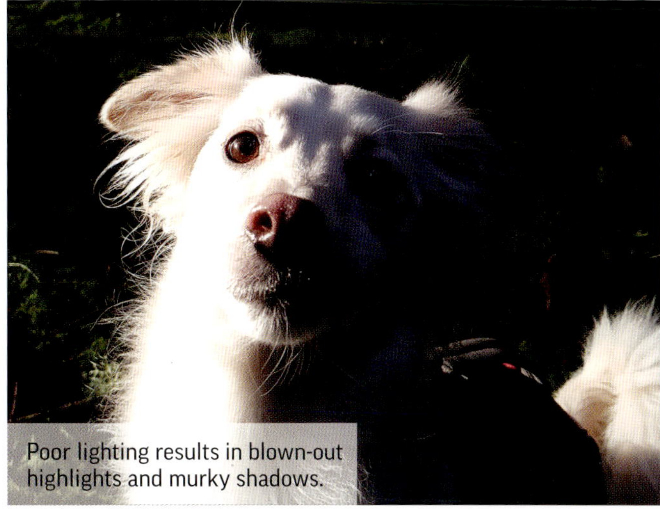

Poor lighting results in blown-out highlights and murky shadows.

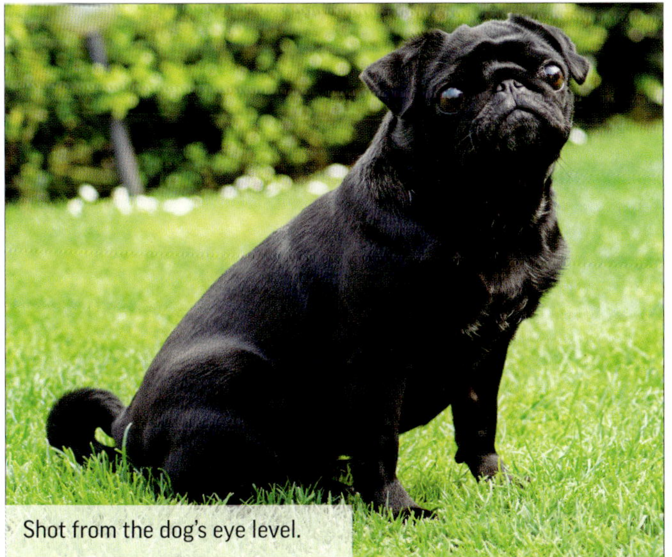

Shot from the dog's eye level.

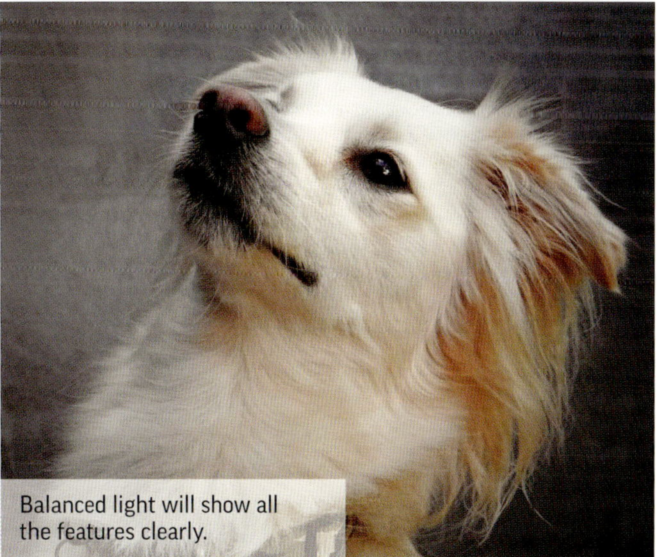

Balanced light will show all the features clearly.

Get down to their level

A lot of pet photographs are taken from above so it can give your subject a skewed look. While this viewpoint can be quite interesting, it's best to get down to the animal's eye level for the best portrait photographs. When taking your reference photographs, I highly recommend wearing an outfit in which you don't mind lying down in the mud or grass.

Choose the right light

Bright sunshine or using a flash is a complete no-no when taking photographs. You will get glare and blowout if the lighting is too bright. The best lighting should be natural light on a cloudy day. This will enable you to get true coloration of the fur and the perfect balance of light and dark.

DIGITAL EDITING AND COMPOSITION

Ahead of selecting my colours for a piece I will first of all edit my photographs. Sometimes this is as simple as removing a distracting background, but if I want to include more than a single subject in a piece, being able to create a digital mock-up from my reference photographs helps to give a better idea of how the finished piece may look. Being able to utilize digital software can save so much time and also helps you in the creation process further down the line.

Combining photographs

Imagine that you want to include two animals together in one portrait, but one has passed away and only a few photographs remain. If you are able to take some new photographs of the second animal in roughly matching lighting, the two can then be put together in one composition, as in the example below, through the use of a photo-editing program or app. It is a great tool, useful if you need to include two, three or even more subjects together in one piece; or if you simply want to see what a different colour background might look like.

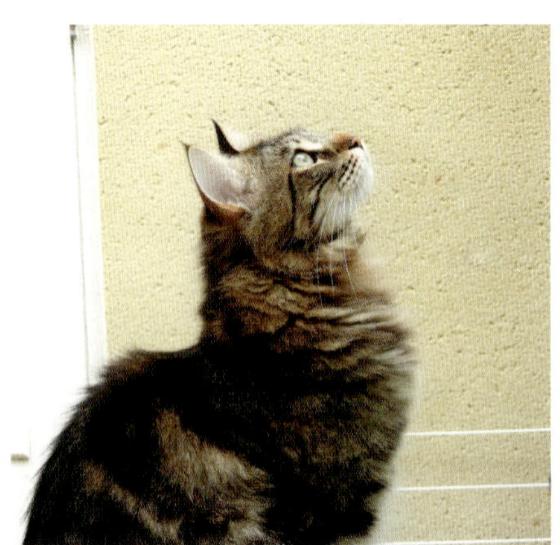

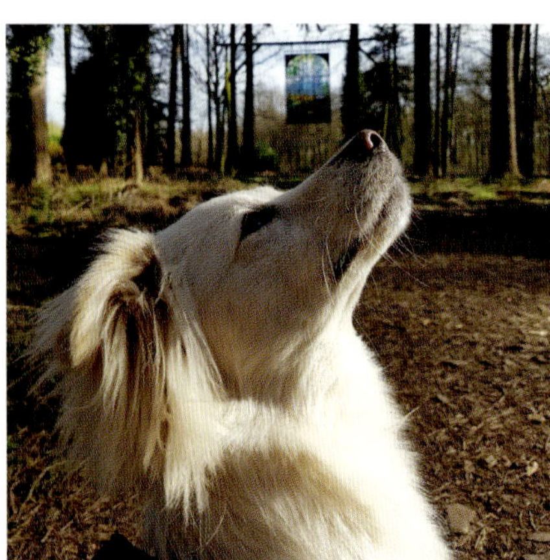

The original reference photographs.

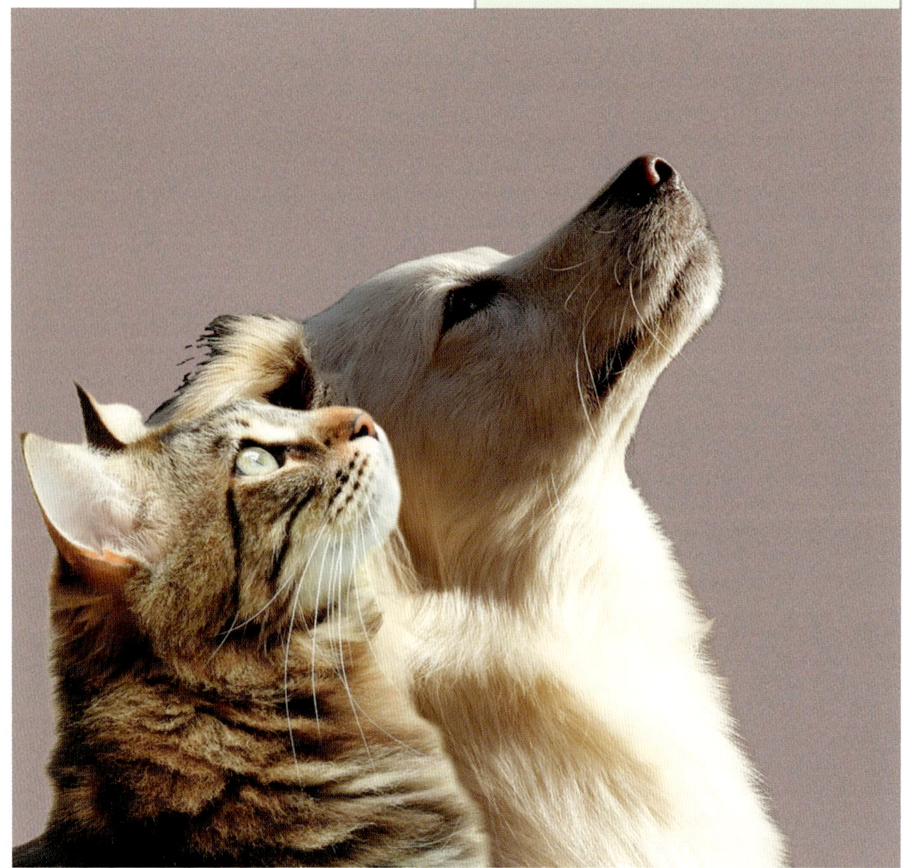

The resulting mock-up, ready to be used as the reference photograph. For this scenario I used BeFunky (see the tip above) to separate out my individual subjects into layers, which I then aligned and resized until I got the composition I liked and the relative proportions correct.

Having similar lighting in each reference photograph is essential, but you'll still need to make intelligent choices and adjustments when combining photographs digitally.

Changing backgrounds

You can use the same programs to put together a scene or add other objects in. For example, the owner of this dog didn't like the original green background, and described her spaniel as a very girlie doggy. I went out with my camera and my eye fell on a beautiful cherry tree in full blossom – and pink, the owner's favourite colour. By using BeFunky I was able to edit the blossom with a *bokeh* effect (that is, a soft, out-of-focus look), then place the dog over the top to create a quick mock-up of what the portrait might look like.

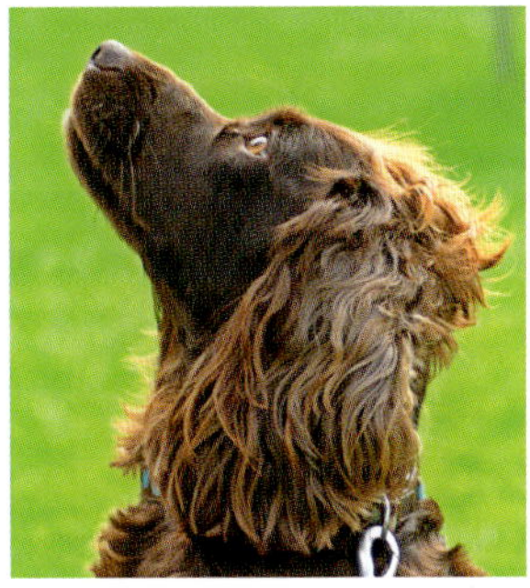

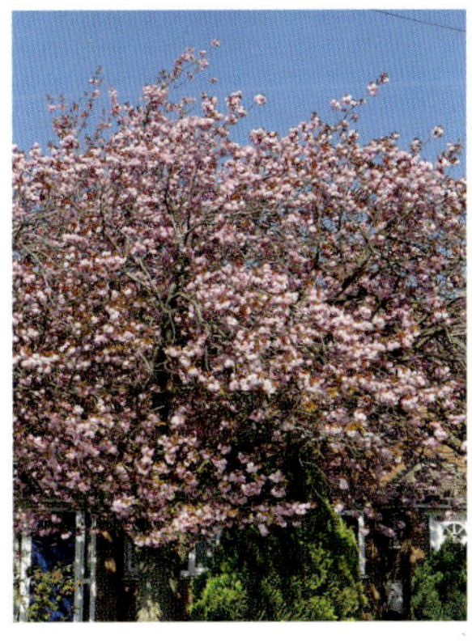

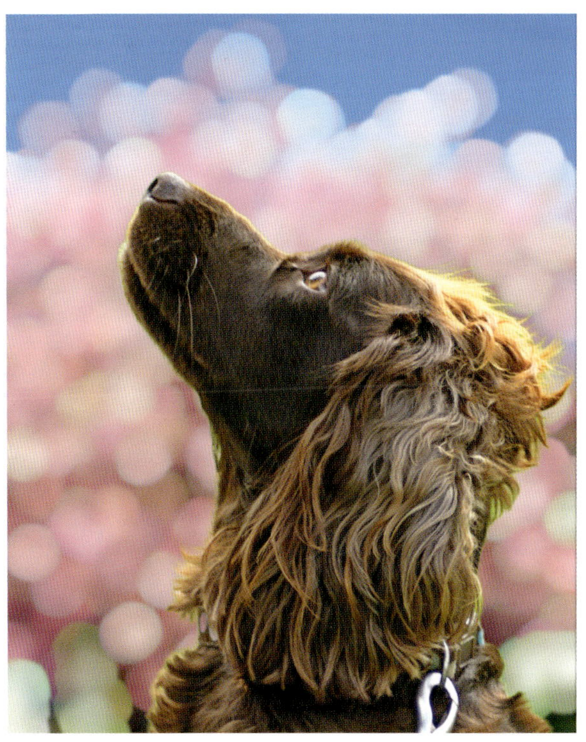

Editing photographs for your artwork

The other thing that I always do ahead of starting a piece is to make some adjustments to my main reference photograph to make it easier on my eyes as I work on my piece. I increase the saturation of the photograph to make the colours pop even more. Sometimes, especially with white or black fur, this can make the hidden colours become more apparent.

The other thing I do is turn my photograph into black and white and then increase the contrast. This is a great way of showing the values and means that I don't have to strain to see them as much when working.

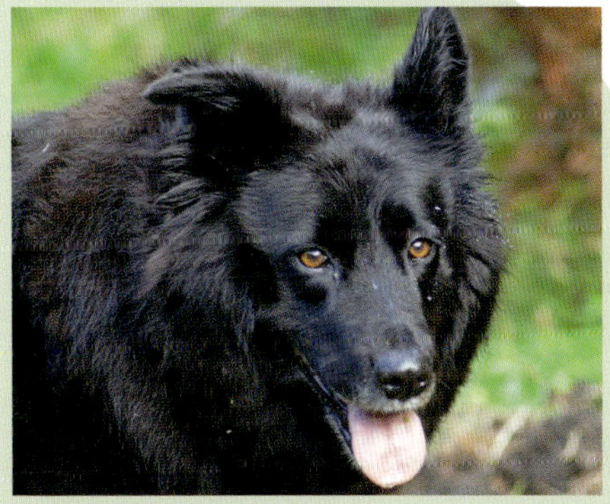

Original reference

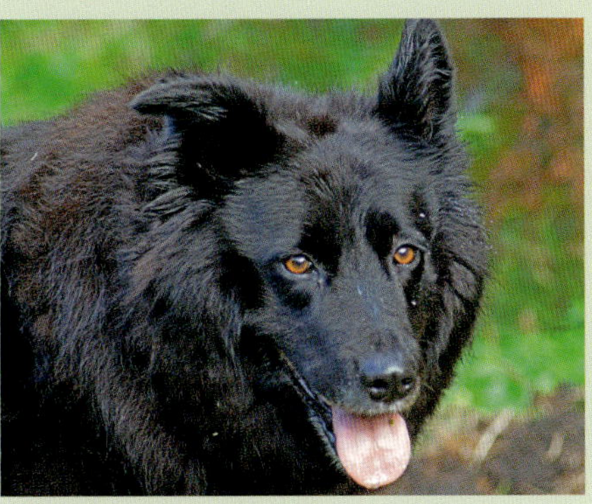

Increased saturation

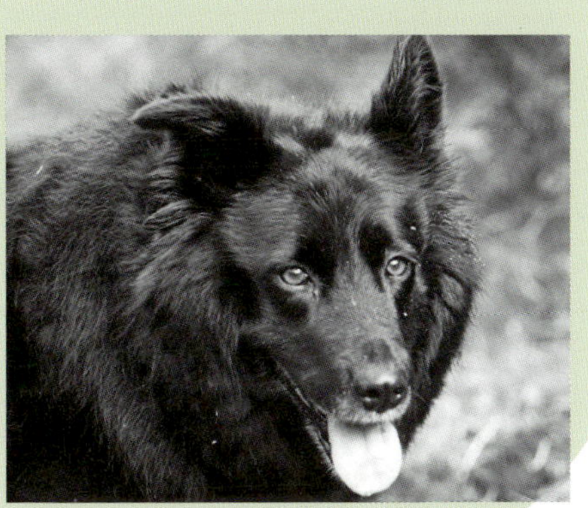

Black and white

FROM PHOTOGRAPH TO LINE ART

You have your reference photographs at the ready. You have selected which support and materials you want to use... but how on earth do you get that wonderful composition onto your paper?

Creating your line art

Depending on how confident and capable you are at drawing, you might wish to draw your line art yourself, using graphite pencil or pen and cartridge paper. If, however, you want to skip this step, you can use tracing paper. You will need a print-out of the reference image at the size that you want to use it – this is easily done on your computer, or you can enlarge it on a photocopier.

1 Place your tracing paper over your reference image and anchor it into place with tape so that it does not move.

2 Identify the key placement marks and shapes that you need to transfer across. These include the main outline, the highlights, the blocks of fur shapes and any details such as the eyes, nose and identifying markings that need to be portrayed in a particular position. Use a pencil to outline them, using a solid weight of line for clarity.

3 Add in some hints of the fur direction in each area, but avoid adding too many, as this will overcomplicate things.

4 Before lifting away your tracing paper, take a moment to ensure that you have captured all of those key marks and feature placements.

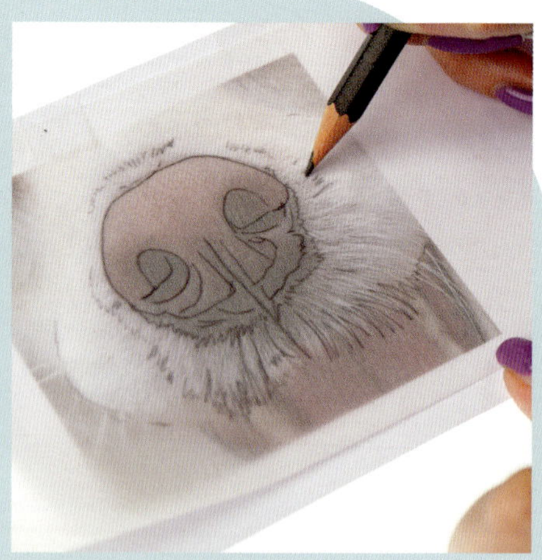
An HB graphite pencil is well-suited to creating line art.

How much detail?

A key question is how much detail to include in your initial drawing, and the short answer is that you can add as many or as few lines and details as you like. However, there is a balance to be struck between having just a few guide marks and adding every detail from your reference. Including too much detail can lead to confusion further down the line, while not having enough information can affect how true-to-life the finished image is. Both extremes can be confusing, so I suggest it's best to aim for a middle ground.

The colour blocking technique (see page 37), where we squint at our reference image to eliminate all the detail, can also be used to help you identify the basic shapes to make your line art.

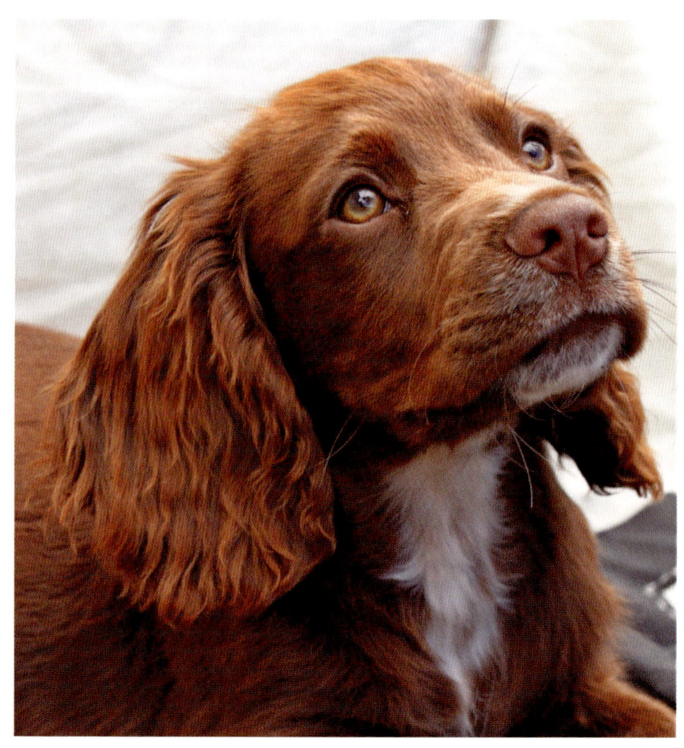

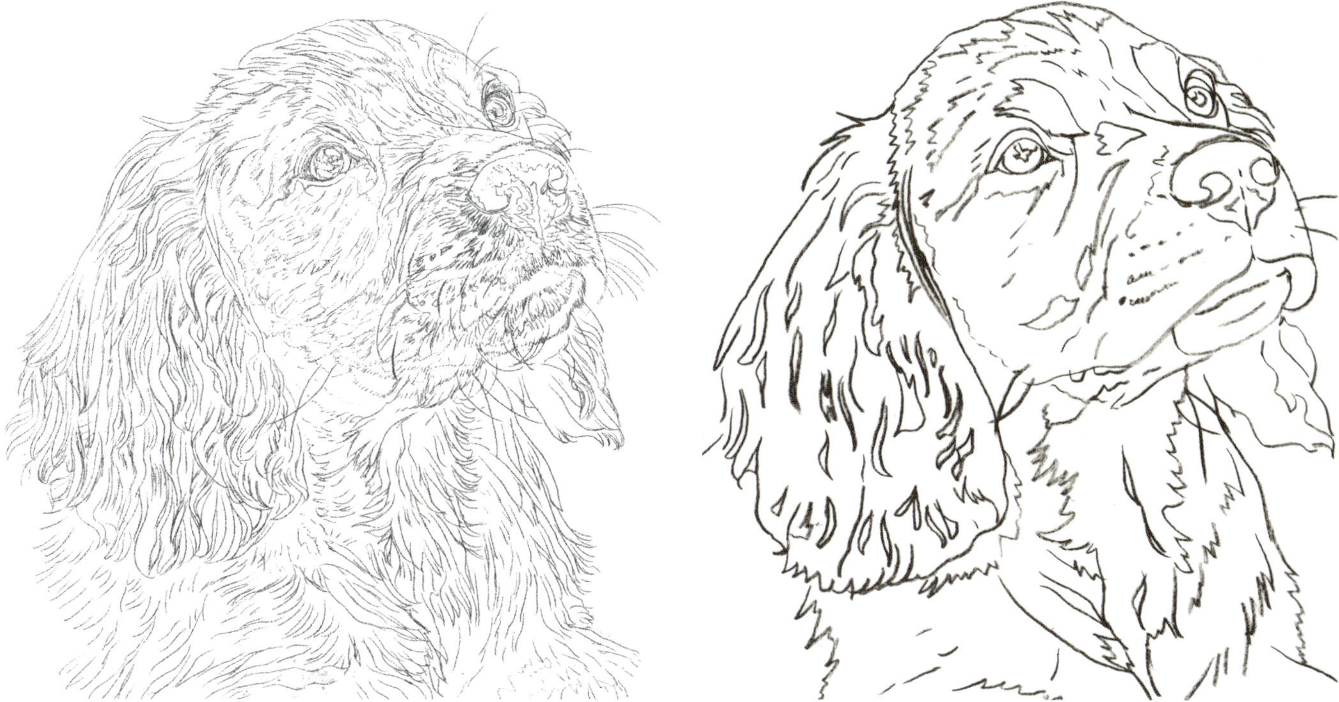

Two possible starting points

Here are two line drawings produced from the reference photograph opposite. The left-hand drawing includes all the detail you could possibly need, showing the direction and length of the fur, along with exacting marks around the features. However, the right-hand drawing, which has less detail, is perhaps more immediately useful for coloured pencil work. Built up using a twist on the colour blocking technique on page 37, it includes the key areas of tone, and is much more easily understood at a glance.

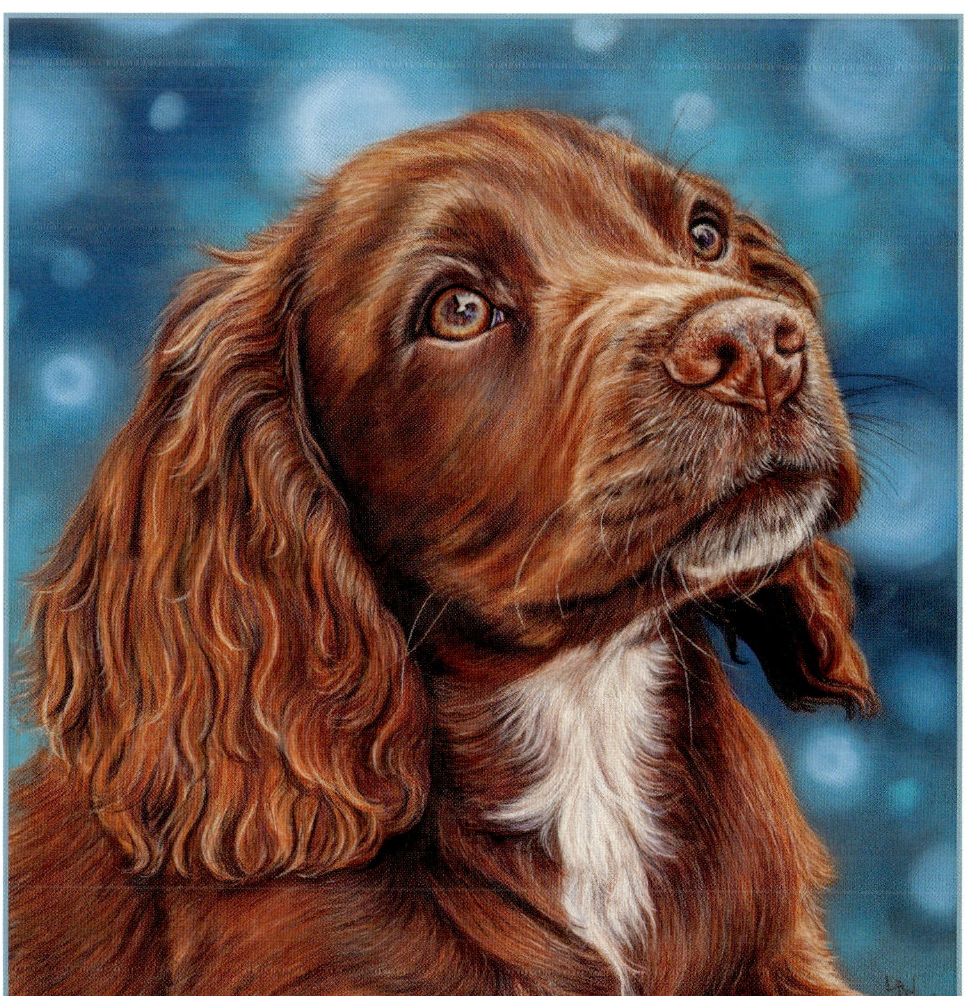

Mocha Pup

The resulting artwork, built up from the starting point above right. In general, the complexity of an animal portrait is best built up through layers of colour, rather than through the initial drawing.

This was a project created for my first workshop tour of the US. I used watercolour pencils both wet and dry, and added a bright PanPastel background to give the piece some extra fun.

Digital help

An alternative method to creating your line drawing is to digitally convert your photograph. The precise method will vary depending on which program you use, but most image editing software will allows you to use similar preset functions to convert it to a sketch outline or line art.

Here is an example using Gimp, a free-to-download graphic editing program. It may look like a lot of things to click but this process really does take less than a minute to do. If you have a different app or program, then look for the convert to outline or sketch function.

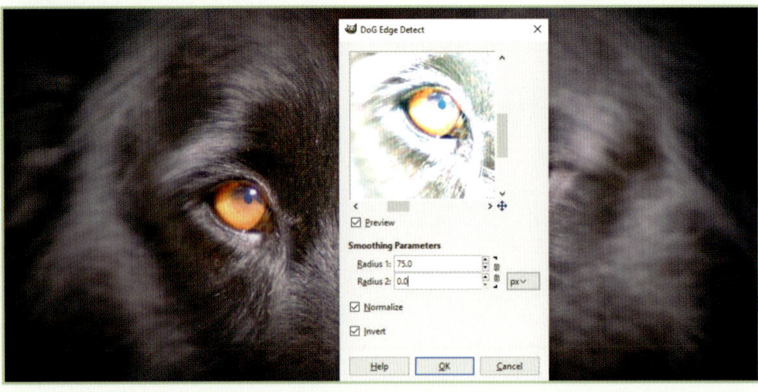

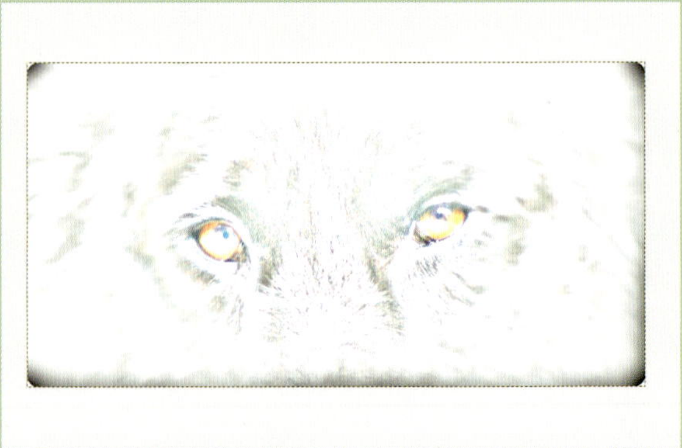

1 Open your reference photograph in Gimp and click on Filters – Edge Detect – Difference of Gaussians. Move the sliders until the image box is over an area with detail such as an eye. Ensure both the normalize and the invert boxes are ticked. Change radius 1 to a value of around 75 (you may want to tweak this figure higher or lower) and change radius 2 value to 0.

2 Click OK, and the image will now look somewhat like this. We now need to refine the image a little to make the picture useable.

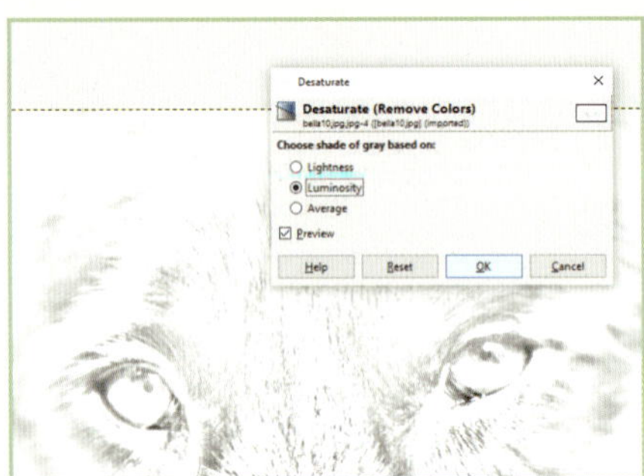

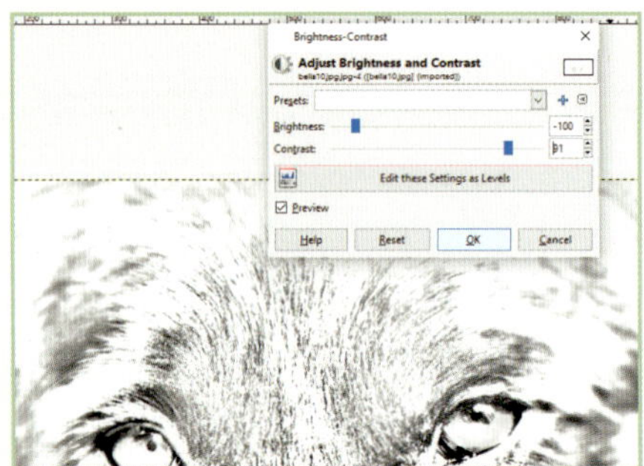

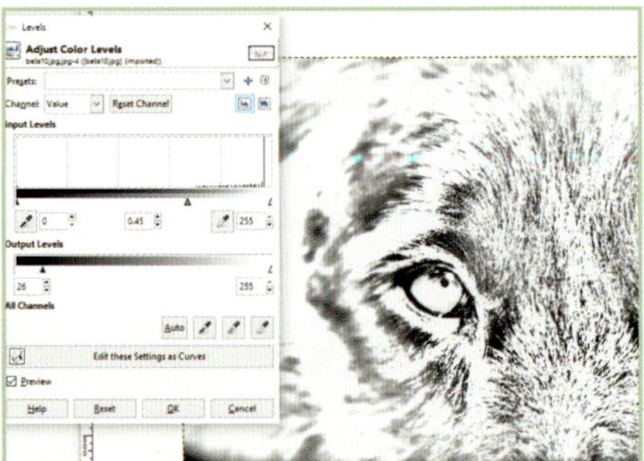

3 Select Colors – Desaturate, and select the Luminosity option, then click OK. This will strip out the colour.

4 Next, select Colors – Brightness and Contrast. Change the brightness value to -100 and the contrast value to +95, then click OK to strengthen the contrast in tone.

5 Select Colors – Levels and adjust the sliders until you have a sharp image, then click OK.

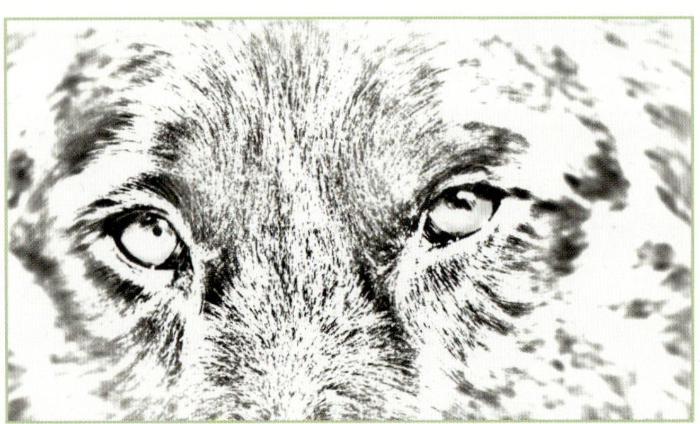

6 This gives you your line art. Once you have printed a copy, you can use it either with the indenting method (see opposite) or to place underneath your drafting film when working on that as a support.

TRANSFERRING LINE ART TO YOUR SURFACE

Time now to transfer the line art to your chosen support. Here are some of my preferred methods. It may be that you want to work smaller or larger than the original reference size, in which case you can scan or photograph your line art and reprint it at the size that you need.

The most important thing with all of these methods is to ensure that you have the line art securely affixed to your support across the top edge only. This will keep the line art in place as you work and also allow you to flip it up to check progress.

Indenting method

This is my preferred way of transferring the image, as it preserves the outline for longer than the other methods. Rather than being lost under the first layer or two of pencil, the indented outline remains visible as you work.

1 Secure your drawing to your surface and, pressing as hard as you can with the tip of the stylus, draw over the lines.

2 This will indent the surface – lift the drawing away to check all the lines have transferred.

3 Glaze the surface (see page 36 for the glazing technique) with a colour appropriate to your picture – you'll see the image appear, with the indented lines left clean.

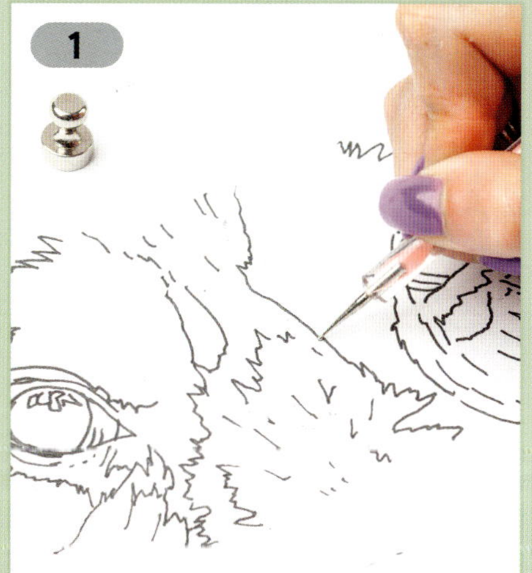

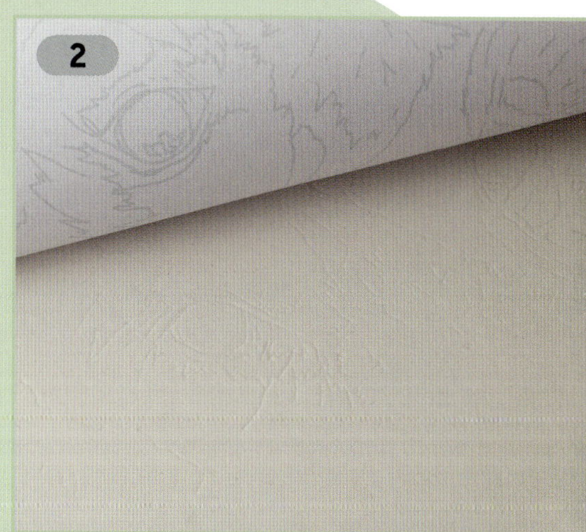

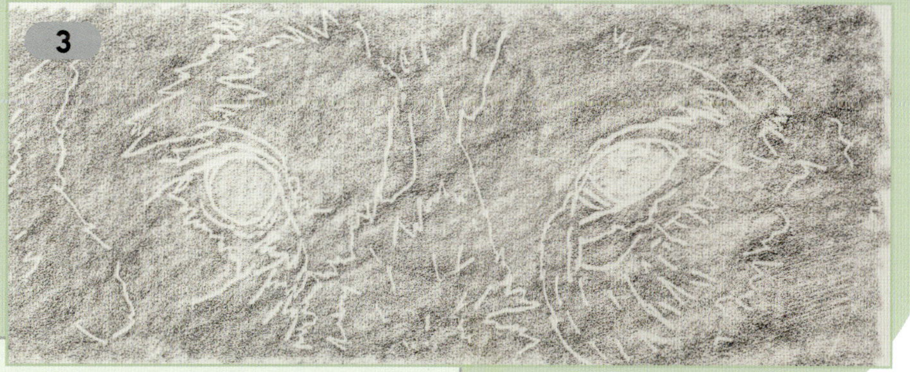

Tracing paper method

This method helps to ensure that the lines you make will be lost or blended smoothly into the finished piece, rather than remaining visible at the end. This is achieved by transferring the lines using the same colour as in your planned piece.

1 Secure your original line drawing to the surface and lay a sheet of tracing paper over the top.

2 Use a pen or pencil to trace over all the lines, then turn the tracing paper over and repeat the process on the back, this time using a coloured pencil of the colour and type you will be using for the final piece.

3 Turn the tracing over once again, and secure it onto your support. Use a stylus to work over the lines one final time, transferring the coloured pencil onto the surface. Apply enough pressure to transfer the pencil without indenting the surface – try an unobtrusive area first, to check.

4 Lifting away the tracing paper will reveal the faint image on the surface. It's worth checking that all the lines have transferred clearly – replace the tracing paper and repeat if necessary.

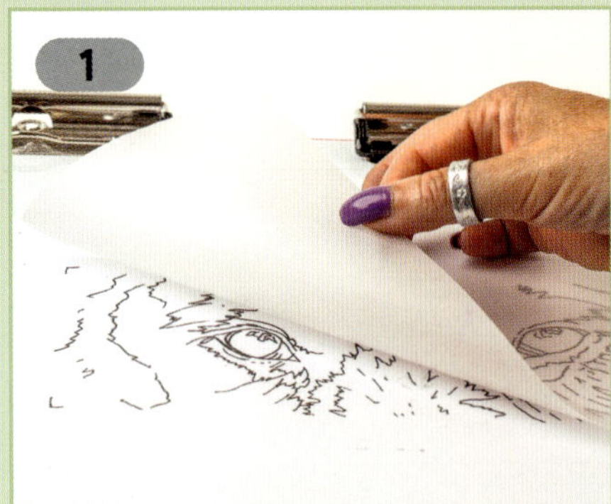

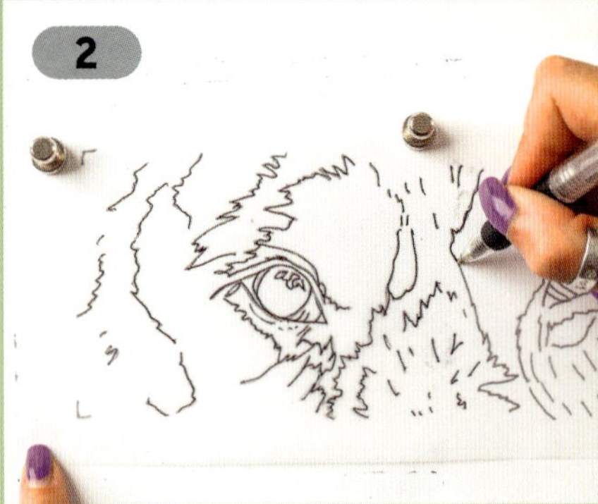

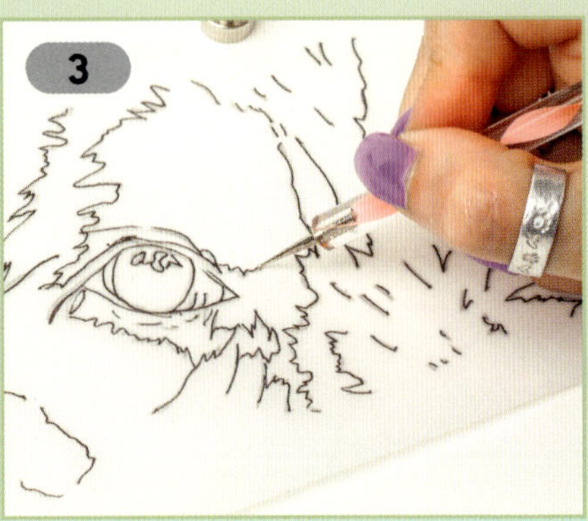

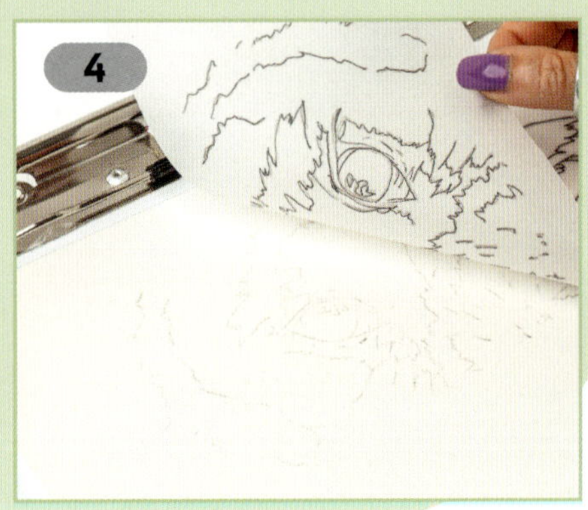

Tip

If you have access to a lightbox, this makes transferring images to drafting film really easy – just tape it over the top of your reference photograph and copy the lines. In fact, this allows you to skip creating line art on separate rough paper completely – you can go straight from photograph to final surface.

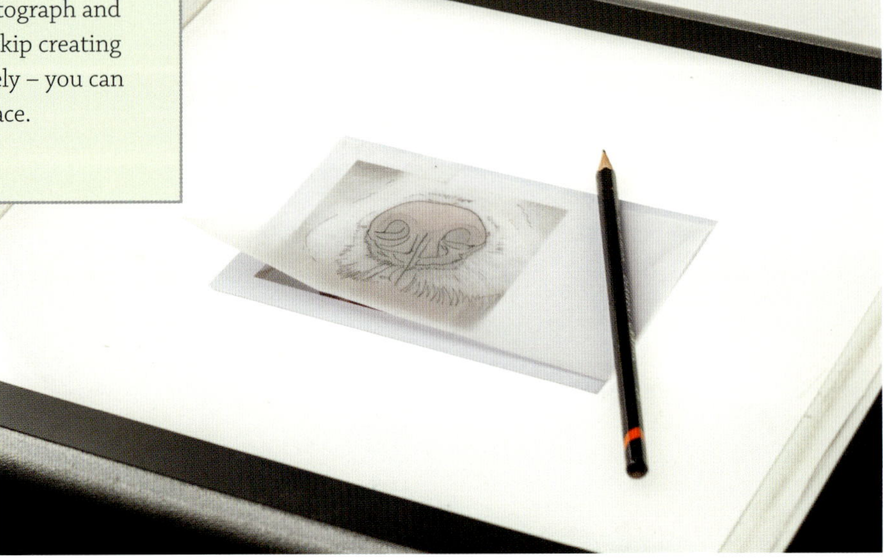

Tracedown paper method

The approach has the benefits of speed and simplicity, though it's not as clean as the others.

1 Secure your line drawing to the surface, then slide a piece of tracedown paper in between the line drawing and surface.

2 Use a stylus to work over the lines. Press just hard enough to transfer the lines, and not to indent or damage the surface. You can lift off any excess graphite powder or marks using a putty eraser.

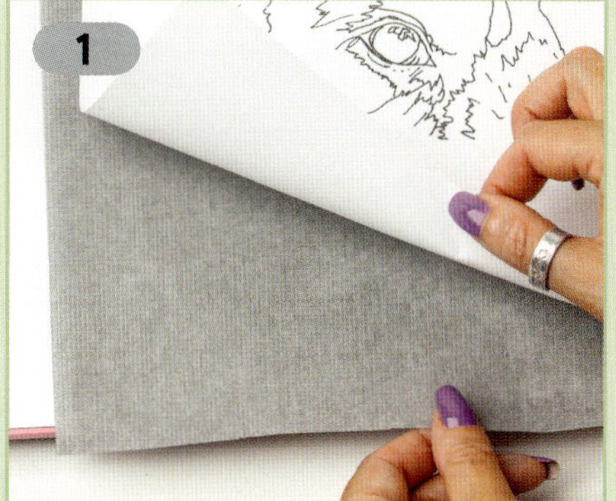

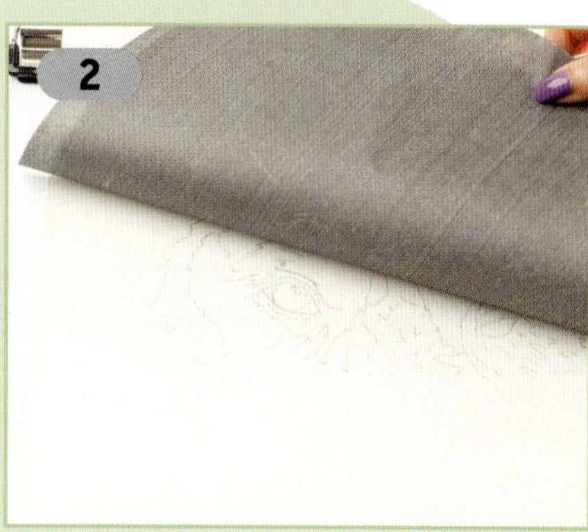

Tip

If you want the line transferred in a different colour, you can simply rub pastel on the back of the line drawing in the appropriate hue; then carry on as normal for the technique – simply leaving the tracedown paper out.

MASKING TAPE FRAME

Once you've transferred the line drawing to your working surface, run strips of masking tape around your picture area to create a frame. Not only will this keep the edges crisp and clean when removed at the end of working, but it will also help you to stay within the area, avoiding accidentally altering the proportions or simply wasting your time detailing areas that won't be visible.

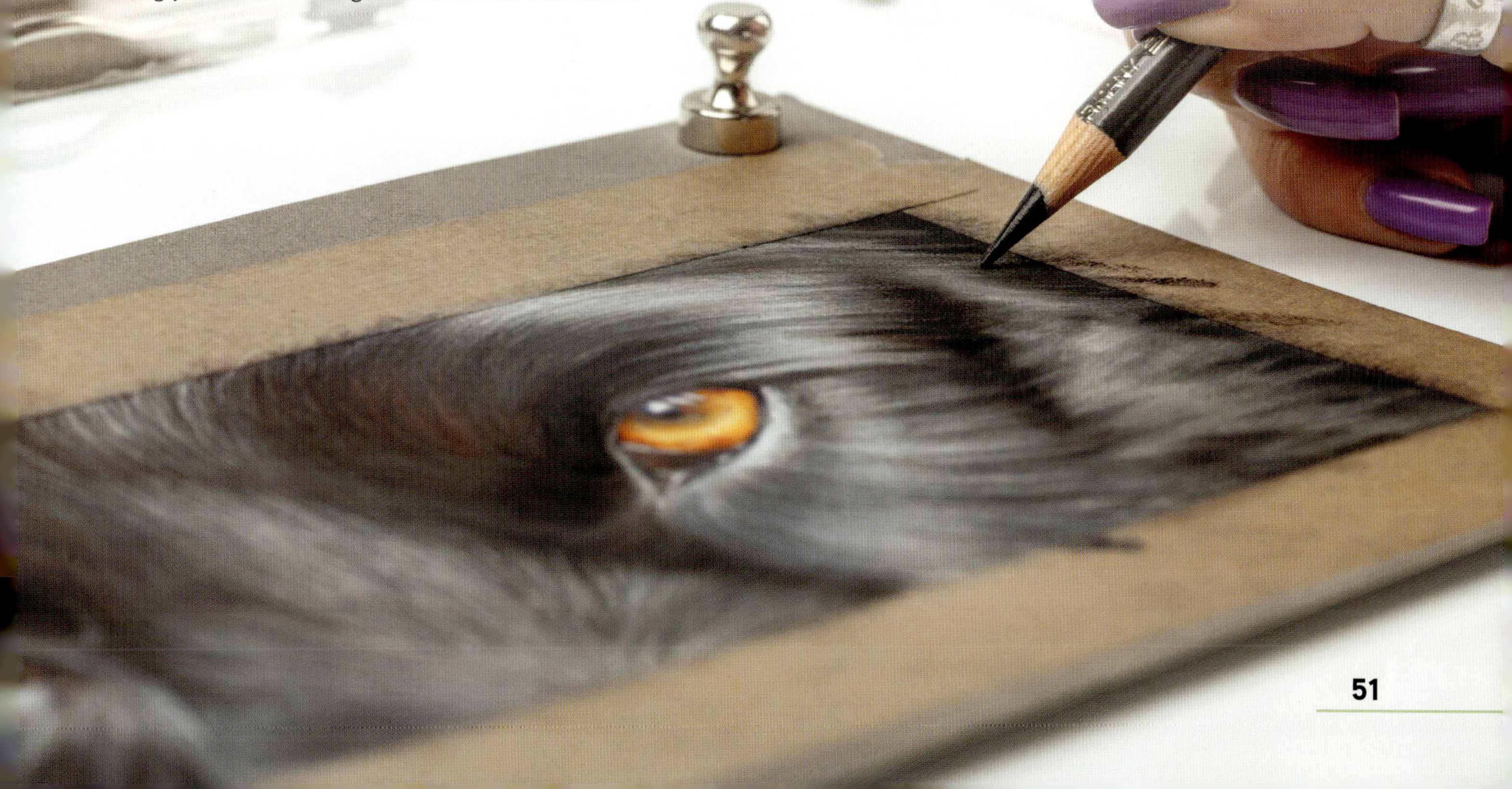

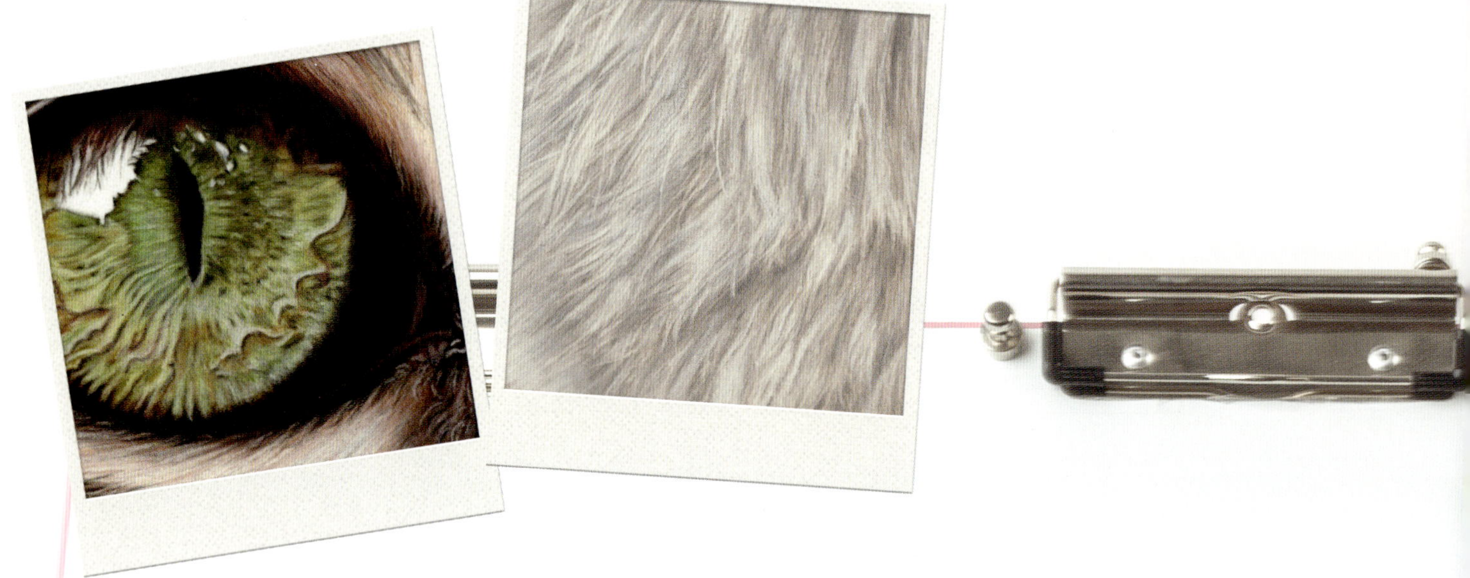

STUDIES

Having read up to this point, you're now ready to start putting all you have learnt together. When starting out, it can seem overwhelming to jump straight into a full portrait, so I have designed these studies as a gentle way to practise all of the techniques explored earlier in the book.

Once you have finished these studies, you will have gained even more confidence ahead of embracing some full portraits. Of course, there is nothing to stop you going straight for a full portrait if you feel ready. Nonetheless, I highly recommend that you work through the studies first or come back to them for reference as you work on the bigger project pieces later in the book.

Each study has been designed to encompass the different supports, pencil strokes and subtraction techniques that have already been mentioned. If you don't have the exact same pencils or colours, that's fine. You can refer back to the basic techniques and materials chapters to help you work through them with the materials you have to hand.

Each study focuses on a particular feature or detail of an animal, such as eyes, noses or fur. Some, like the cat's eye, are fairly specific, while others, like clumped fur, are more general.

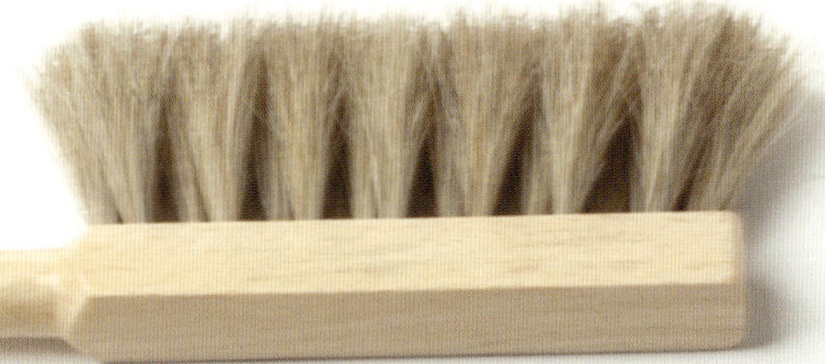

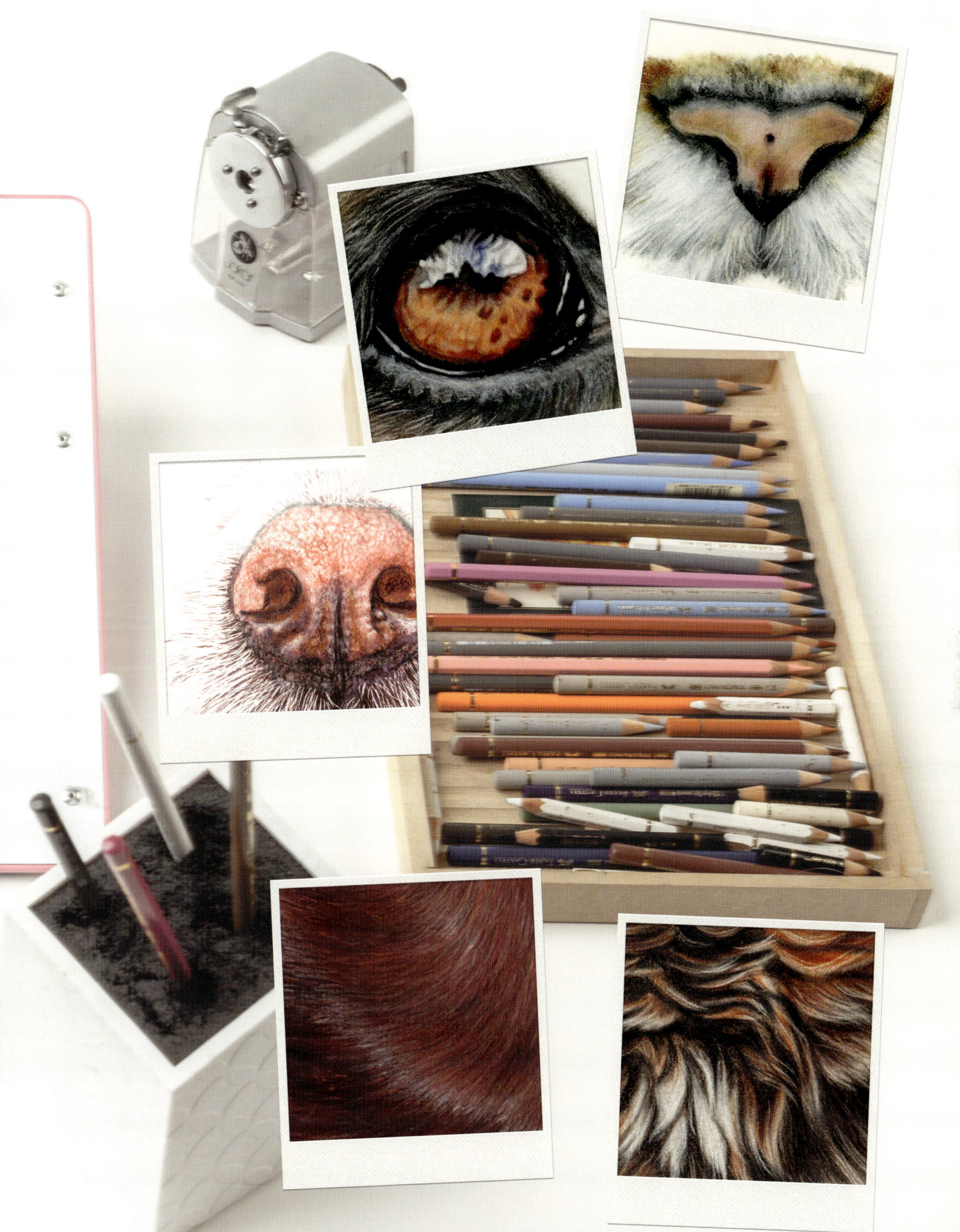

GOLDEN EYE: DOG

This study focuses on consistent pressure of pigment laydown along with rotating between the scumbling and back-and-forth strokes. The aim is to create the smoothness of the eyeball.

Building layers on Pastelmat and working from dark to light allows you to really get to grips with these essential techniques on a smaller scale. Please note that a frame of fur has been added to the finished study but the main focus here is the eye itself.

You will need

Support: Clairefontaine Pastelmat paper – dark grey colour, 10 x 10cm (4 x 4in)

Faber-Castell Polychromos pencils: 181 Payne's grey, 199 black, 157 dark indigo, 175 dark sepia, 169 caput mortuum, 186 terracotta, 190 Venetian red, 109 dark chrome yellow, 102 cream, 191 Pompeiian red, 103 ivory, 151 helioblue reddish

Caran d'Ache Pablo pencils: 001 white

Caran d'Ache Museum Aquarelle pencils: (used for the fur) black, Payne's grey, Prussian blue, brown, French grey and white

Other materials: Tracedown paper and stylus or sharp pencil to transfer line drawing, pencil sharpener, glassine paper, soft dusting brush, waterbrush

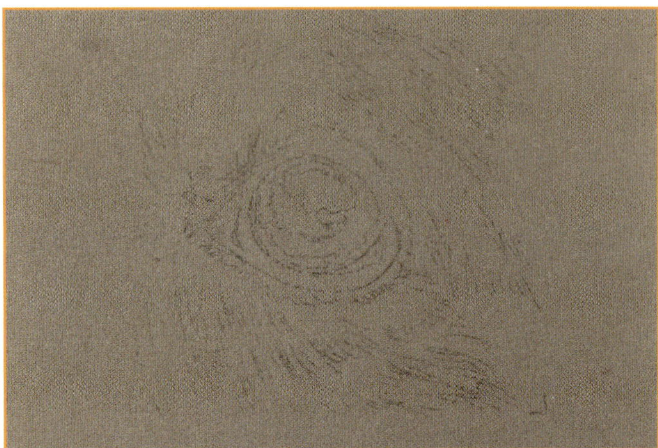

1 Transfer the image to your surface using a variation on the tracedown paper method (see page 51): glaze the back of your outline with Payne's grey pencil, place it on the surface and use a fine stylus to work over the lines. This transfers only coloured pencil onto the surface, rather than graphite, which will contaminate the light areas of the eye. With the image in place, run a frame of masking tape around the picture.

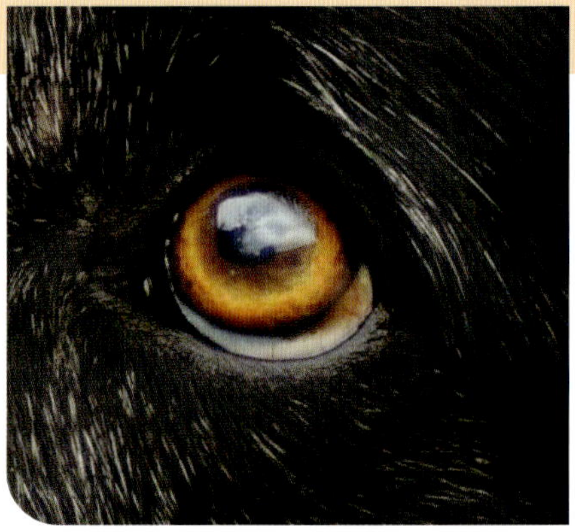

The reference photograph for this study.

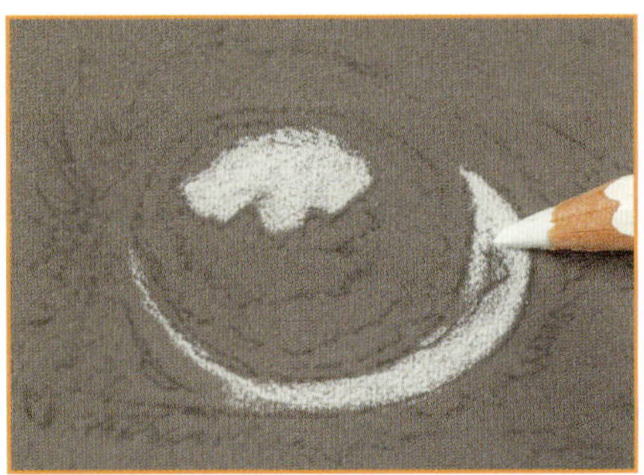

2 Use the Pablo white (this is more opaque than the Polychromos white) to mark in the highlight in the eye and the white of the eye itself with a scumbling technique. Build up two or three layers in each area to create a foundation.

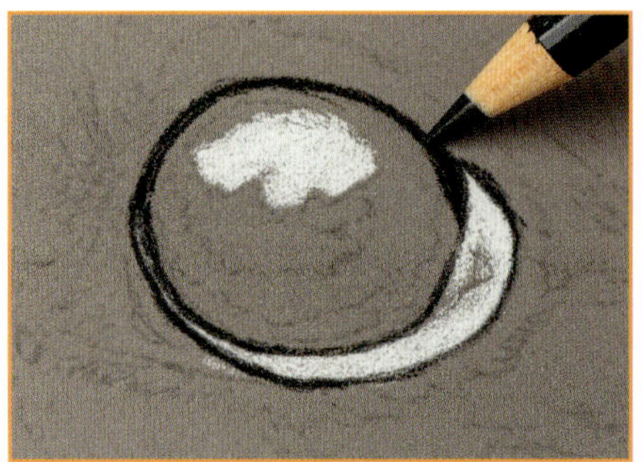

3 Outline the eye itself using black. This will create a nice frame to work within.

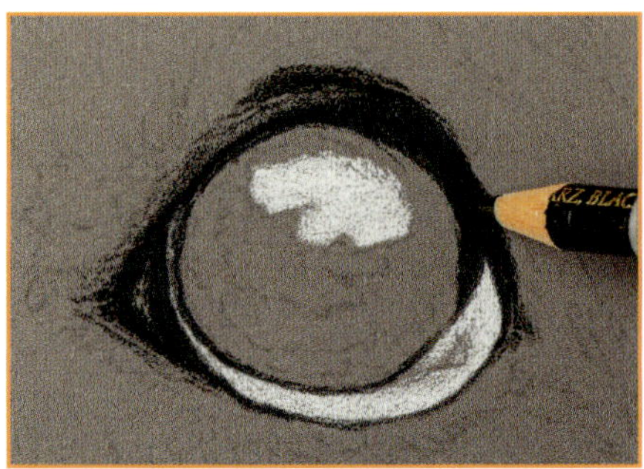

4 Extend outwards from the outline to fill in the tear duct and shadow of the eyelid. Developing these deep shadows around the eye will help the area to recede, throwing the eye forward and suggesting its spherical form.

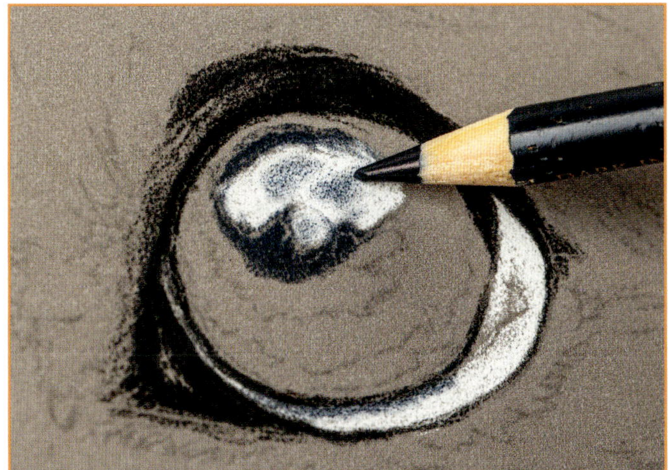 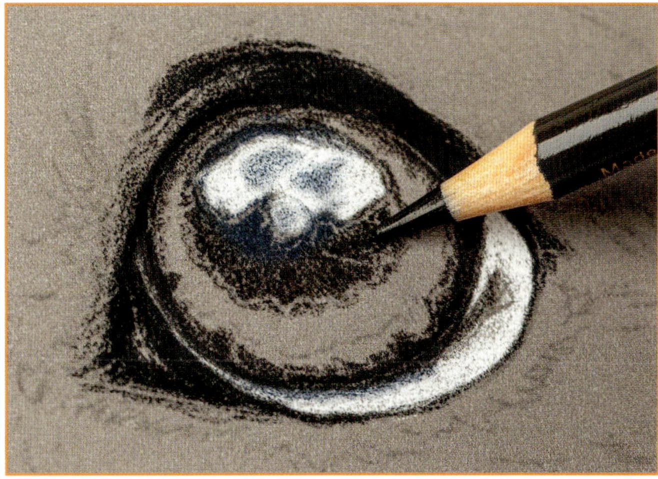

5 Use dark indigo with a scumbling technique to add the first layers to the pupil. Use the same colour to add a hint of colour on the white of the eye on the lower left; a contrasting hint above the highlight; and to pop in some subtle reflected shapes in the highlight itself.

6 Swap to dark sepia and scumble the lower edge of the iris itself. Surround the pupil with scumbling marks of the same colour, overlapping the edge of the pupil as you do so.

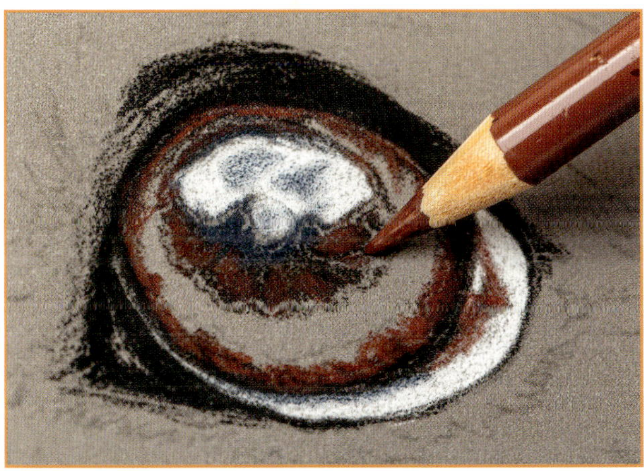

Some dogs' eyes show more obvious flecks and lines that converge on the pupil. For these, you might want to use a back-and-forth motion – if so doing, be careful that you follow the curvature of the eye, bearing in mind that it's spherical. Flat, straight lines will give a flat effect.

7 Gradually working in from the edge and outwards from the pupil, scumble caput mortuum over the previous areas on the iris, overlapping the dark sepia parts and covering more of the iris.

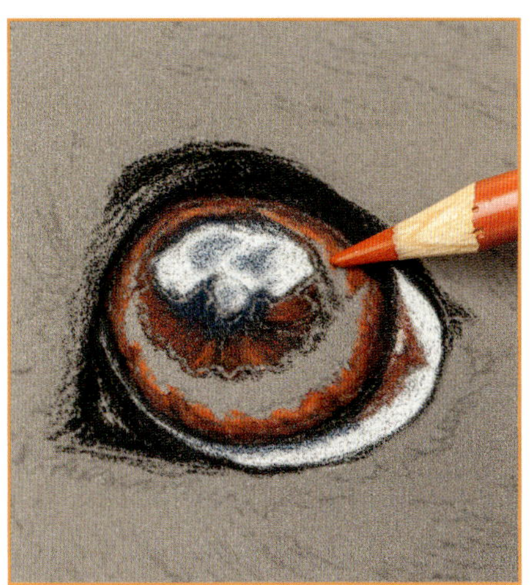 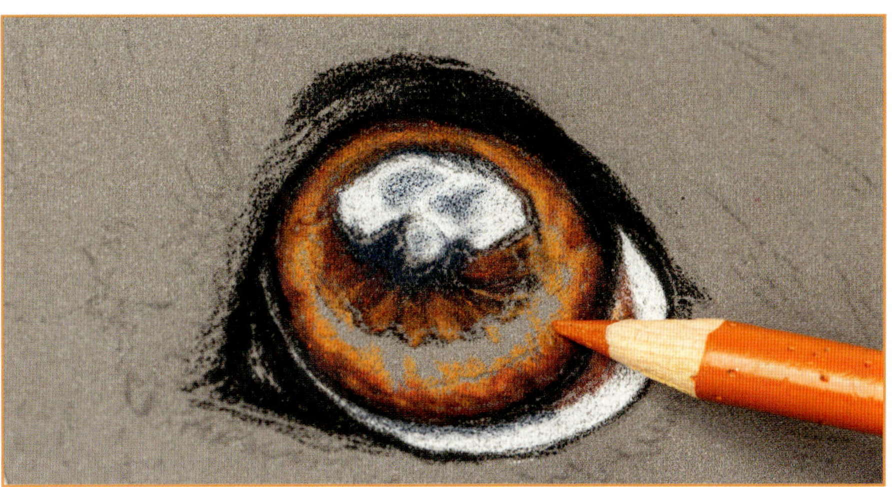

8 Repeat the process using Venetian red, overlapping the caput mortuum area.

9 If you look closely at the reference, you'll see orange flecks within the yellow ring. Scumble these in using terracotta. Work terracotta up and over the top of the eye, and then continue filling in the iris outwards from the pupil and inwards from the white area.

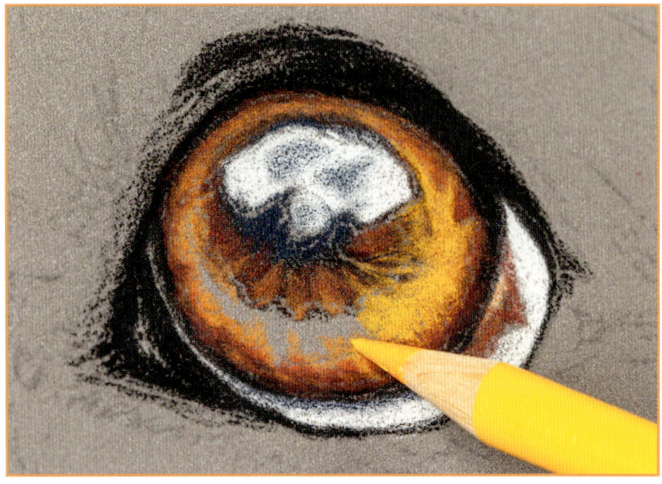

10 Use dark chrome yellow to scumble the remainder of the area within the iris.

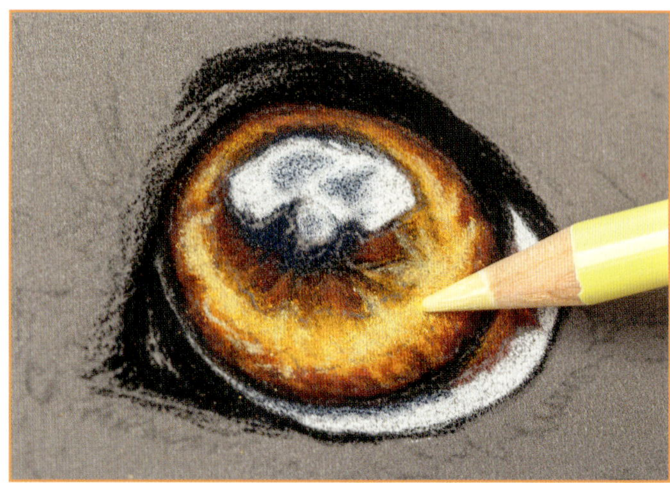

11 Use cream to scumble another layer over the lightest part of the eye. This completes the underlayers.

12 Begin to layer the eye, repeating the process of scumbling in turn with the following colours: Polychromos black, Polychromos white, dark indigo, dark sepia, and caput mortuum. When you come to the red stage, introduce Pompeiian red in place of Venetian red. This adds a punchier, enriched red – useful to take account of the surface colour.

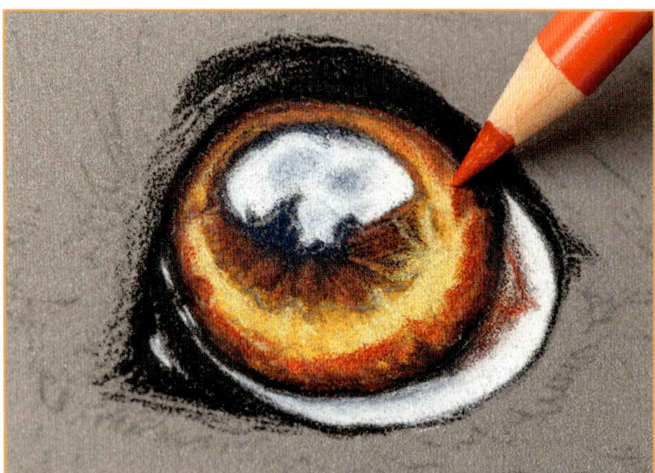

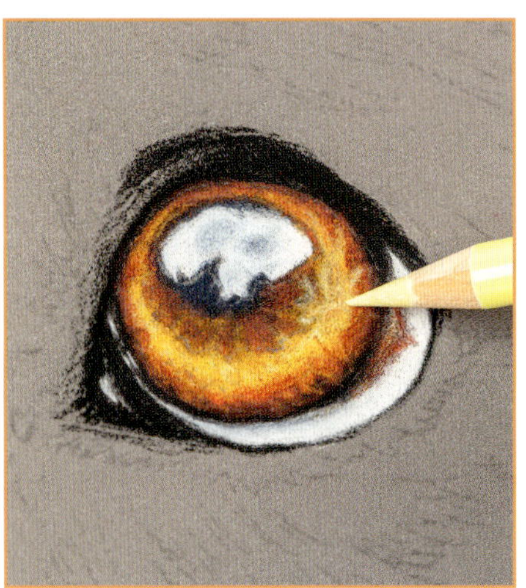

13 Continue scumbling, adding terracotta, dark chrome yellow and cream in turn. Use ivory for a new layer of highlight within the iris.

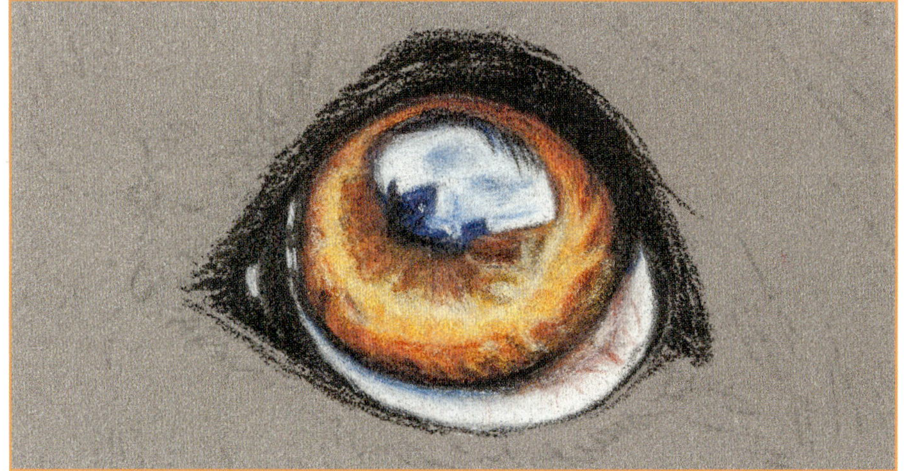

14 At this stage, the surface is at the halfway stage (see page 25), with small touches of the surface still visible close-up. You will also be able to feel the pencil being resisted ever so slightly by the surface. Continue layering and tweaking your tones. As before, the more you refine, the more you're likely to see. Don't be afraid to adjust your colours in response. I've introduced helioblue reddish at the top of the pupil.

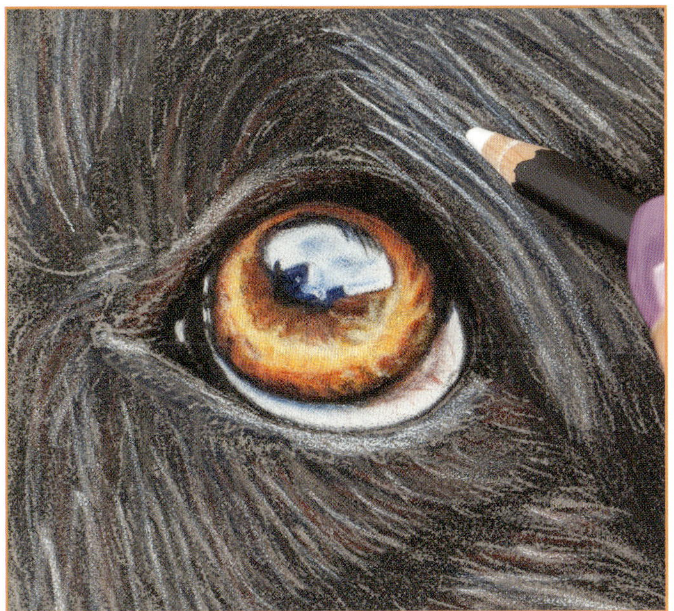

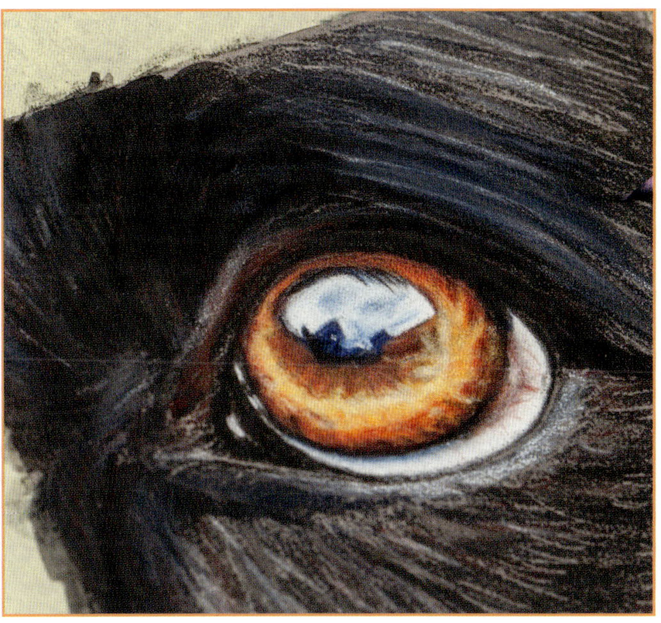

15 Before you reach the buttery stage, but when the eye is at ninety per cent completion, add the surrounding fur using the following watercolour pencils (Caran d'Ache Museum Aquarelle): black, Payne's grey, Prussian blue, brown, French grey and a touch of white. This frames and contextualizes the eye, allowing you to better judge the hue and tone of any final adjustments as you take it to the buttery stage.

16 With the watercolour pigment in place, use your waterbrush to draw back over in the direction of the fur. To dissolve the binder, it's important not to work back and forth, but to make single strokes in one direction only.

The finished study

Once the image is fully dry, repeat the colour blocking on the fur area. Gradually work on the smaller shapes within the bigger shapes, working dark to light. Repeat until the saturation, tone and colour are looking right. Then, with sharp pencils, you can start to add a hint of some fur detail. Remember, however, that the focus of this study is the eye itself and the smooth reflective surface there.

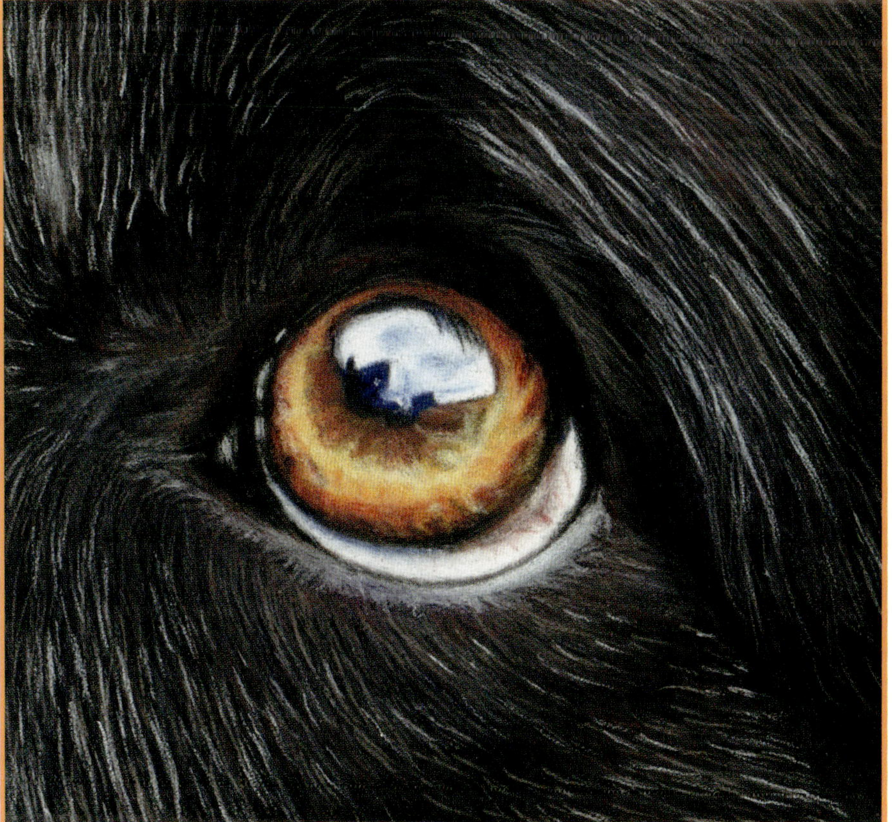

GREEN EYE: CAT

In this study the focus will be on how to create the glossy effect of a green cat eye on Pastelmat, a surface which many struggle with. This study will help you to overcome any fears that textured papers will not take more layers and will give you confidence that you can work light over dark with your pencils. As with the golden eye earlier, a frame of fur has been added to the finished study but the main focus of this study remains the eye itself.

Transfer your line art to your surface. Add in as many or as few lines as you prefer. I used graphite transfer paper for this tutorial. Even though the study is worked on white paper, add in white pigment to the highlight areas first. Use a scumbling stroke with a standard pressure. Keep repeating to build up the pigment.

You will need

Support: Clairefontaine Pastelmat paper – white colour, 14 x 12.5cm (5½ x 5in)

Caran d'Ache Pablo pencils: 001 white, 491 cream

Faber-Castell Polychromos pencils: 199 black, 169 caput mortuum, 157 dark indigo, 186 terracotta, 278 chrome oxide green, 174 chromium green opaque, 173 olive green yellowish, 268 green gold, 178 nougat, 172 earth green, 168 earth green yellowish, 270 warm grey I, 271 warm grey II, 103 ivory, 102 cream, 175 dark sepia, 189 cinnamon

Other materials: Graphite transfer paper and stylus or sharp pencil to transfer the line drawing, pencil sharpener, glassine paper, soft dusting brush, small paintbrush or cotton bud and kitchen paper

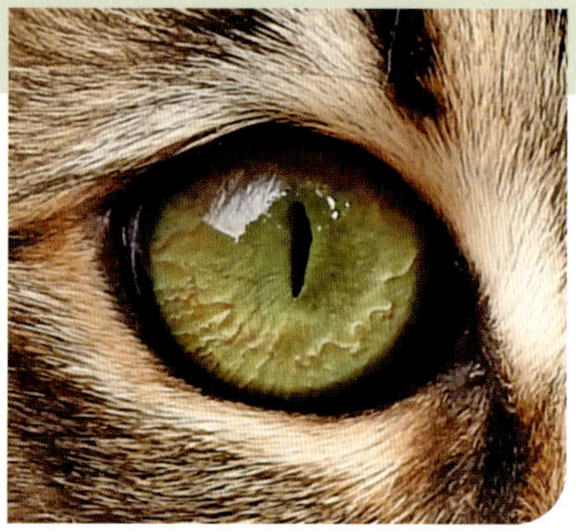

The reference photograph for this study.

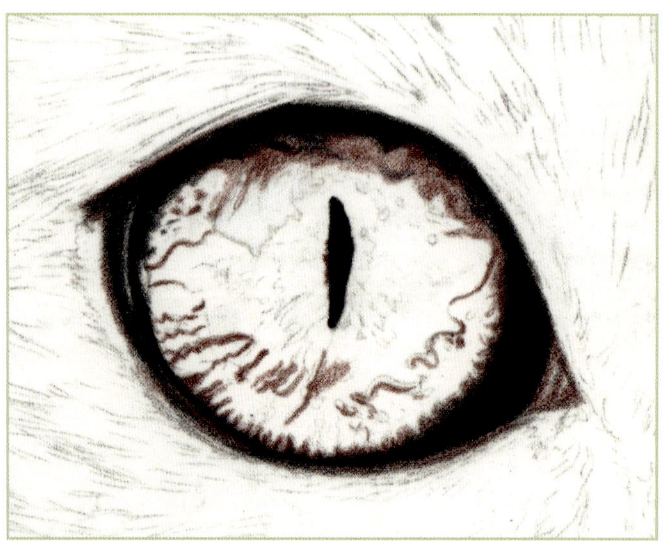

1 Transfer the image using the tracedown paper method on page 51. Use black to outline the eye itself and also the slit of the pupil. Glaze over the top of the outside area in towards the iris using caput mortuum, dark sepia and dark indigo, and with a back-and-forth stroke. Lightly map in all of the dark reddish markings on the iris using caput mortuum. This is our 'darks' stage.

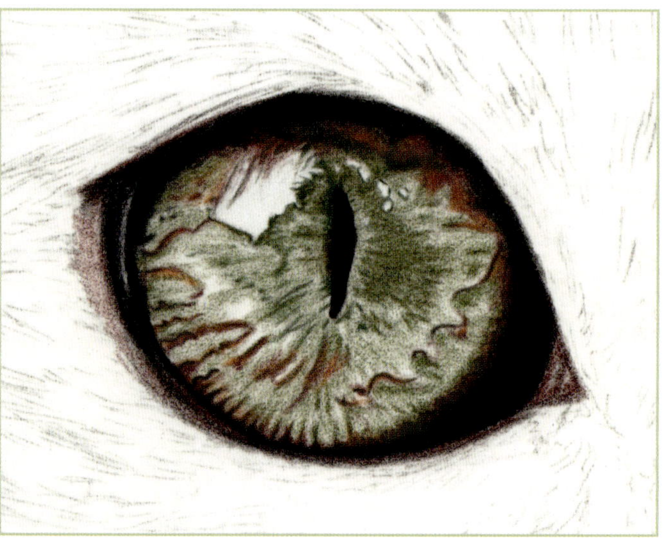

2 Start to build up the green of the iris using a mix of scumbling and small back-and-forth strokes, always working in towards the centre of the eye, never in circles around the pupil. Chrome oxide green and chromium green opaque form the darker undertones of the main iris. Add in touches of terracotta around the outside areas of the caput mortuum markings.

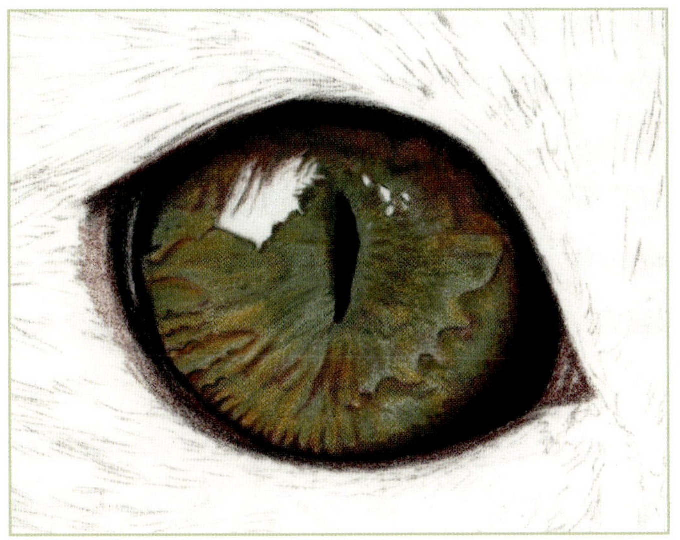

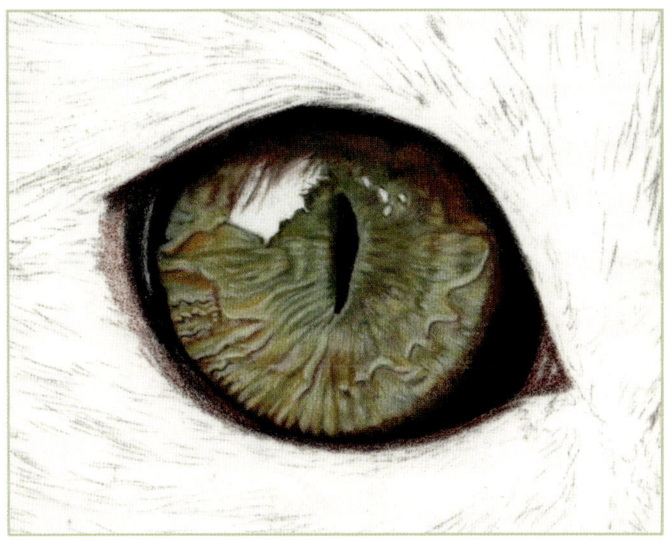

3 Add touches of green gold around the outer edges of the iris. Continue to scumble or use the back-and-forth motion as you lay down the pigment. Glaze over the whole eye using a mix of nougat in the browner- or greyer-looking areas, and earth green over the rest of the iris. This is our mid-tone stage.

4 On to our lights now. Continue to glaze using Polychromos cream and warm grey II in the slightly more yellow areas such as the outer edges of the iris. For the centre of the iris, use warm grey I and ivory. Look closely at the markings but do not worry if you do not match the reference photograph exactly.

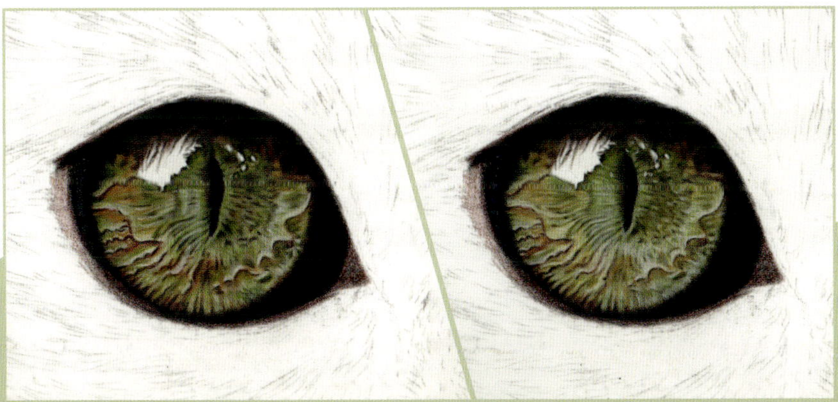

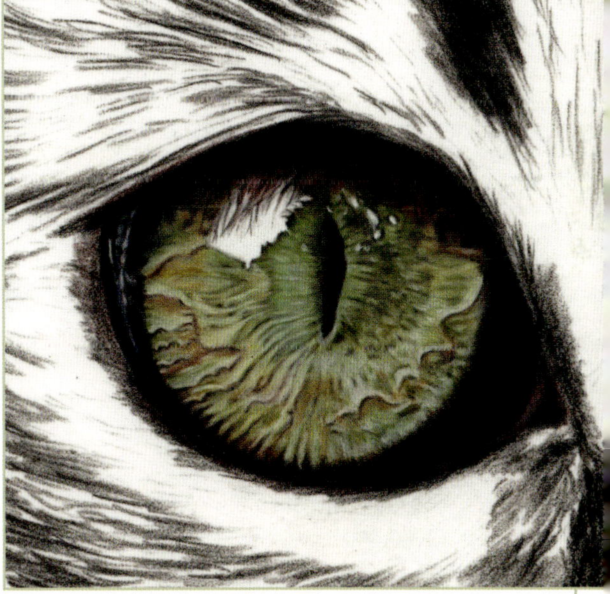

5 Repeat steps 2–4 again. Keep repeating and refining with each layer until you have built up the pigment enough that it starts to feel buttery on the surface and you can no longer see the grain of the tooth. You will be placing the tip of your pencil and simply 'wiggling' it in places to add in touches of highlights.

Tip

Trust the properties of the Pastelmat that it will allow you to keep building up layers.

6 Keeping your pencils super sharp, use caput mortuum and dark sepia to form a hint of the eyelash reflection in the main highlight. Next, use dark indigo and caput mortuum to add in a hint of the outer rim of the eyelid. Glaze over the top using the warm greys and white to create a slight highlight there. Use black to add in some of the dark shapes of the fur – we'll take this further in the next step.

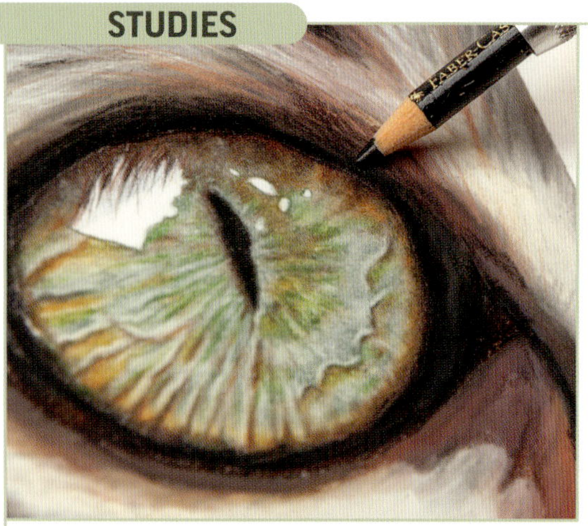

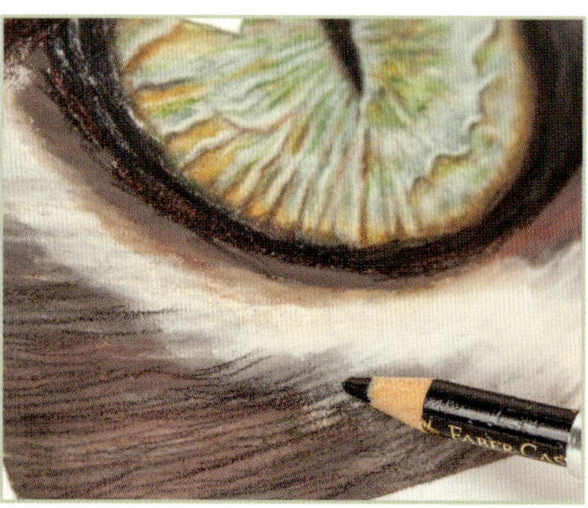

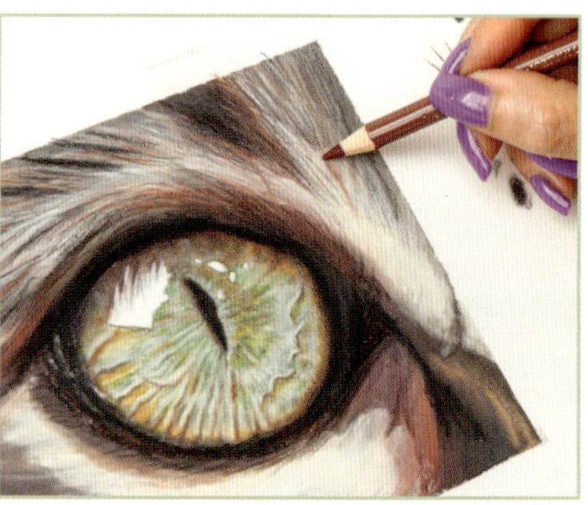

7 Build a rough hint of fur texture to frame the main subject using the following pencils: dark sepia, caput mortuum, terracotta, dark indigo, cinnamon, ivory; and Pablo cream. Use black with a back-and-forth motion to re-establish the shapes and to strengthen the depth of tone in the fur – in particular, the skin surrounding the eye.

8 Start to break up the larger shapes with strokes of black, using striking or tapering marks that follow the direction of the hair growth.

9 Add caput mortuum to the fur with striking or tapering marks.

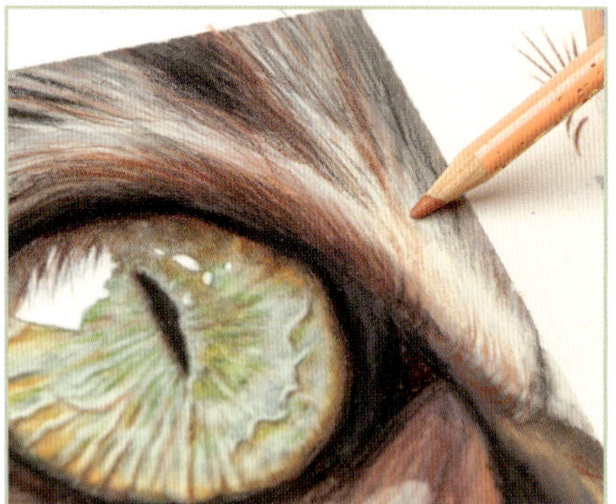

10 Use cinnamon to continue developing and refining the fur with striking or tapering marks.

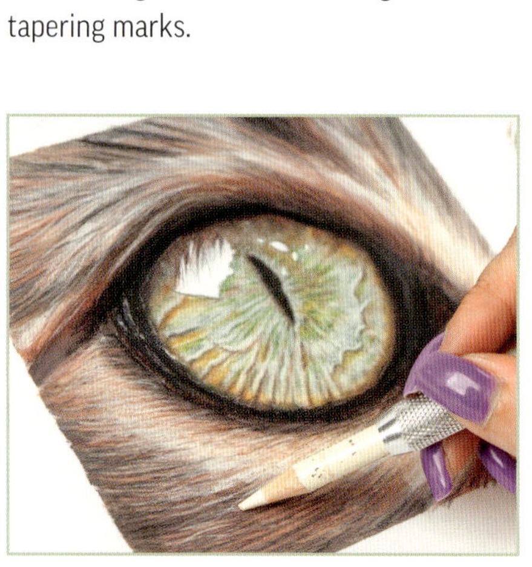

11 Use a small brush to blend the fur layers with solvent and then work again with the pencils from step 7 when dry.

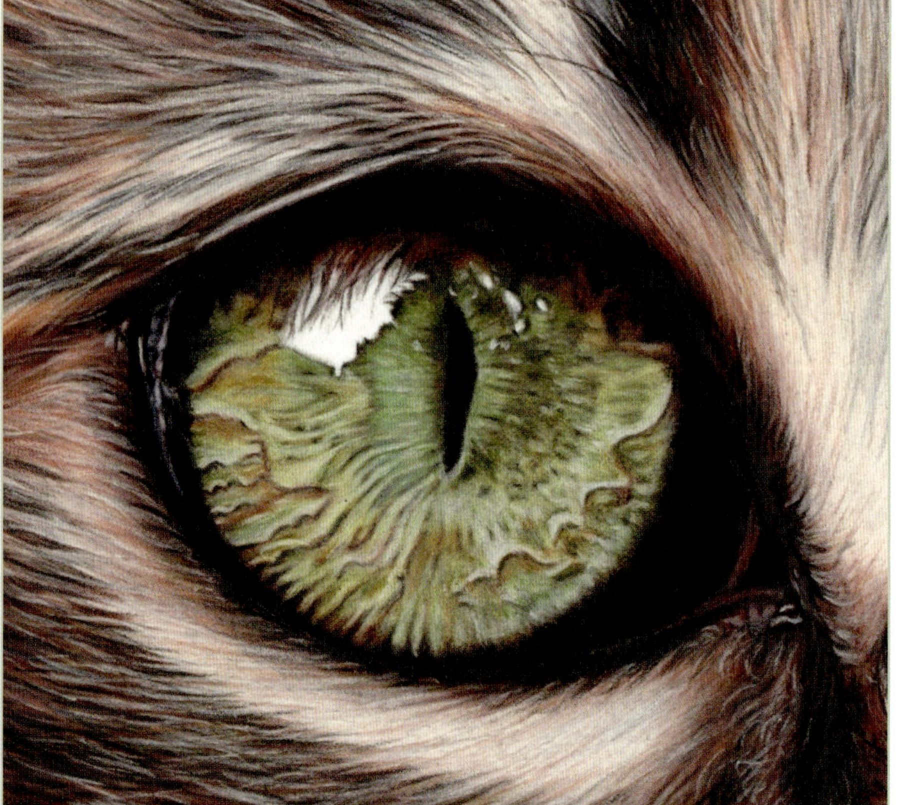

12 If you need to re-balance the eye itself, do so at the end. Do not worry if your details or colours do not match the reference photograph exactly. This is about learning how to create an effect and using a technique that you may not have tried before.

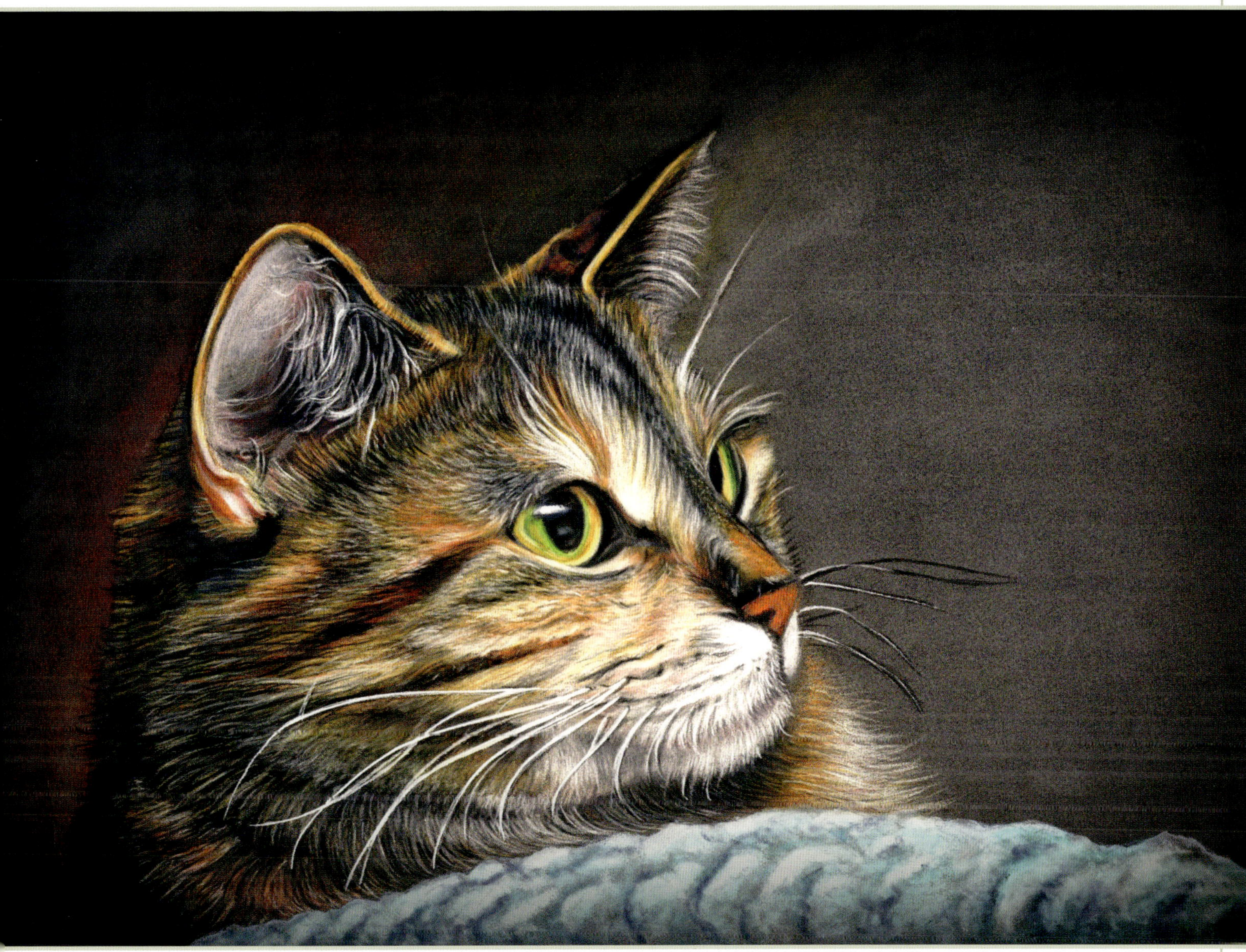

Amber glow

Watercolour pencils, used wet and dry, on Pastelmat. Cats are
nighttime predators, so the slit of their eyes expands and contracts
to allow in more or less light. It can, however, also show fear, so
do consider how you want to portray the eye. This is another good
reason to have lots of supporting reference images.

BROWN EYE: DOG

You can work this study at different sizes, but working a little bit bigger than life size will push you to really refine your dark-to-light layering techniques on Pastelmat. It also allows you to add in more details if you choose.

When you subsequently work on eyes within a full portrait, they will almost always be much smaller than in this study, but you will be aware of just how much detail they actually hold.

You will need

Support: Clairefontaine Pastelmat paper – white colour, 12.5 x 12.5cm (5 x 5in)

Faber-Castell Polychromos pencils: 199 black, 157 dark indigo, 175 dark sepia, 169 caput mortuum, 247 indanthrene blue, 188 sanguine, 186 terracotta, 101 white, 271 warm grey II, 102 cream, 103 ivory, 192 Indian red

Caran d'Ache Pablo pencils: 001 white

Other materials: Graphite transfer paper and stylus or sharp pencil to transfer line drawing, pencil sharpener, glassine paper, soft dusting brush

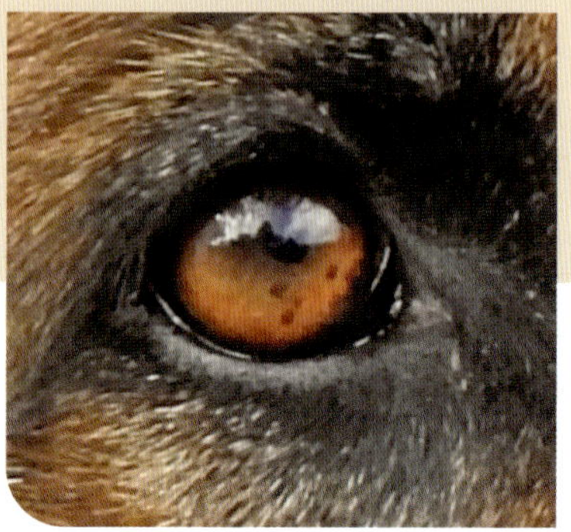

The reference photograph for this study.

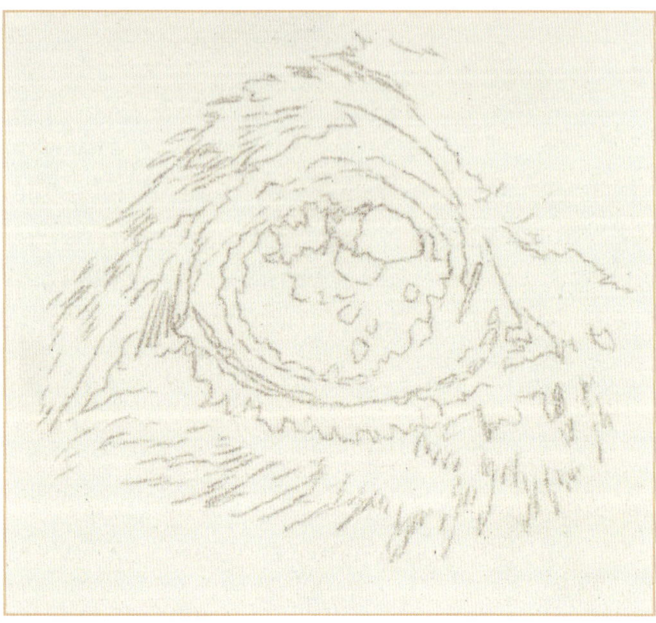

1 Transfer the image to your surface using a variation on the tracedown paper method (see page 51): glaze the back of your outline with dark sepia pencil, place it on the surface and use a fine stylus to work over the lines. This transfers only coloured pencil onto the surface, rather than graphite, which would contaminate the light areas of the eye. With the image in place, run a frame of masking tape around the picture.

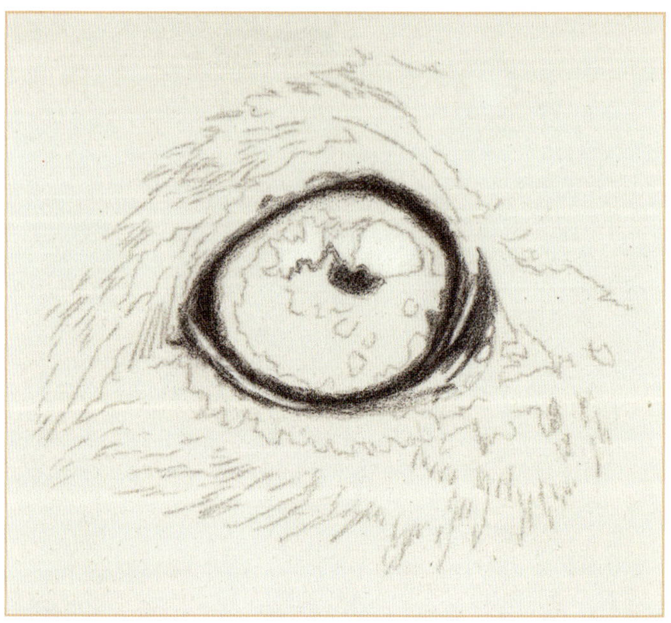

2 Use the Pablo white to mark in the highlight in the eye and the lighter line of the lower eyelid. With dark sepia, mark in the dark outline of the eye itself, including a hint of the pupil. Darken up some of these lines with black.

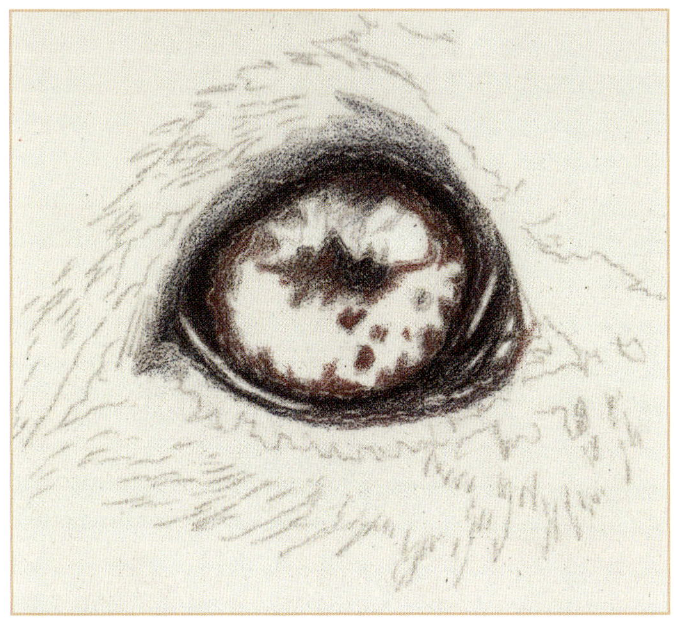 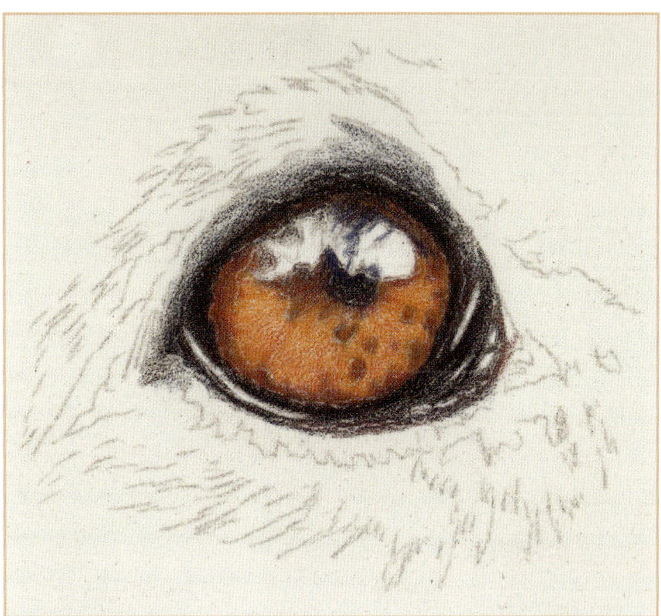

3 Begin using dark sepia with a back-and-forth technique to add the first layers to the outer edge of the iris, then overlap the dark outline with this layer and add a hint through the white highlight area. We now continue to work from dark to light, with repetition to build up the layers: glaze the dark sepia in the iris area with caput mortuum, then build the dark of the outline with dark indigo, black and caput mortuum.

4 Add the darks flecks in the iris using caput mortuum, then use the same colour to scumble around the edge of the iris, overlapping the dark outline. Glaze over this edge area with sanguine. Use terracotta in a back-and-forth motion, in towards the pupil and out towards the outline, to apply a glaze over the whole iris (except the highlight). Add a touch of indanthrene blue into the highlight area.

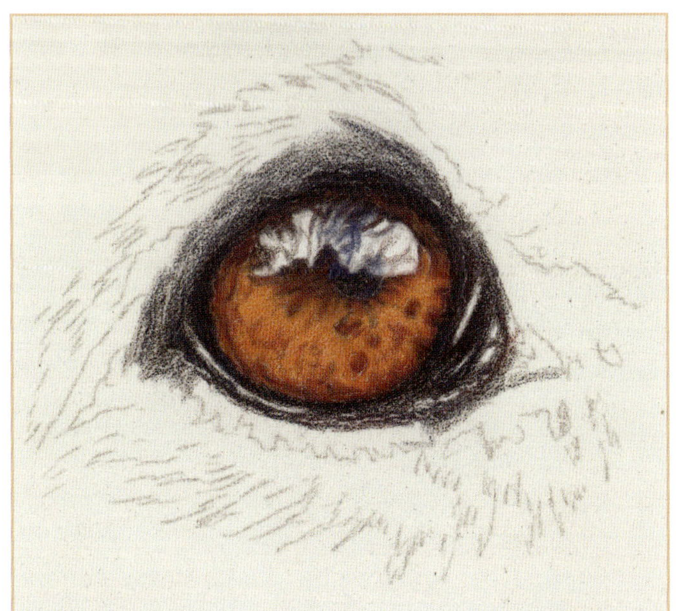 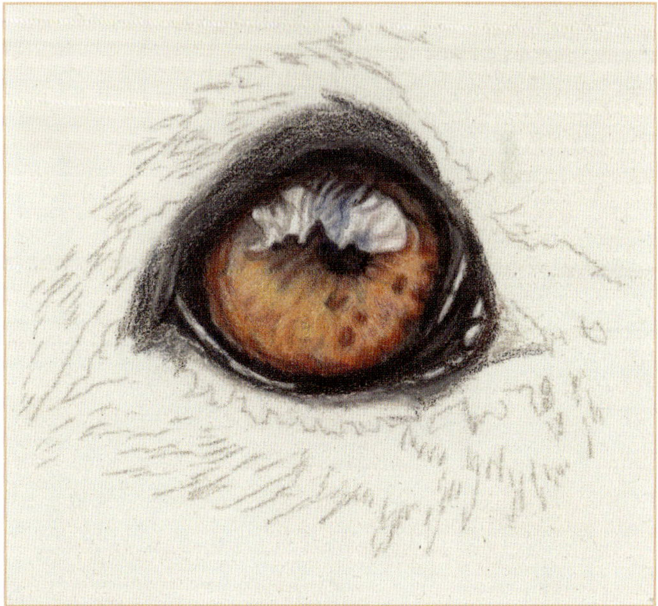

5 Glaze over the highlight with Polychromos white to soften the marks. Repeat steps 3 and 4 until the tooth of the paper starts to fill. With each layer, sharpen your pencils more and add in a few more of the markings on the iris using caput mortuum. Mark in the hint of eyelash reflection using dark sepia and indanthrene blue.

6 Soften the top edge of the highlight and around the pupil with warm grey II. Do the same with cream, using a back-and-forth stroke outward from the pupil into the orange areas. Glaze over the whole of the iris, except the highlight, using ivory. Use black to extend the lid outwards into the surrounding fur area with a light layer to widen the frame of the study.

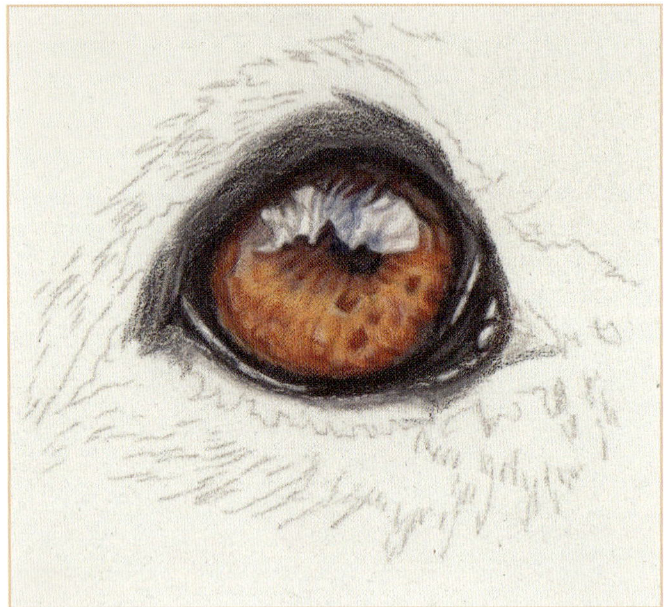

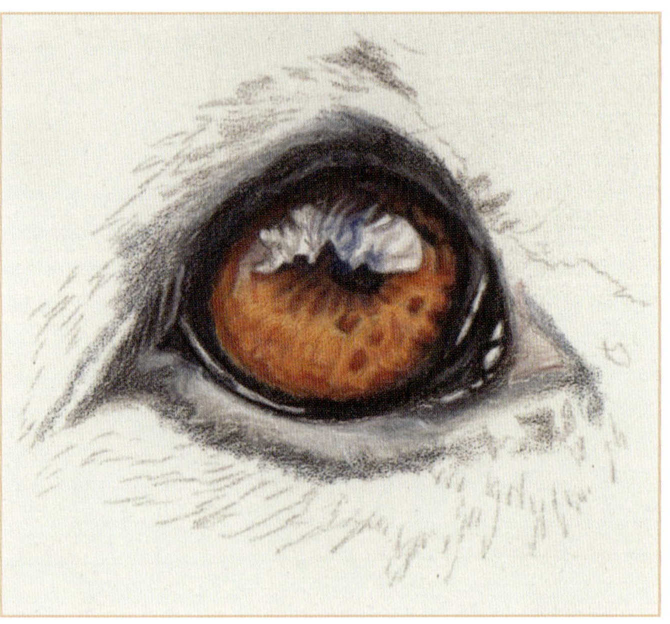

7 Bring back the orange colour using sanguine. Add touches of Indian red over the initial caput mortuum markings to intensify the red. Rotate between sanguine, caput mortuum and Indian red to build the saturation, always overlapping each colour.

8 Keep repeating the previous steps to build the saturation and detail. If you lose a colour or tone, just add it back in. To prepare for a hint of fur to be added in the area outside of the eye, block in using a combination of black, dark sepia and caput mortuum.

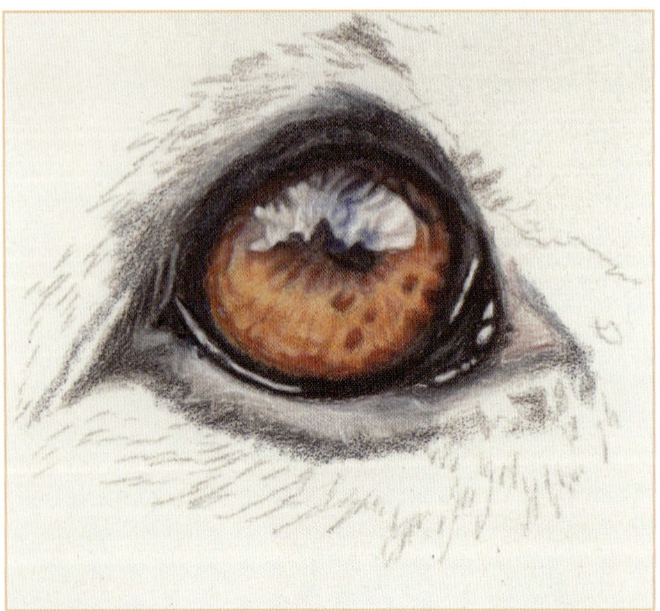

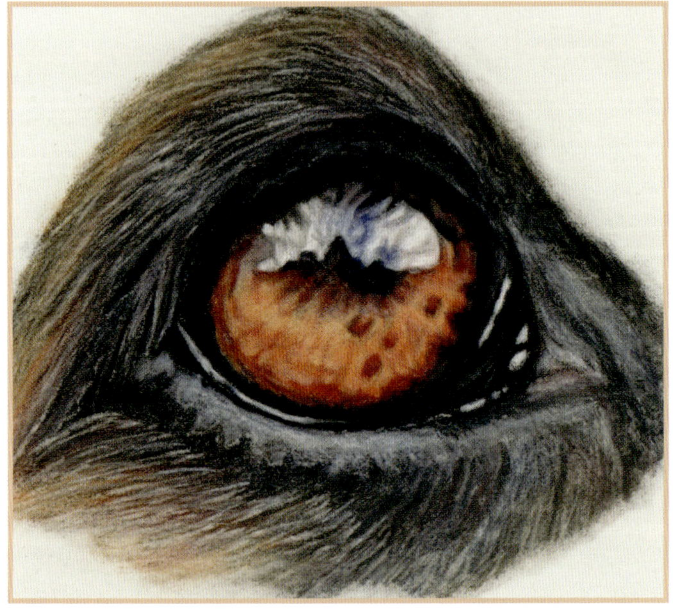

9 Soften the lower lid with a glaze of warm grey II. With sharp pencils, add back in any missing flecks of colour to the iris using caput mortuum, then glaze with terracotta. Next, use Pablo white and ivory to strengthen any highlights within the iris. Keep glazing and adding colour or tone until you are happy with the eye itself. You can tweak and balance further after the fur surround is in place.

The finished study

To add a touch of fur, start by using a stylus with a tapered flick to create some indented hair texture lines. Glaze over this with dark sepia and the lines will appear. Repeat until you have a nice even dark tone. Glaze over the brown areas using terracotta to soften the look, then add in dark indigo and caput mortuum. Repeat to build the saturation. Next, use warm grey II and white to soften the whole area. Repeat working from dark to light, sharpening your pencils with each layer until you have built up a buttery surface. Once buttery, work dark through to light using short flicks of the pencil to achieve the fur texture lines. Once you are happy, the study is complete.

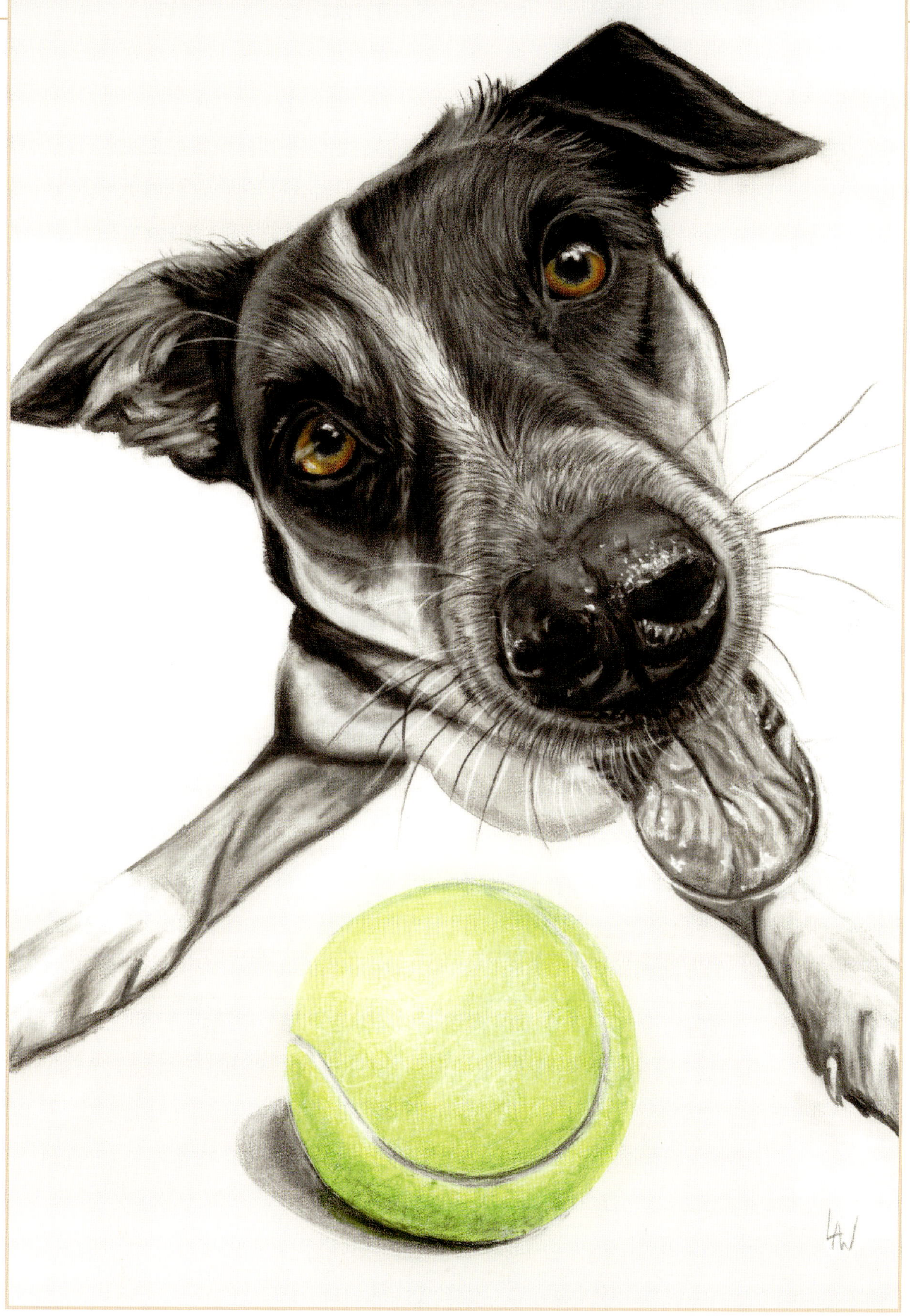

Lucy

Watercolour pencils, used wet and dry, on Pastelmat. As this is one of my own dogs,
I was able to have fun and be creative. She has the most amazing brown eyes, so
I stripped away all the colour from the piece in order to create a tonal portrait; only
then did I add the colour to her eyes – and of course into her favourite ball!

PINK NOSE: CAT

This study focuses on the pink nose and surrounding fur of a cat's muzzle. Working once more on Pastelmat paper, you will use a combination of smooth scumbling on the nose itself and a following touch of colour blocking, indenting and tapered strokes for the hint of fur texture.

You will need

Support: Clairefontaine Pastelmat paper – white colour, 7.5 x 6.5cm (3 x 2½in)

Faber-Castell Polychromos pencils: 189 cinnamon, 181 Payne's grey, 274 warm grey V, 169 caput mortuum, 180 raw umber, 103 ivory, 132 beige red, 231 cold grey II, 101 white

Other materials: Stylus, pencil sharpener, glassine paper, soft dusting brush, Slice craft knife

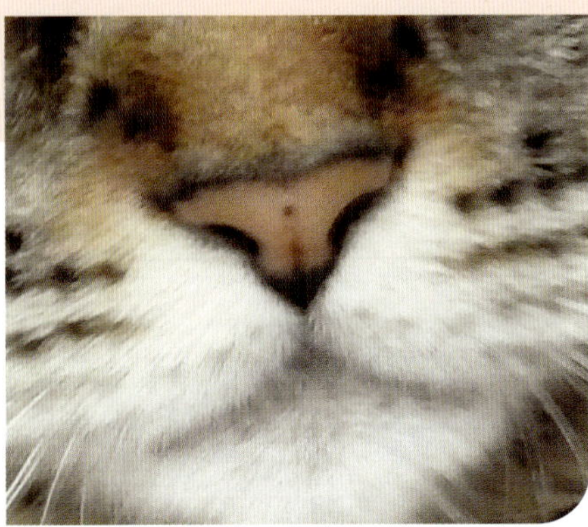

The reference photograph for this study.

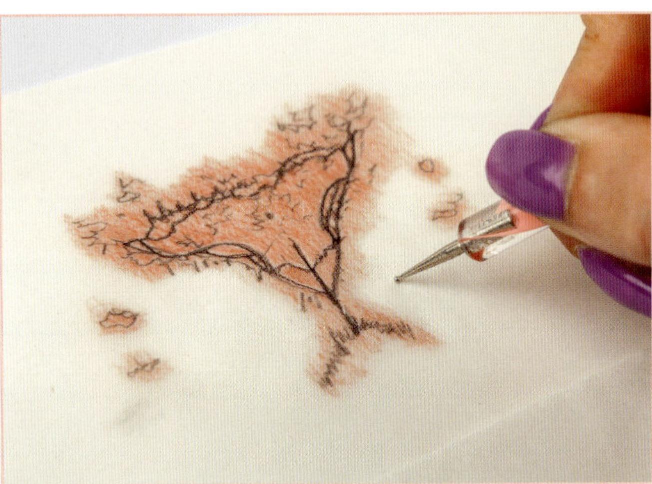

1 Using the tracing paper method on page 50, transfer the main lines onto white Pastelmat using a sharp Polychromos cinnamon (or other colour from within the nose). Transfer the hints of texture too. These fine wandering marks are subtle, but important. Use the fine stylus to indent a hint of fur around the nose. This will allow you to work the nose study up into a full picture, if you decide to.

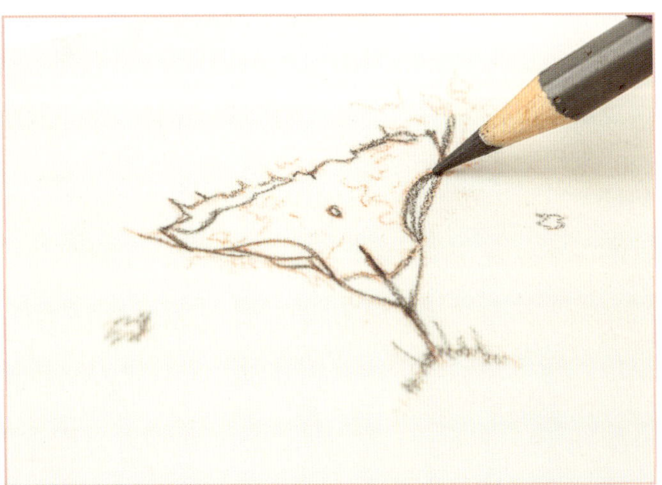

2 Using sharp Payne's grey and warm grey V pencils, mark in the dark outline shapes; don't fill these in at this stage.

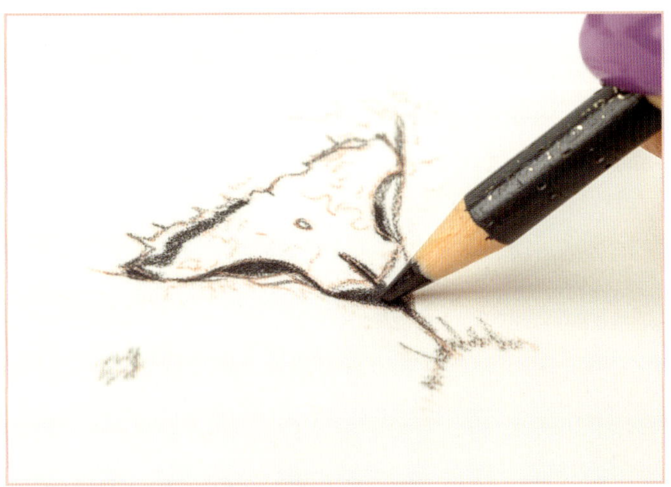

3 Colour block using Payne's grey and warm grey V to fill in the main areas of dark around the nose.

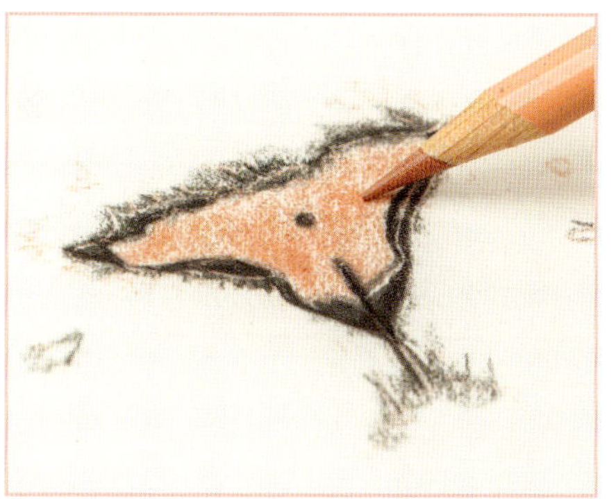 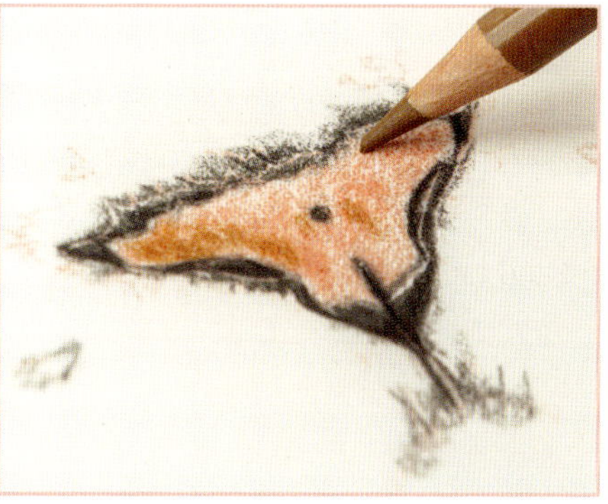 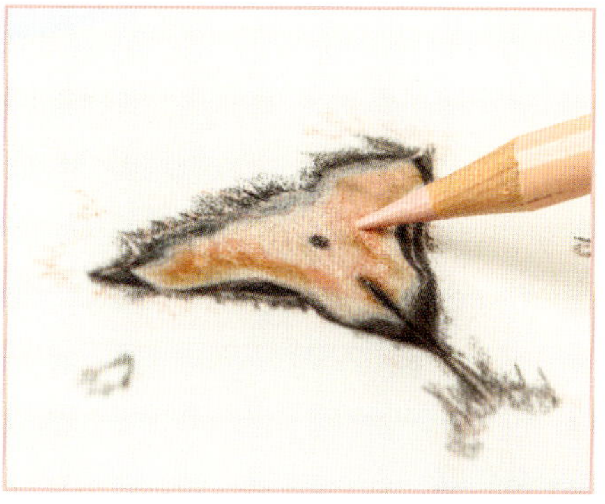

4 With the darks in place, switch back to the cinnamon pencil and scumble over the whole of the nose itself.

5 Use a sharp caput mortuum pencil to add a further layer of reddish scumbling towards the sides of the nose. Repeat with raw umber to add yellowish tones.

6 Scumble the nose using ivory over the lightest areas, and beige red over the pinker areas. Take the glaze over the edges of the dark surround.

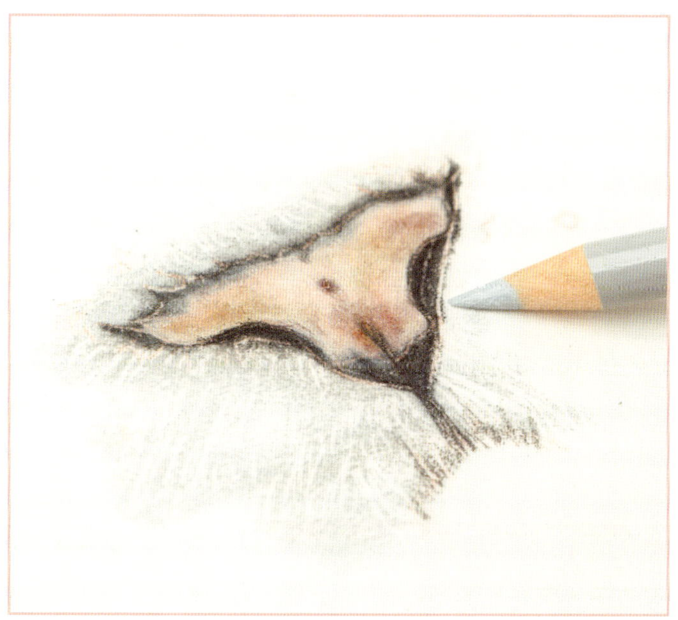 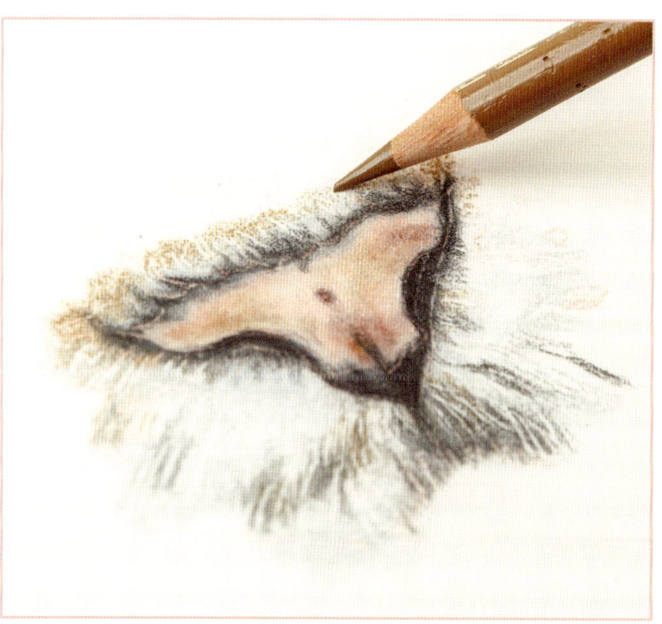

7 This brings the nose itself to around ninety per cent completion. Before we finish it off, we need to add a subtle frame of fur to put it in context. Once this is in place, you can better judge if any colours or tones on the nose itself need adjusting. Using Payne's grey, strengthen the darks in the nostrils and at the bottom of the nose, then swap to cold grey II and glaze over the area around the nose to pick out the indentations.

8 Use Payne's grey to add depth to the fur in the shadows, and scumble hints of raw umber for warmer areas – pay close attention to the reference photograph for placement.

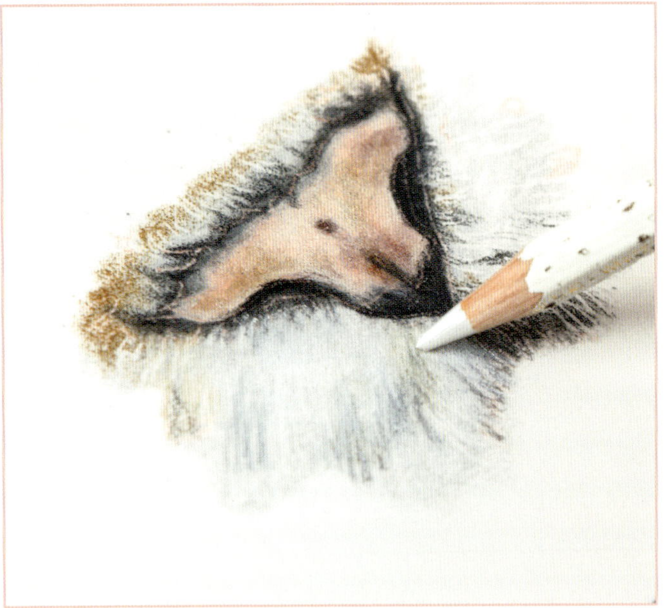

9 Add a layer of white over the muzzle area using tapered strokes in the direction of the fur.

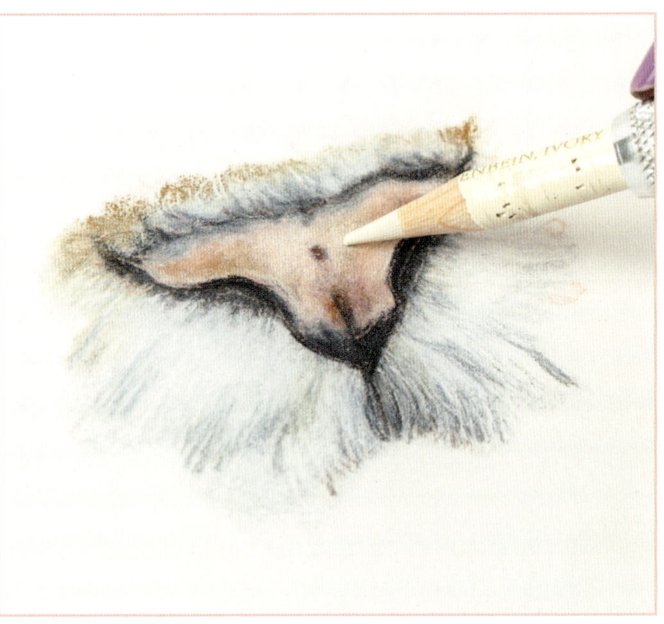

10 With the fur in place, check the reference photograph and, if necessary, rebalance the nose using the colours listed earlier, along with pure white.

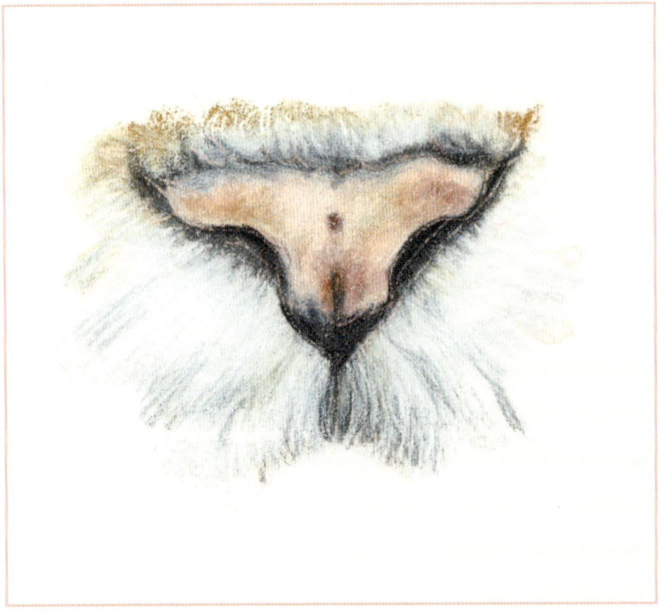

11 Continue to repeat the dark to light layers on the fur and use the Slice knife to add in more texture where needed. Repetition is key to the refinement.

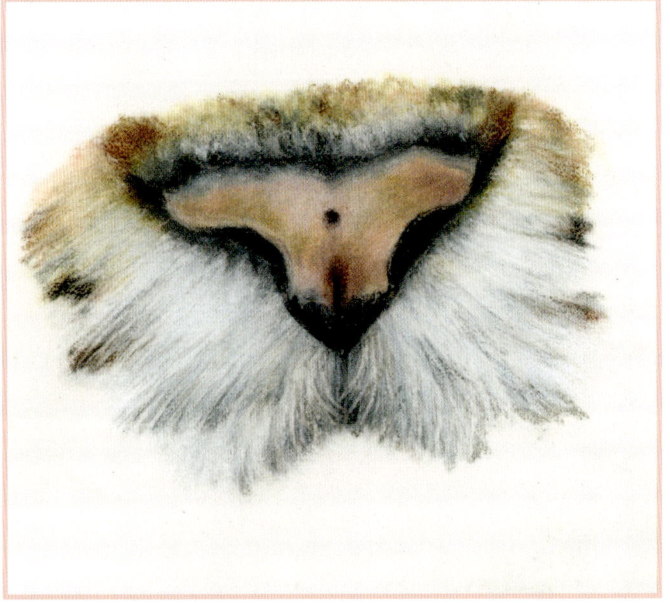

The finished study
The finished effect should be soft, so once you find the balance of detail and effect, then it is time to stop.

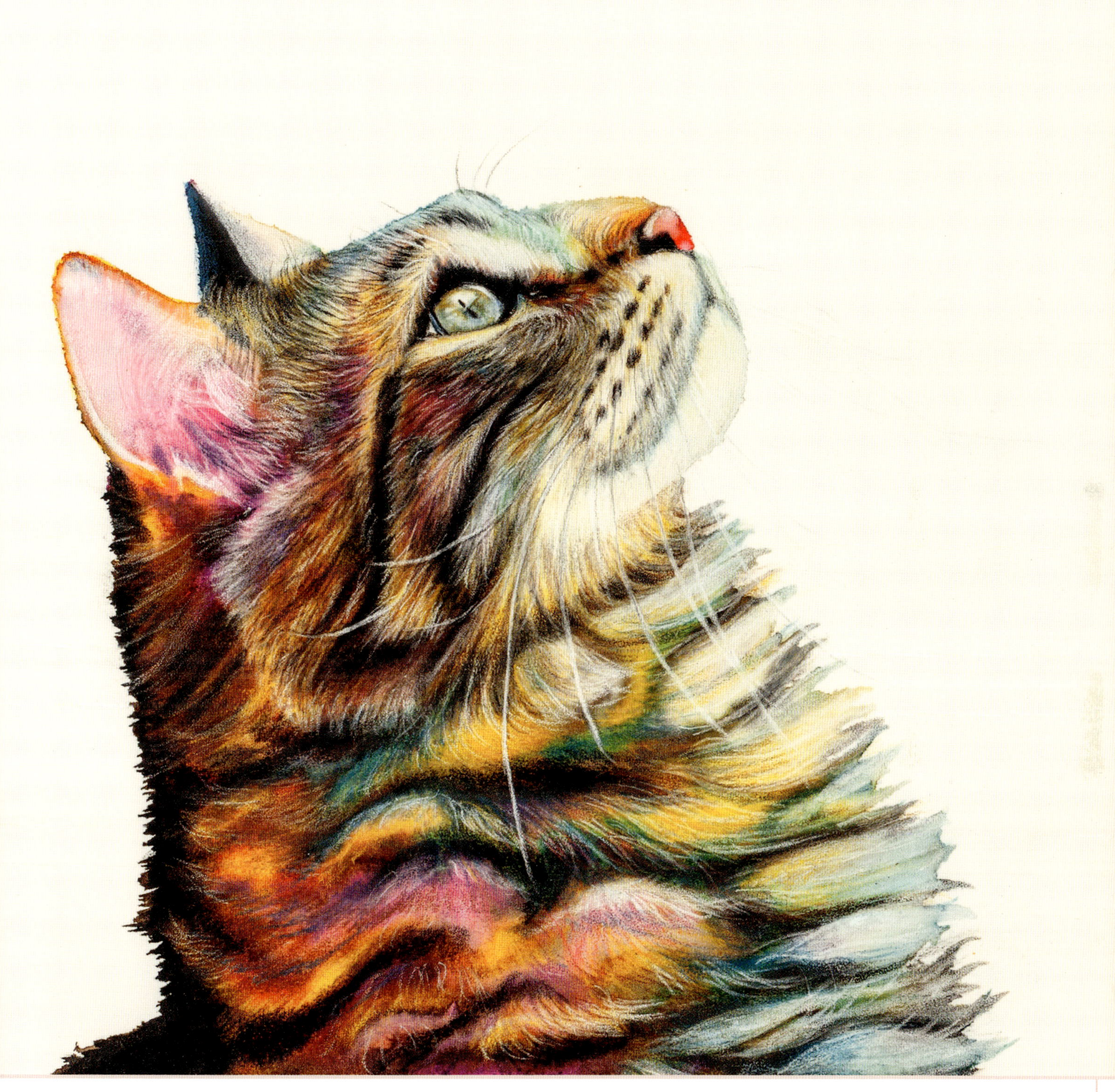

Inky Cat
This is the perfect example of the fun that can be had when combining inks with coloured pencils. You don't always have to be realistic with your colour choices! Your subject doesn't always need to be looking straight at the viewer either.

BLACK NOSE: DOG

This study will teach you how to balance the darks, lights and colours with repetition and the dark colour of the surface will make you focus and approach things a little differently. The key techniques here include back-and-forth and tight scumbling strokes as well as a touch of stippling to create a different texture.

You will need

Support: Clairefontaine Pastelmat paper – anthracite colour, 7.5 x 7.5cm (3 x 3in)

Faber-Castell Polychromos pencils: 199 black, 169 caput mortuum, 151 helioblue reddish, 178 nougat, 231 cold grey II, 272 warm grey III, 233 cold grey IV

Caran d'Ache Pablo pencils: 001 white

Other materials: Stylus to transfer line drawing, pencil sharpener, glassine paper, soft dusting brush, Slice craft knife

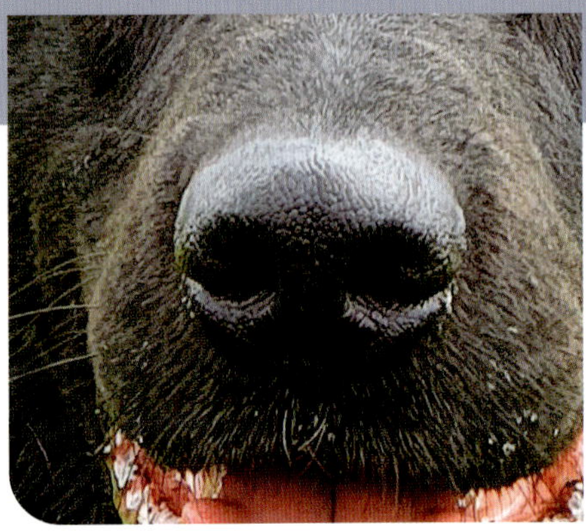

The reference photograph for this study.

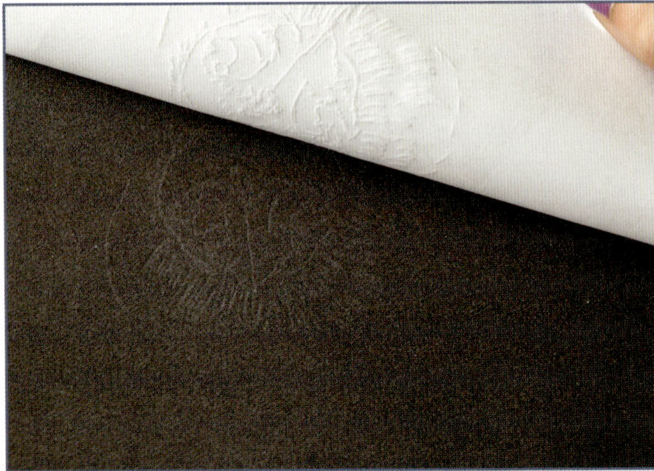

1 Transfer your image to anthracite Pastelmat using the indenting method on page 49. When working on a dark surface, be conscious to transfer the darker lines, rather than the highlights. Were you working on a white surface, you would do the opposite. Transferring using the indent method means you can also sink some of these dark lines and features down at the start.

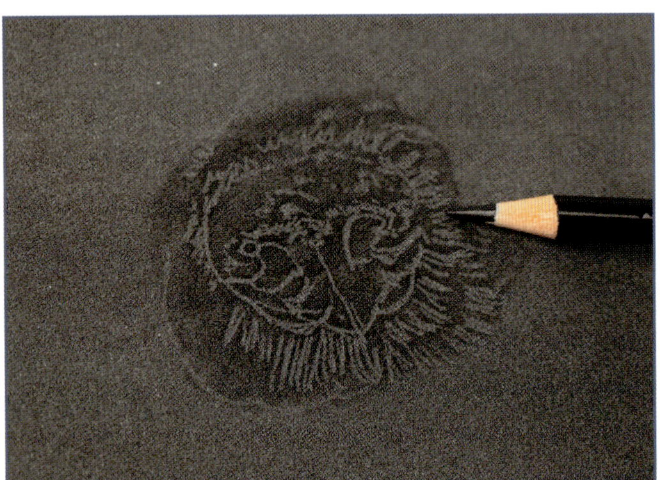

2 Make the indentations pop by glazing the whole area, highlights and all, with black – you can apply this fairly quickly, with loose strokes; there's no need to follow the fur direction with this.

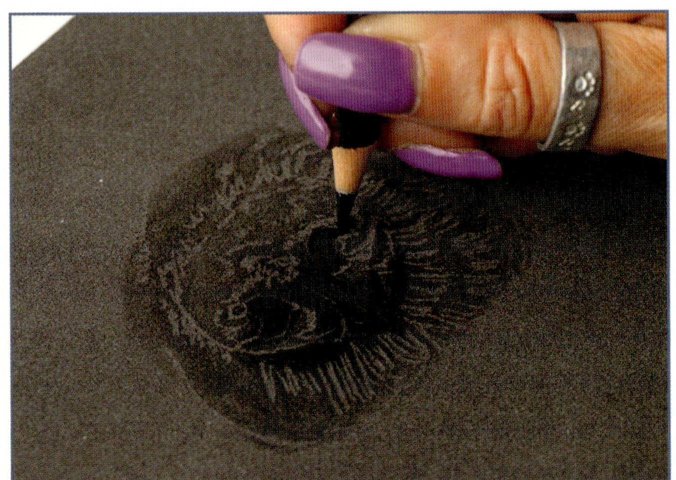

3 Once this initial layer is in place, use a second glaze to build up the darkest areas. Sharpen the black pencil and use it to fill the indentations of the nostrils and on the line between them.

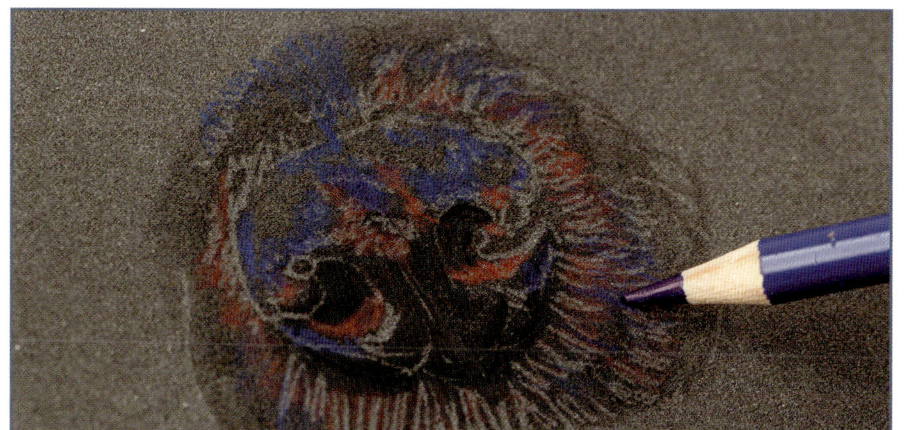

4 Use caput mortuum to pick out the hints of pinky flesh on the nostrils and tip of the nose with the scumbling technique. Don't be alarmed by its boldness; we'll knock it back later. Swap to helioblue reddish to pick out the blue-tinged areas on the nose. Whilst focusing on these colours, you'll likely spot hints of the same in the surrounding fur. While you're attuned to them, pop in some marks using a back-and-forth motion and the same colours.

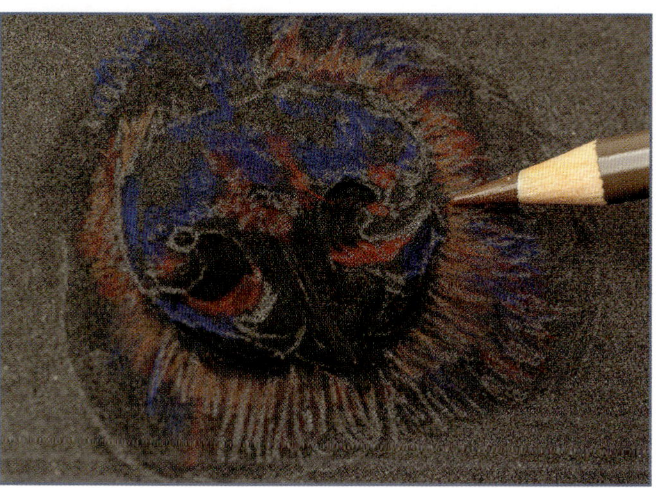

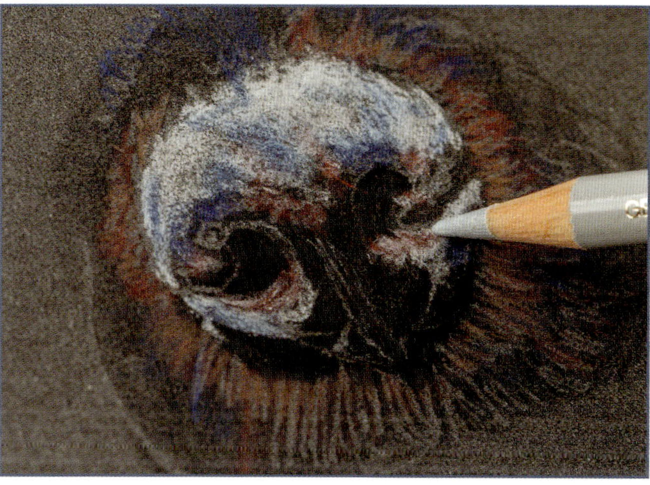

5 Using nougat – one of my softening pencils (see page 35) – make short, tapered strokes to represent the fur around the outside outline of the nose. Remember to always make these marks in the direction of the fur. This is typically away from the nose, but always check your reference photograph before committing.

6 Using a cold grey II pencil and a tight scumbling action, start to add in highlights to the nose itself. The paper will still be grainy at this point. Don't try to fill the grain too quickly; it needs to build up with repeated layers of all the colours.

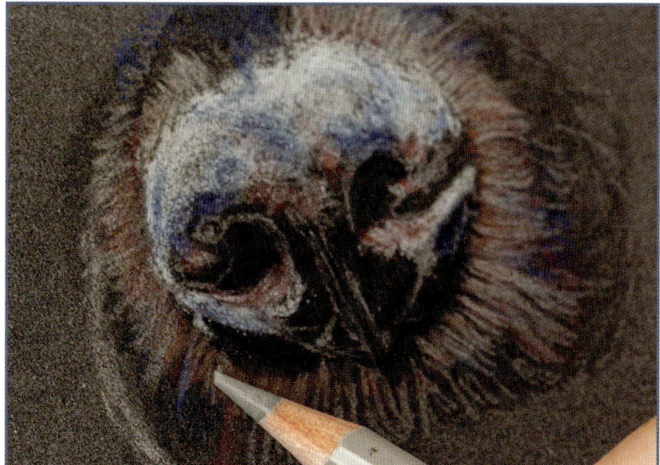

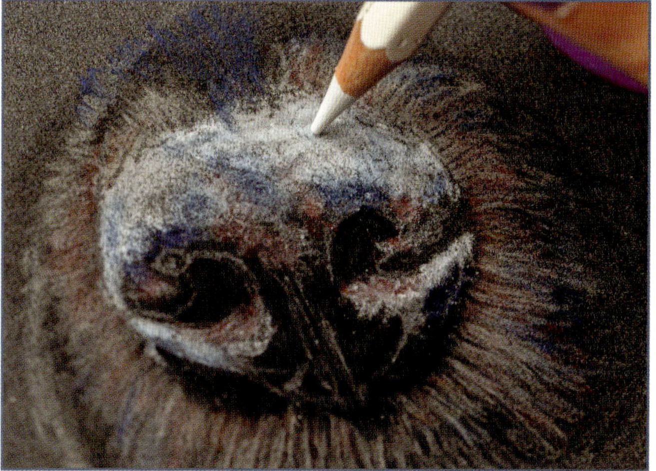

7 Don't over-focus on a particular area; try to stay aware of the overall image as well, to ensure things remain balanced. Swap to a warm grey III to work another layer of short tapered strokes over the fur framing the nose.

8 Using Pablo white (this is more opaque than the Polychromos white) and a stippling action, add highlights to the top of the nose and where the bottom of the nostrils catches the light. This completes the initial layer.

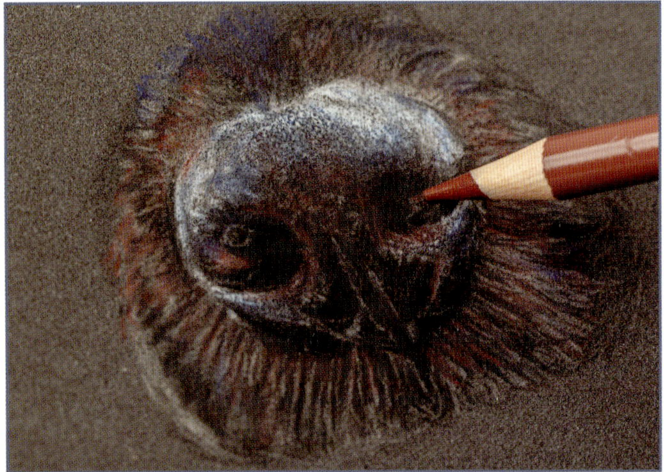

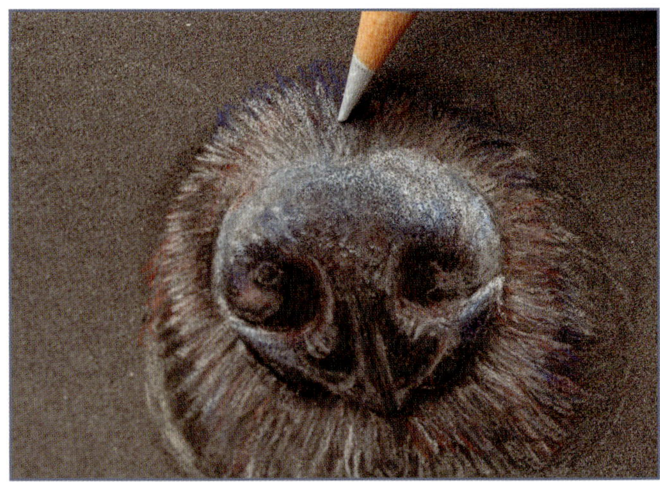

9 Returning to the black pencil, start to work more slowly and precisely in your application. Using a combination of scumbling and back-and-forth strokes, build up and refine the dark areas on the nose itself, working into and over the colours in place. Change to tapered strokes on the surrounding fur. Switch to caput mortuum to begin re-establishing the warm areas.

10 Continue using caput mortuum alongside helioblue reddish to reinstate the warm and cool colours over the black once more, and build up the layers. Bring back the lights – the white areas and highlights – using cold grey IV and cold-grey II. Aim to bring back the balance across the whole area, rather than getting blinkered on the highlights.

Tip

Get into the habit of looking at your reference photograph more than the picture you're drawing. Keep it close by to make this easy.

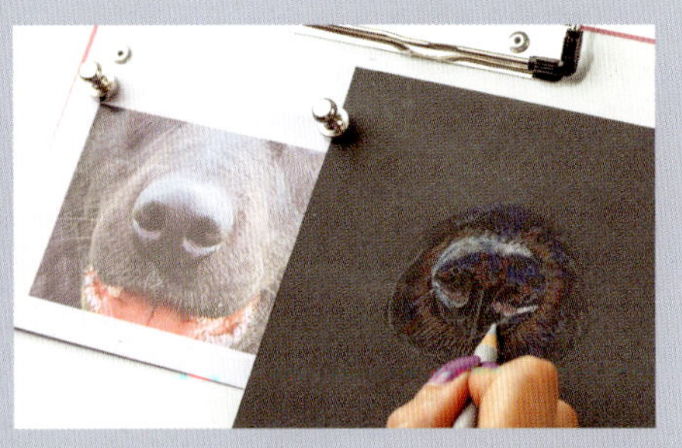

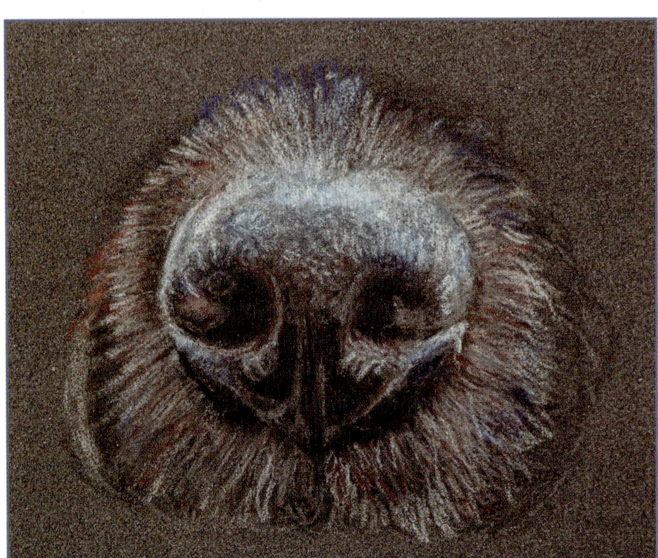

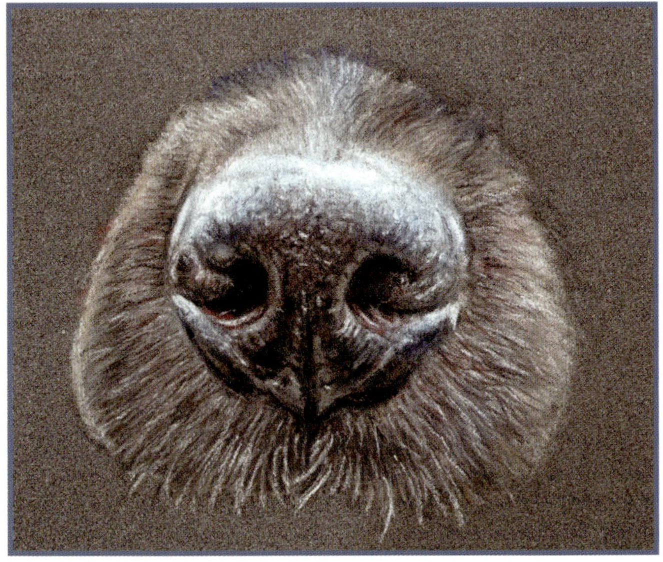

11 Use Pablo white to build up the extreme highlights, finishing this stage with a little stippling.

The finished study
Continue to rotate through your darks, mid-tones and lights until you have built up a rich saturation of pigment, colour and tone. Use the Slice knife to lift away to create fine details and then sink sharp pencils into those areas to soften.

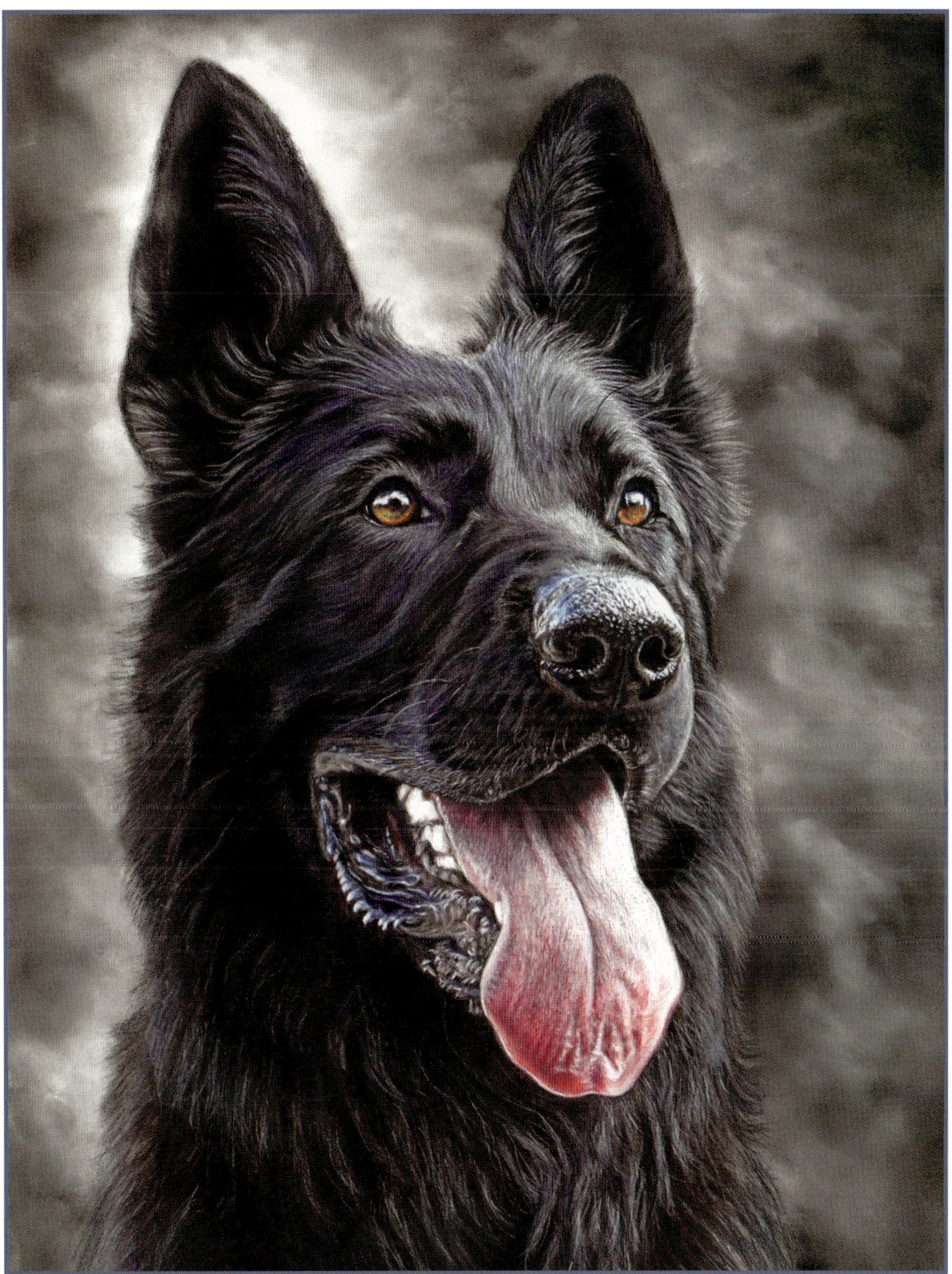

Mac, Black GSD

Coloured pencil on Pastelmat with PanPastel background. Whether it's black, pink or even spotty, the techniques used for a dog's nose are largely the same, regardless of colour. Always look for the shapes, block in the shadows and the colours (see page 37) and then save the texturizing until the final layers. Always try to get the highlight matching the direction of the light.

PINK NOSE: DOG

One of the big appeals of drafting film is that you can work on the front or the back. Colours applied to the back will show through slightly muted on the front, giving you access to a range of different effects. You can work both sides to intensify tones, too – useful, as drafting film doesn't have much tooth: as it won't hold many layers on one side, using both doubles the intensity available to you. The key thing is to ensure you have double-sided matte drafting film.

Keep a strip of the same film near to your reference photograph, and you can test how colours appear on either side, simply by turning it over.

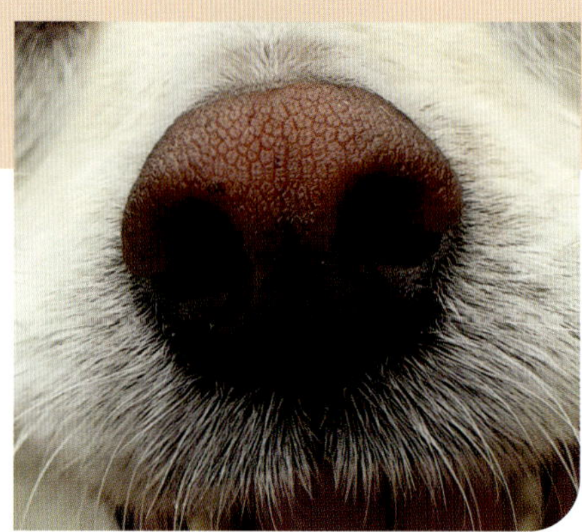

You will need

Support: Grafix 0.05mm double matte drafting film 9 x 7.5cm (3 x 3½in)

Derwent Lightfast pencils: Venetian red, Mars black, cloud grey, merlot, dusky pink, Mars violet, mist, white

Other materials: Pencil sharpener, glassine paper, soft dusting brush, Slice craft knife

The reference photograph for this study.

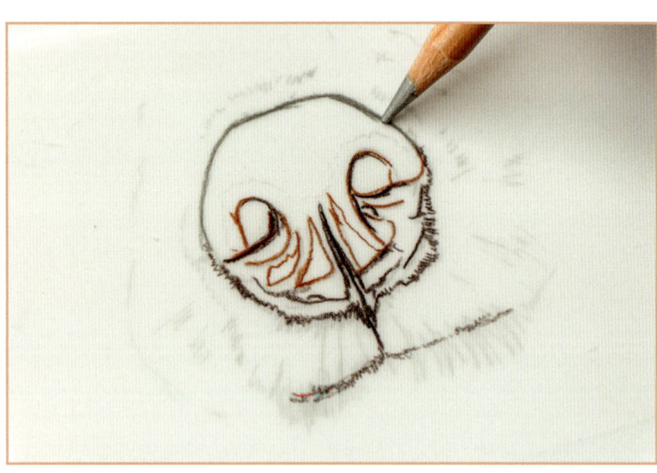

1 Lay the drafting film over your line art and transfer the outline of the nostrils and some shapes on the front of the nose using Venetian red and the tracing paper method on page 50. Transfer the darkest lines inside the base of the nose using Mars black, then follow the outline of the top edge of the nose with cloud grey.

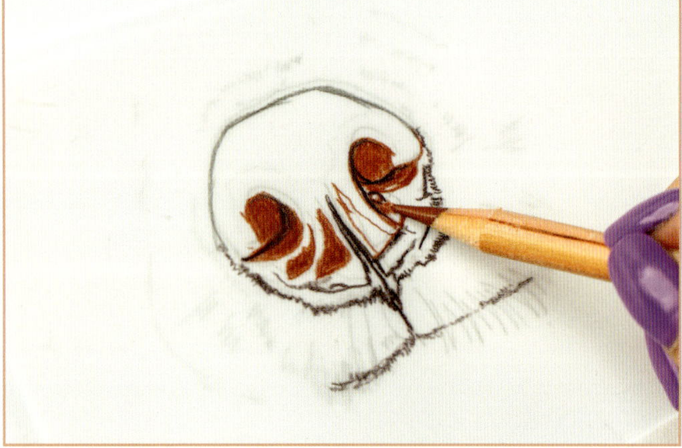

2 Use a combination of scumbling and back-and-forth marks to fill in the nostrils and marks on the front of the nose with Venetian red.

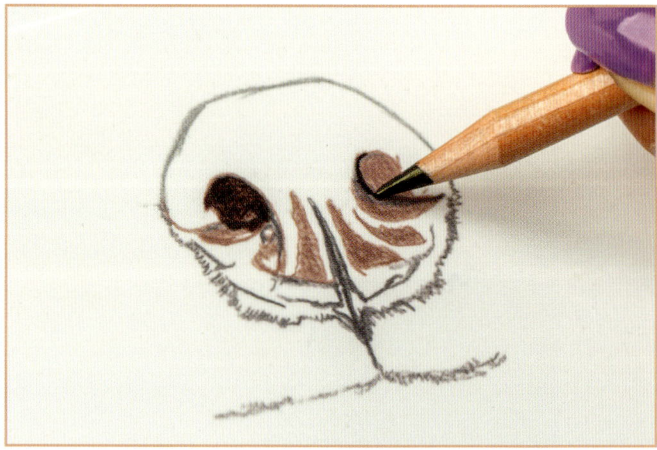

3 Take the film and outline drawing off the surface and turn the drafting film over. On the back, use Mars black to scumble a couple of layers inside the nostrils to intensify the colour, then work over the black lines at the bottom and sides.

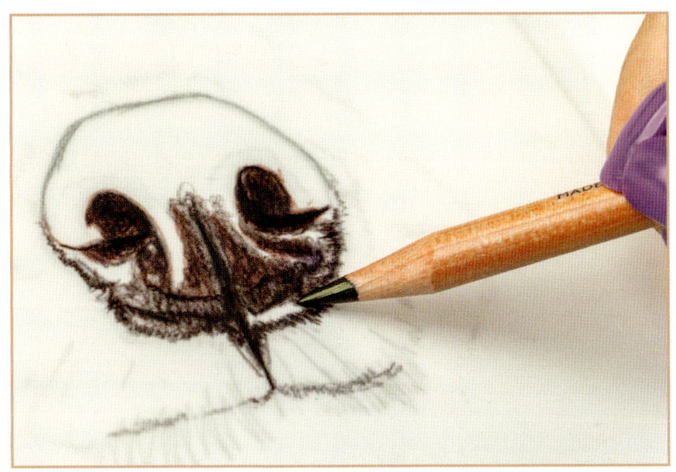

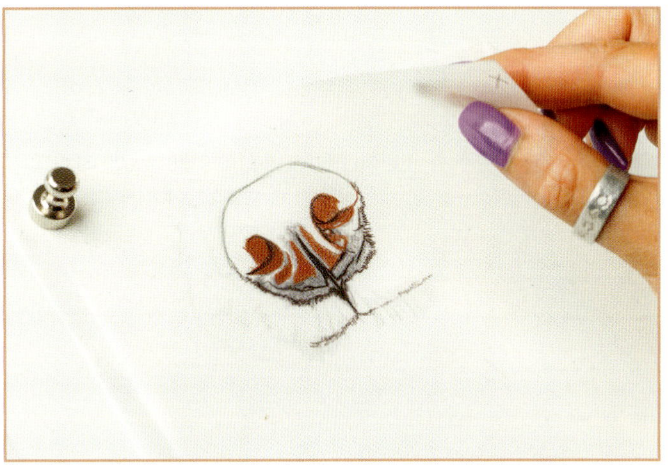

4 Still working on the back, scumble a single layer over the red part of the nose.

5 Turn the drafting film back over, replacing the outline drawing in position behind.

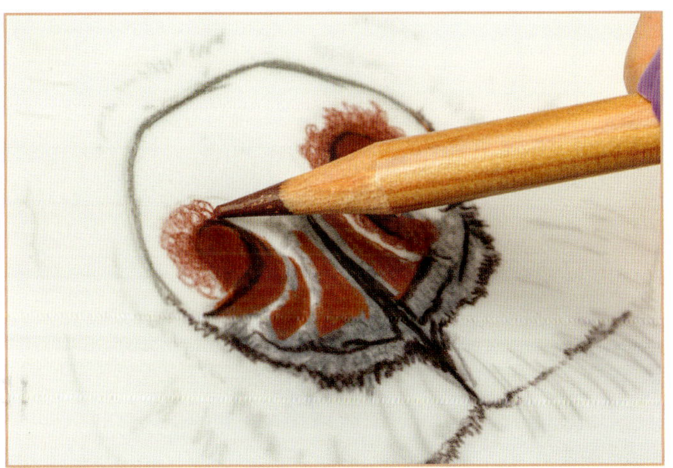

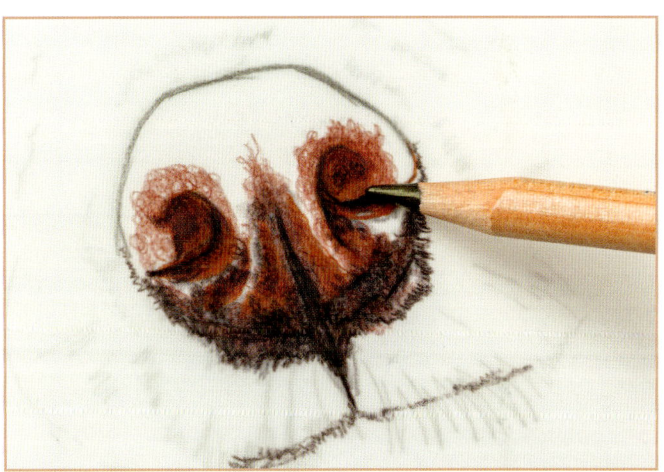

6 Intensify the red inside the nostrils, and a little around the edge, using merlot. Apply the layer with small, loose, circular strokes.

7 Using a mix of scumbling and back-and-forth strokes, add a very light layer of Mars black into the nostrils to shade the areas shown.

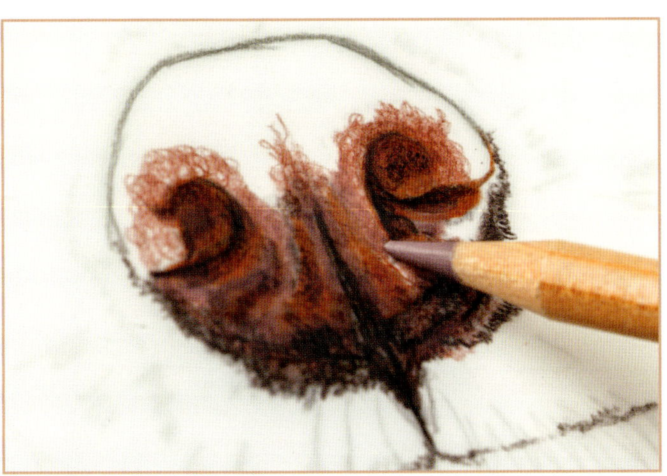

8 Time for smooshing! (See page 37 for the technique.) Use Mars violet to smoosh the colours on the front and lower part of the nose.

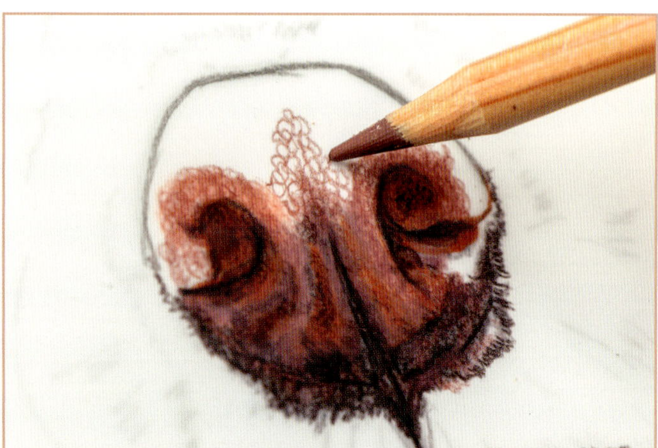

9 Swap to merlot to add the texture of the upper part of the nose. Use a wandering line of tight circles to build up the pattern of the skin.

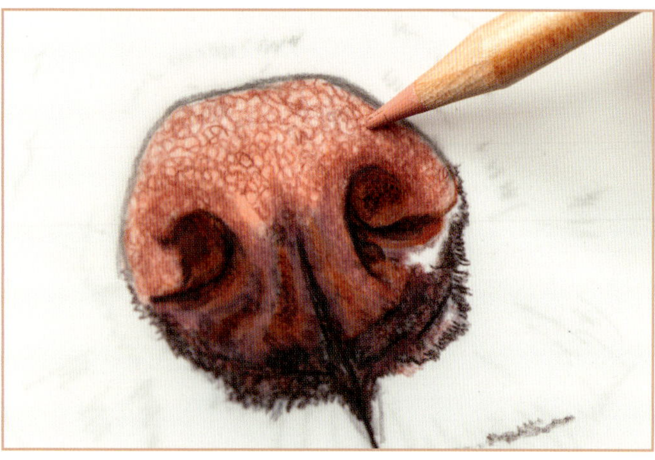

10 Use dusky pink to smoosh outward from the nostrils, and over the top of the nose.

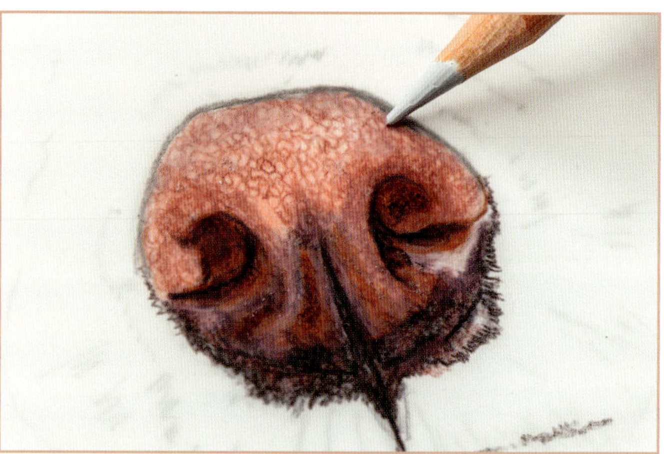

11 Using cloud grey, add another layer of smooshing over the top of the nose and to the sides of the top of each nostril. Next, jump to the slight highlights under each nostril.

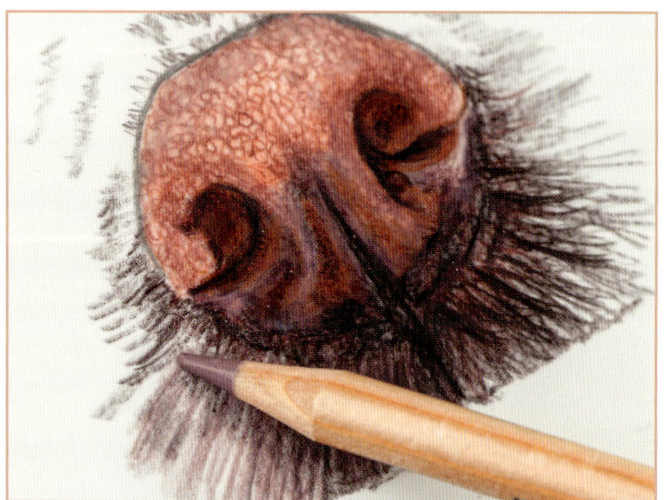

12 Establish the fur framing the nose by layering Mars black, then merlot, then Mars violet. Use back-and-forth strokes that follow the direction in which the hair grows.

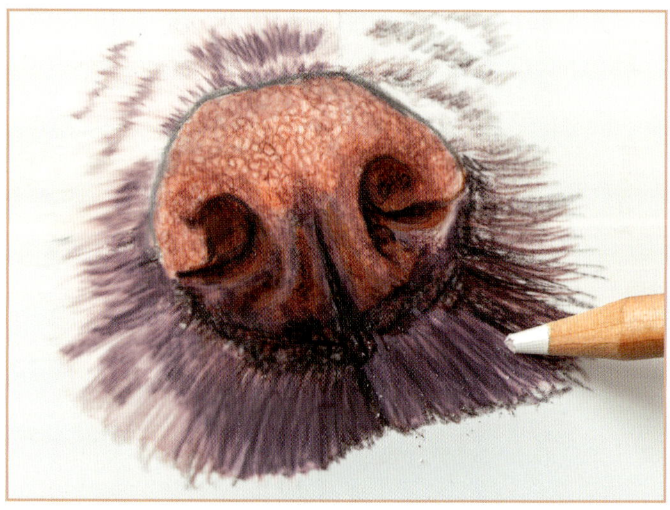

13 Use white to smoosh all of the fur; again using a directional back-and-forth stroke.

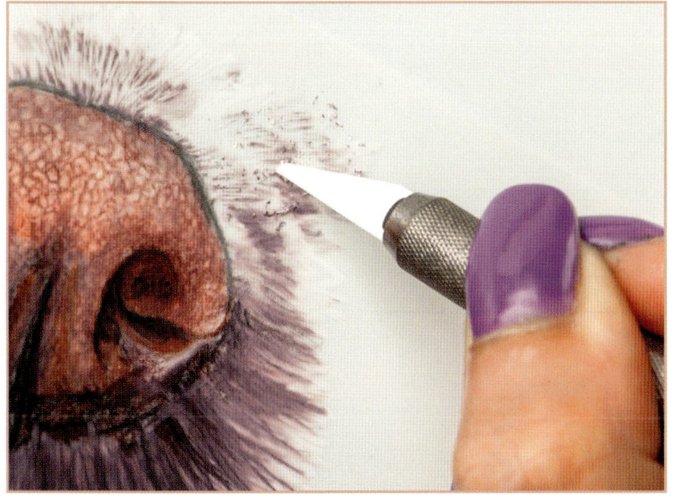

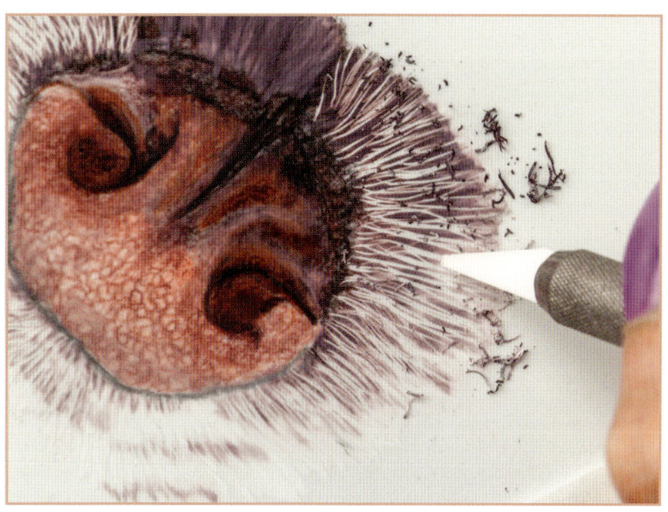

14 Turning the paper as you go (to follow the direction of fur growth), use the back of the knife to start to create the white fur by scratching away the established colour.

15 Continue working round, creating the white fur. Follow the length and direction of the hairs, referring to your reference photograph throughout.

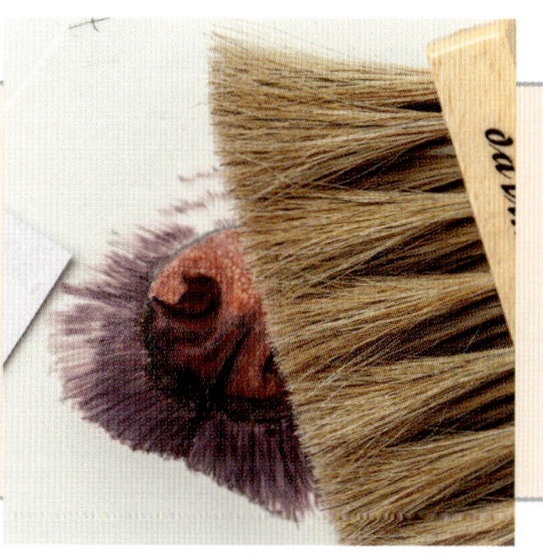

Tip

Use a large soft dusting brush to clear any scrapings from the surface.

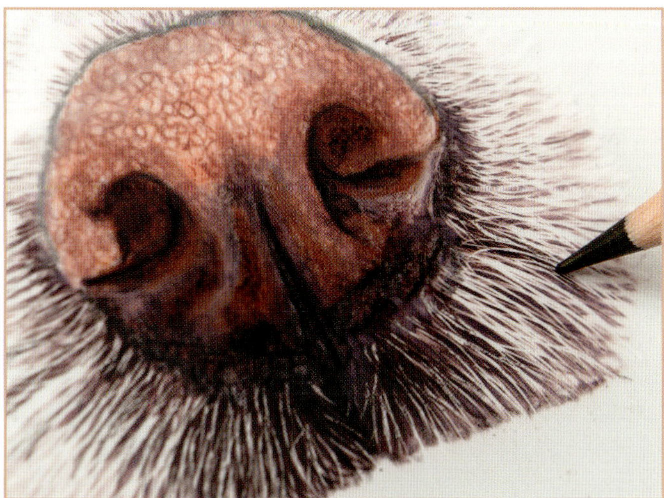

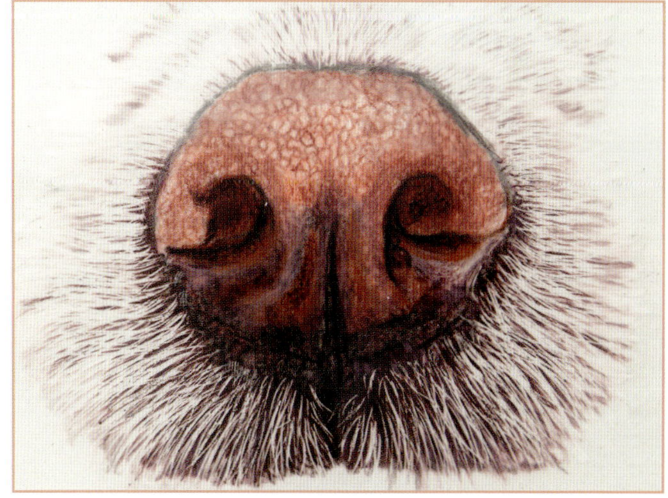

16 Work over the cutmarks with Mars black, flicking outwards from the roots of the hairs. The pencil will skip over the slice marks as long as you apply with the standard pressure; the result is that the areas near the roots become slightly softened and darker. This helps to avoid the white hairs appearing to sit flat on the surface.

17 Smoosh the fur with white again, then repeat the process of creating the fur with the knife, adding black at the roots, then smooshing with white.

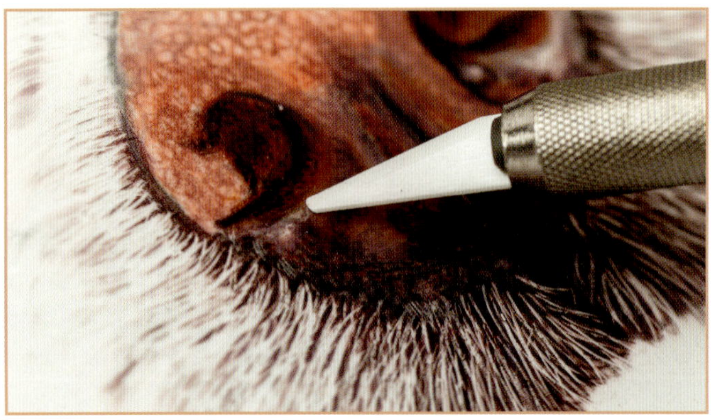

18 Use the knife to refine the highlights on the nostrils using light pressures and a mix of scumbling and stippling. This creates the soft highlights. You're aiming to remove one or two layers of underlying colour, rather than strip right back to the surface of the drafting film.

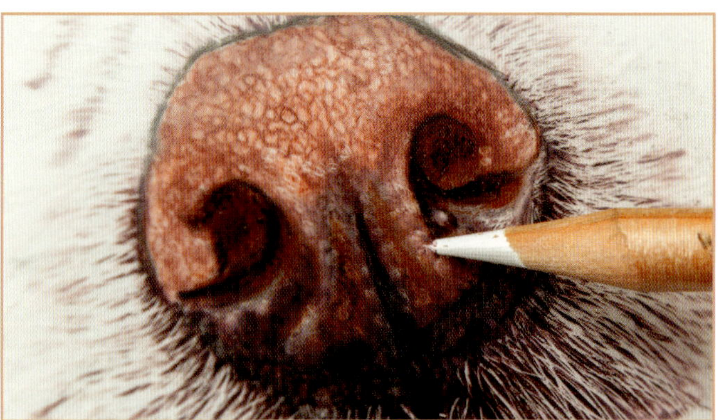

19 Lightly texturize the front of the nose with the knife in the same way. Soften this with a touch of white.

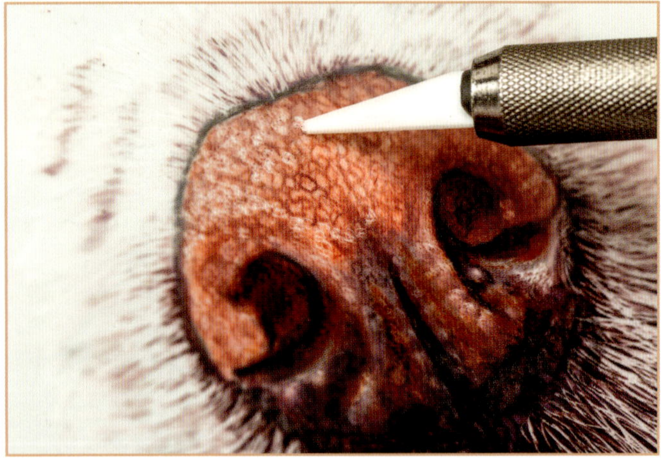

20 Use the knife with a very light pressure to overlay the texture on the top of the nose with similar wandering circular marks as are already in place.

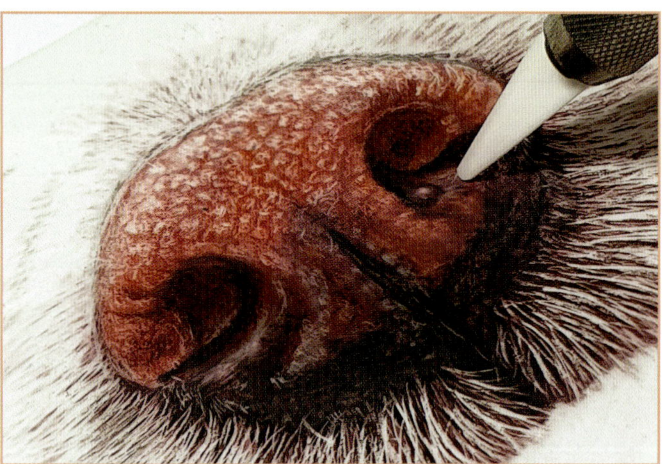

21 Keep repeating the pencil layers until you are happy with the hues and tones. Use your knife tool to lift away the pigment to enhance those fine details.

The finished study

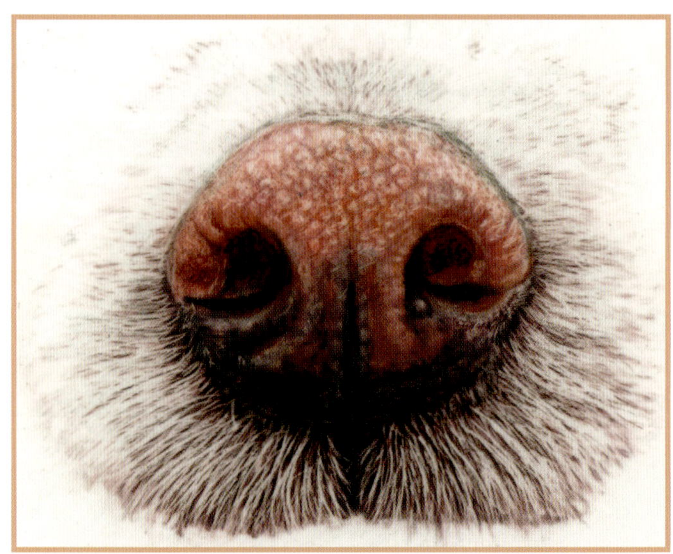

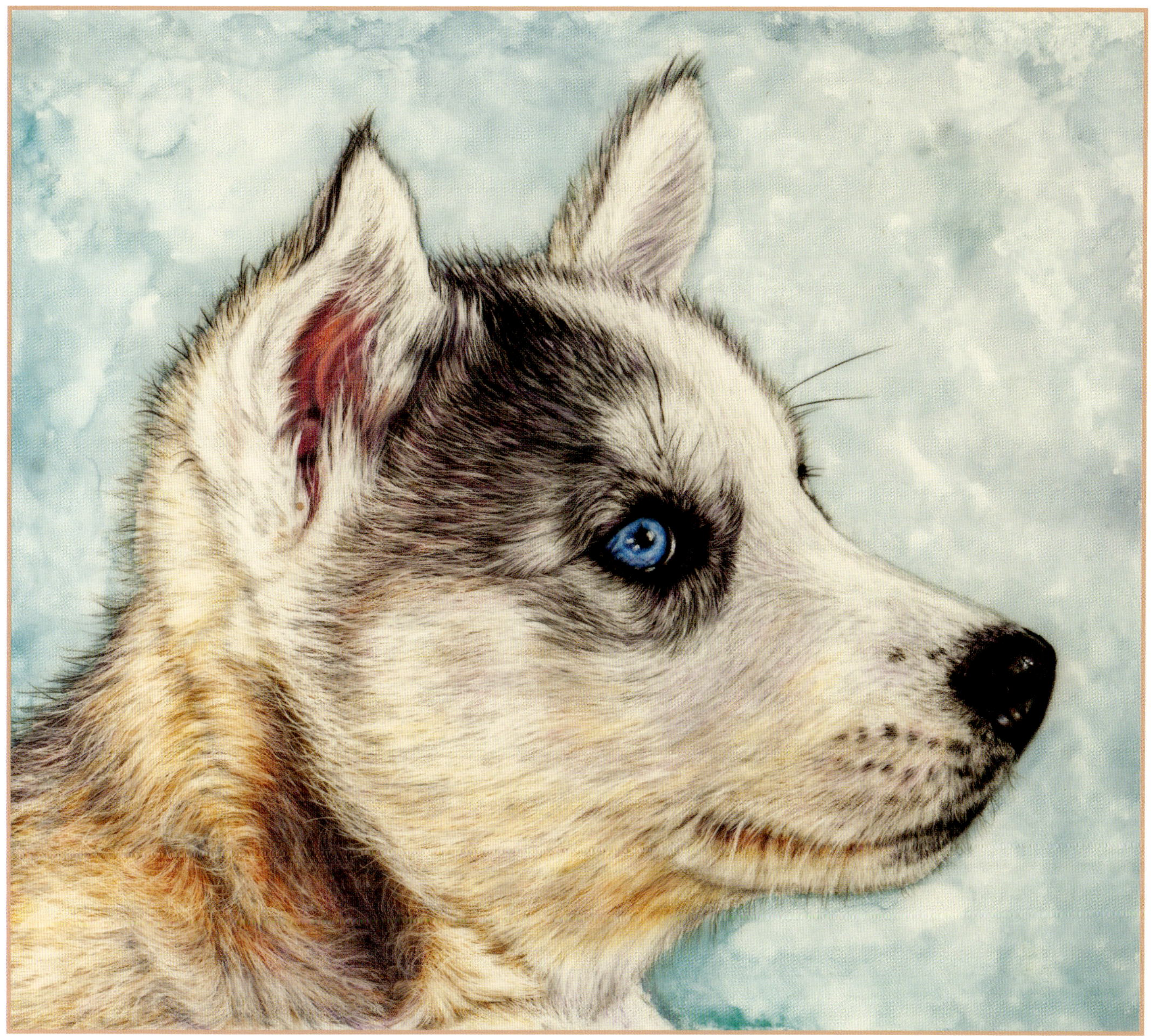

Husky Pup
Coloured pencils on drafting film with a watercolour pen background. I love working on profile portraits as they always add an element of 'what is she looking at?' to the piece. When working a profile piece, always be careful to draw what you see. A common mistake is to try to get both nostrils in view, and the slightest wrong curve line can completely throw the shape of the nose out. Secondly, always think of where you want the focus to go to first. For this one, it was the beautiful blue eye and then the fur detailing that were most important, so the nose was left less detailed.

CLUMPY FUR

Different supports work better for particular types of fur. This fur study is on suede mat board, the fibrous properties of which instantly help to create the desired fluffiness of the texture.

The other key thing to take from this study is the importance of simplifying your reference image and focusing on the shapes within. You can still work from dark to light, but rather than focusing on it being fur you simply need to work on depicting shapes and transitioning between shadows to highlights to create depth.

You will need

Support: Crescent suede mat board – thicket colour, 10 x 11.5cm (4 x 4½in)

Caran d'Ache Pablo pencils: 496 ivory black, 059 brown, 045 Van Dyke brown, 403 beige, 491 cream, 401 ash grey, 001 white

Other materials: Stylus, pencil sharpener, glassine paper, low-tack tape

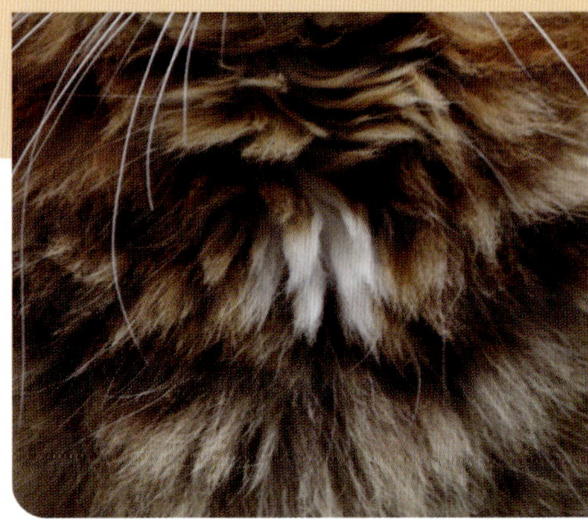

The reference photograph for this study.

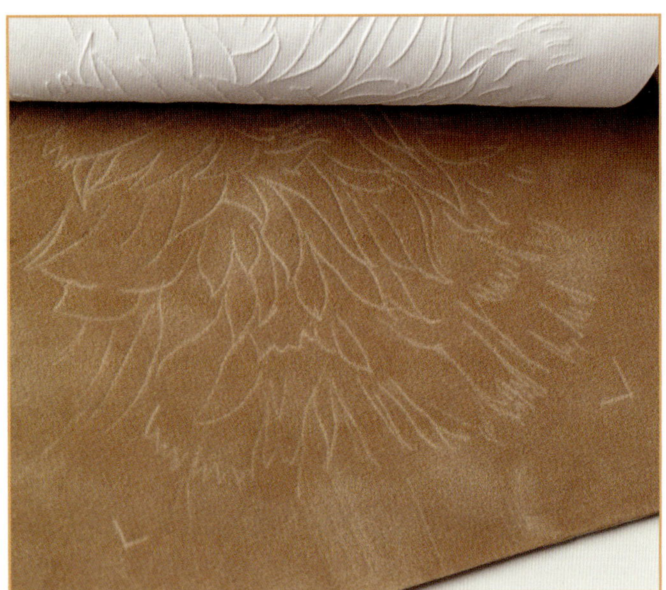

1 Transfer the outline to the surface with a stylus, using the indenting method on page 49. Try to avoid thinking of the pictue as fur. Instead, look to identify larger shapes. The underlying forms here are effectively bendy triangles.

Tip

I've taped the outline to the surface here. This is to fix it in place. Unlike papers, where the fibres are permanently indented, suede mat board won't retain the marks of the stylus. As soon as you work over it, the fibres will spring back into place and you'll lose your mark. By fixing the outline at the top, you can fold it over, out of the way. If you lose your marks, you can simply fold it back into place and reinstate them.

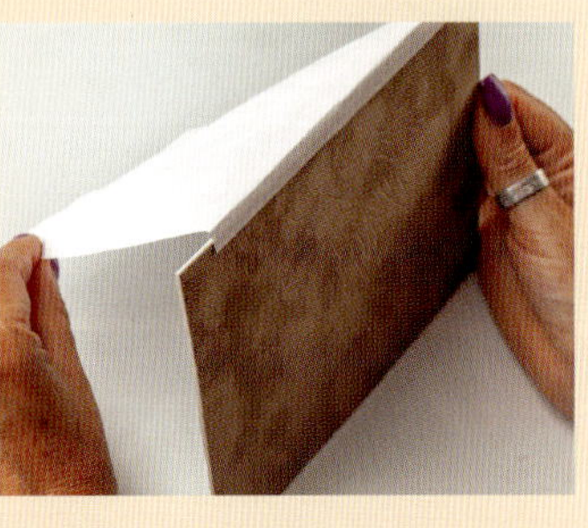

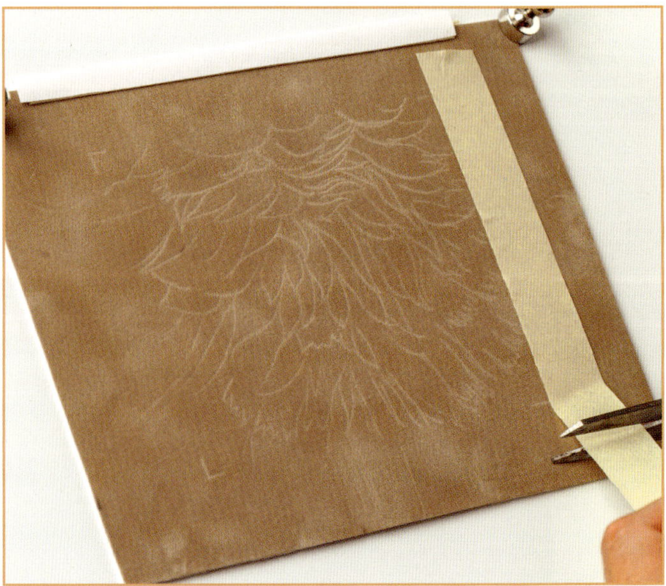

2 Run low-tack tape around the image to create a frame to work up to.

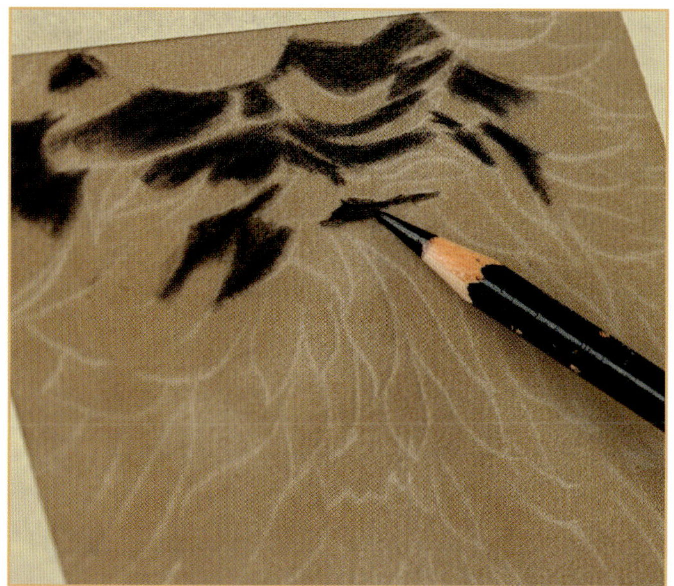

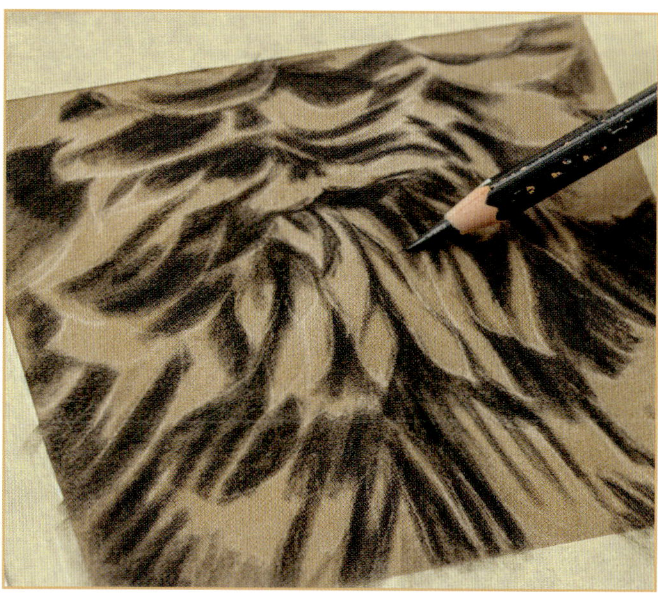

3 Start to block in the darkest shapes using ivory black, with a back-and-forth motion that follows the direction of the fur. Using a sharp point risks scratching the surface, so use either a blunt pencil or the side of a rounded tip, as shown.

4 Continue building the shadows up. As you press down in the direction of the fur, the pile of the surface will begin to lie down, enhancing the impression.

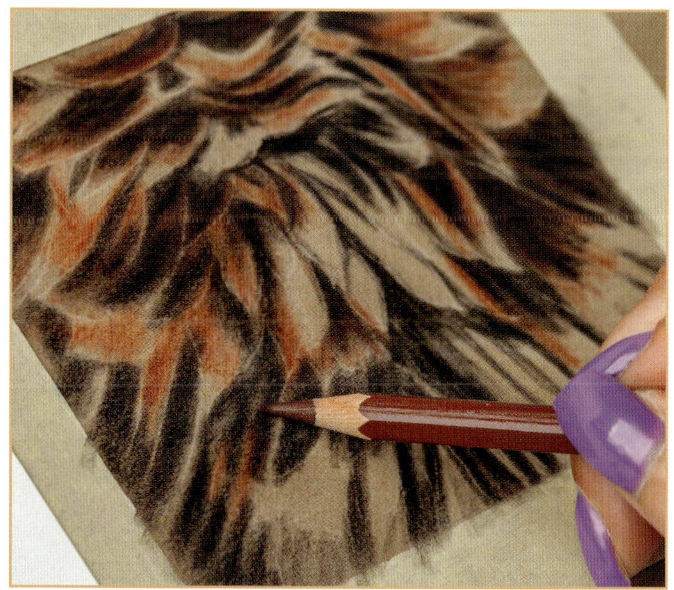

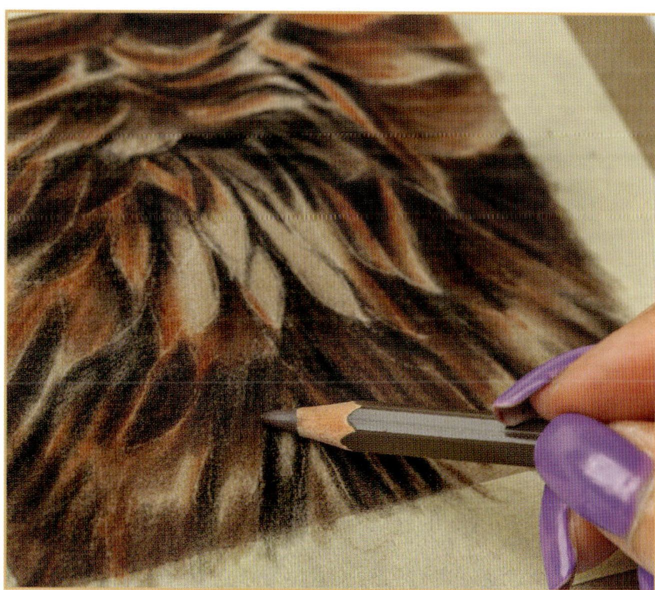

5 Look for the reddish-brown tinges and block in these areas using brown pencil. Overlap with the black areas where appropriate. The colours will mix on the surface.

6 Swap to Van Dyke brown and work this over some of the black and ginger areas. Start within the coloured area and outwards onto the untouched surface. This creates a natural transition in colour.

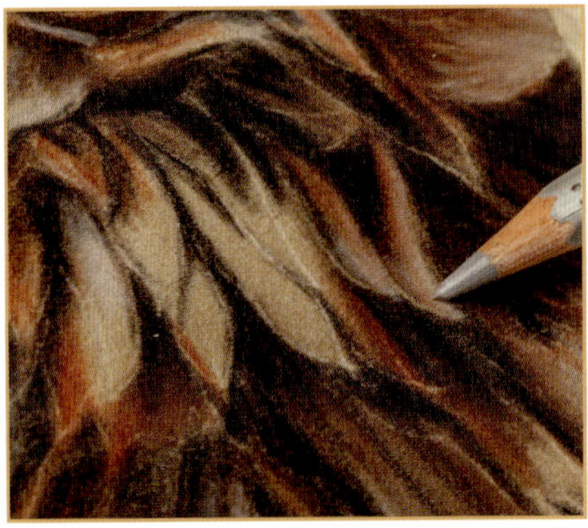

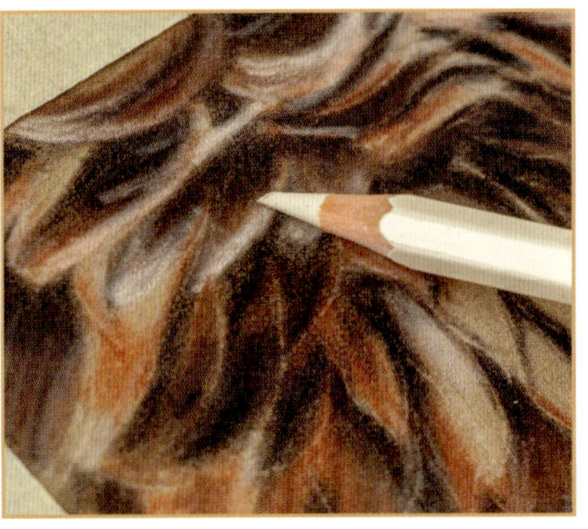

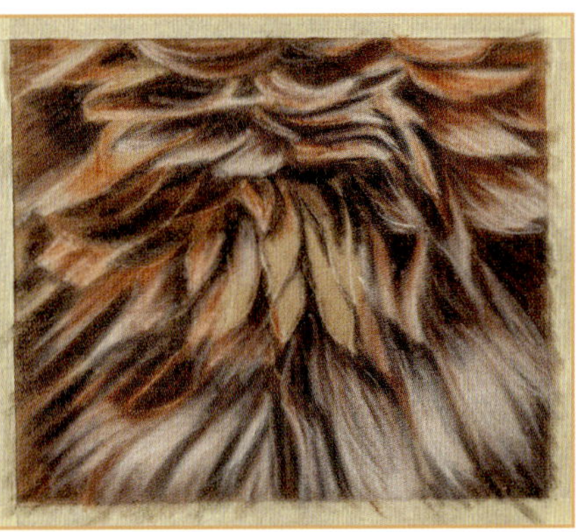

7 Use beige to add the lighter sections. Again, transition from the Van Dyke brown areas by starting within them and working onto the virgin surface of the suede mat board.

8 Add the tips of the light hairs at the top of the picture using cream. Start working from within the previous colours, again creating that smooth transition.

9 Repeat the process on the grey tips of the hair near the bottom, using ash grey. Increase your pressure as necessary to get an even layer of pigment down.

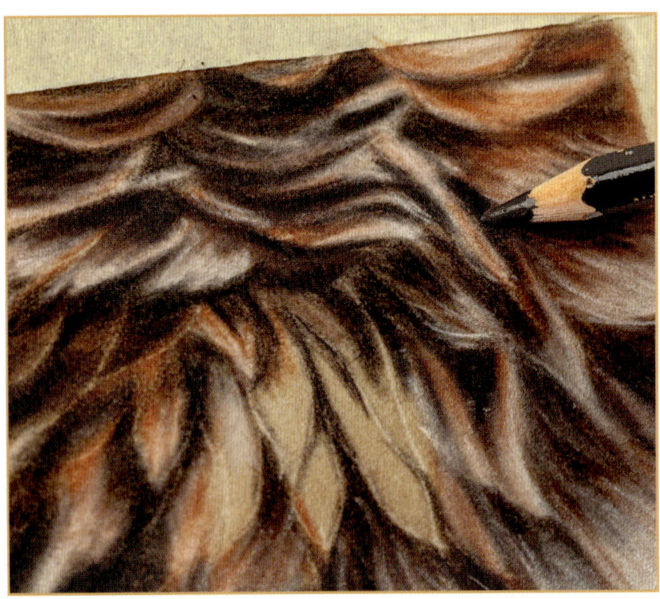

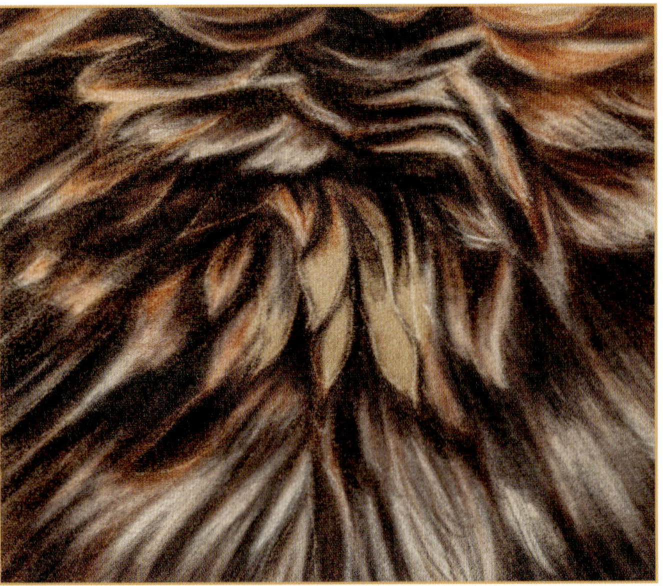

10 Reinforce the black areas as before using ivory black.

11 Repeat the process with brown, Van Dyke brown and beige. The brown and ginger areas can be built up with the same directional back-and-forth strokes as before, but as you come to the lighter hairs, supplement this with the use of striking or tapered marks that follow the direction of the fur.

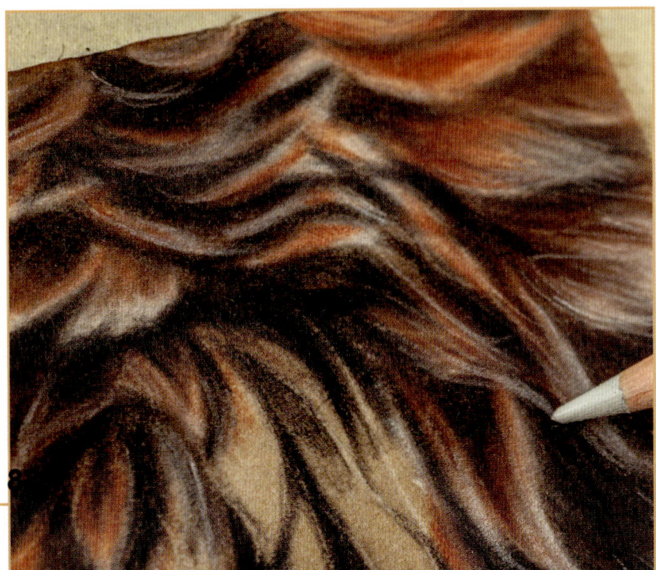

12 Add more striking or tapered marks with cream and ash grey.

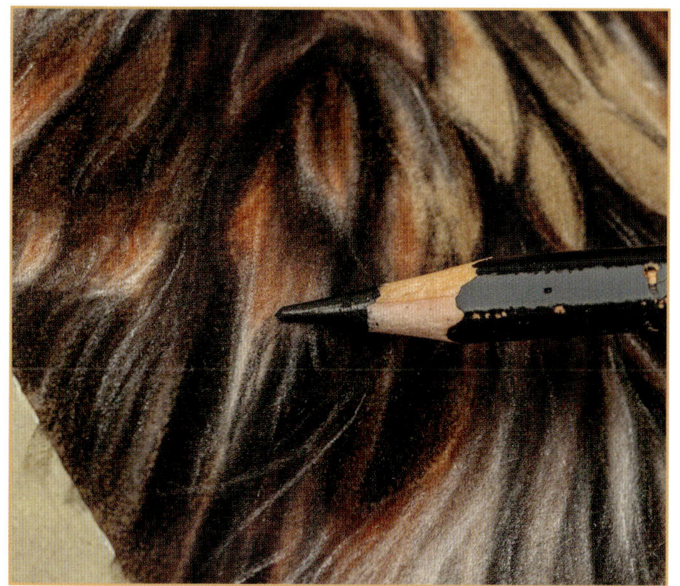

13 Pull the darks out of the shadows and break up the clumps with ivory black. Be selective with these marks; don't overwhelm the other colours.

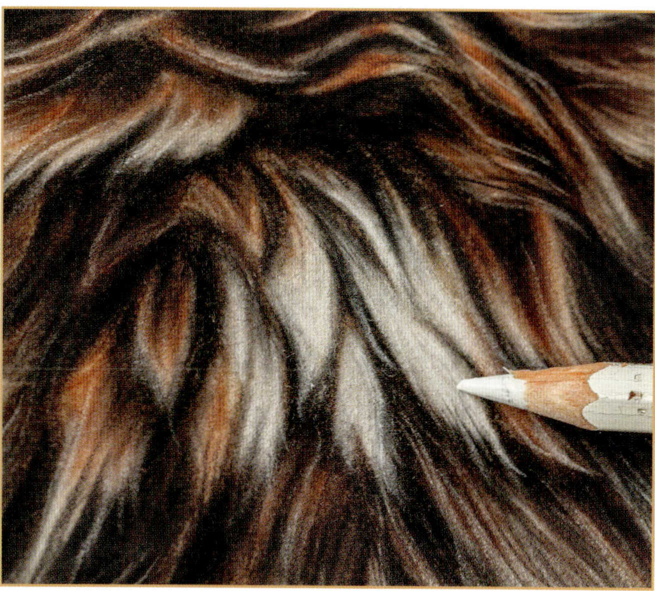

14 Add the bright white flash with white. As this area is still virgin surface, it'll take some time to build up the coverage. Don't be tempted to increase the pressure; just work patiently with repeated layers.

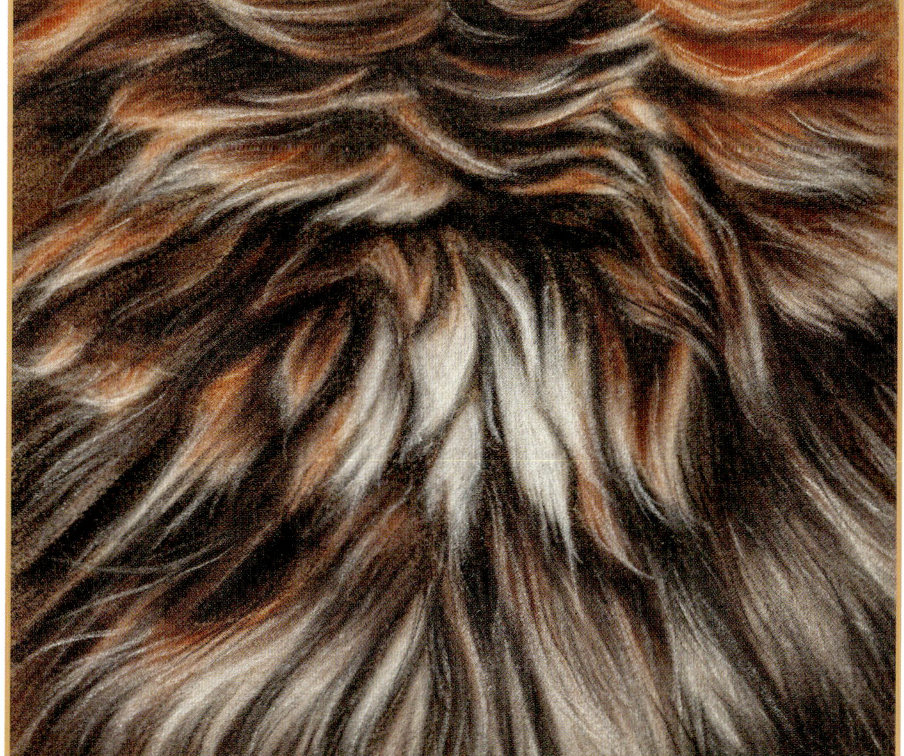

The finished study

LONG WHITE FUR

For this coloured pencil on Pastelmat study, it's important to remember your preparation stage. If you struggle to see the colours in your reference photograph, use a colour picker tool (see page 34) to pull them out of the white fur before matching them up to your pencils.

Work from dark to light and do not panic when your piece looks too dark or too bright. Each glaze of white or lights will soften back any of the undertones.

You will need

Support: Clairefontaine Pastelmat paper – white colour, 11.5 x 10cm (4½ x 4in)

Caran d'Ache Pablo pencils: 001 white

Derwent Drawing pencils: 7010 warm grey, 7120 cool grey, 7200 Chinese white

Faber-Castell Polychromos pencils: 181 Payne's grey, 175 dark sepia, 270 warm grey I, 272 warm grey III, 273 warm grey IV, 230 cold grey I, 232 cold grey III, 178 nougat

Other materials: Stylus or sharp pencil to transfer line drawing, pencil sharpener, glassine paper, soft dusting brush, Slice craft knife, low-tack tape

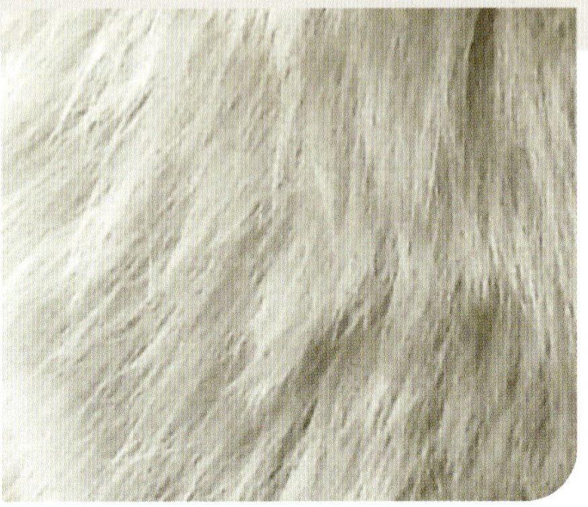

The reference photograph for this study.

1 Transfer your line art to your support using the tracedown paper technique on page 51.

2 Using the more opaque Derwent Drawing pencils, start to block in the bigger darkest shapes using standard pressure and a back-and-forth stroke. Use both the warm and the cool grey and look for those big shapes. They resemble bendy triangles in the reference. Take your pencil over the lines into the surrounding areas.

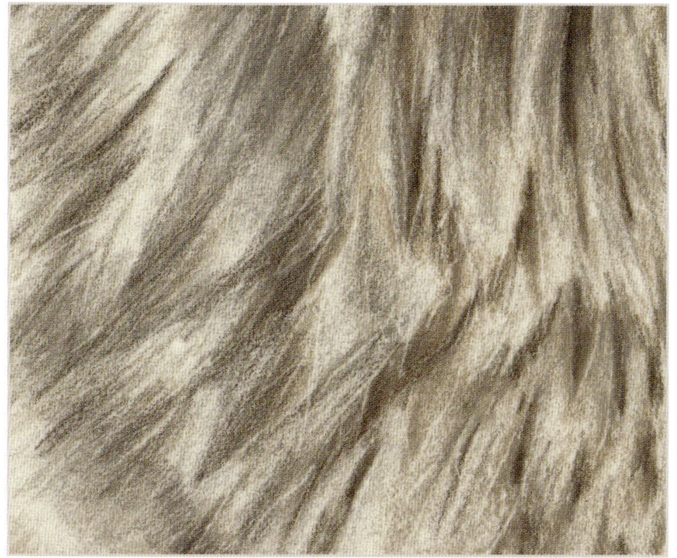

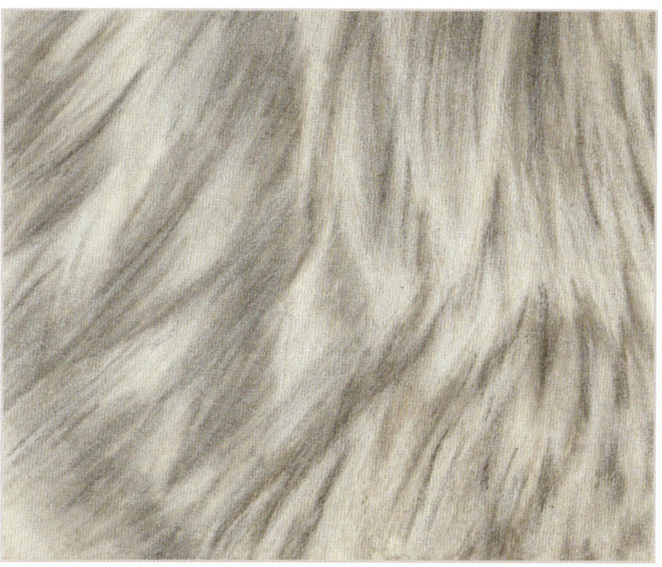

3 Take the darkest shapes even deeper in tone, using warm grey IV on the right-hand side of the study and warm grey III on the left. If you need to take any of the shadows a touch darker, use Payne's grey and a touch of dark sepia. Add a light glaze of cold grey III to the whole piece to begin to soften the darks.

4 Use Derwent Drawing white to glaze over the whole piece. You will really notice the darks softening here. Another benefit to this thicker pencil is that it will help to fill the tooth faster.

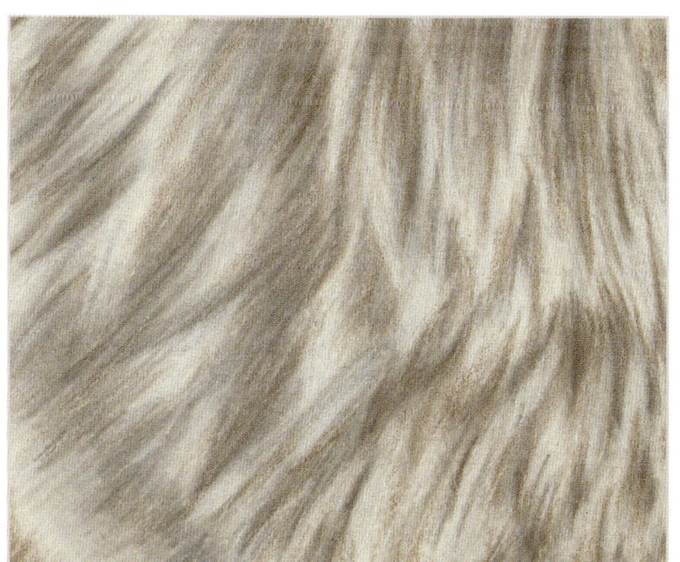

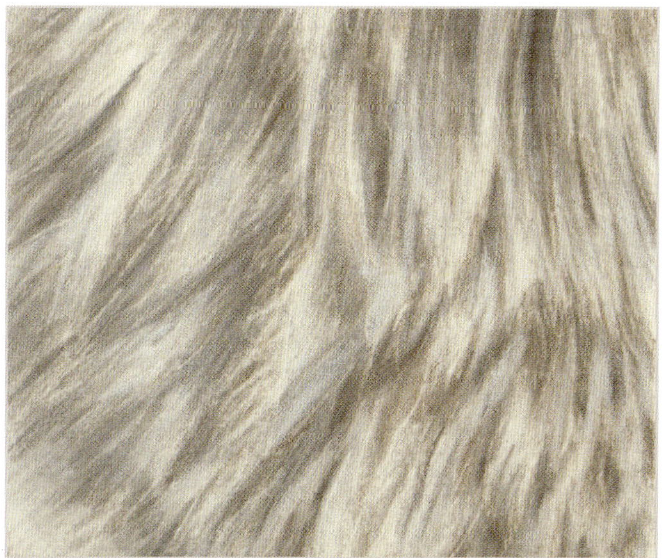

5 Darken the shadows again, this time using nougat. Keep using standard pressure with a back-and-forth motion, but begin to be more precise, picking out the smaller shapes within the bigger ones.

6 Time to use a subtraction technique to lift away some pigment and regain the white of the paper. Gently place low-tack tape over the lightest tone areas and then rub over it gently with the stylus, using a mix of back-and-forth strokes and tapered strokes. This will begin to form the initial texture of the fur.

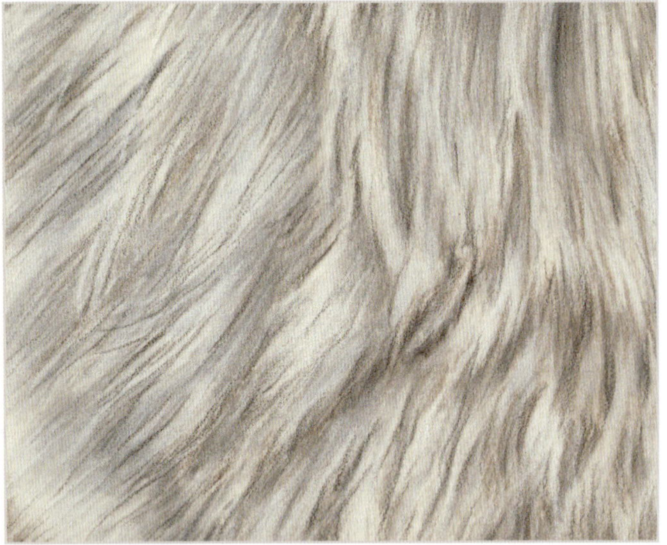

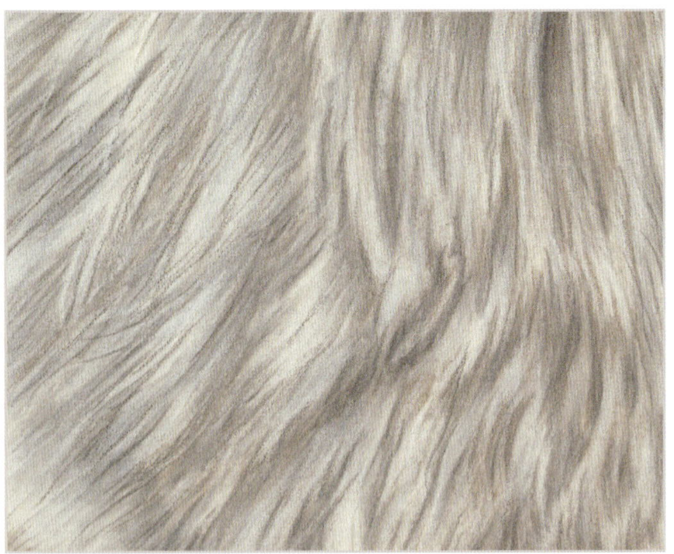

7 Using the Pablo white, break up the shapes even more with a tapered flick stroke to suggest the fur texture. Keep the pencil sharp as you add detail with the long strokes, and use more pressure if you need to. Glaze over the bigger light shapes on the left-hand side using cold grey I, then do the same on the right-hand side using warm grey I. The darker shadows will now be too light, so re-establish them with the nougat and dark sepia, using a sharp nib and long tapered strokes.

8 Glaze and soften once again, using warm grey I and cold grey I.

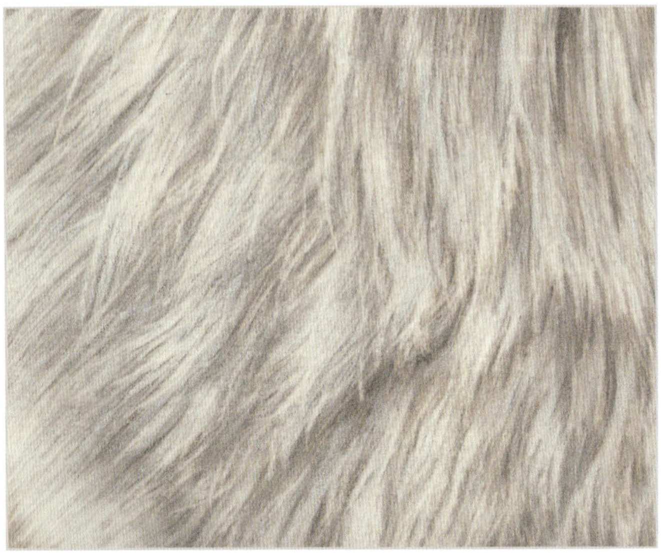

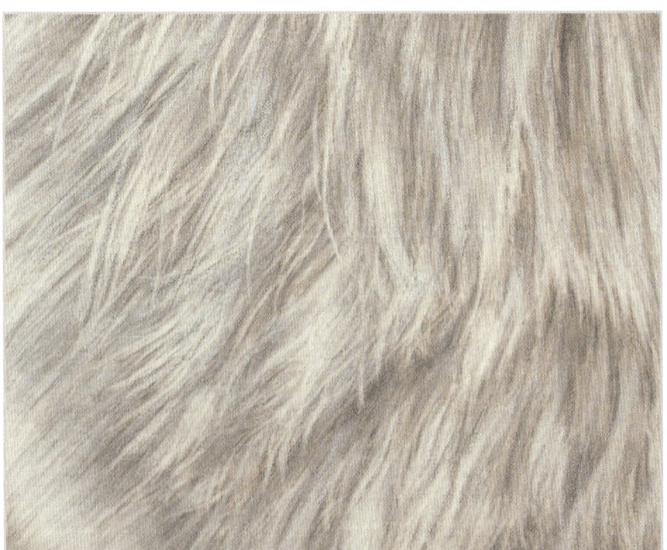

10 As you near to the finish, you need to be more precise with your application. Push the values back down again in the shadow areas using nougat. Note that the nib will skip over the knife lines. Lift the fine highlights back up using a sharp Pablo white, the cold grey I and warm grey I.

9 Time for knife work. Use a firm pressure on your ceramic blade and long tapered strokes to cut through all of the shapes and create the long white hairs of the fur. Brush away any excess dust as you go. Use the sharp nib of the Pablo white to sink some pigment into the brightest lines lifted away by the knife strokes.

Tip

When you lift pigment from the surface of your support, it will enable the colour of the paper to show through.

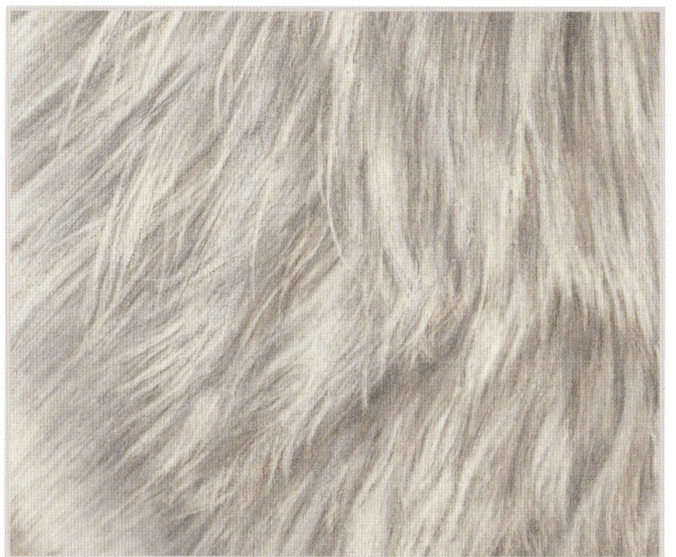

The finished study

11 Repeat any of the previous steps using sharp pencils to increase the shadows or highlights and to soften them back again. Bring the knife back in to add even more detail to the texture too. The study is finished when you feel happy with the result.

Jamie

PanPastel and coloured pencils for the dog itself, watercolour pencils for the bed and PanPastel for the floor – demonstrating that you shouldn't be afraid to mix your media. This was another commission piece that combined lots of techniques.

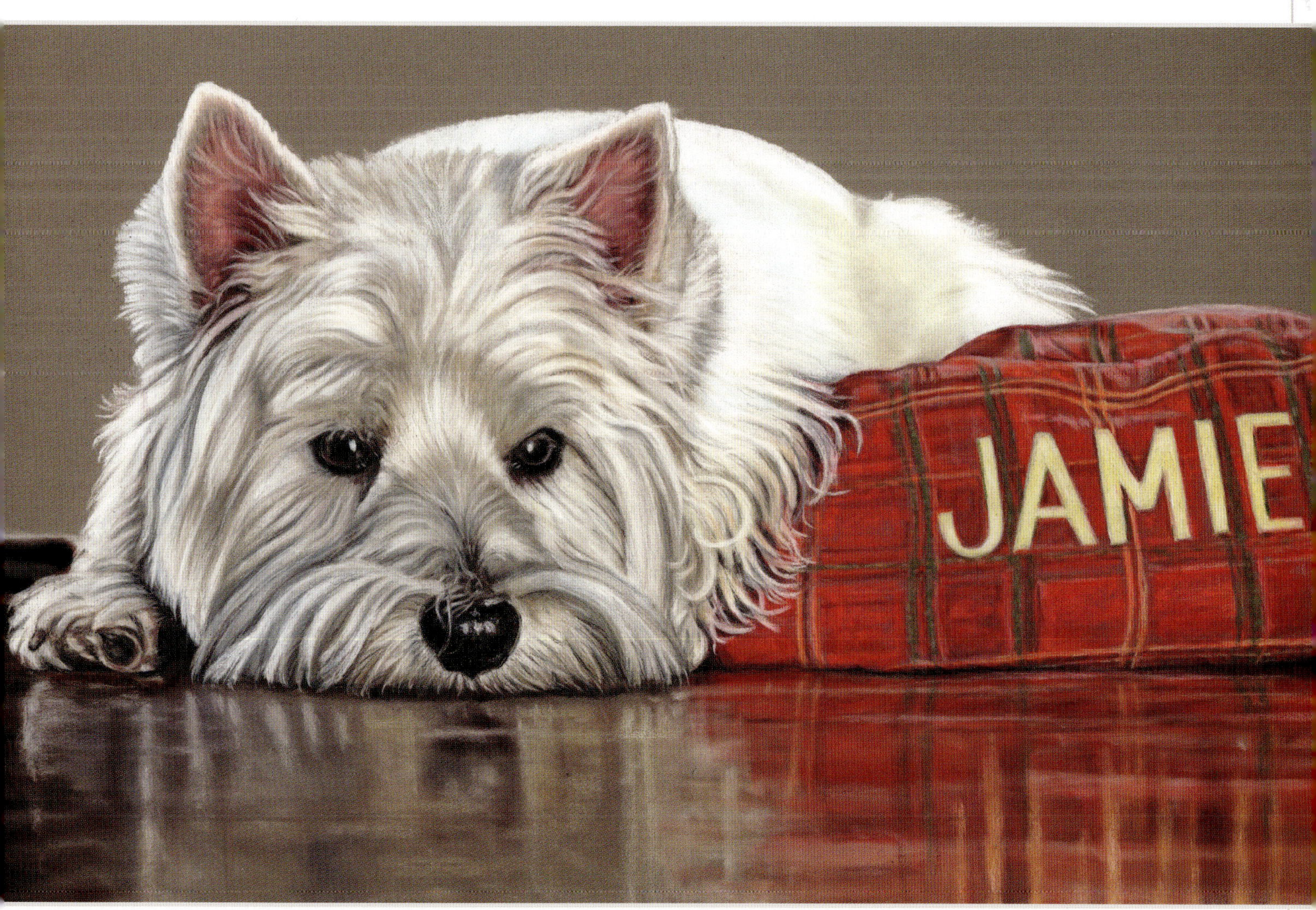

SHORT SHINY CHESTNUT FUR

As with the previous two studies, the key here is to forget that this is fur texture. You are simply looking for the shapes. To start, look for the biggest shapes and the darkest tonal value areas. It is too easy to think that a dark shadow must be added with black at the very start – but instead, this study shows you how to look for the colours that mix together to make that dark area. We use a Prismacolor pencil here, too – showing that it's always useful to keep your eye out for specific pencils in different ranges. You can pick these up open stock.

When working with solvent, always apply it in a well ventilated room. Less is definitely more when adding solvent, especially on Pastelmat.

You will need

Support: Clairefontaine Pastelmat paper – sienna colour, 7.5 x 7.5cm (3 x 3in)

Faber-Castell Polychromos pencils: 263 caput mortuum violet, 157 dark indigo, 190 Venetian red, 188 sanguine, 133 magenta, 189 cinnamon, 132 beige red, 233 cold grey IV

Caran d'Ache Pablo pencils: 002 Silver Grey, 062 Venetian red, 491 cream, 409 charcoal grey, 001 white

Sanford Prismacolor pencils: Black cherry

Other materials: Glassine paper, Slice craft knife, soft dusting brush, sharpener, stylus, transfer paper to transfer the line drawing, odourless mineral spirit and brush or cotton bud (Q-tip) for applying, plus paper towel

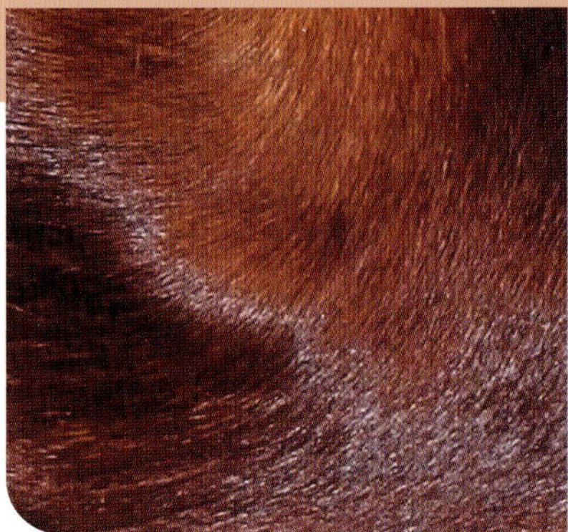

The reference photograph for this study.

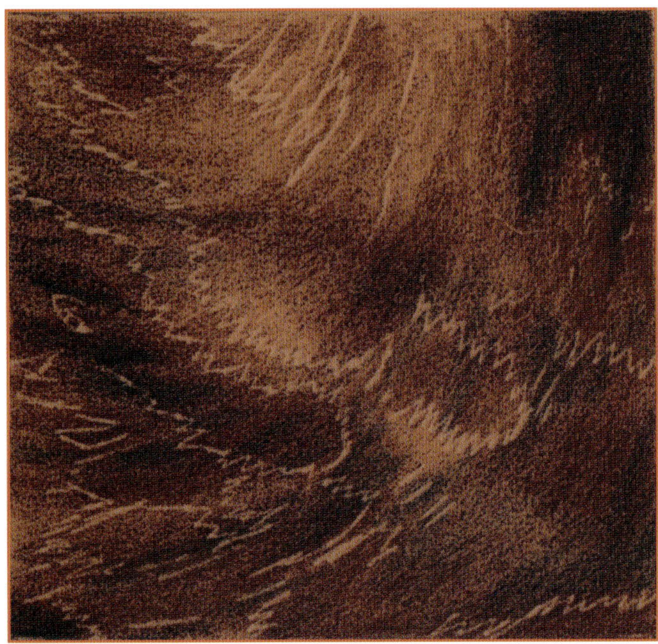

1 Transfer your line drawing using the indenting method on page 49. Rub a pencil lightly over the surface first to make the lines appear more prominently. Next, as always, start by adding the darks. Look for how the colours combine to make the dark areas, and use caput mortuum violet, black cherry and dark indigo to block in these initial dark shadow shapes with standard pressure. Repeat with the black cherry and caput mortuum violet to increase the dark tone.

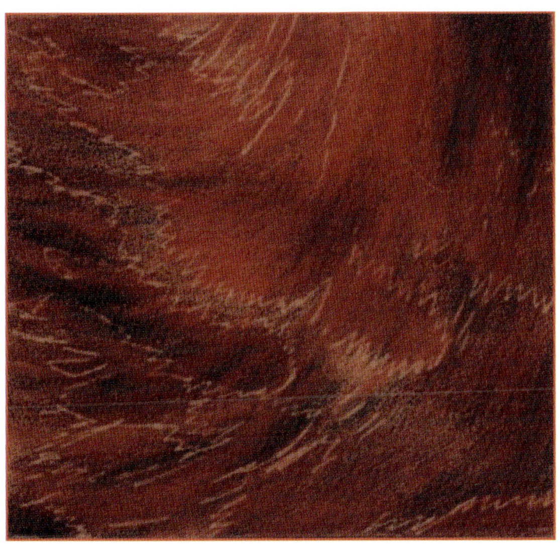

2 Add the mid-tones by glazing over some of the initial darks. Aim to create a chestnut hue in the main reddish areas. Start with the Polychromos Venetian red to glaze over the whole piece, continuing to work in the direction of the fur using that same standard pressure of application. Add a few touches of magenta in the areas where there is a purplish-red glow to the undertones. Next use cinnamon as a softener in the areas where the darks transition into the highlights. Enhance the orange areas with Pablo Venetian red. Go back in with the cinnamon if any areas need more softening.

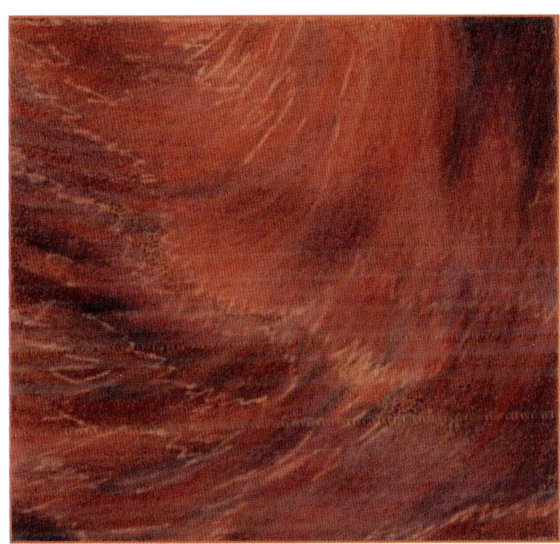

3 Create the effect of the greyish hues with a little cold grey IV above the main reflective line and some of the same colour in the bottom right-hand corner. Next, add beige red along that reflective line and in some of the upper block of colour. Follow this with silver grey once more along that reflective line, and also to block in the main area of highlight in the bottom right-hand corner. Use the cream in the top, warmer highlight areas. Go back and repeat any of the previous tones or colours that may now seem diminished.

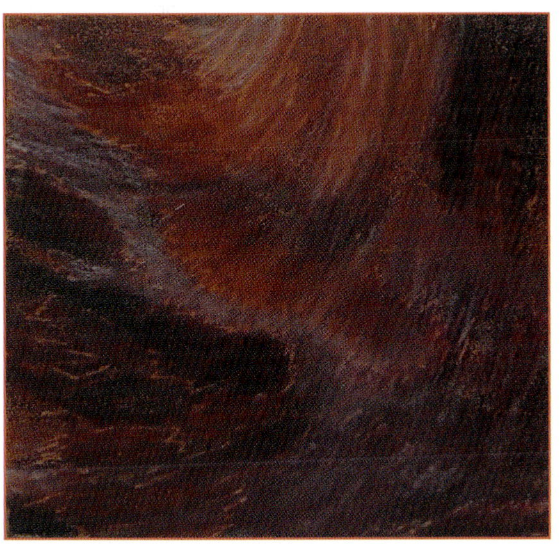

4 Now that there is a build-up of layers, it is time to add solvent to blend the areas together. Dip a brush or a cotton bud (Q-tip) into the solvent, then remove any excess liquid onto a sheet of kitchen paper before touching the brush to the surface. Start in the areas of lightest tone and move on to the darks, each time cleaning your brush on kitchen paper before loading it with solvent. While the surface is damp (not wet), go back in very gently with your pencils. Rub the nib onto the surface and it should release pure pigment down into the area being touched. Leave the piece to dry for at least twenty-four hours before continuing.

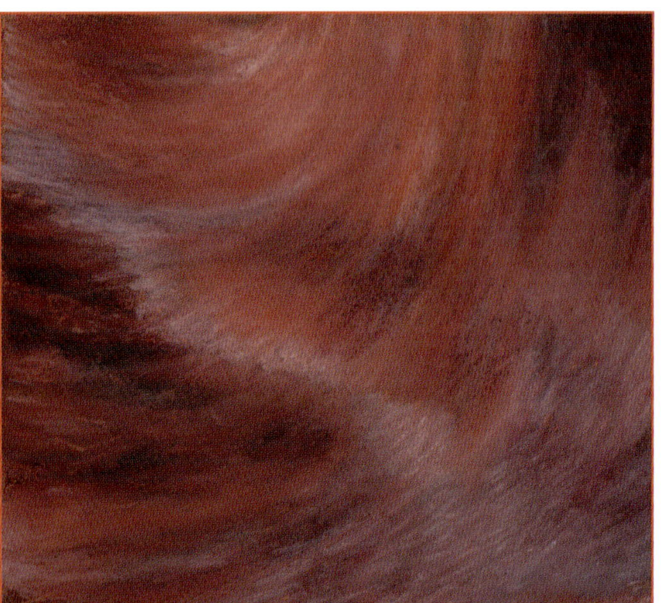

5 Repeat steps 1–3 and keep repeating them until you elimate the grainy tooth of the surface and it starts to feel buttery. Bring in the charcoal grey to really push the dark tonal values (black is a little bit harsh to use here). Keep adding darks until you are happy with the tonal depth. This may take two or three repetitions.

Tip

Ensure that your pencil strokes are always in the direction of the fur, and that you make them the same length as the fur itself at this stage.

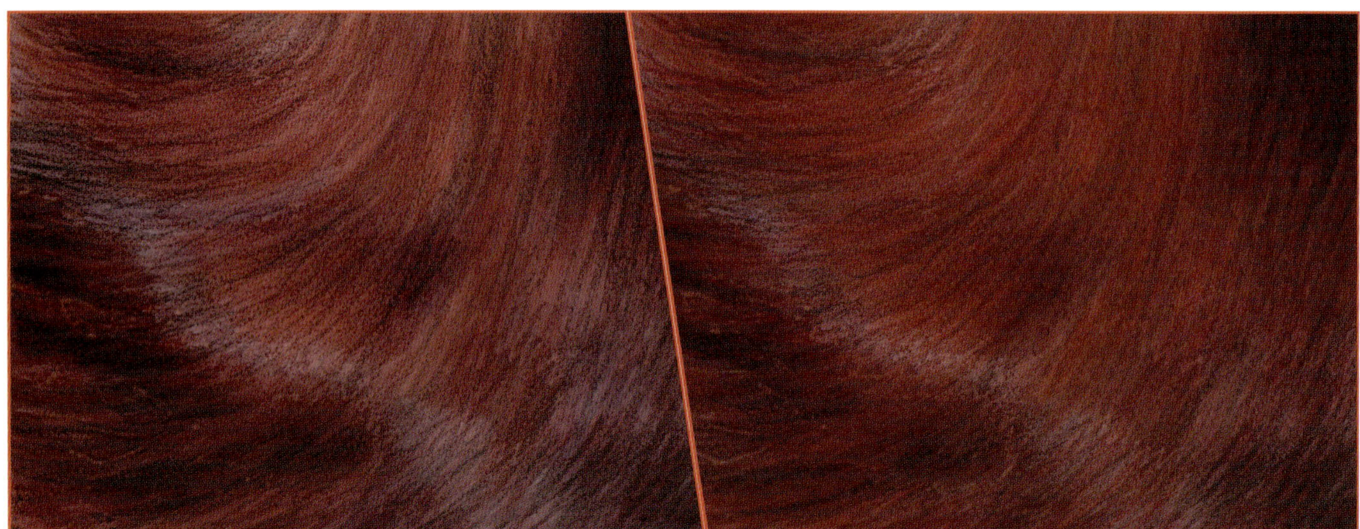

6 Repeat the mid-tones next. Bring in sanguine to really give the most orange areas a boost, mainly across the top area of the study. Follow this with Polychromos Venetian red, then magenta, then Pablo Venetian red and finally cinnamon. Keep rotating through these mid-tones until you have built up a lovely rich, red value. Each time you feel like you have lost a colour, pop it back in. By the end of this stage (see above right), the darks should just be undertones to the reds.

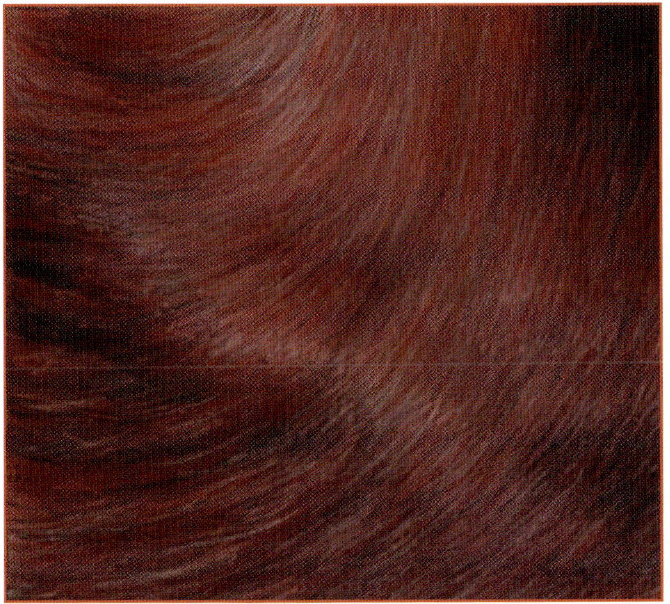

7 Finally, move on to adding the lights now. If you have built up enough depth with your darks and mid-tones, then this is where your hard work will really pay off. Rotate between your lights which are cream, beige red, silver grey and white. The first layer will be in blocks but bring in a couple of other darker pencils to break up these clumps. Use light flicks of the pencil in the direction and the length of the fur itself. All through this stage, it is important to keep your pencils super sharp.

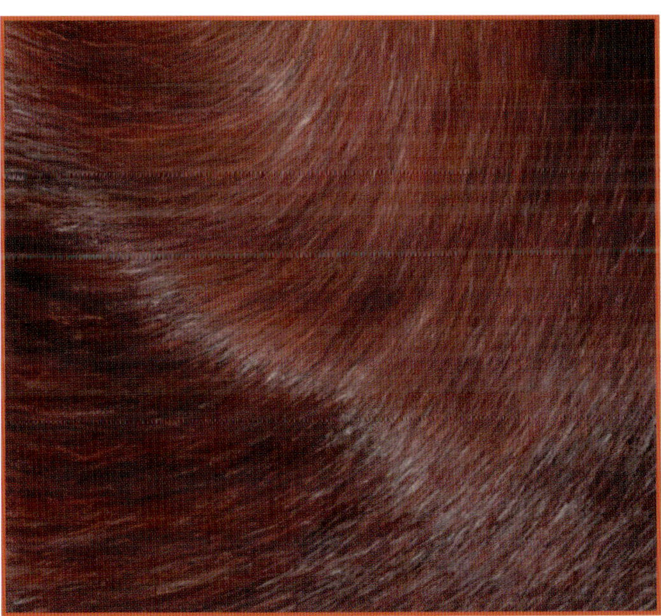

The finished study

8 Use your ceramic blade to create some superfine fur texture. Turn your paper so that you are flicking the blade away from you in the most natural manner and use it the same way as you do your pencils to create fur strokes with a standard pressure. Using sharp pencils of the relevant colour, go back into the lines scraped out with the blade to create even finer marks. You can continue to tweak as much as you like, repeating any of the previous layers until your fur is refined, textured and shiny.

Tip

You need to think about what colour paper you are using when considering where to make strokes with your knife. If the underlying surface is dark, you'll reveal a dark mark; if it's a light surface, you'll create a fine highlight.

CURLY BLACK FUR

This study is also a good way to practise eliminating the grain of the paper. Working black pigment onto white Pastelmat will push you to build your layers to the buttery stage.

As with the other fur studies, this one will help you to practise picking out semi-abstract shapes. Curly fur can usually be simplified into 'bendy triangles' or S-shapes.

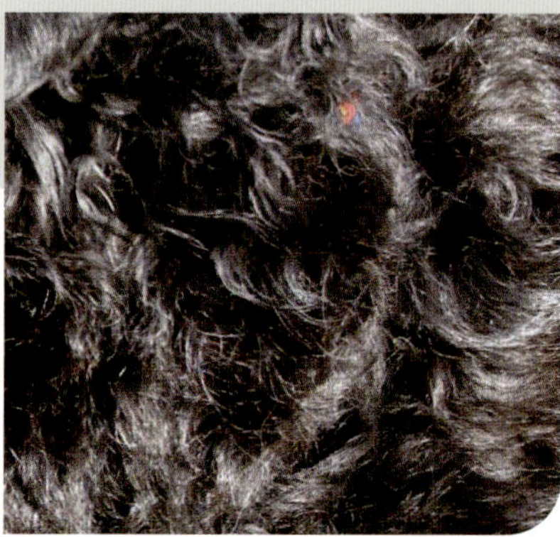

The reference photograph for this study.

You will need

Support: Clairefontaine Pastelmat paper – white colour, 12.5 x 10cm (5 x 4in)

Caran d'Ache Pablo pencils: 001 white, 401 ash grey, 003 light grey

Derwent Drawing pencils: 6700 ivory black

Faber-Castell Polychromos pencils: 199 black, 169 caput mortuum, 157 dark indigo, 249 mauve, 272 warm grey III, 133 magenta

Other materials: Stylus or sharp pencil to transfer the line drawing, sharpener, glassine paper, soft dusting brush, Slice craft knife

Tip

Use a colour picker (see page 34) if you struggle to see the different hues in the reference.

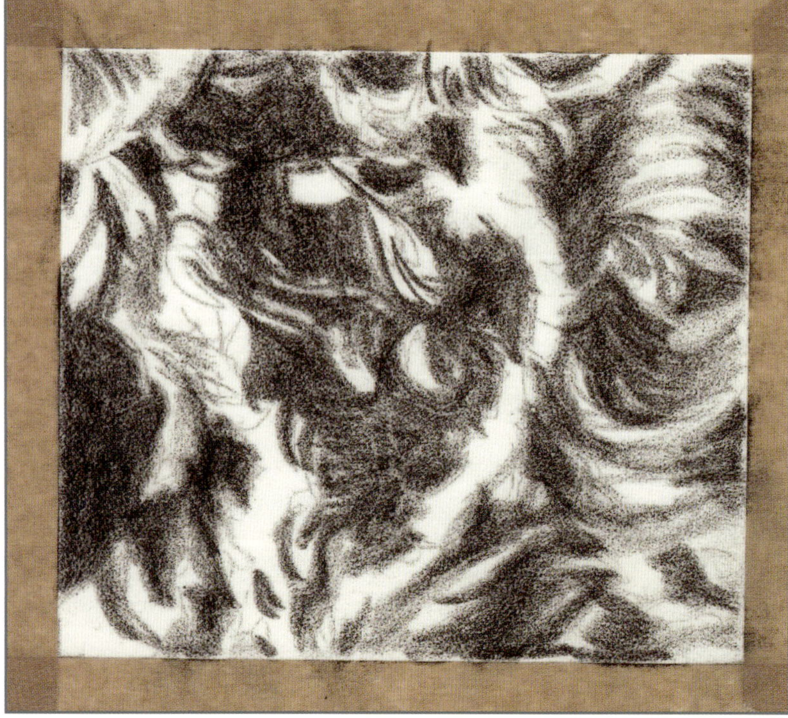

1 Approach this study with the same method of dark to light using a back-and-forth motion to colour block in your base layers. With this being black fur, you can use ivory black initially. Use a standard pressure and a back-and-forth stroke to lay down this first layer.

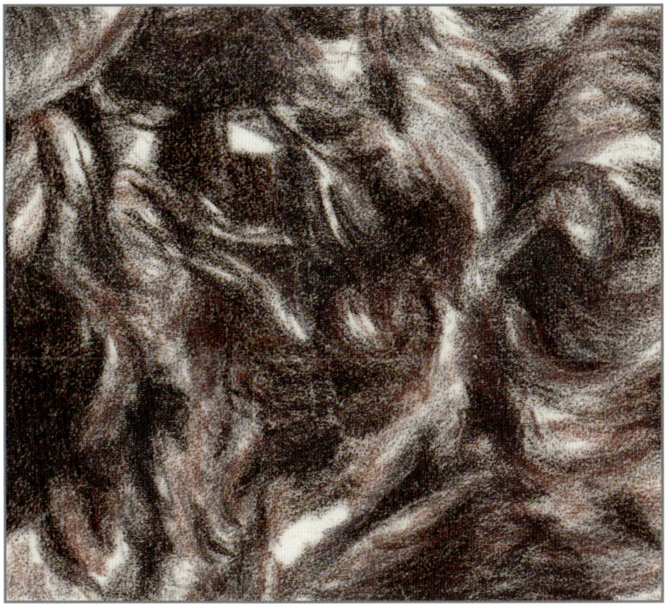

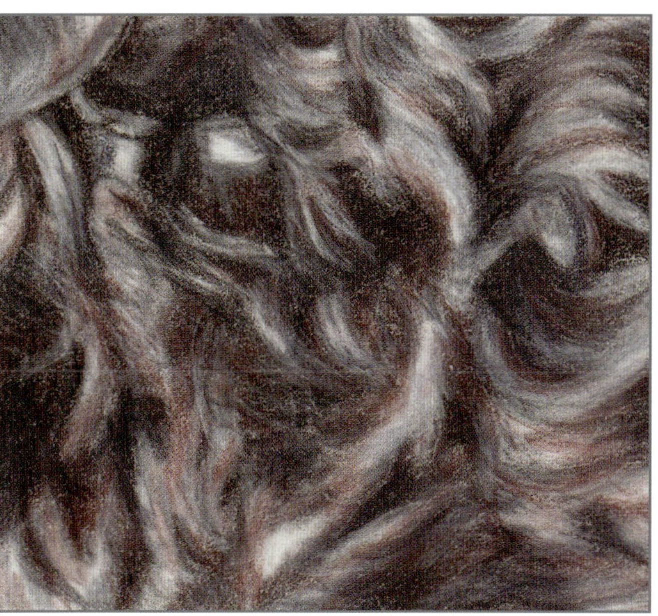

2 Continue to block in the darkest shapes by bringing in your caput mortuum and dark indigo to mix with the black.

3 As this is a soft textured fur, glaze using warm grey III over all of the surface, except the really dark shapes. This will help to soften the transitions from dark to light in the curls.

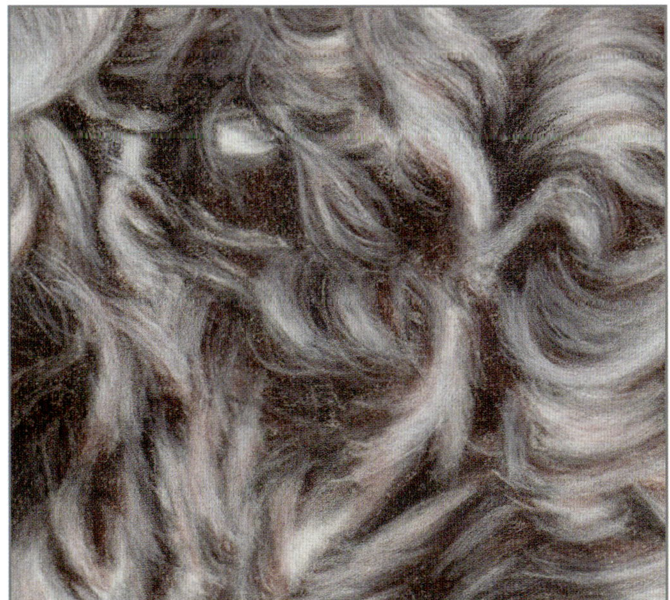

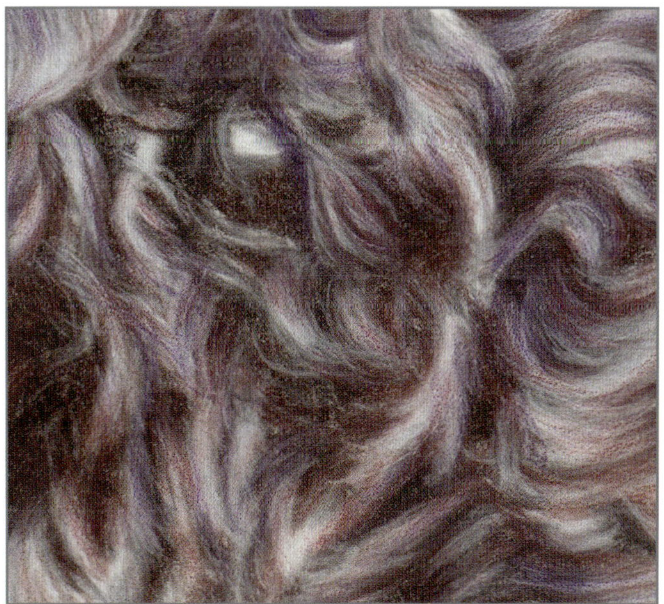

4 Repeat this by adding ash grey, light grey and white to the brightest areas, allowing some of it to glaze over the mid-tone grey too.

5 If you see any bright colours appearing as you stare for longer at the reference photograph, add them in now. For this study I used a touch of mauve and also magenta – but go with the colours that you can pick out by eye. It might look scary but these will be toned down again with the following layers.

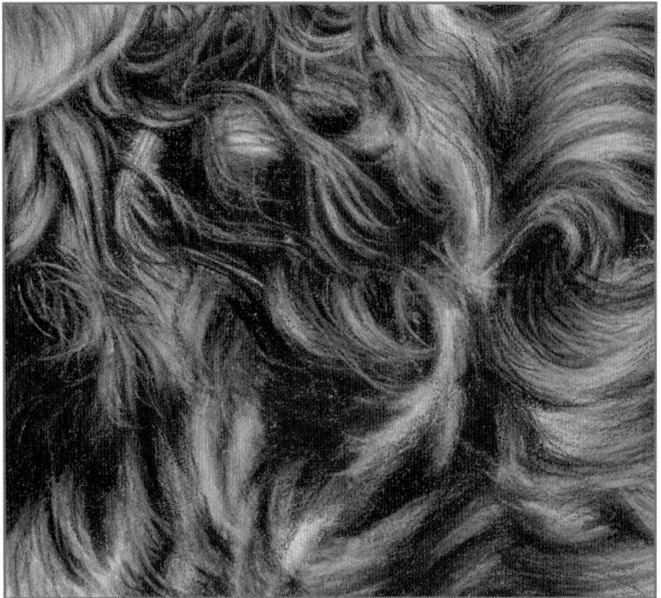

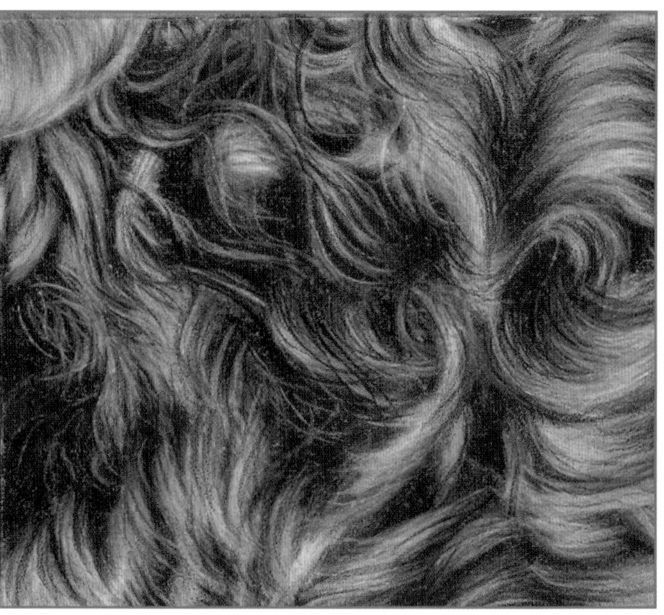

6 Repeat steps 1–5, working once more from darks to lights and touching back in any colours that now seem lacking. Continue to use the same standard pressure and keep your pencil to the paper following the length and direction of the fur shapes.

7 Sharpen your pencils with each layer and slowly progress from using the back-and-forth technique to the tapered flick. Keep your pencil strokes long to match the length of the fur.

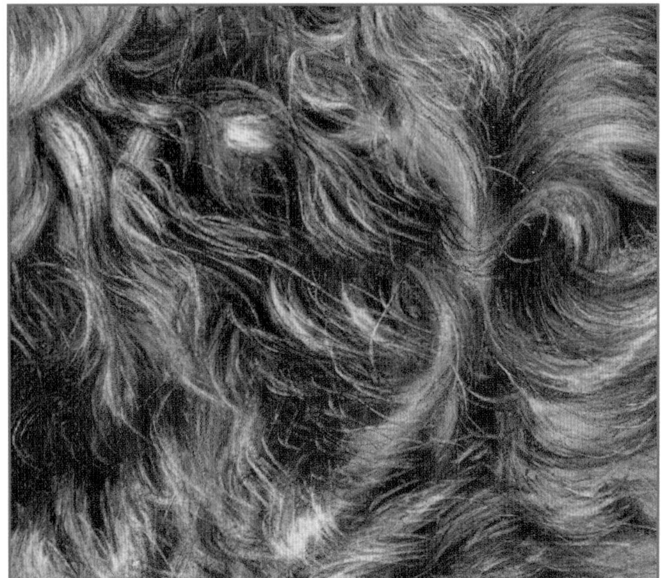

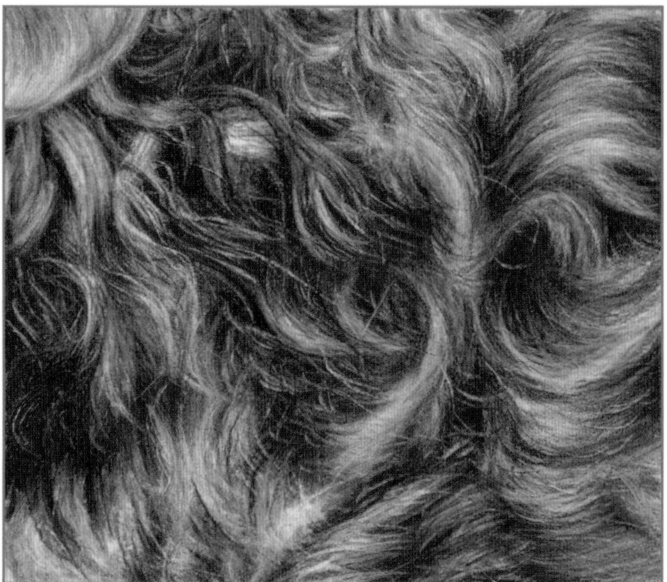

8 Once the tooth of the paper looks and feels buttery, use your knife to create extra fine detailing in the hair texture. Remember to vary the strokes and the pressure to create different lines on the support. More pressure will lift all the way back to the white of the paper, whereas lighter pressure will simply lift the last layer or two of pigment.

9 Go back in with sharp pencils to break up any clumps of fur still visible or any curls that need softening. If necessary, repeat this texturizing a couple more times, alternating between the knife work and pencils. Don't be afraid to push the tones more with your final tweaks

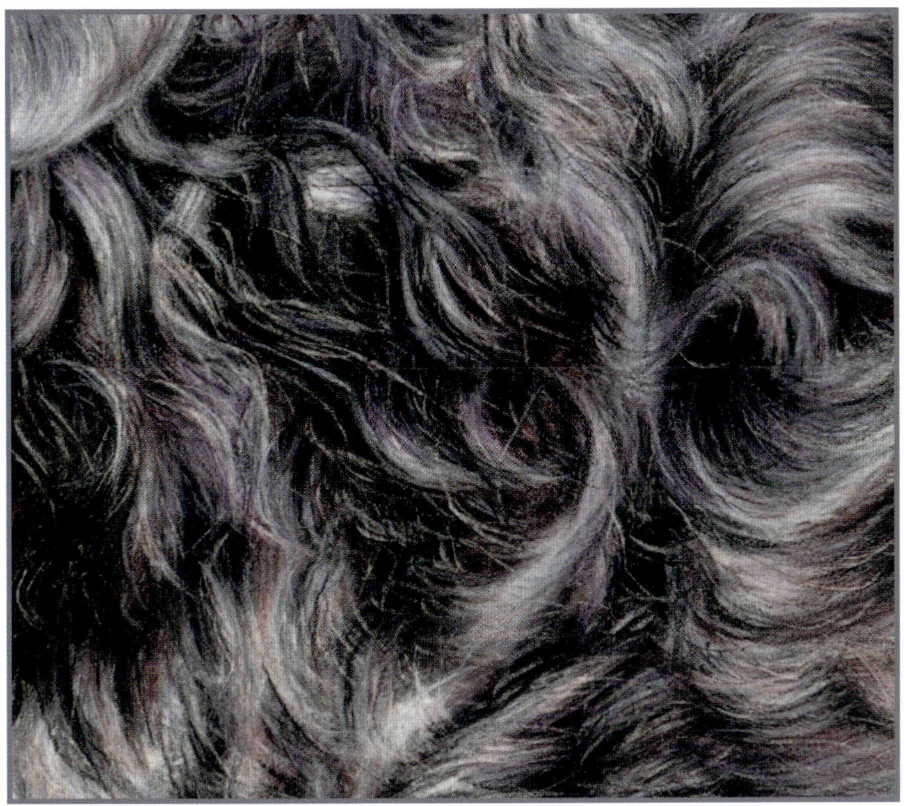

The finished study

Kyloe

Watercolour pencils wet and dry on Pastelmat. When depicting a full body portrait (and sometimes even with a head and shoulders), there is a good chance that the texture of the fur will differ across the body – it could be long and wiry in places and short and smooth in others.

Using the different strokes and application techniques will help you to depict these perfectly, but you must remember to look hard at your reference photograph.

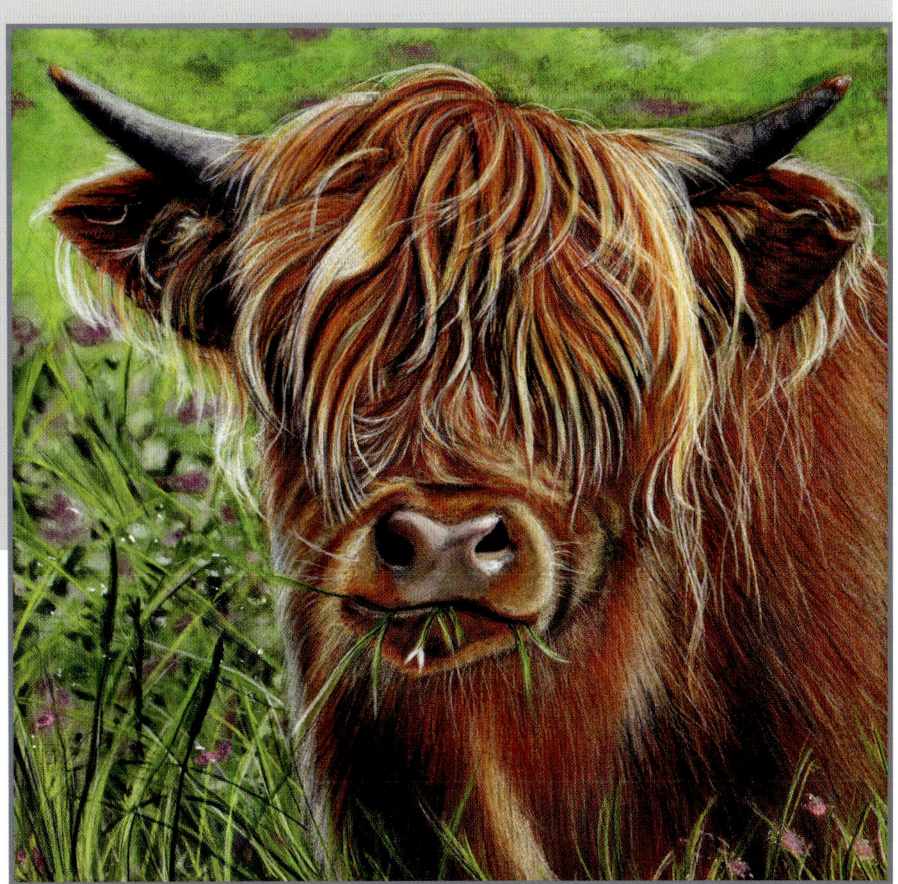

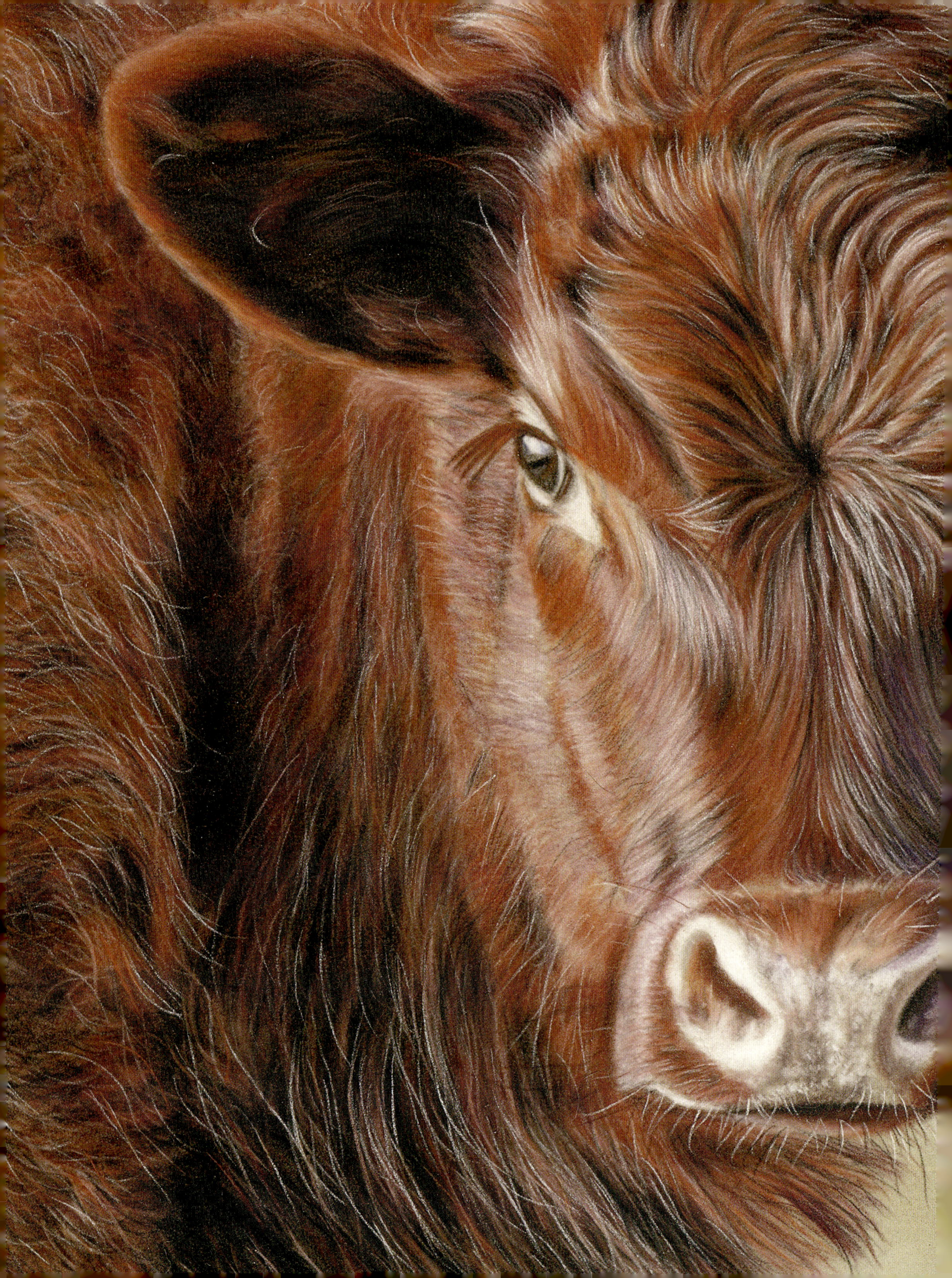

PORTRAITS

With the techniques and studies under your belt, you're now equipped with the knowledge, the skills and the confidence to tackle complete portraits. Using the step-by-step guidance and illustrations in this chapter you will now be able to render a complete animal portrait.

I have selected a range of projects that feature different types of domestic animals to help you try out and decide which of the many supports, materials and techniques you wish to pursue. My hope is that you will use these projects to help you enjoy your own compositions and animal portraits.

My tips for success in working through these projects are:

- **Don't rush** Coloured pencil is a slow medium. If you rush to the finish then you will be disappointed with the result and it might put you off trying again. Be patient. The more layers that you add, the more refined and realistic your piece will be.

- **Keep learning** These projects are still part of your learning curve. If you make a mistake here then you will learn even more by working out how to put it right. This is how I learnt, by trial and error.

- **Feel free to adapt** If you don't have the exact materials suggested in the list for each project, you can go with what you have to hand. My students continue to astound me by adapting the materials and techniques to suit their own resources.

- **Avoid pressure** If you feel overwhelmed, step away and take a break. Think about what it is that you are frustrated by, and go back and remind yourself of the basics: shapes, tones and colours.

- **Be humble** Don't try to create a masterpiece with your first go! This puts enormous – and unnecessary – pressure on you to be perfect at every stage.

Most of all, remember to enjoy the process and make each finished piece your own. I am here to share my knowledge and techniques with you. How you embrace them and utilize them to create your own renditions of the reference images provided will see you on the path to developing your own style. This is what makes art and creativity so special and so individual. I hope that you enjoy the projects as much as I did in creating them.

AURA

NORWEGIAN FOREST CAT

This beautiful cat is one that I have rendered many times using different techniques and supports. For this version, she is worked in a cropped portrait format on drafting film. There is a lot of knife work involved in this piece so you must make friends with your Slice tool. The key to this portrait is to treat the front and back sides of the film with equal importance – this will give the proper balance to the piece.

You need richly pigmented pencils, and also a range that blends smoothly: the Polychromos and the Derwent Lightfast pencils are a perfect match. Whatever the range, your pencils must be kept sharp at all times for this project.

You will need

Support: Grafix double matte drafting film 0.005m, 20 x 15cm (8 x 6in)

Derwent Lightfast pencils: Champagne, Venetian red, sienna, wheat, flesh pink

Faber-Castell Polychromos pencils: 199 black, 175 dark sepia, 101 white, 268 green gold, 186 terracotta, 173 olive green yellowish, 187 burnt ochre, 174 chromium green opaque, 168 earth green yellowish, 280 burnt umber, 172 earth green, 102 cream, 192 Indian red, 188 sanguine, 178 nougat, 274 warm grey V

Other materials: Slice craft knife; dusting brush; pencil sharpener; glassine paper; Tombow Mono eraser; sheets of both black and white mount board, cut to size of image to enable both the dark and light lines to be seen while working

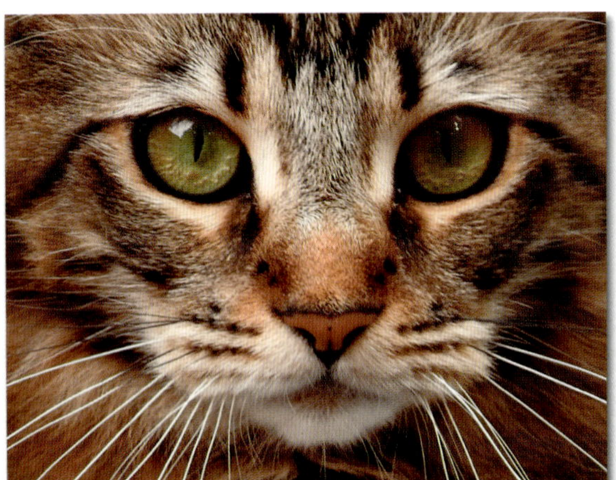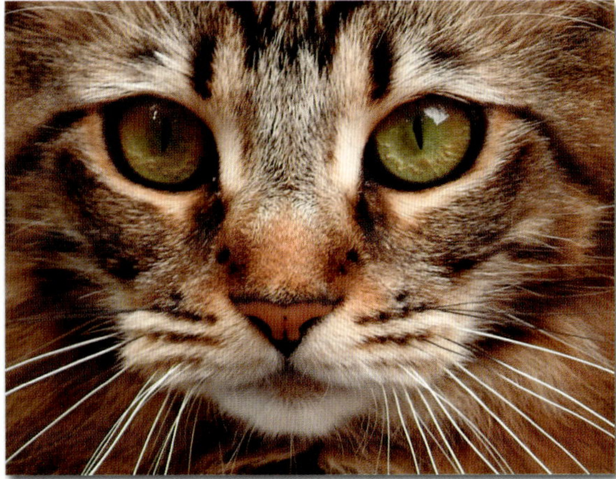

The reference photograph used for this project (left). The reversed version (right) is used when working on the back of the film.

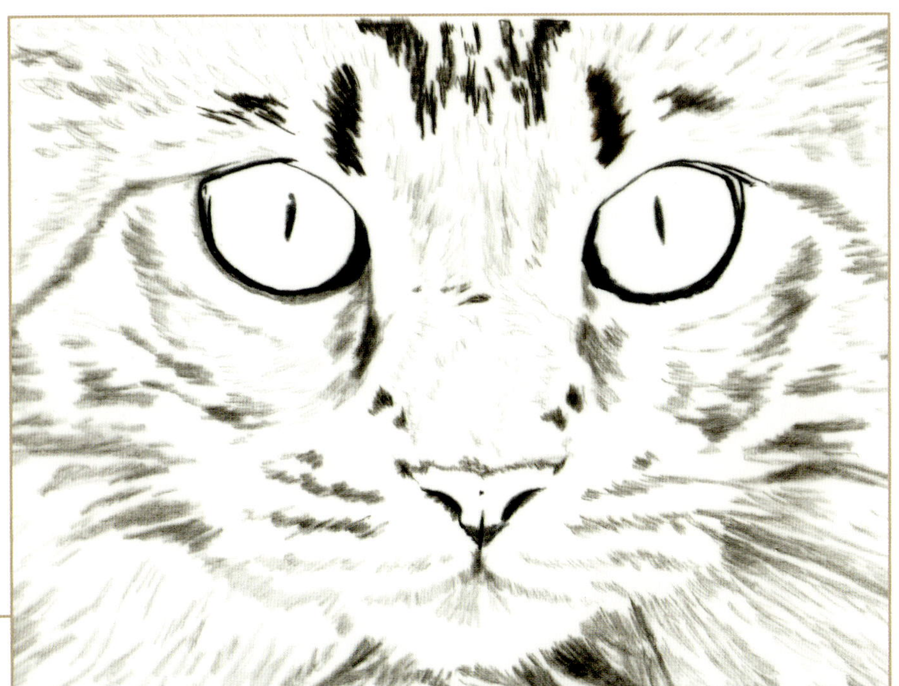

1 Lay the drafting film over the line art and fix it in place. Mark in the corners of the reference image to allow correct placement over the line art at future stages. With a light pressure, use black and dark sepia to map in the dark shapes and lines, then swap to white to map in the lights. Intensify the darks with more layers in the darker areas, especially around the eyes.

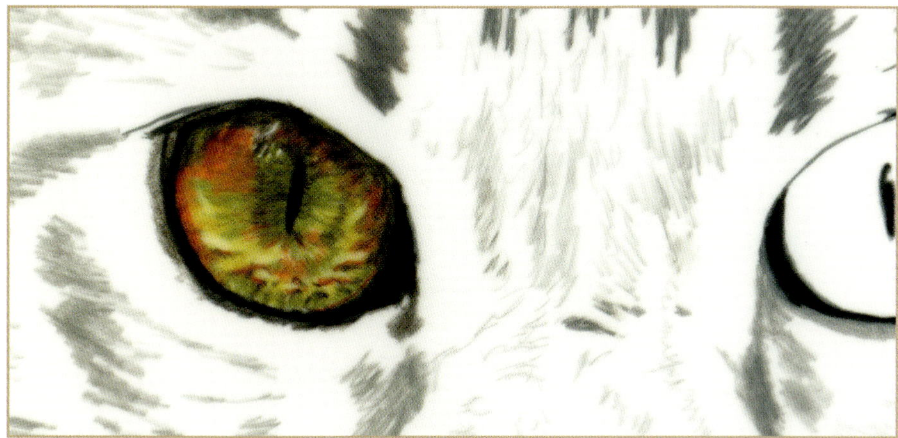

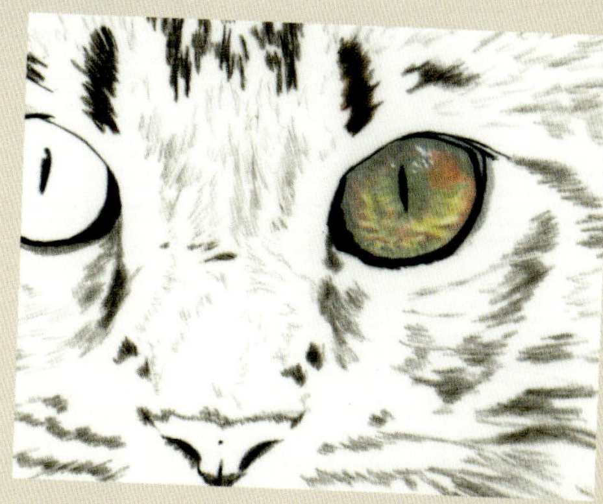

2 Flip the film over to work on the reverse of the right-hand eye (left-hand side once reversed, as shown above). Strengthen the black outline. Glaze green gold and terracotta over the edge of the outline into the iris, going over the edge, not just up to it. Using a back-and-forth application, and working from the outer edge of the iris in towards the pupil, successively apply olive green yellowish, terracotta and green gold, following the markings on your flipped reference image. Add a few hints of the dark markings using dark sepia. Smoosh all over using a back-and-forth motion with champagne.

All work carried out on the reverse is done in order to intensify the colour and depth on the front side, which is shown above. There's no pencil on the front here yet, but you can already see how the colour added behind will add interest and complexity to the finished eye.

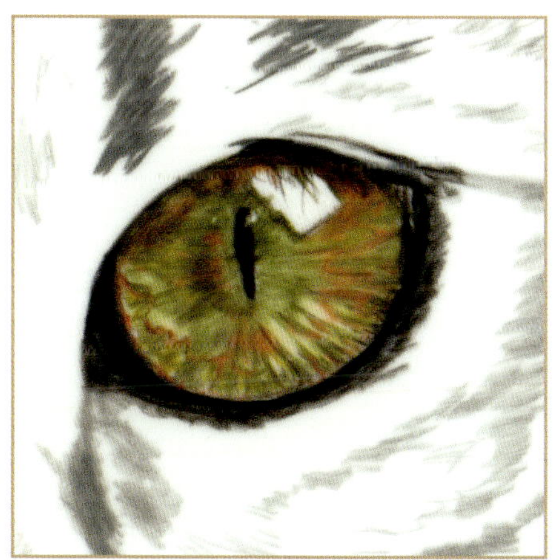

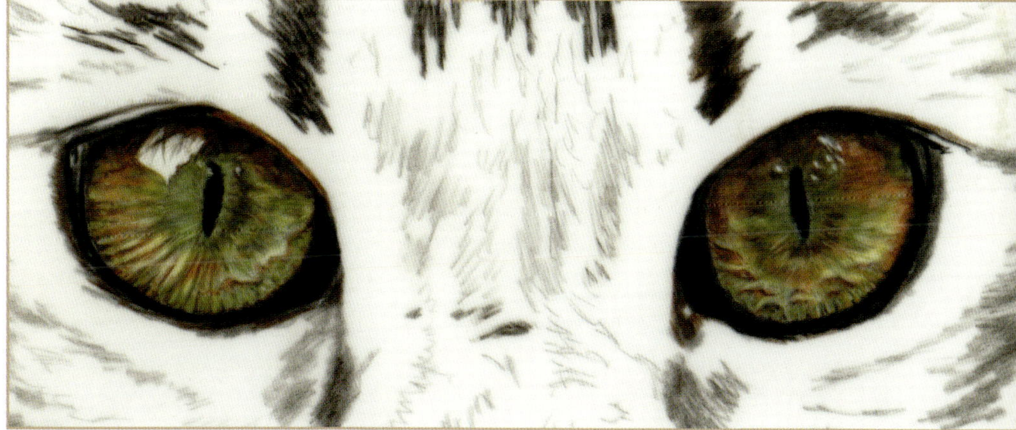

3 Using the same colours, and still working on the reverse side, repeat this process for the second eye. Keep the highlight clear and use less terracotta. Follow the coloration and markings in the reference, always working inwards towards the pupil.

4 Work the front of the eyes next. Use burnt ochre as the main orange colour on the front side (terracotta is too bright). Combine olive green yellowish and chromium green opaque for the darker green markings, then swap to earth green yellowish. Always allow each colour to layer over the edges of the previous one to ensure a smooth finish. Add in the dark markings lightly with dark sepia, before glazing earth green and green gold over the whole area. Transition any of the dark edges and markings coming in from the outer edge of the iris using burnt umber. Add cream to create the lightest of details into the iris. Smoosh with champagne using a consistent pressure and a back-and-forth application. Add cream back into any highlights that need lifting.

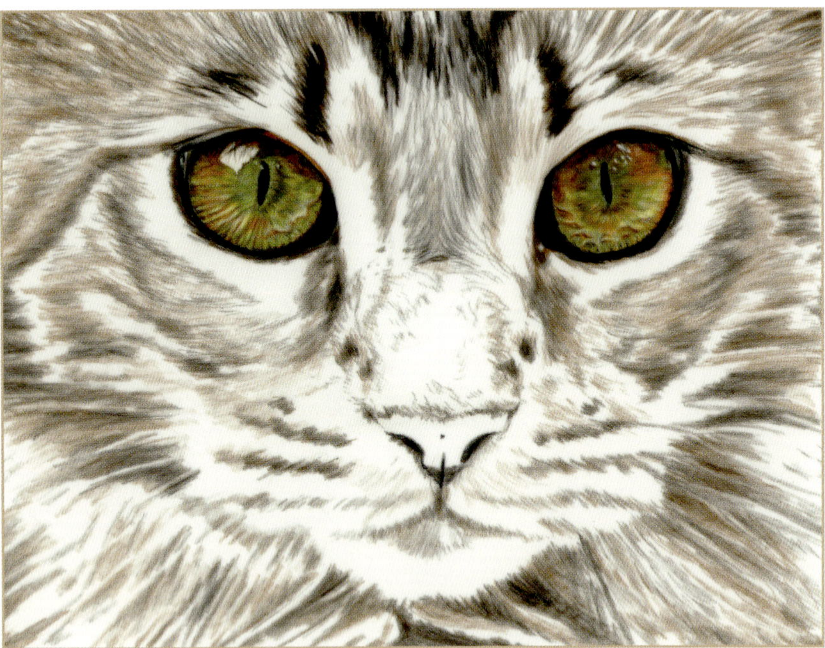

5 With the line art in place, and working on the front side of the film, begin to add in the markings of the fur. Start with the darkest brown markings using dark sepia and burnt umber.

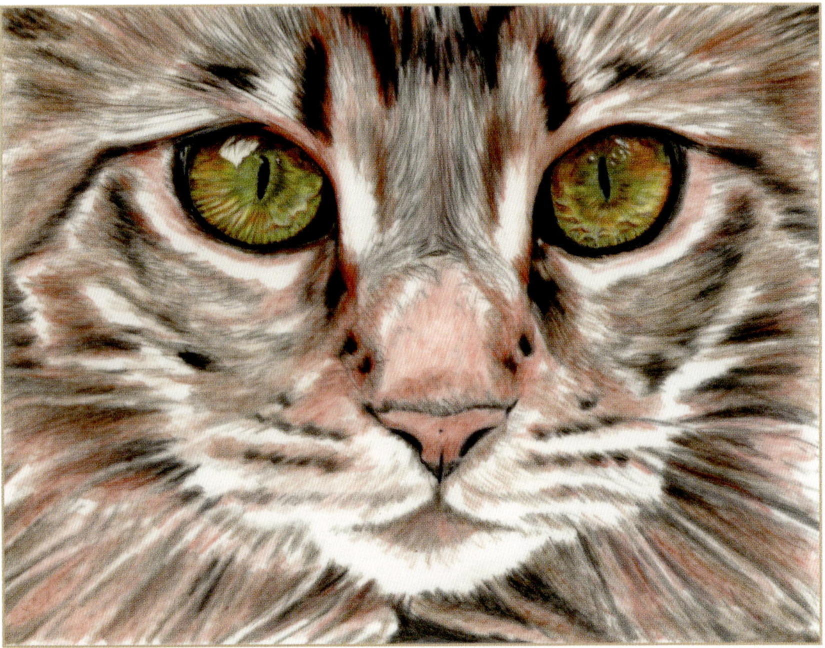

6 Intensify the darkest markings using black and dark sepia on both the front and reverse of the film. Work in the direction of the fur using long tapered strokes. Next, add in the reds on the front side. These will look a little bright to begin with but will soften down in the stages to follow. Use Indian red and Venetian red. When adding pigment to the nose area, use the scumbling technique to keep the application smooth.

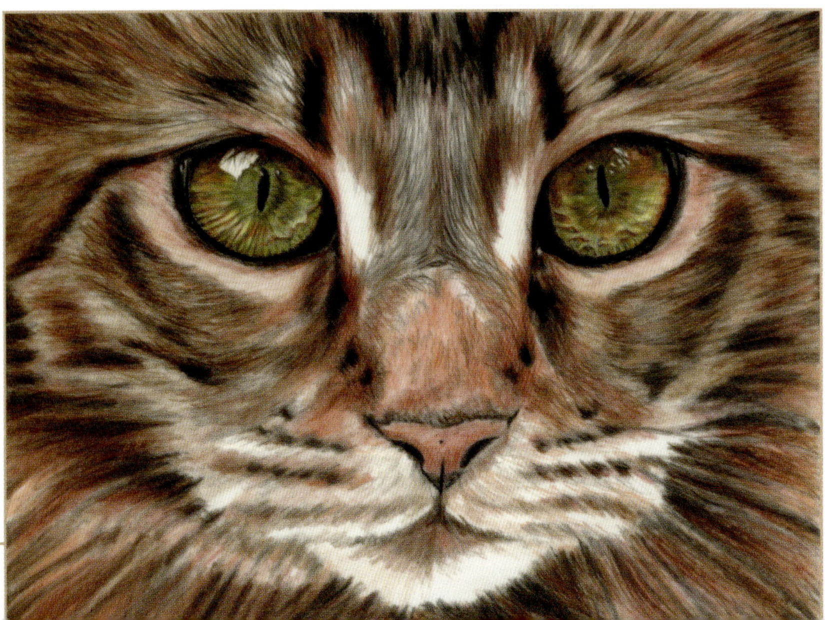

7 Next add in sanguine to the richer, more orange, areas. Glaze with nougat and sienna all over, using a back-and-forth motion with a light pressure in the direction of the fur. Increase the contrast, if needed, with more burnt umber.

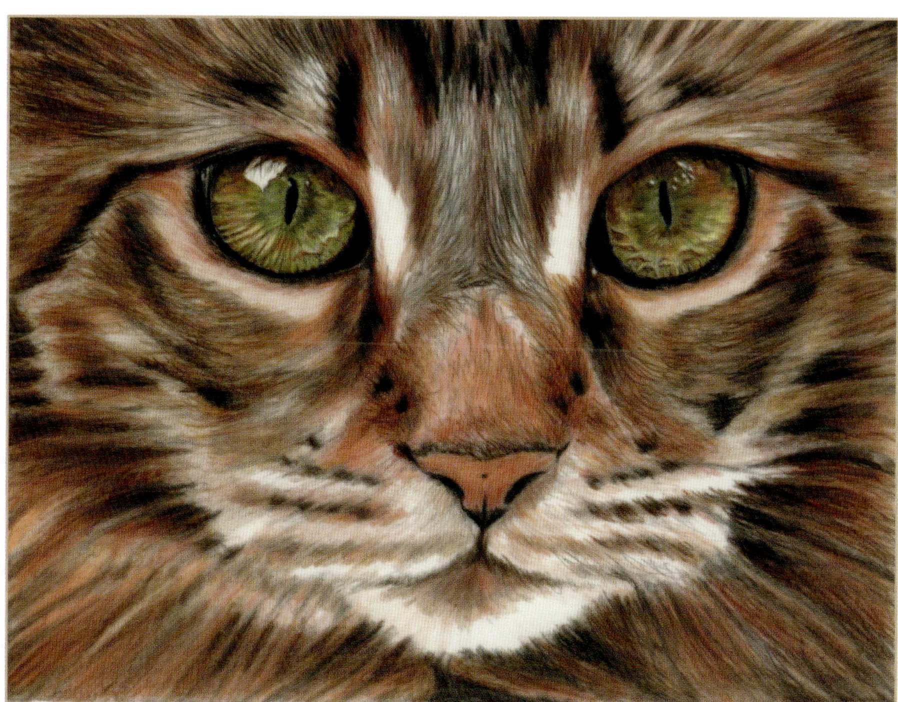

8 Repeat steps 5–7. Bring in more burnt ochre if needed to soften the oranges.

9 Time to smoosh again. Use wheat in the cream and brown areas. Use flesh pink and sienna in the pinker areas.

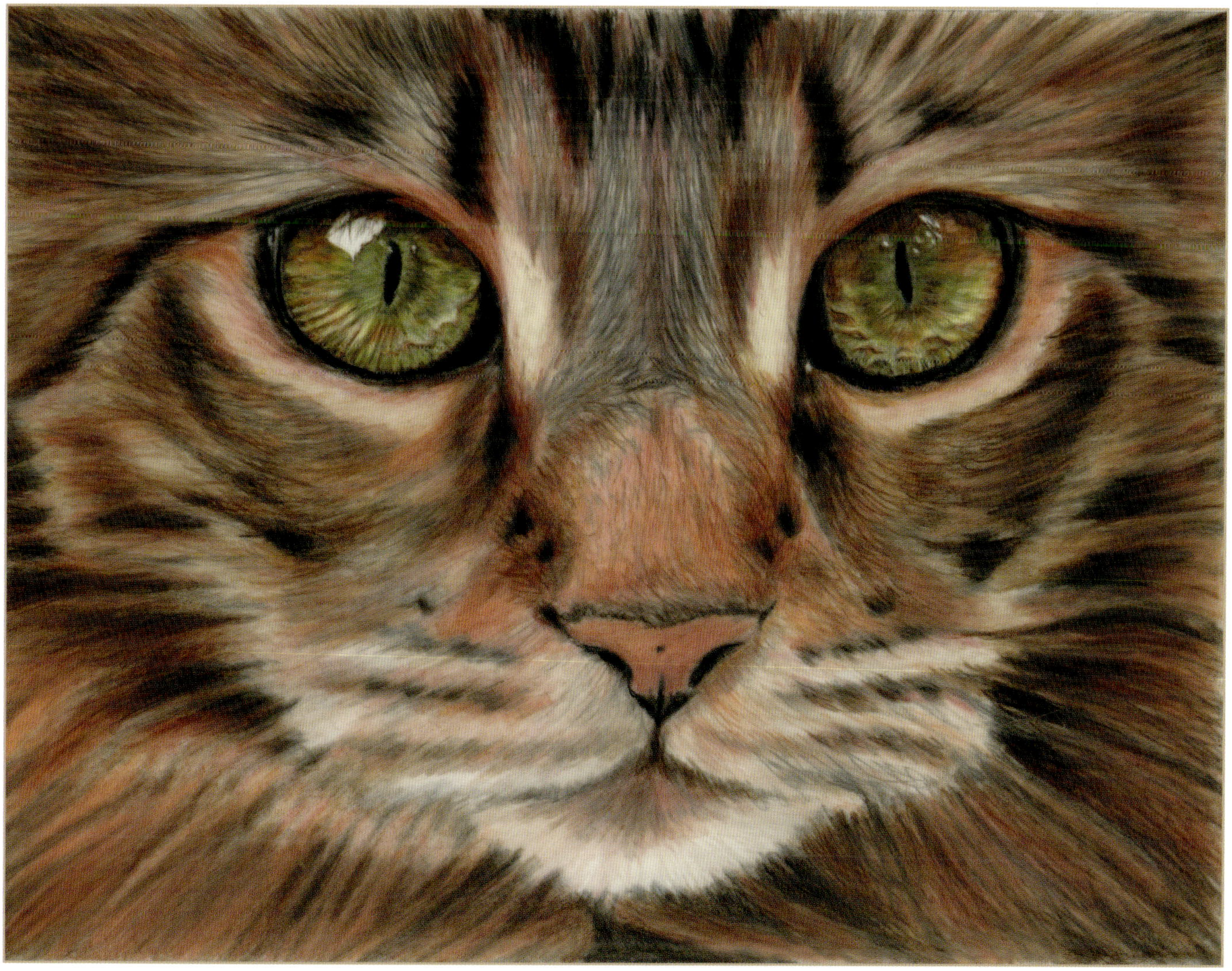

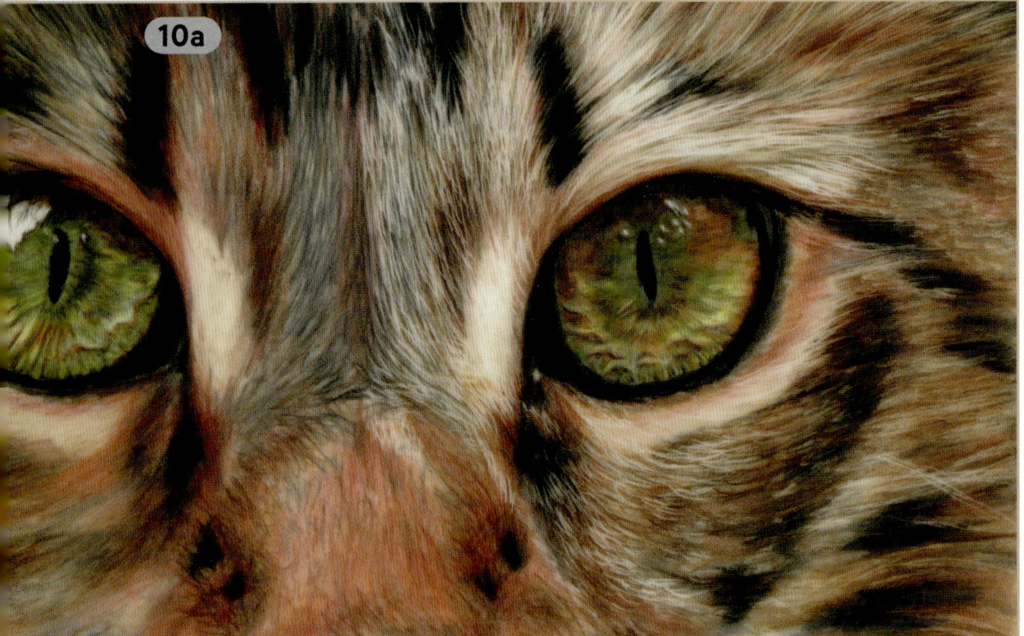

10a

10 Time to move on to the knife work. Using the blade upside-down and starting with the fur around the eye on the right-hand side, make tapered flick strokes in the direction and to the length of the fur (10a). Remember to vary the strokes, pressure and direction to match the fur in the reference photograph. You will remove more pigment than necessary, but the pencil layers will be repeated again later. Move on to the fur around the other eye (10b), then around the centre and nose (10c), and finally the remaining fur (10d, opposite). Follow the progress images here for each area in turn.

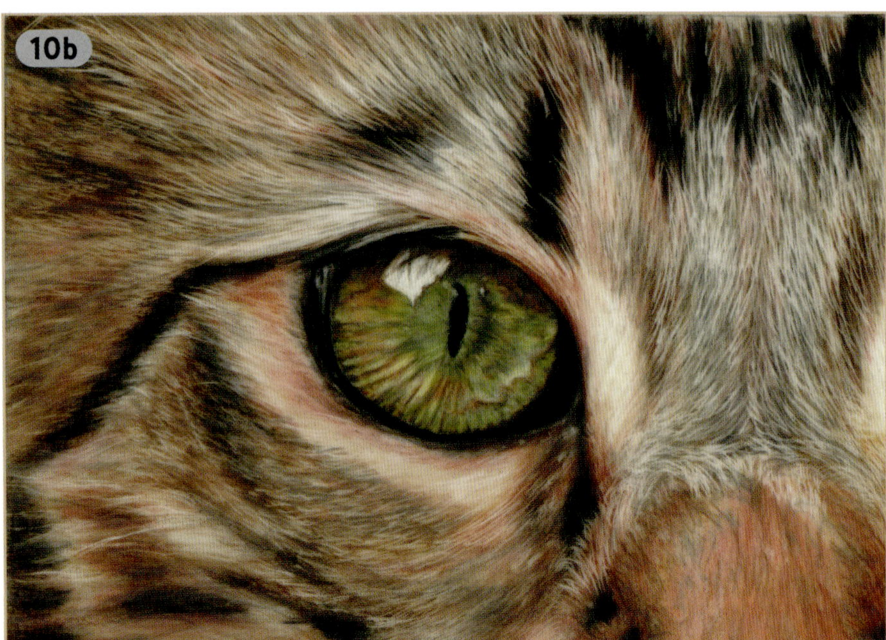

10b

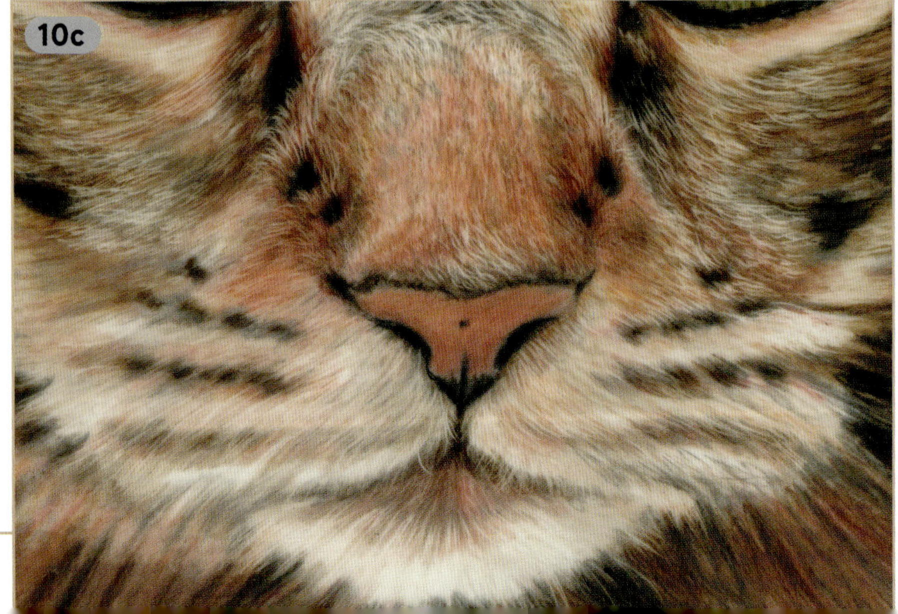

10c

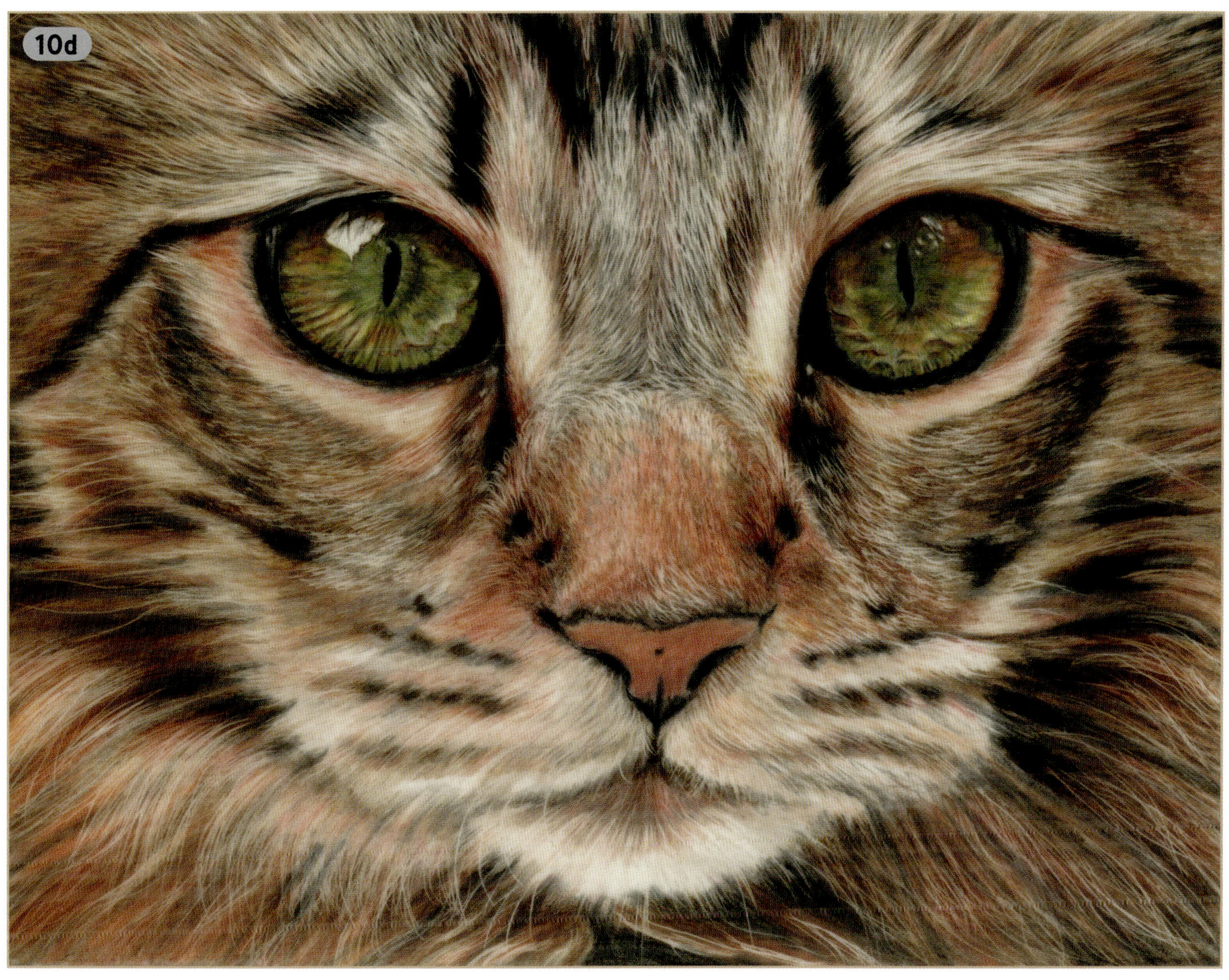

Tip

Have your dusting brush to hand
to sweep away any dust and
pigment, and relax.

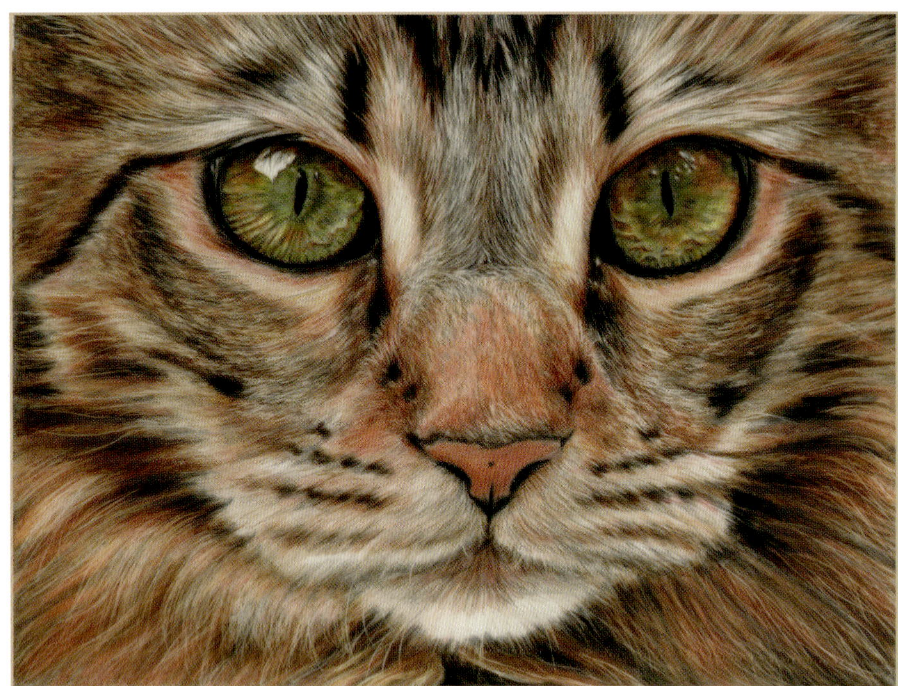

11 Go back to the previous fur stage steps and repeat stages 5–8, adding darks and colours back in. Work on both the front and the reverse while adding pigment back in to intensify the depth of colour and tone.

Tip

Sharpen up those pencils! The sharp pencil should skip over the lines made by the blade.

12 Smoosh again and repeat the knife work.

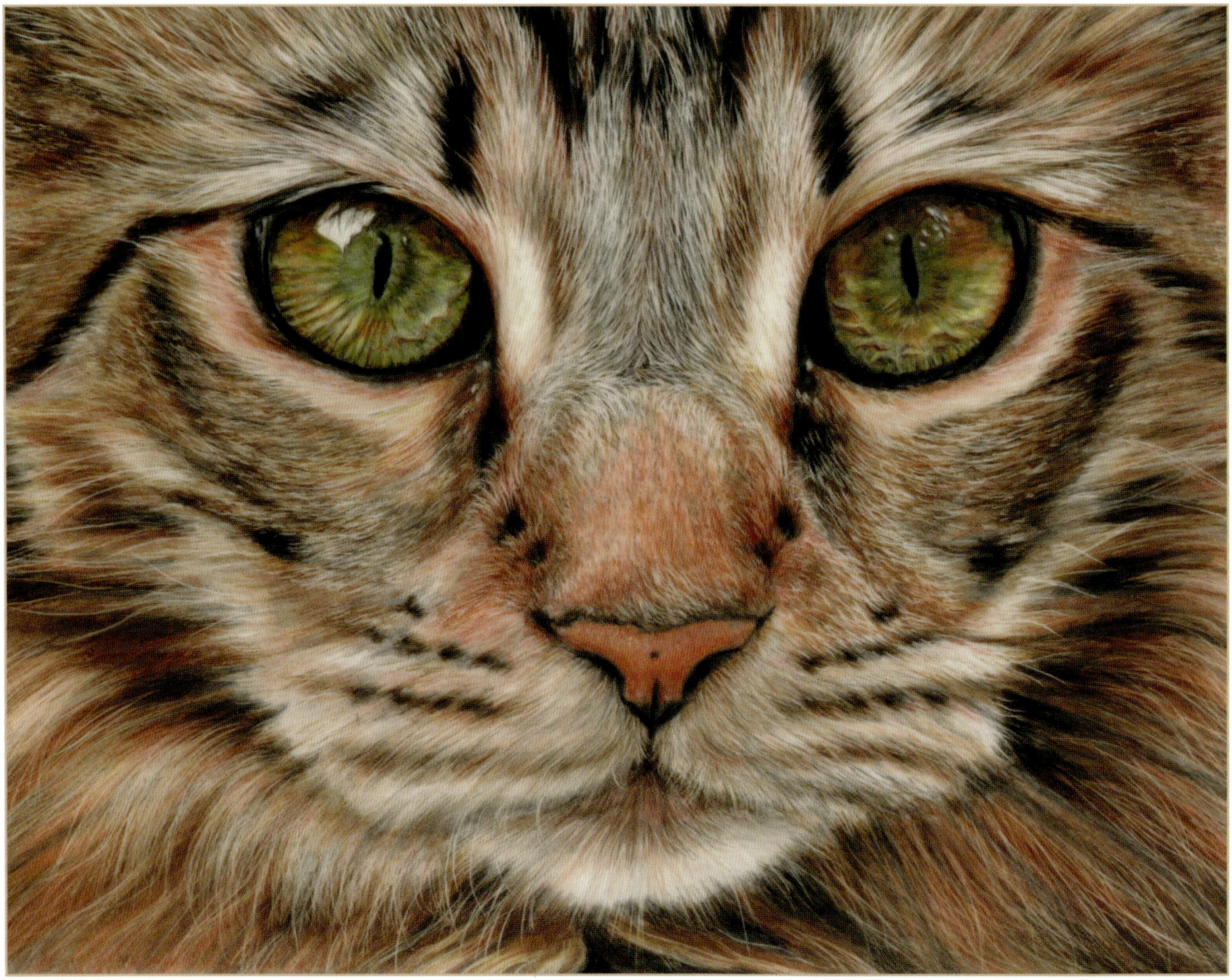

13 To finish the portrait, we need to work the muzzle a little more and add in those fabulous whiskers using warm grey V, white and sienna over the muzzle area. Once these colours are in, smoosh again if necessary, then re-texturize with the knife. Use black and burnt umber to intensify the shadow areas just under the chin. Add the whiskers using the Slice blade. Turn the film in a direction to allow you to flick your hand away naturally in a long, firm tapered stroke. Add white into the whiskers. Tweak the front and back until you are happy. Use a white backing behind your finished portrait to intensify the knifework. And that is this one all finished!

Tip

When adding the whiskers, confidence will help you avoid a hesitant, wavering line. You may find practising beforehand on a spare sheet of film helps build you up to working on your artwork.

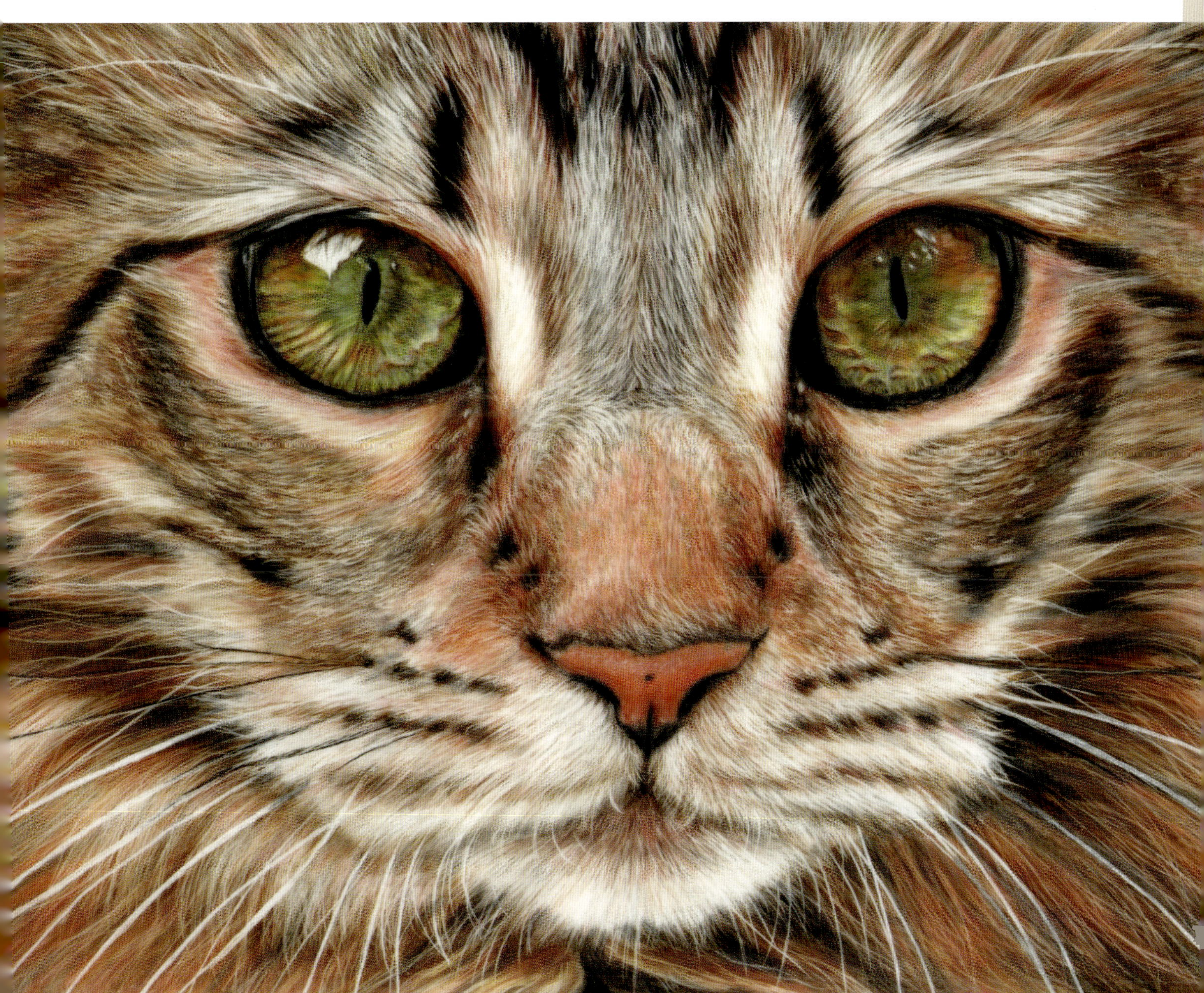

The finished portrait

MILO

XOLOITZCUINTLE, MEXICAN HAIRLESS DOG

The Mexican hairless dog is one of the most ancient breeds of domestic dog. My brother has three of these, so I have had plenty of chance to study them – and enjoy their company. Making a portrait of this breed gives you a perfect chance to practise working on skin texture.

My aim with this project is to show you how to build your pigment smoothly and consistently. Patience is needed for the layers of glazes that you will need to apply. The initial underpainting is watercolour pencils followed by dry layers of coloured pencil.

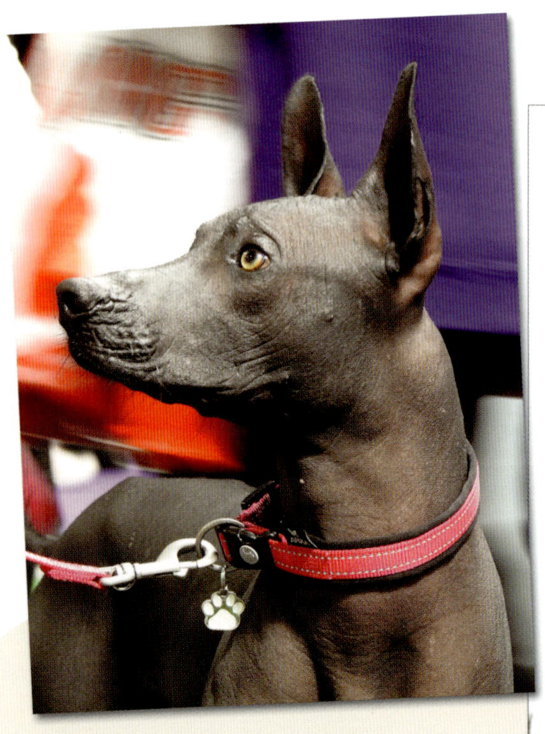

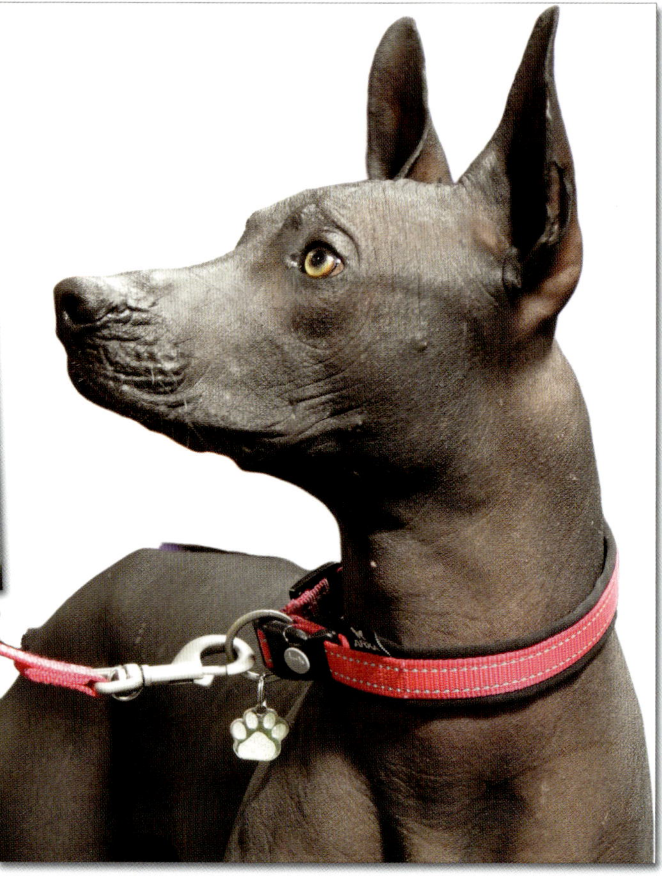

The reference photograph used for this project. I've used a graphics program to remove the background from the original (above). This helps clear out the background clutter and makes it a more useful reference.

1 We will use Albrecht Dürer watercolour pencils for steps 1–5 as we block in the colours. Start by transferring the line art using a stylus and the indenting method (see page 49). Glaze over the transfer with cold grey II to make the lines appear more clearly.

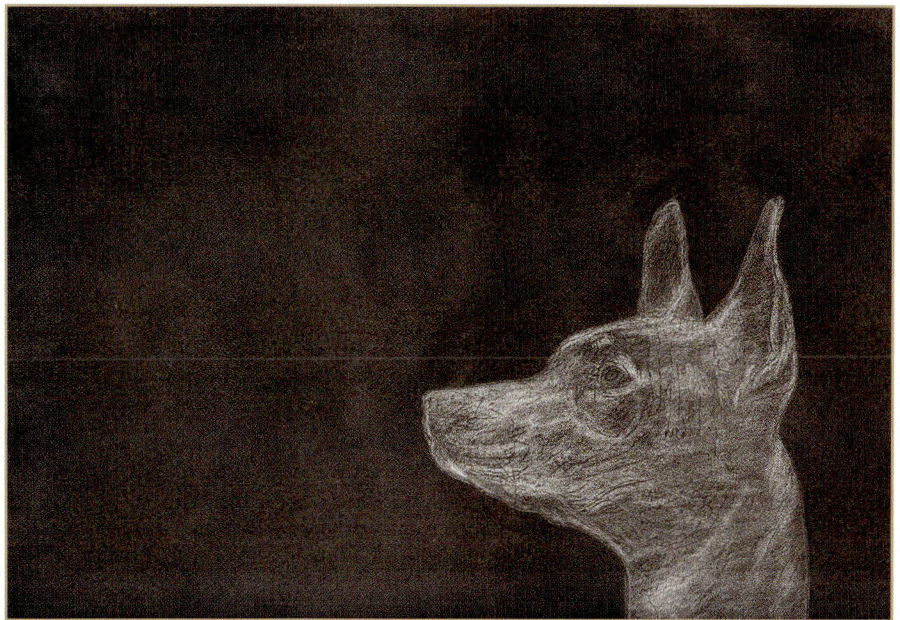

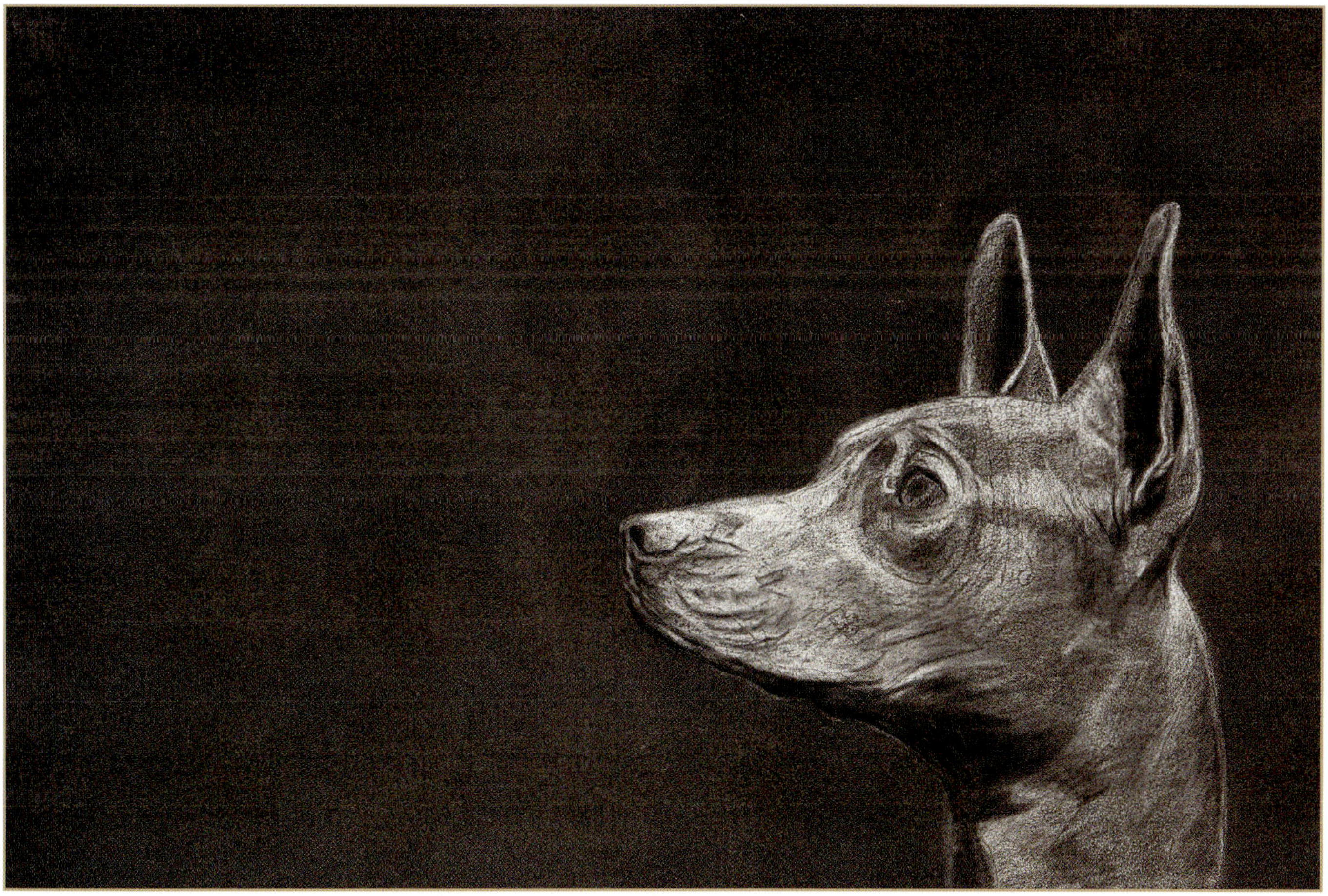

2 Sharpen up the outline using cold grey I, then add in the main highlights. Use black, Payne's grey and dark sepia to map in the main darks. Use Payne's grey in the bluer, cooler areas and dark sepia in the warmer browner ones. Work with a standard pressure using back-and-forth and scumbling strokes.

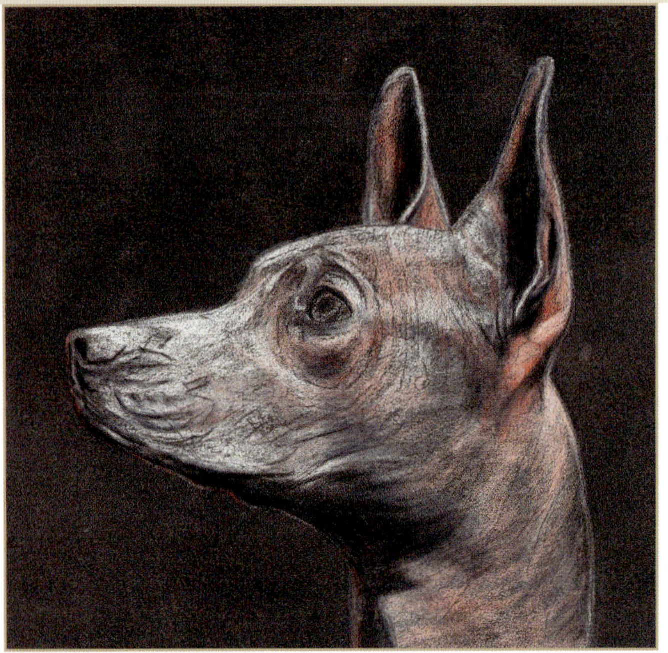

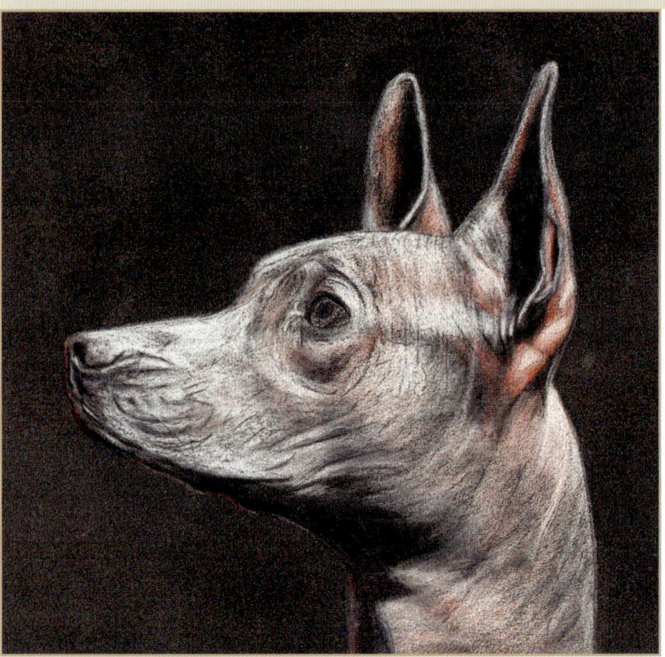

3 Work up through the mid-tones by adding in some colour. Venetian red and cinnamon in the red and pink areas and dark indigo in the bluer ones.

4 Now add in the lights: Use beige red and warm grey II in the pinker areas and cold grey I and white in the cooler, brighter ones.

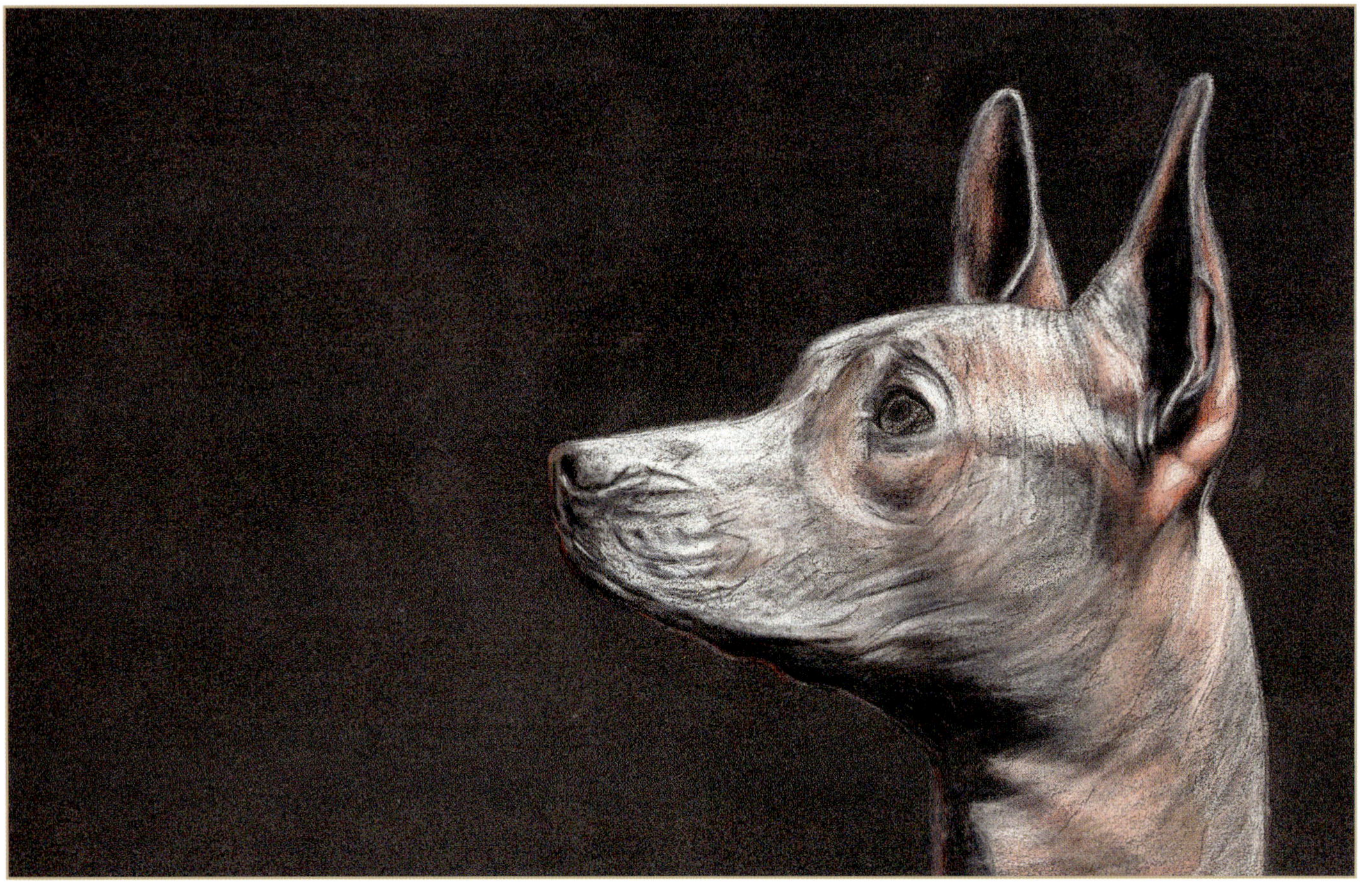

5 When you add water in the next step, all of the pigment laid down on the support will mix and blend and also dilute a little. For this reason, it's important to repeat the previous layers until you are happy with the amount of colour laid down. Pop in some more colour if needed and bring in a touch of nougat to soften some of the browner areas.

Tip

Before moving on, you can take this opportunity to lay down a background if you choose – but this is optional.

I used PanPastels to create a mottled dark background for my piece but you can leave yours blank or create one of your own choice.

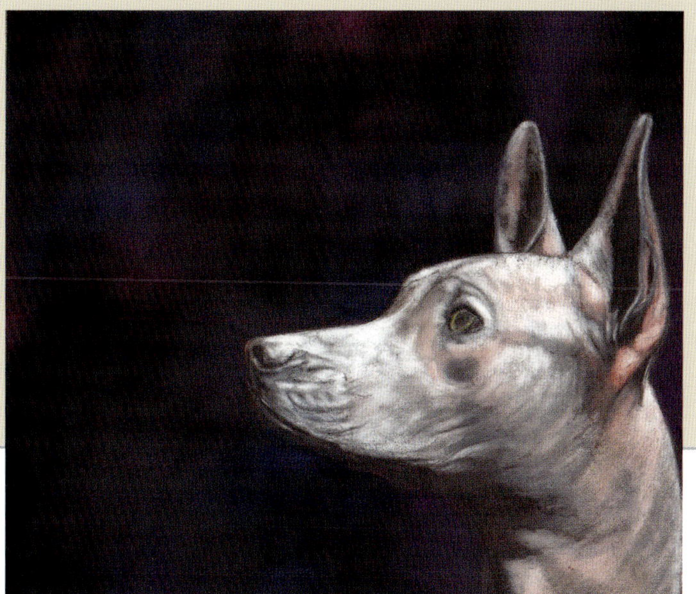

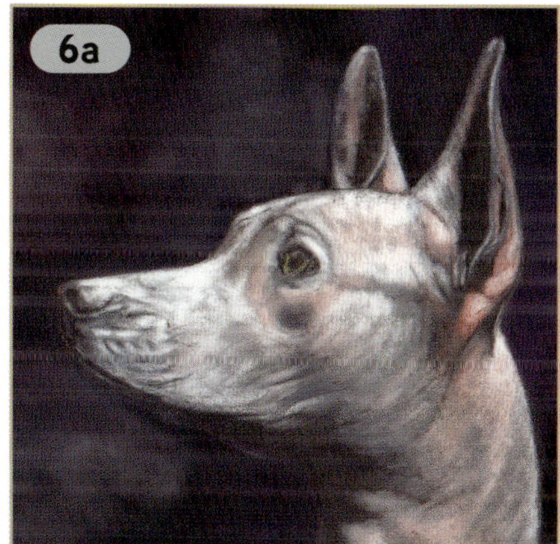

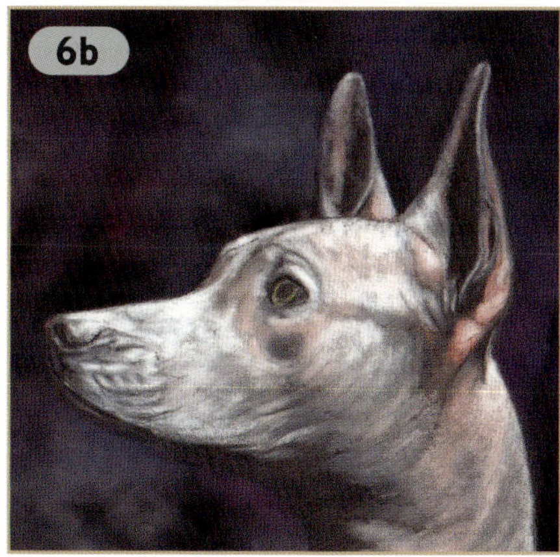

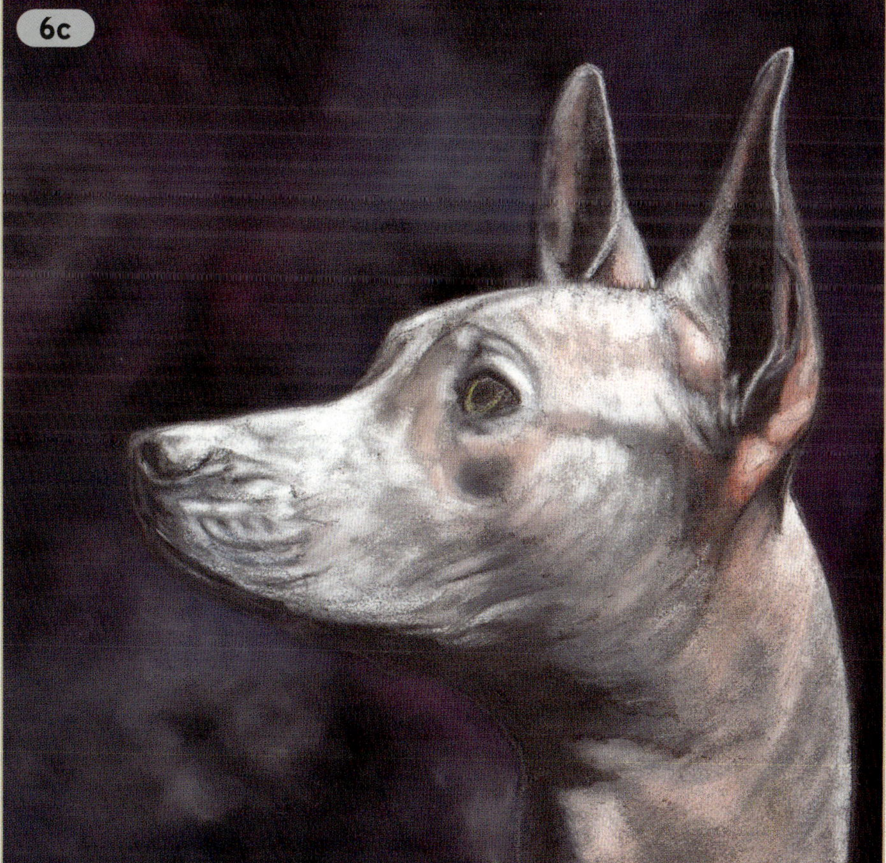

6 Time to add the water. Using a waterbrush (you can use a regular brush instead, but ensure that you have dabbed off excess water onto a piece of kitchen paper before you begin), carefully move the brush tip over the pigment, being careful not to go over any area more than once. The idea is simply to dissolve the binders in the pigment so that it releases into the support. It is very important that you leave the piece to dry overnight before attempting to add any of the subsequent dry layers!

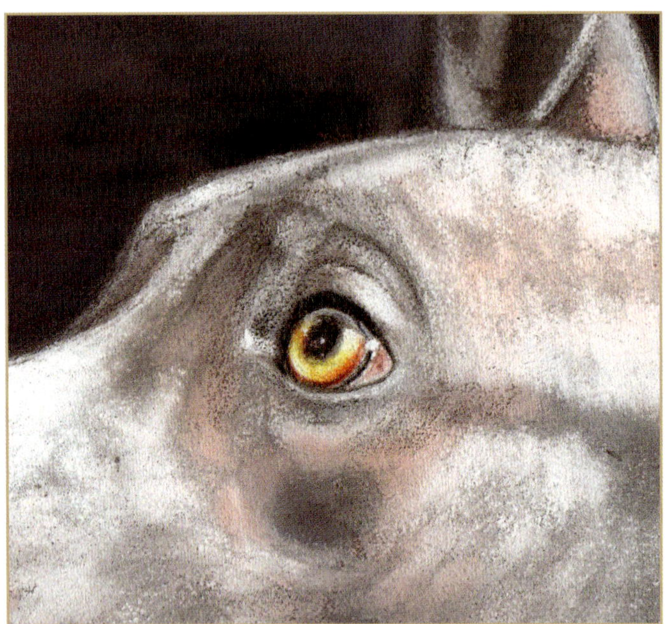

You can continue using your watercolour pencils from this point, but I switched to using the Polychromos and Pablo pencils for the dry layers. Refer back to the study on pages 54–57 for more detailed information on colouring golden eyes.

7 With sharp pencils, and using a mix of back-and-forth and scumbling strokes, add in the eye. Use black to define the outline and the pupil, then use Pablo white to create the highlight. Next, glaze over the whole of the iris with dark Naples ochre before softening the lighter area of the iris with ivory. Create the outer fleshy corner of the eye using cinnamon and caput mortuum and soften with ash grey and Polychromos white. Add a touch of indanthrene blue around the edge of the pupil. Finally, add the red to the outside edge of the iris using vermilion. Sharpen up the pencils and repeat this whole step again until you have a good saturation of colour and pigment. More work will be done on the eye close to the finish of the whole portrait.

After the base layer has dried, it is time to build the pigment layers. Remember that this is not only to create tone and colour, but also to fill and smooth out the tooth of the Pastelmat surface. Depending on the pressure you use, you may have to repeat the next steps several times.

8 Working from dark to light, begin by blocking in using black, dark sepia and Payne's grey. You will see the grain of the tooth appear immediately: it is the smoothing out of this by repetition of layers that we are trying to achieve.

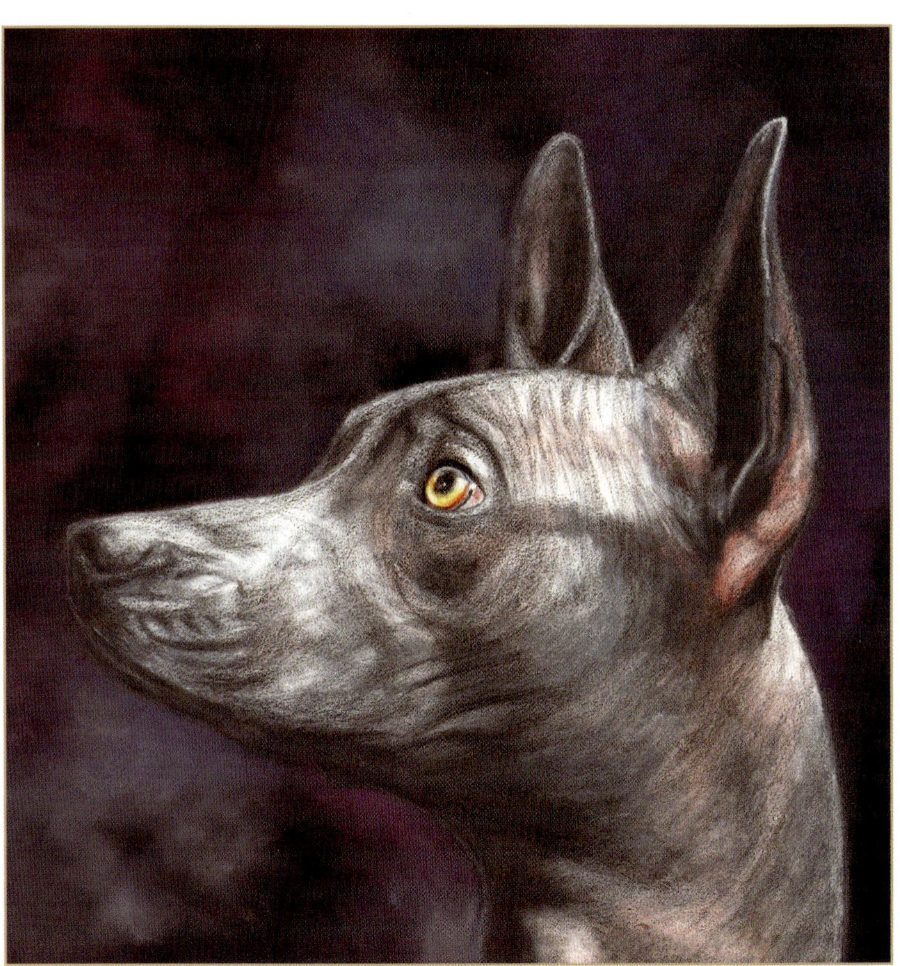

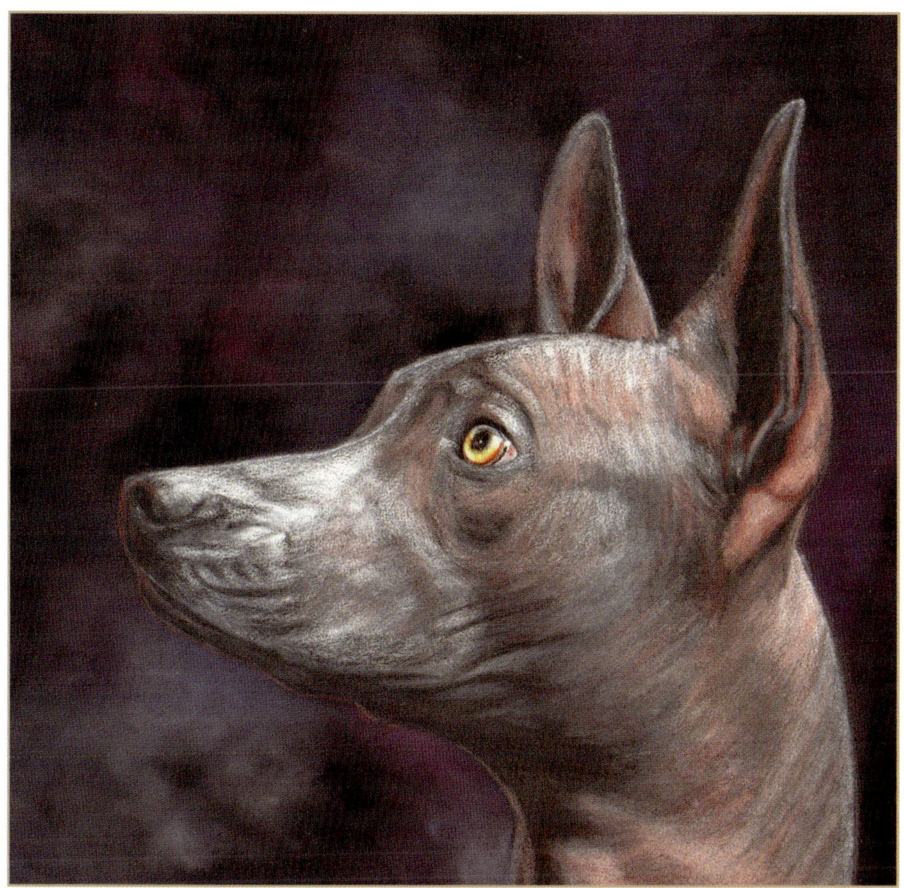

9 Move up through the mid-tones, using the pencils in this order: caput mortuum, greyish black, brownish orange, cinnamon and sepia.

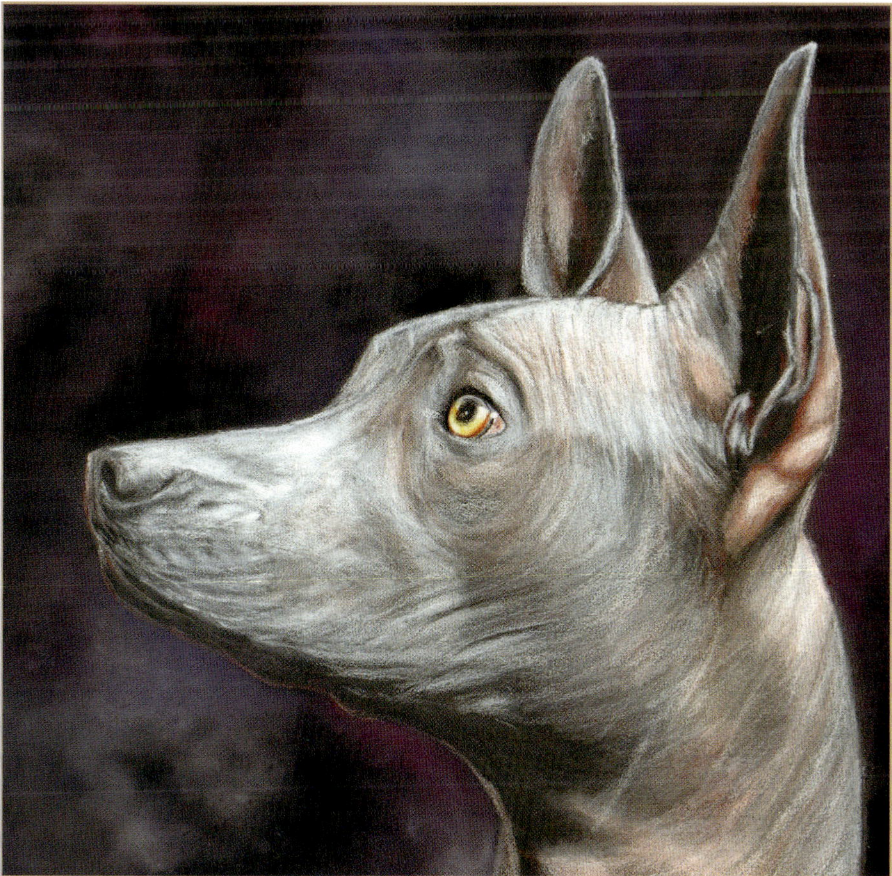

10 Next, move on to the lights in this order: dark grey, beige red, steel grey, ash grey, Polychromos white.

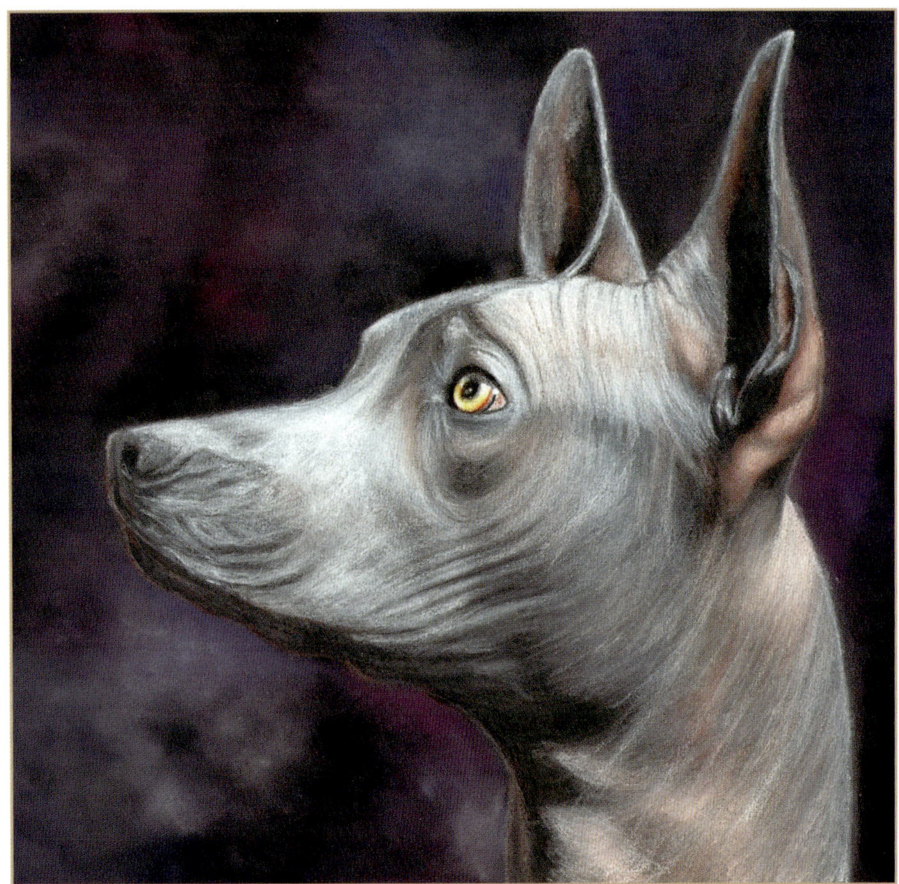

11 Repeat steps 8–10. Use the image here as a guide to where you should be at with your rendition.

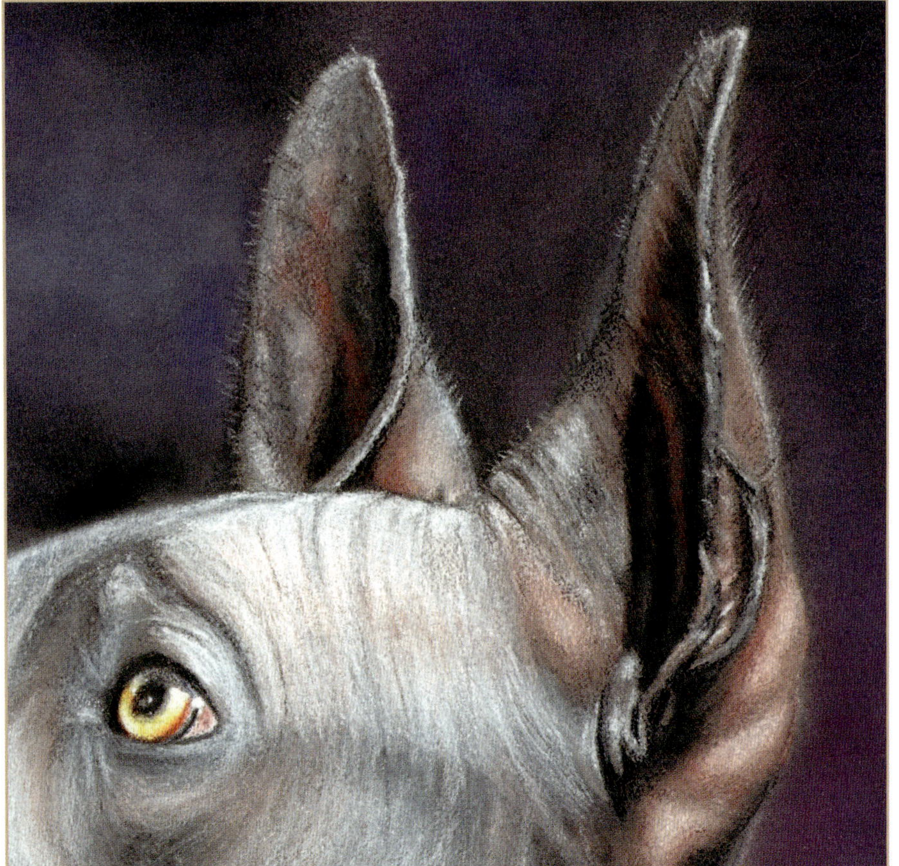

12 It's time to zoom in and refine each area now, starting with the ears. You will need to keep your pencils sharp at all times. Continue to use the scumbling or back-and-forth strokes with a standard pressure. You can vary your pressure and the angle of your pencil a little if you are struggling to get a grip on the support. Work through from your darks, mid-tones and lights, focusing now on the smaller shapes within the bigger blocks. Build up the tone and the colour until the tooth begins to smooth out. Use all of the same colours as before but bring in Pablo cream to thicken the highlights on the fleshy pink areas.

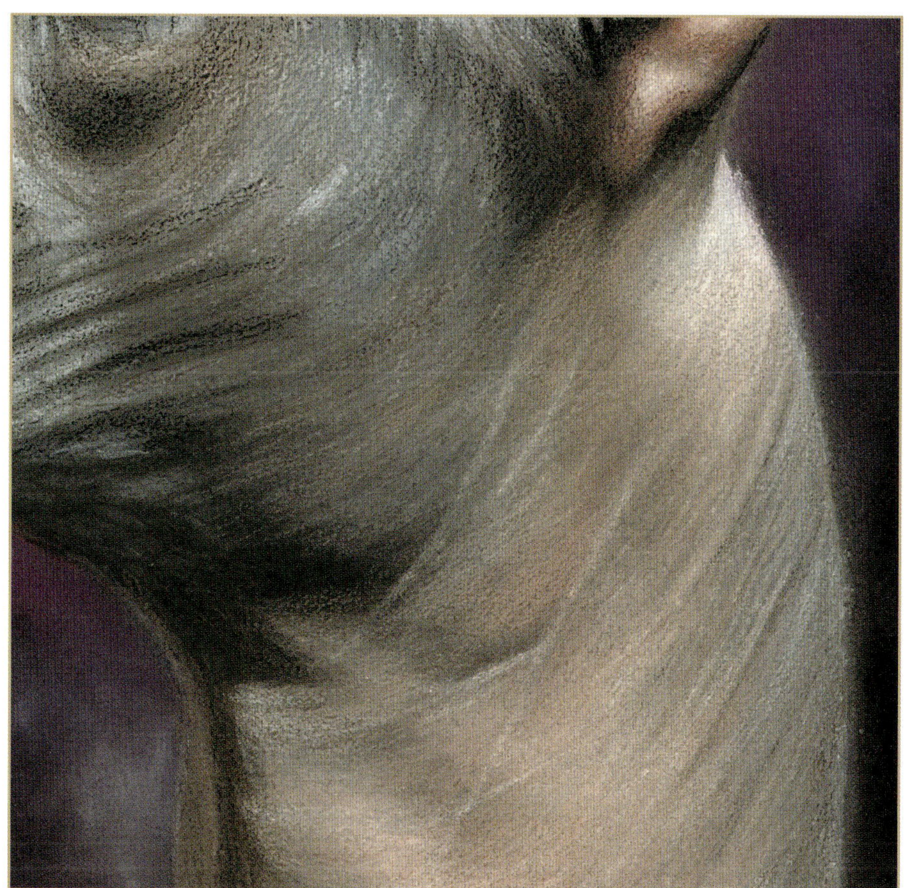

13 Move down to the neck. Using a long back-and-forth stroke with even standard pressure, work in the direction of the lines of the neck. Use black and greyish black for the darker areas. Glaze over these with brownish orange and sepia. Work through to your lights using beige red and ash grey in the lightest areas. Repeat this step again until you see the tooth beginning to smooth out. Mark in hints of the creases of the neck as you go.

14 Move up over the cheek and face using the same techniques as before. Work on the darks first, using black and greyish black to build on the tones. Glaze sepia and brownish orange over the pinker areas and soften with cocoa and brownish beige. Repeat until soft and smooth. Sharpen up the dark sepia and carefully mark in the folds of the skin.

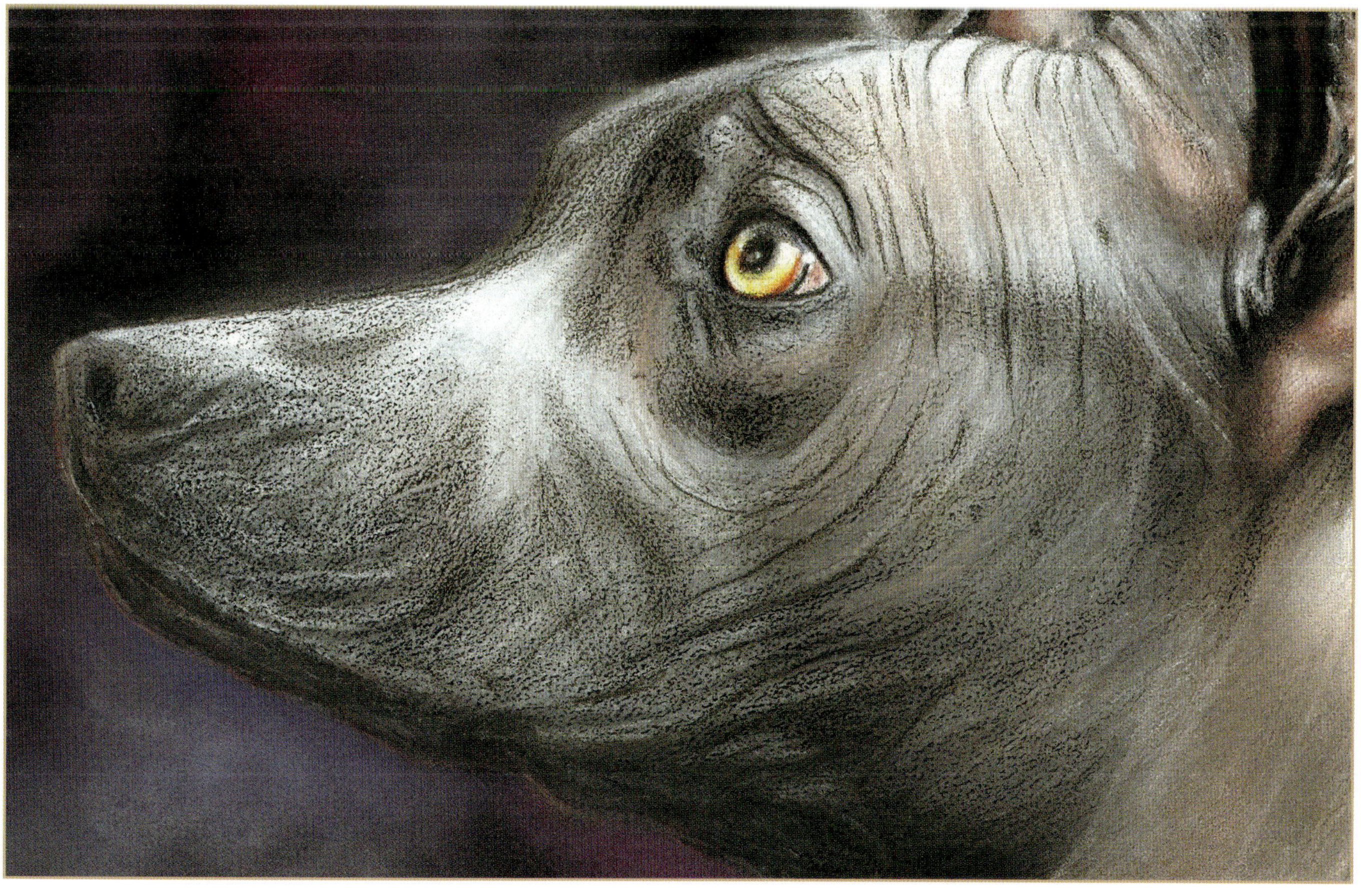

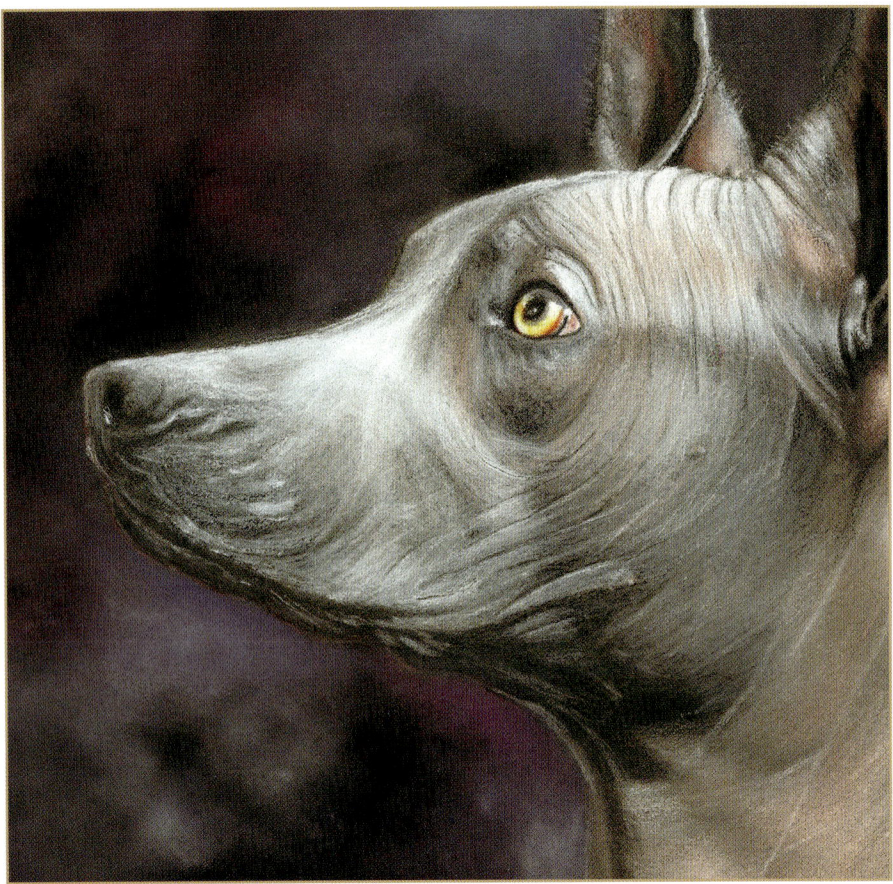

15 Work up through the lights glazing them over the darks. Repeat the mid-tones and then the lights again. Strengthen up any darks as you go along. Glaze with silver grey and white over the muzzle and across the top of the head. Use the warmer hues across the brown/pink areas.

16 Keep working the muzzle repeating the dark-to-light method. Use a mix of back-and-forth and hatching strokes. The tooth of the paper can be embraced a little here as it lends itself to the texture of the skin. Carefully start to add in the markings of the muzzle using black. Use the various warm and cool greys to lift the highlights.

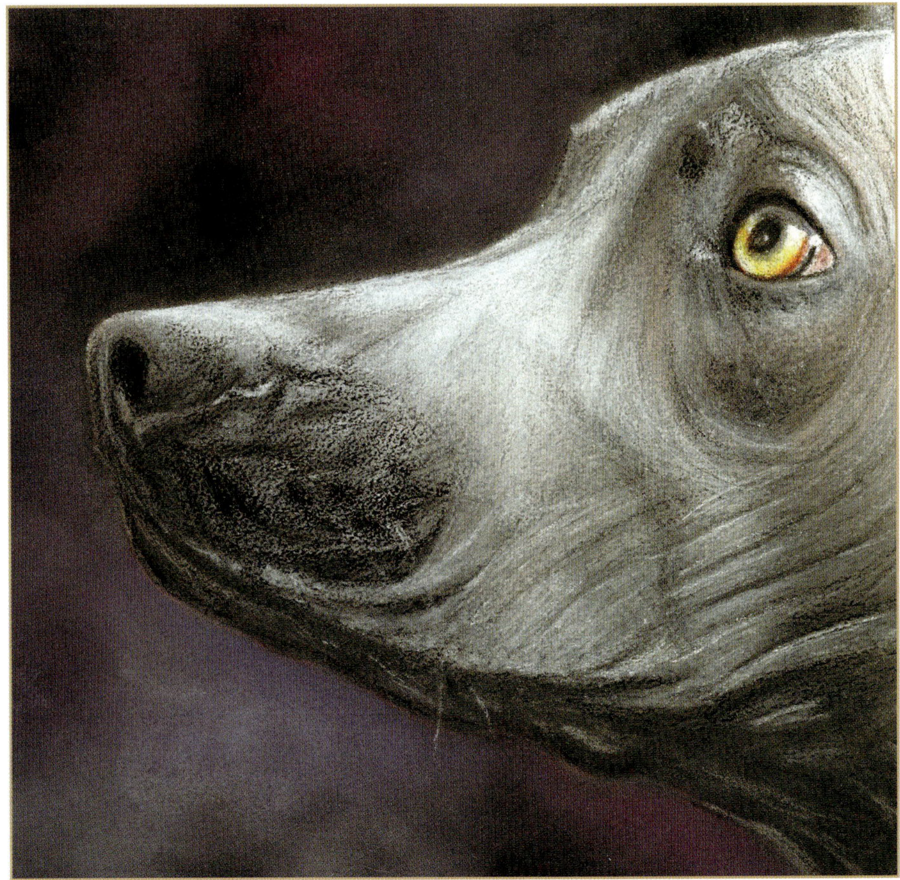

17 Sharpen those pencils all the time now as you work towards the final layers and tighten up the placement of markings. Work your highlights and shadows to as much depth as you are happy with. You can leave the skin with a hint of texture as I have done, or keep working it, adding more and more texture details. The choice of how detailed you take the final look is yours. Once the skin is textured to your liking, add in the whiskers, softening them back where necessary. A final top-to-toe tweaking session and you should be there.

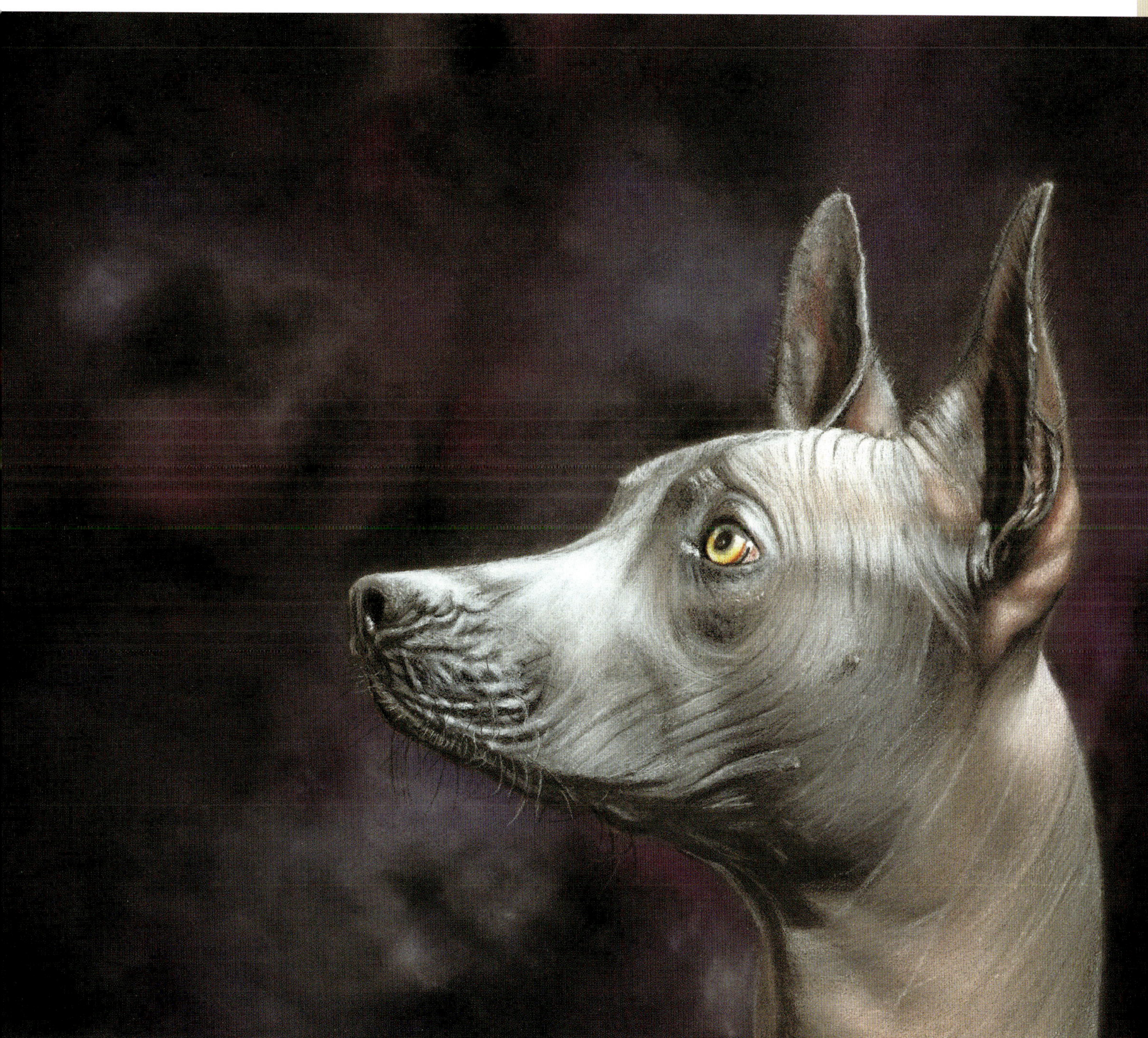

The finished portrait

SADIE

SHETLAND SHEEPDOG

Long white fur is often described as one of the hardest to depict and this little girl gives the opportunity to portray it in abundance. You will need a lot of patience as you seemingly apply pigment only to lift it away again, but the results are well worth the hard work. If you can master the chest fur on this girl, then you shouldn't fear white animals ever again.

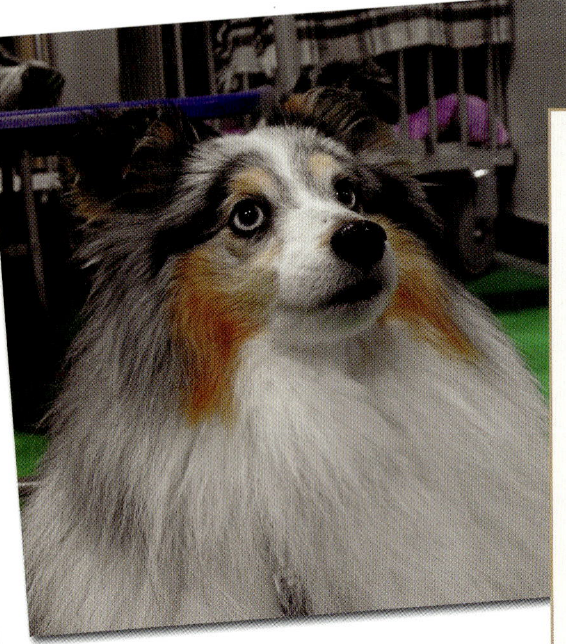

The reference photograph used for this project.

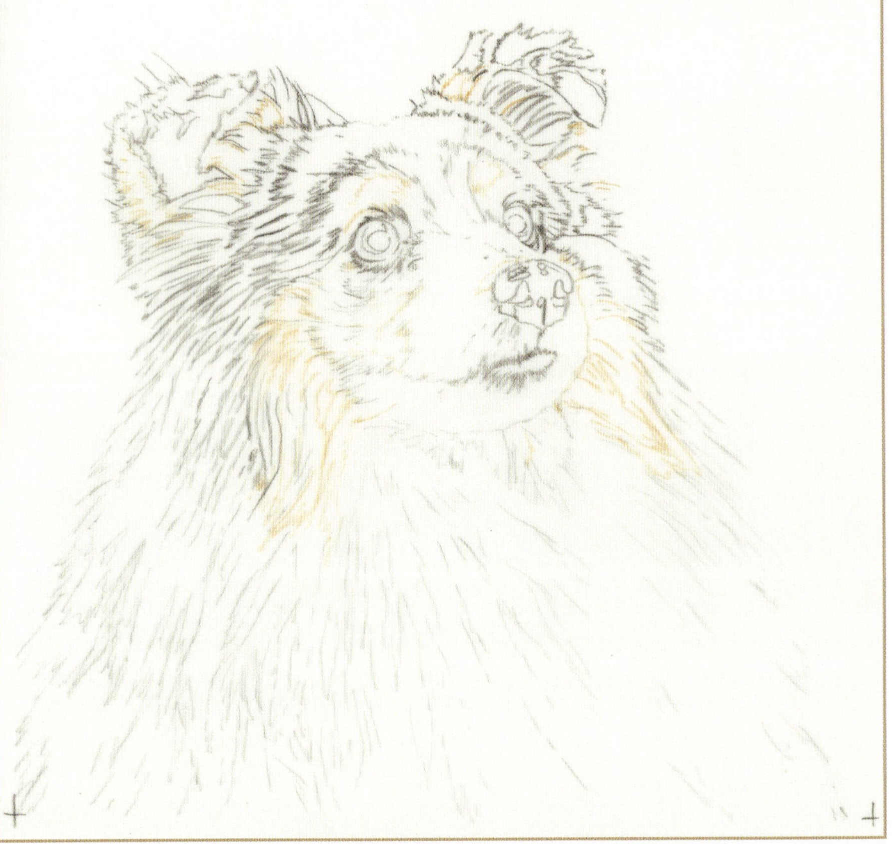

1 Lay the drafting film over the line art and affix into place. Mark in the corners of the reference image to allow you to place it correctly over the line art at future stages. With a light pressure, start to use cold grey VI to map in the dark shapes and lines. Next, use white to map in the lights and burnt ochre to map in the orangey areas.

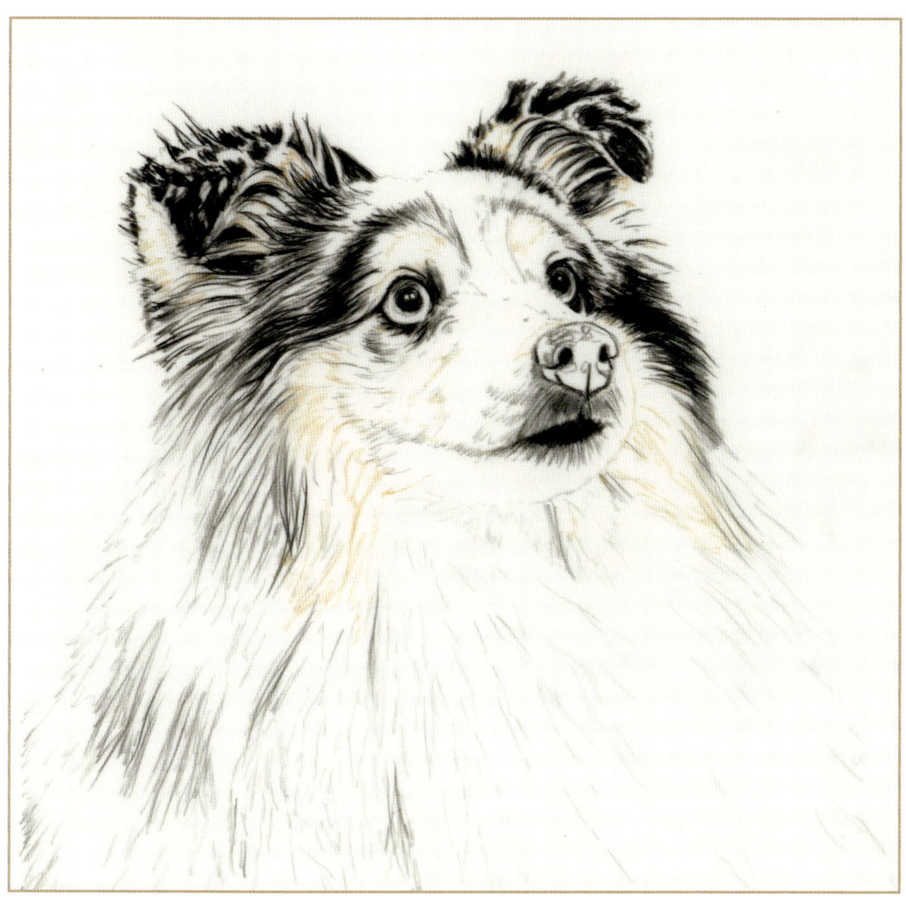

2 Using a back-and-forth stroke, strengthen the tone of the dark areas using black and cold grey VI.

Tip

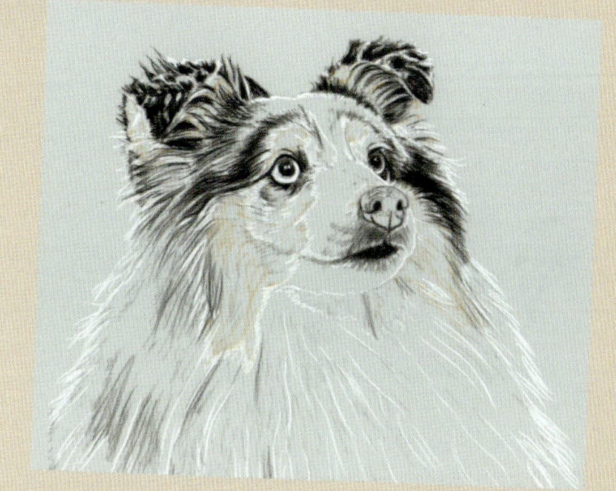

You may be wondering why you need white and black mount board cut to the size of the image. These are used to enable both the dark and light lines to be seen clearly while you work.

Swap between white and black backing as you work to make things easier. This picture shows the drafting film on top of the black mount board, which makes seeing the cold grey VI marks much more clear.

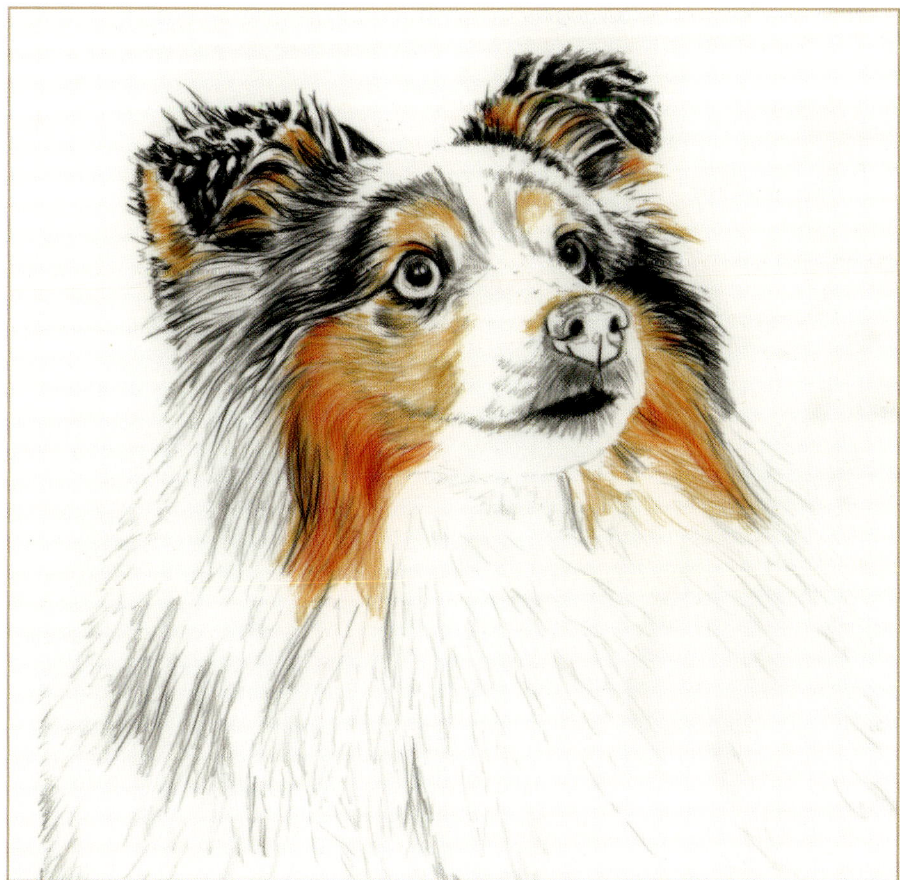

3 Once again using the back-and-forth stroke, fill in all of the orange areas with burnt ochre, and increase the vibrancy using sanguine in the brightest parts. Add a touch of Indian red in the neck area. Soften the cheeks with a glaze of burnt ochre.

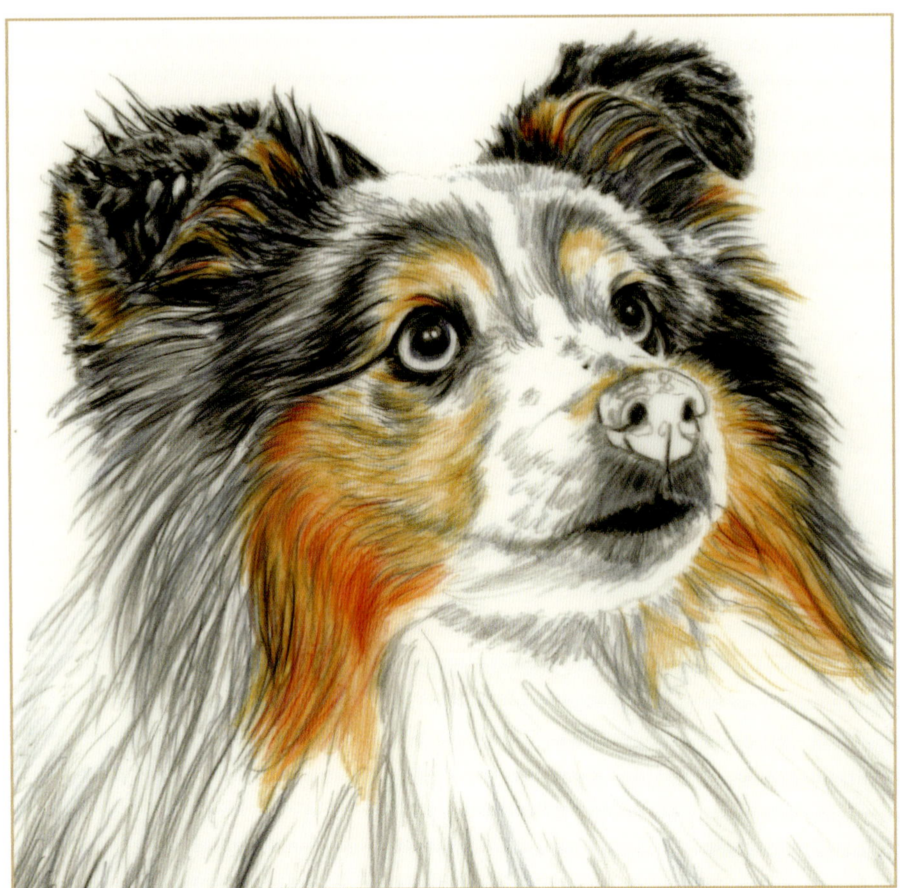

4 Add a fine touch of dark indigo around the iris on both eyes. Combine with Payne's grey throughout all of the darker fur where you see any hint of a bluish tinge.

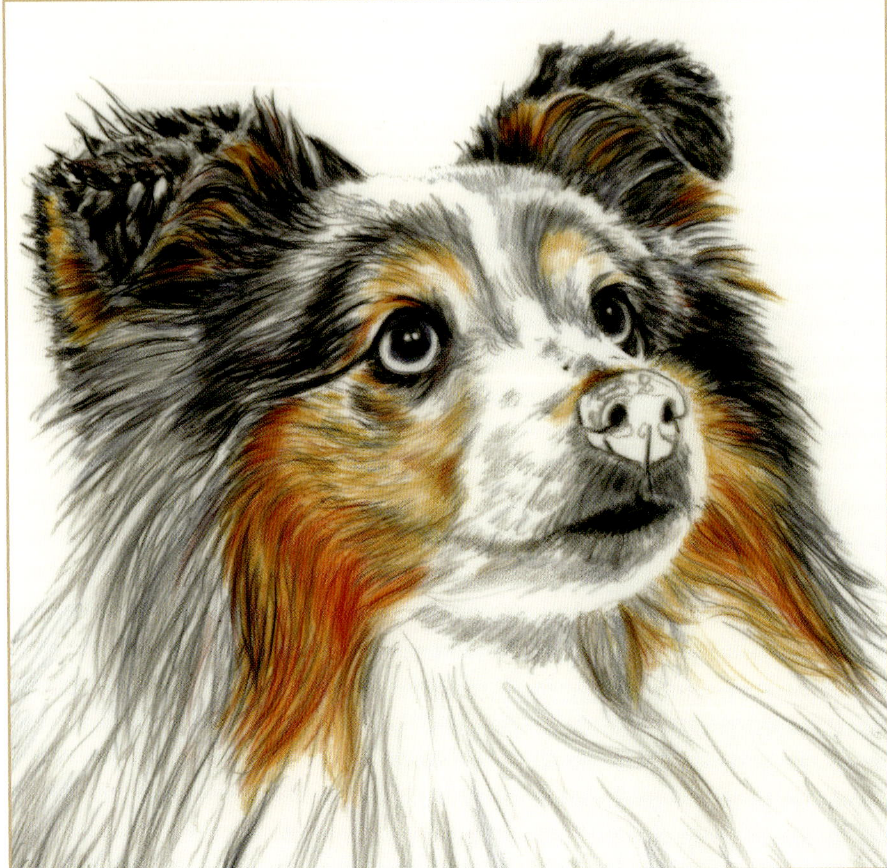

5 Enhance the darker lines in the orange areas using burnt umber. Pick out the reddish tinges in the ears and across the top of the head with caput mortuum.

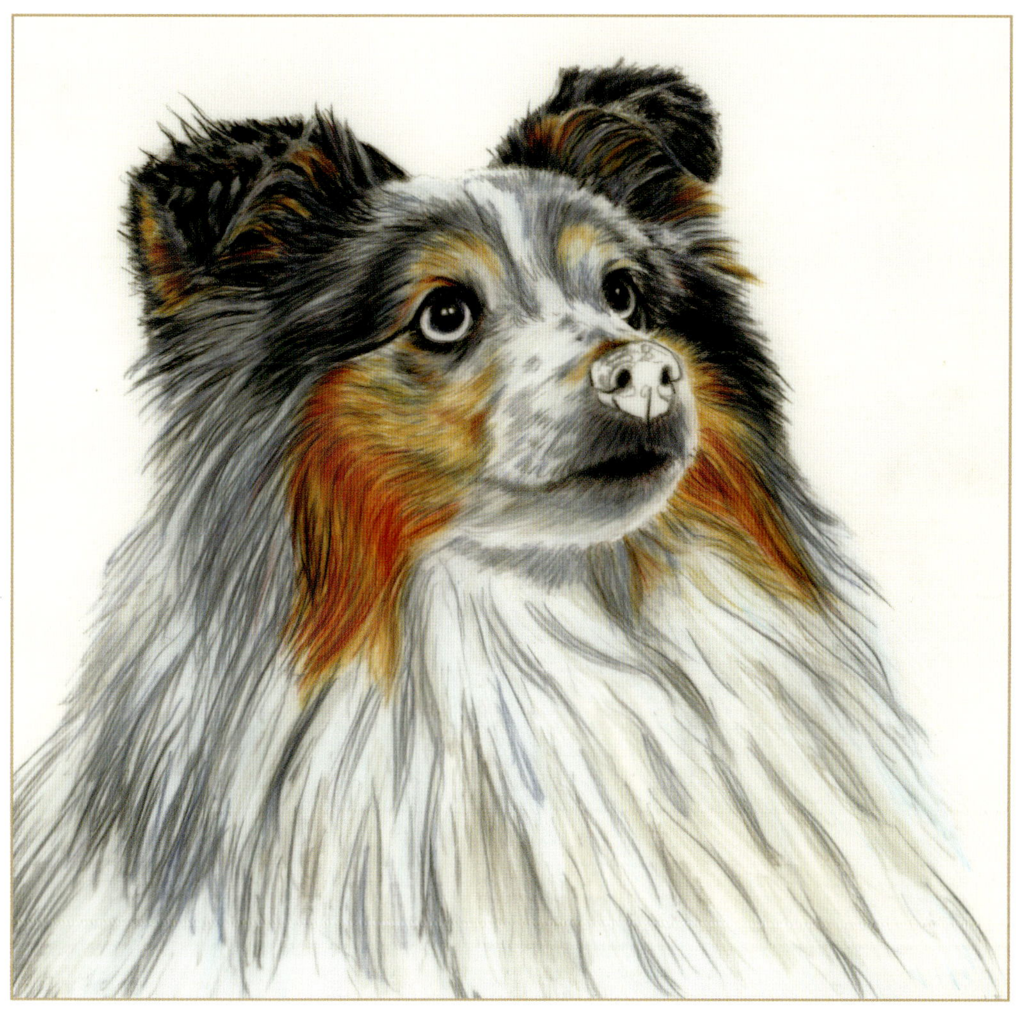

6 Time to smoosh the pigment together now. With a firm pressure and your softer pencils, use the back-and-forth motion in the direction of the fur to smooth and blend all of the pigments. Use platinum over the ears, arctic over the white areas and wheat on the orange areas.

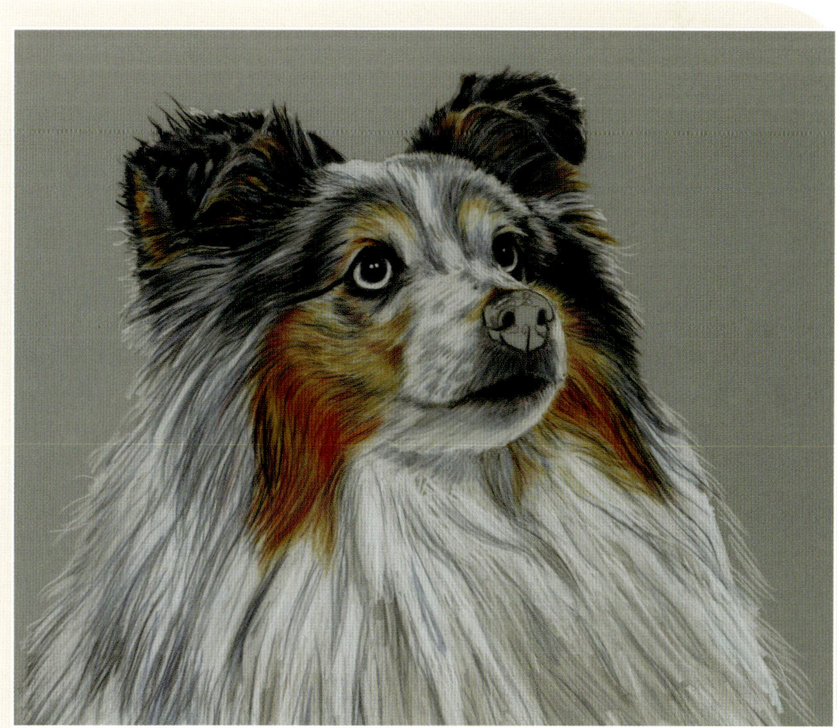

The same stage pictured on black mount board.

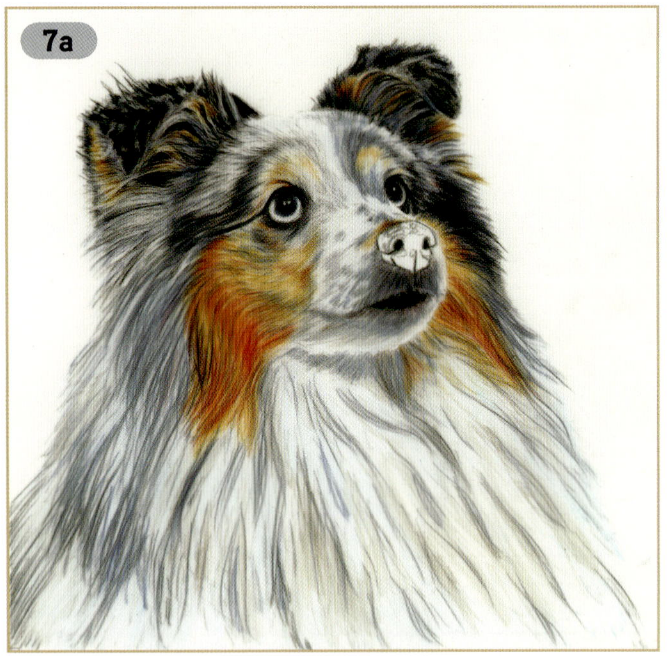

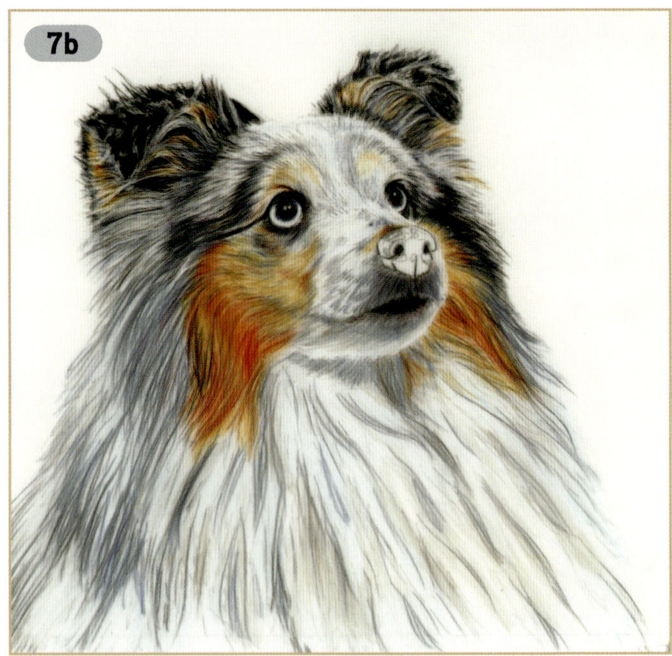

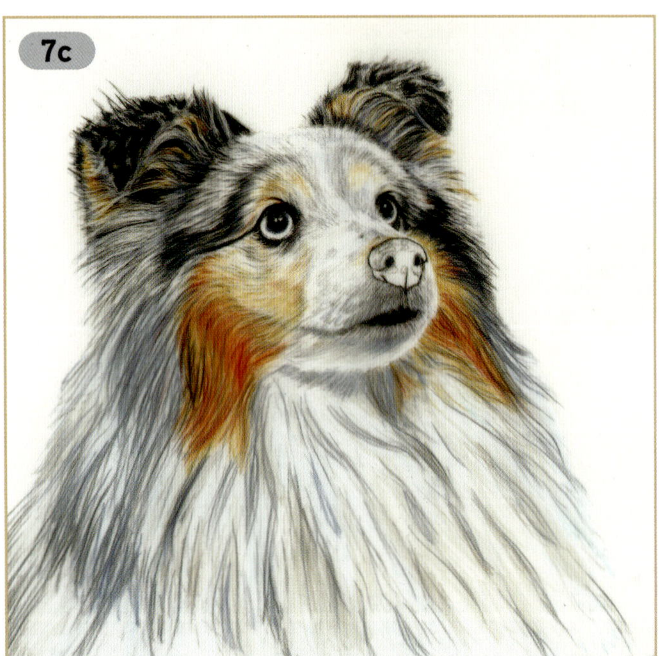

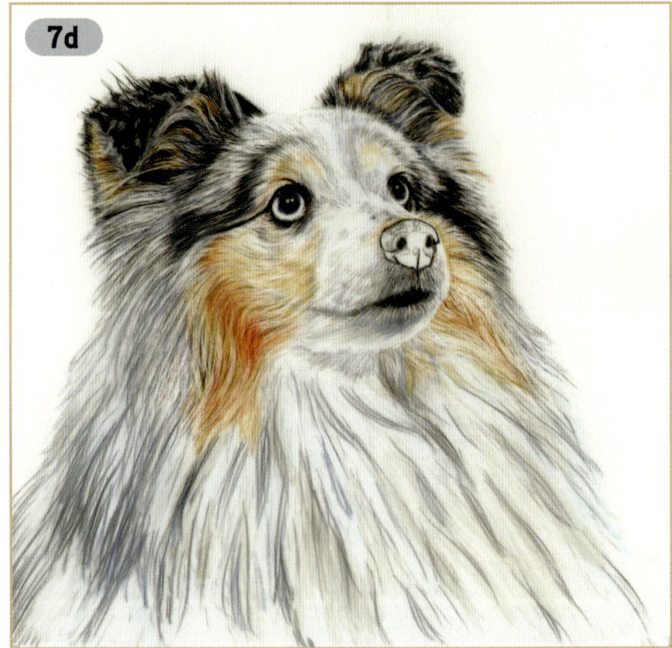

7 Now onto the knife work. Have your dusting brush to hand to sweep away any dust and pigment. Relax and, using the blade upside-down, make tapered flick strokes in the direction and to the length of the fur.

To remove chunks in an area, use a back-and-forth motion with the blade. You will remove more pigment than necessary, but the pencil layers will be repeated again. Follow the progress images for each area. Remember to vary the strokes, pressure and direction to match the fur in the reference photograph.

Work over the top left area of the head (7a) and then move onto the right-hand side (7b). Continue down through the face and cheeks (7c) before finally working on the body (7d). For the main body fur, use long tapered flicks.

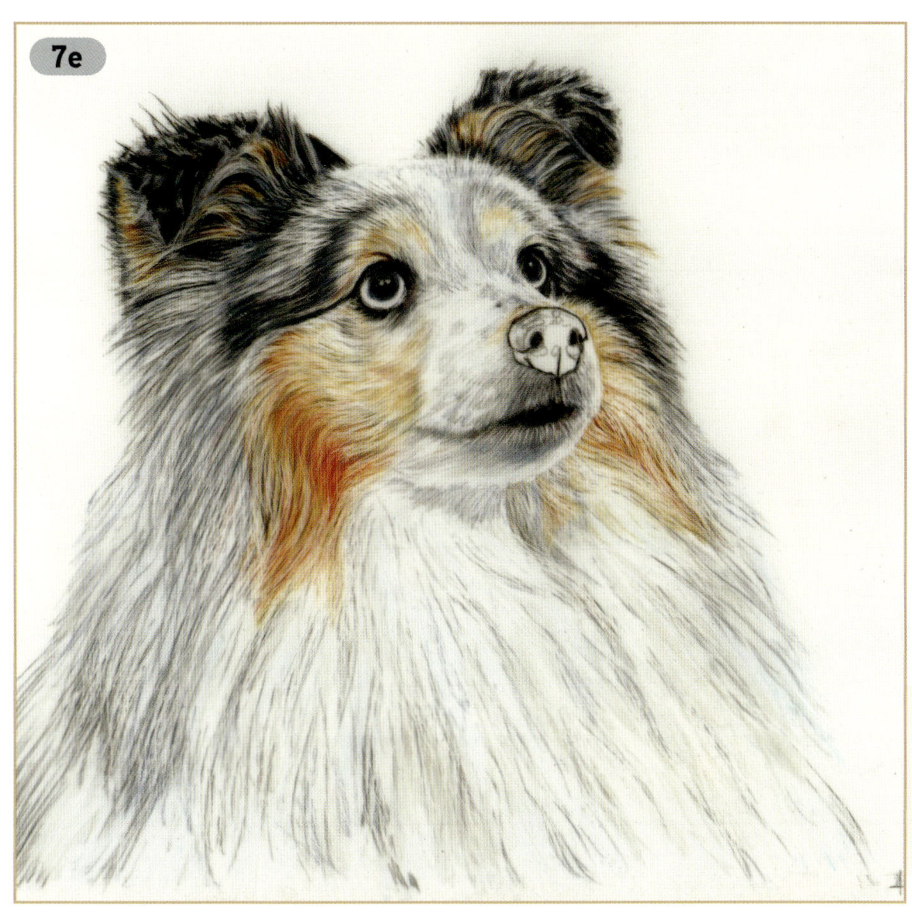

The picture at the end of step 7
Don't be concerned by the amount of colour removed – this is essential to achieving the correct finished result.

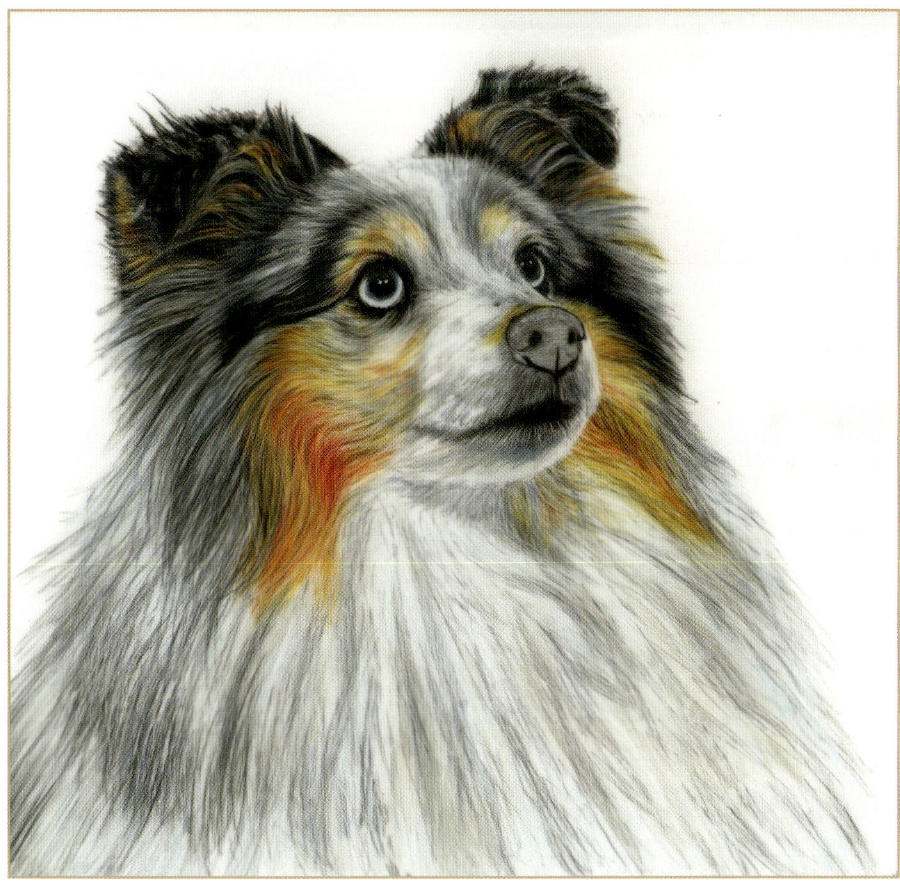

8 Repeat steps 2–5, bringing in more burnt ochre if needed to soften the oranges. Next, it's time to smoosh again. Use Lightfast arctic in the whitest areas and wheat in the orange. This time, also use mist in the greyer areas.

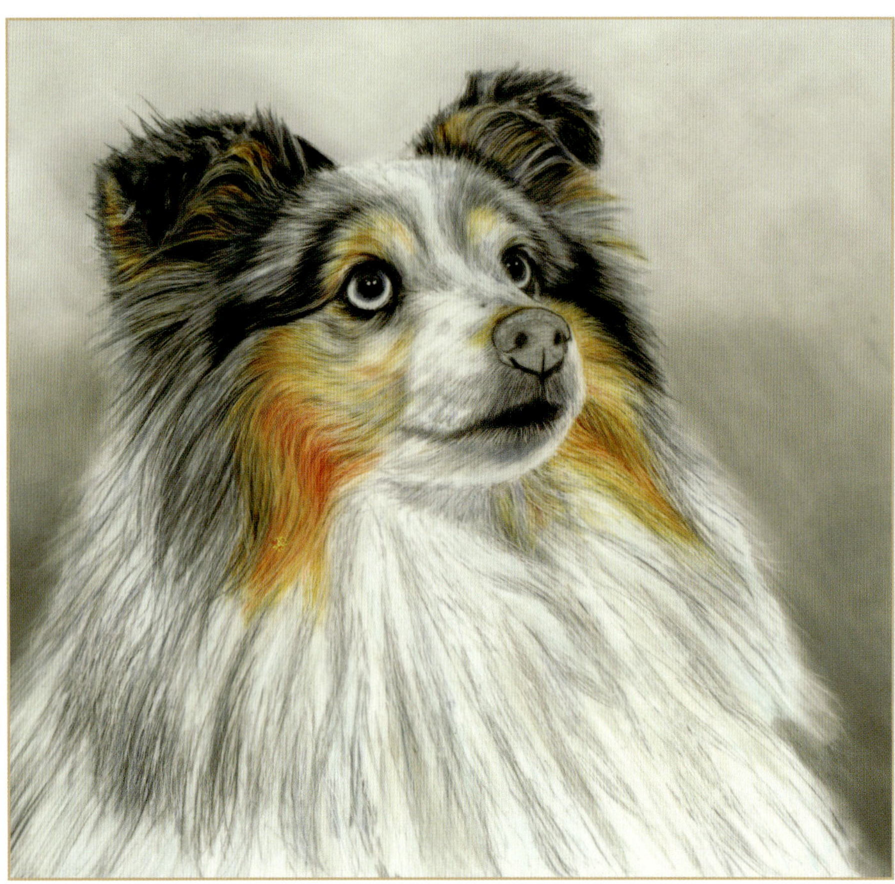

9 Add in a hint of a background using PanPastels. Gently brush on and blend layers of neutral grey tint and Payne's grey.

The background is optional – feel free to leave it plain if you prefer. Alternatively, you might like to choose your own colour palette

10 Time to work each area in detail, rotating between pencils and knife as you go along. Start at the top of the head and work the ears and forehead first, using black, cold grey V and warm grey II. Add pencil, texturize with blade and brush away, repeating as necessary. Your pencil will be skipping over the lines made by the blade.

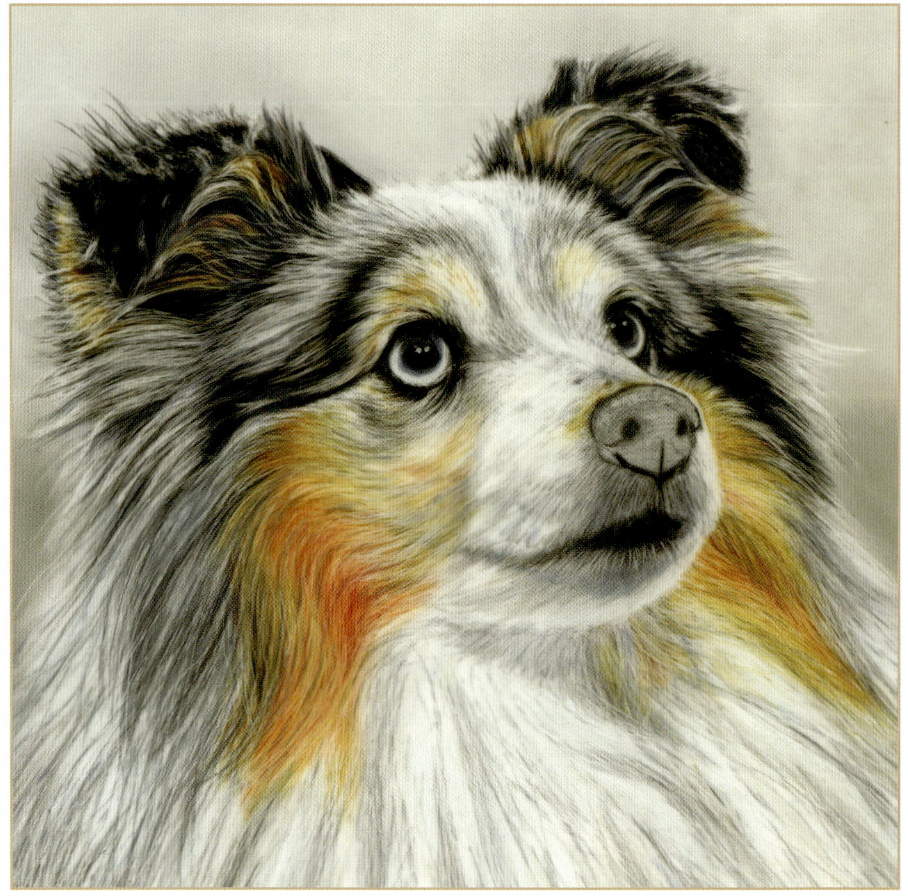

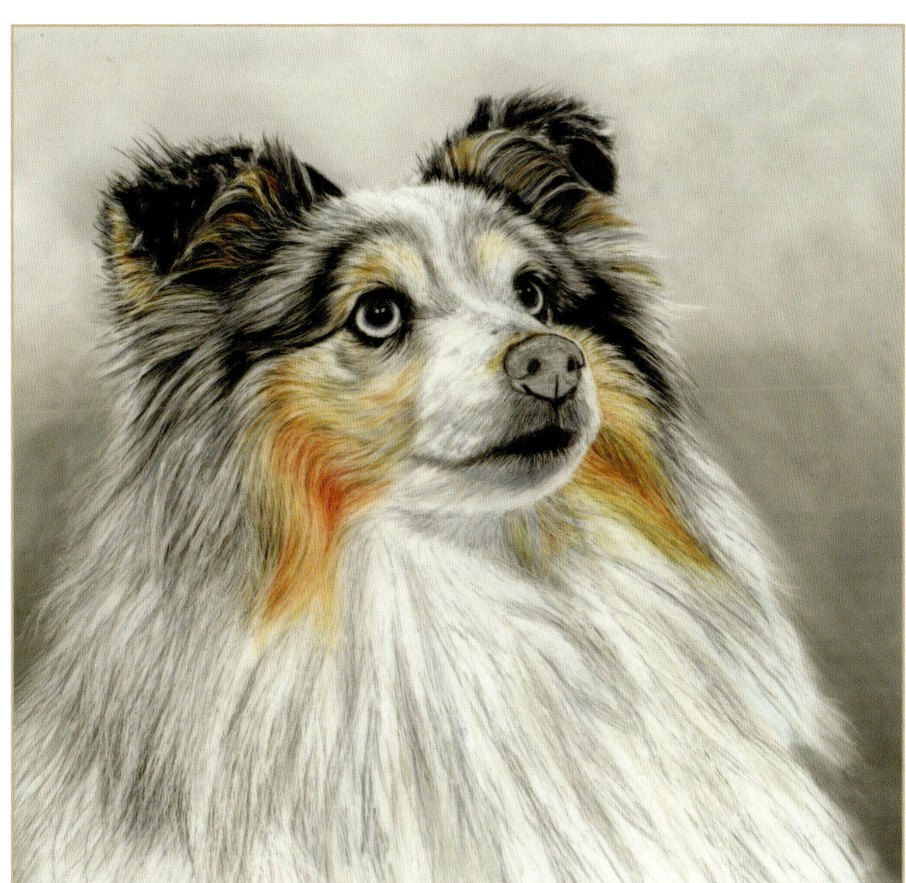

11 Continue to work in this way down the left-hand side of the body, across the middle and up the right-hand side.

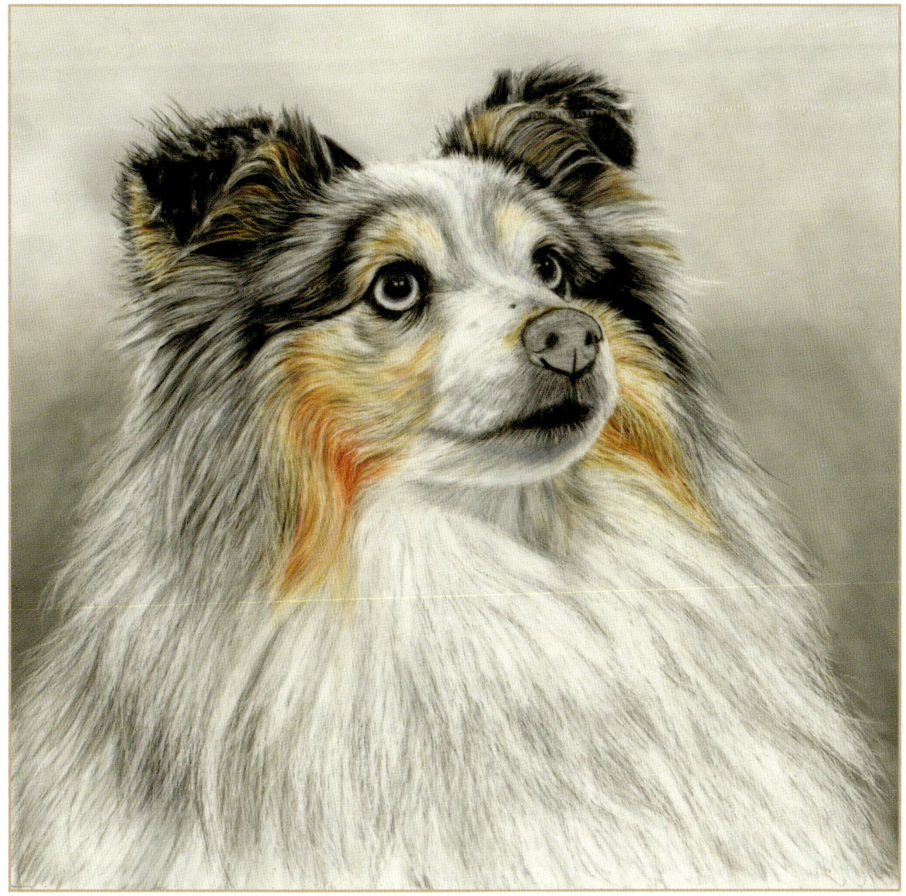

12 Soften the body fur using white and warm grey II.

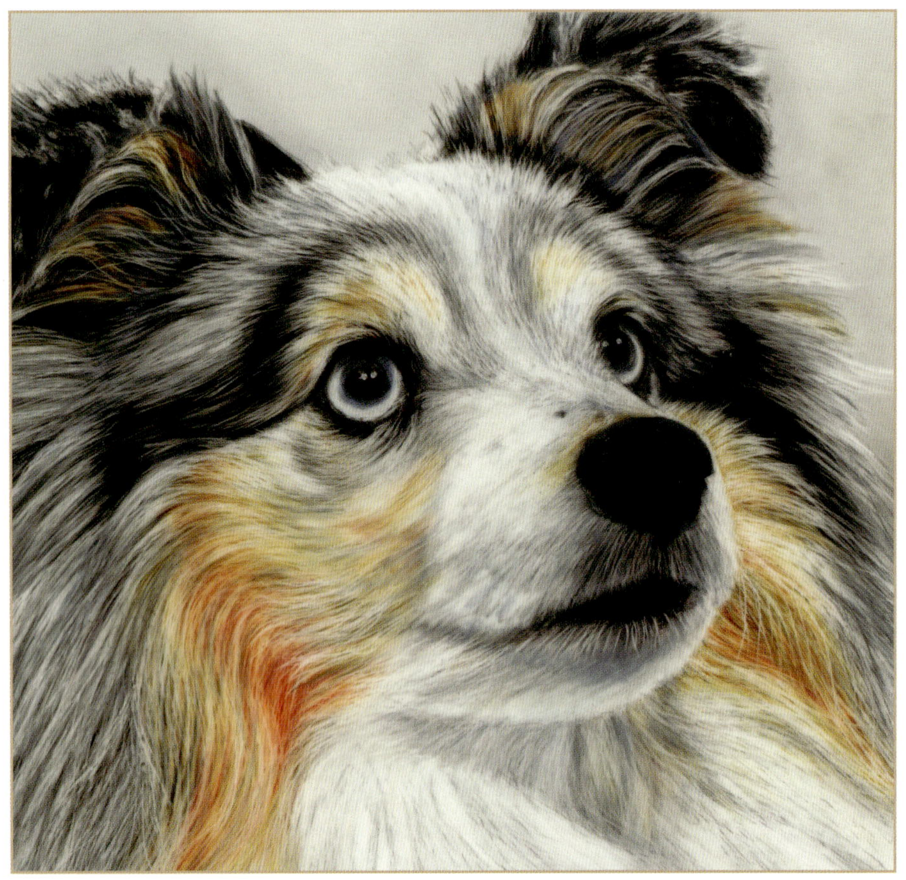

13 Add black into the nostrils and intensify the depth by adding a touch to the reverse of the film too. Using a scumbling stroke, lightly glaze black all over the nose area, building up the tone in areas by adding more layers. Add a touch of dark indigo to the top of the nose and a hint of caput mortuum to the base. Use white over the black to create the hints of grey markings. While intensifying this dark area, you may also want to increase the saturation of darks elsewhere on the portrait for balance, as your eye is drawn to these areas.

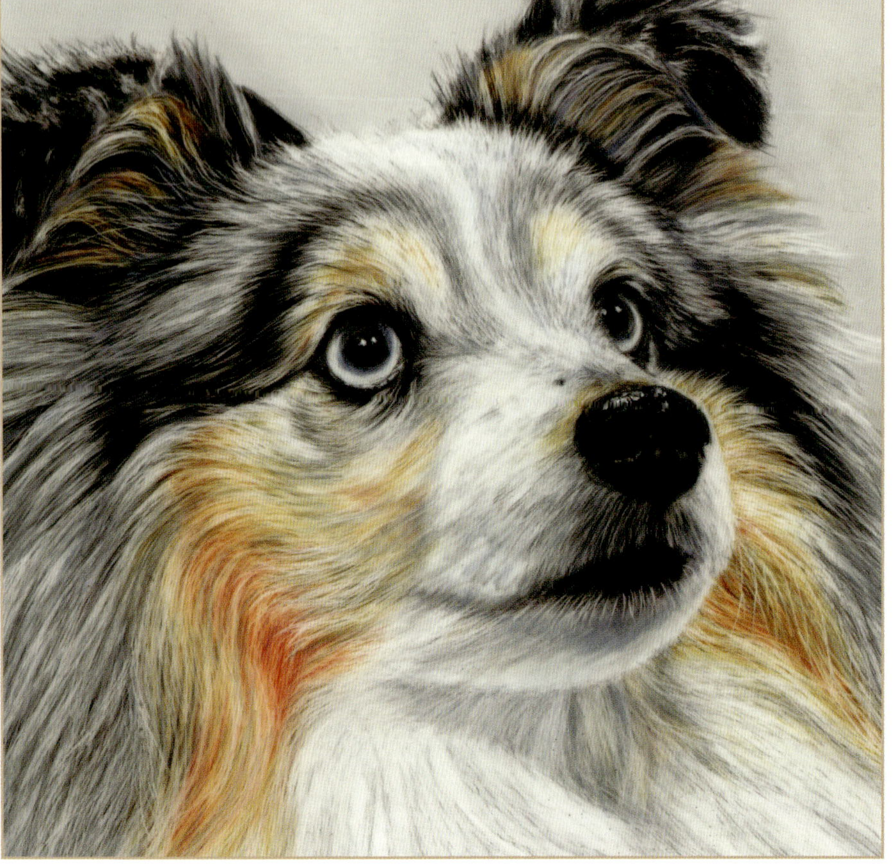

14 Texturize the nose, using the knife to lift off pigment and create the white highlights. Begin to work out from the nose into the immediate area of the muzzle to ensure continuity. To finish the portrait, all you need do is to work the muzzle a little more.

OPPOSITE:
You can repeat any of the previous fur stages to re-establish tone, colour, smoothness or texture until you are happy. Turn the film in a direction to allow you to flick your hand away naturally and confidently, then make long, firm tapered strokes to add the whiskers in. Use the Slice blade for the white whiskers and a super sharp Payne's grey for the dark ones. Next, add white into the whiskers before tweaking the front and back until you are happy. Use a white backing behind your finished portrait to intensify the knifework.

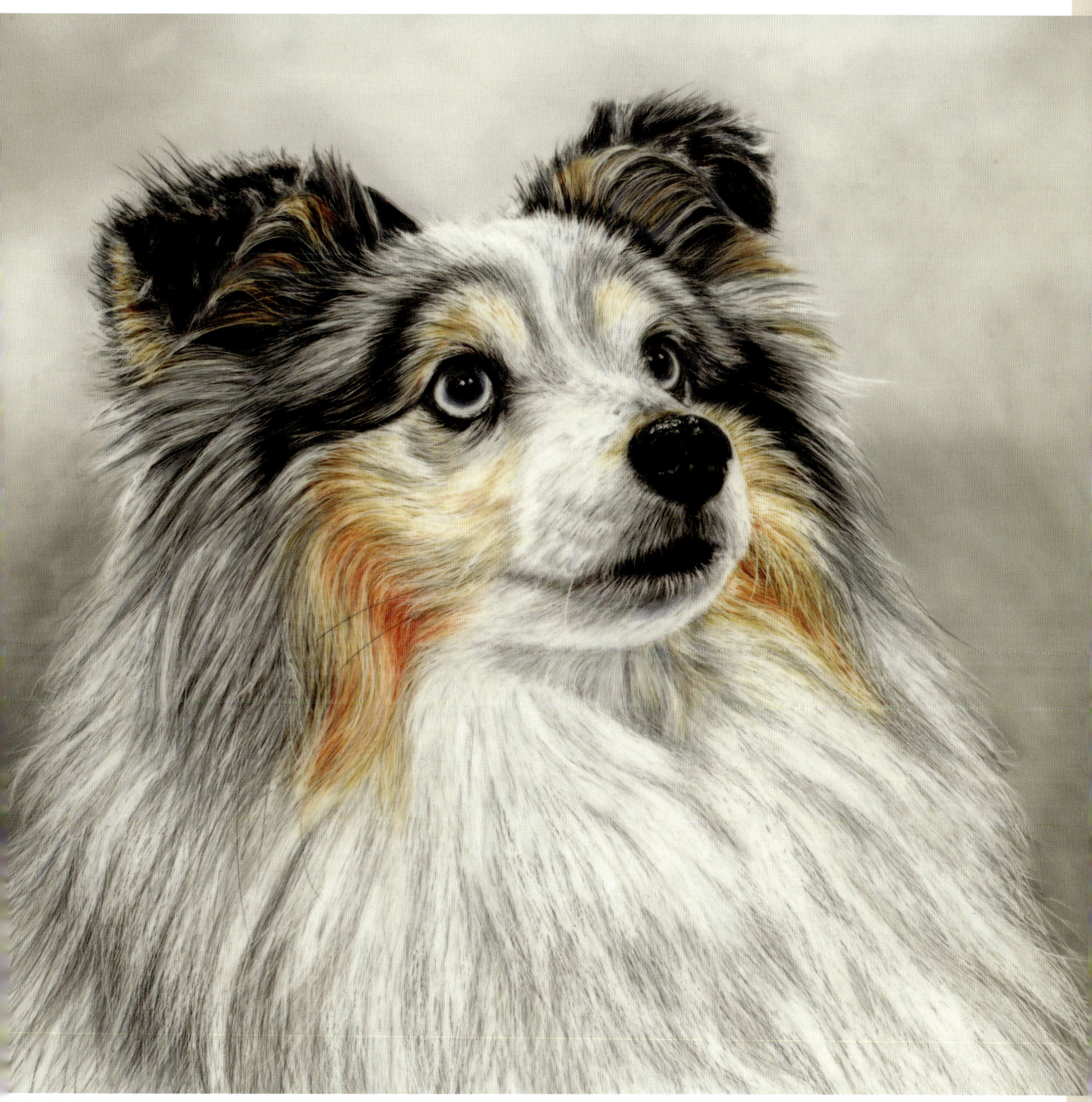

The finished portrait

BLUE

GYPSY COB HORSE

I spotted this horse quite by accident one day and his blue roan coat caught my creative eye. I chose to work him using a combination of the PanPastels and coloured pencils, working on a smooth surface.

The project combines subtraction techniques and softening using the pastels. It is a fantastic opportunity for creating lots of different textures with both short and long hair.

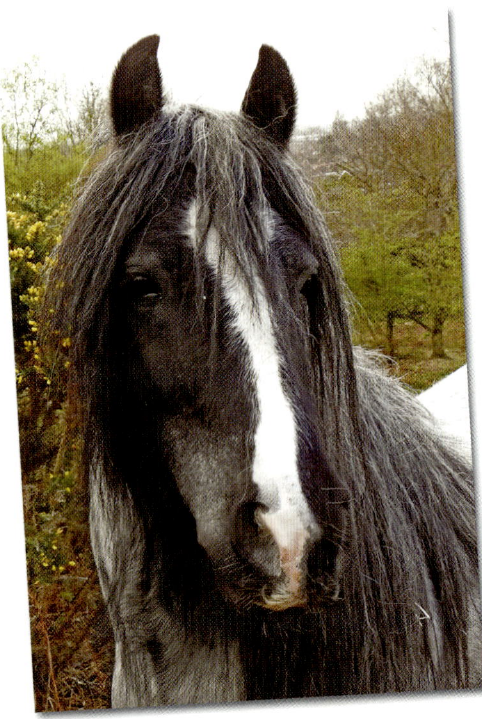

The reference photograph used for this project.

1 Transfer the line art using a stylus and the indenting method described on page 49. The lines appear very faintly on the surface, so the colour in this picture has been exaggerated for the sake of clarity.

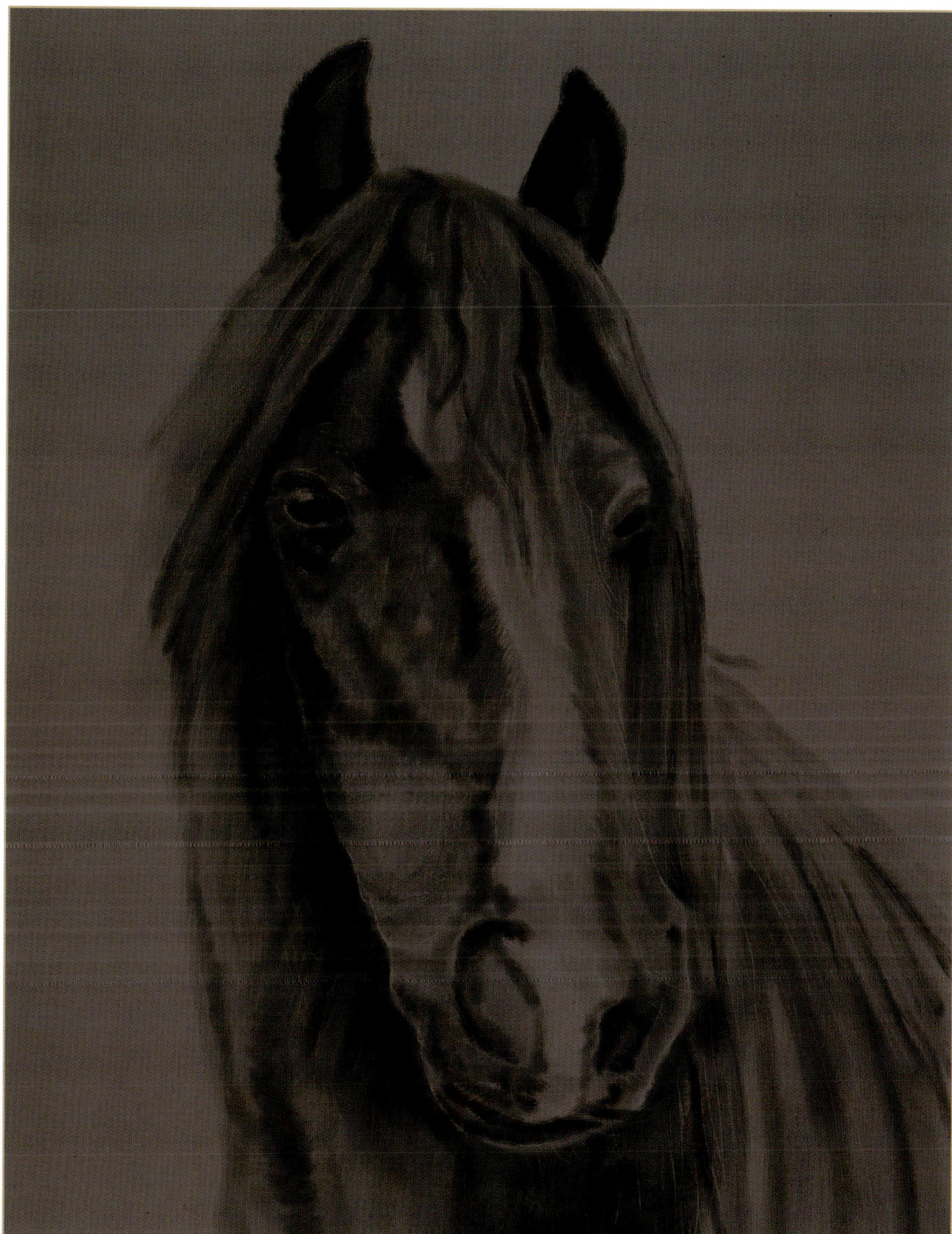

2 Begin by adding tone using black PanPastel. Pick up a small amount
of pastel onto the Sofft tool applicator and then add a light layer to
the surface. Using a dabbing method to apply the pastel. This helps to
press the pastel into the tooth and avoids any dust or contamination
as the layers build. Add more layers in the darker areas to build the
depth of tonal value.

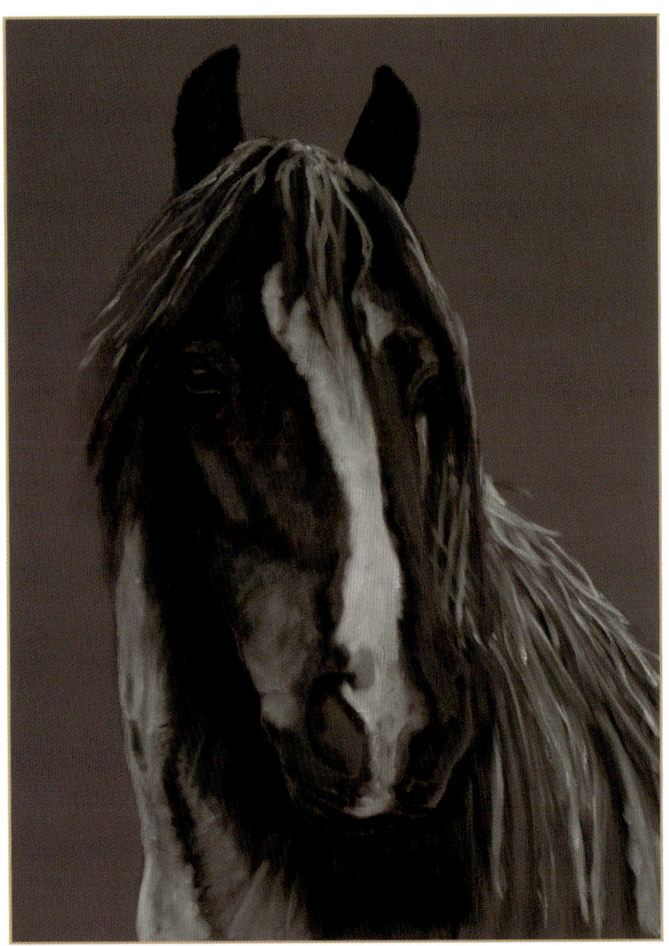 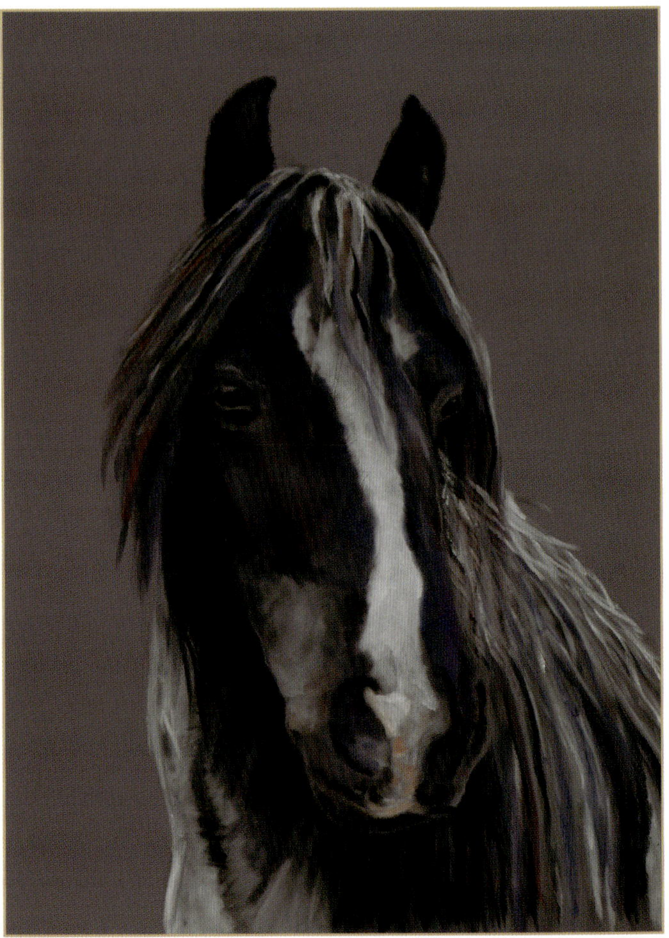

3 Next add in the highlight areas using white PanPastel, following the same method as for the black. Use the flat of the sponge applicator as well as the sides and tip.

4 Add some colour now, continuing with the dab application method. Begin with Payne's grey in the darkest blue-tinted areas, ultramarine blue extra dark in the brighter blue areas, violet shade where there are purplish hues, and red iron oxide shade where you see reds in the reference photograph.

5 Time to utilize those subtraction techniques now, using the eraser and the knife. This is done ahead of any of the pencil work in order to break up the bigger chunks of pastel. Start within the mane, using the eraser first and then the knife. The latter will help to form some fine channels for the pencils to lay down in. Use the eraser on the face if you need to lift any pigment or correct any mistakes. When you lift any pigment, it is the colour of the underlying surface that shows through – bear this in mind if you are using a different colour support.

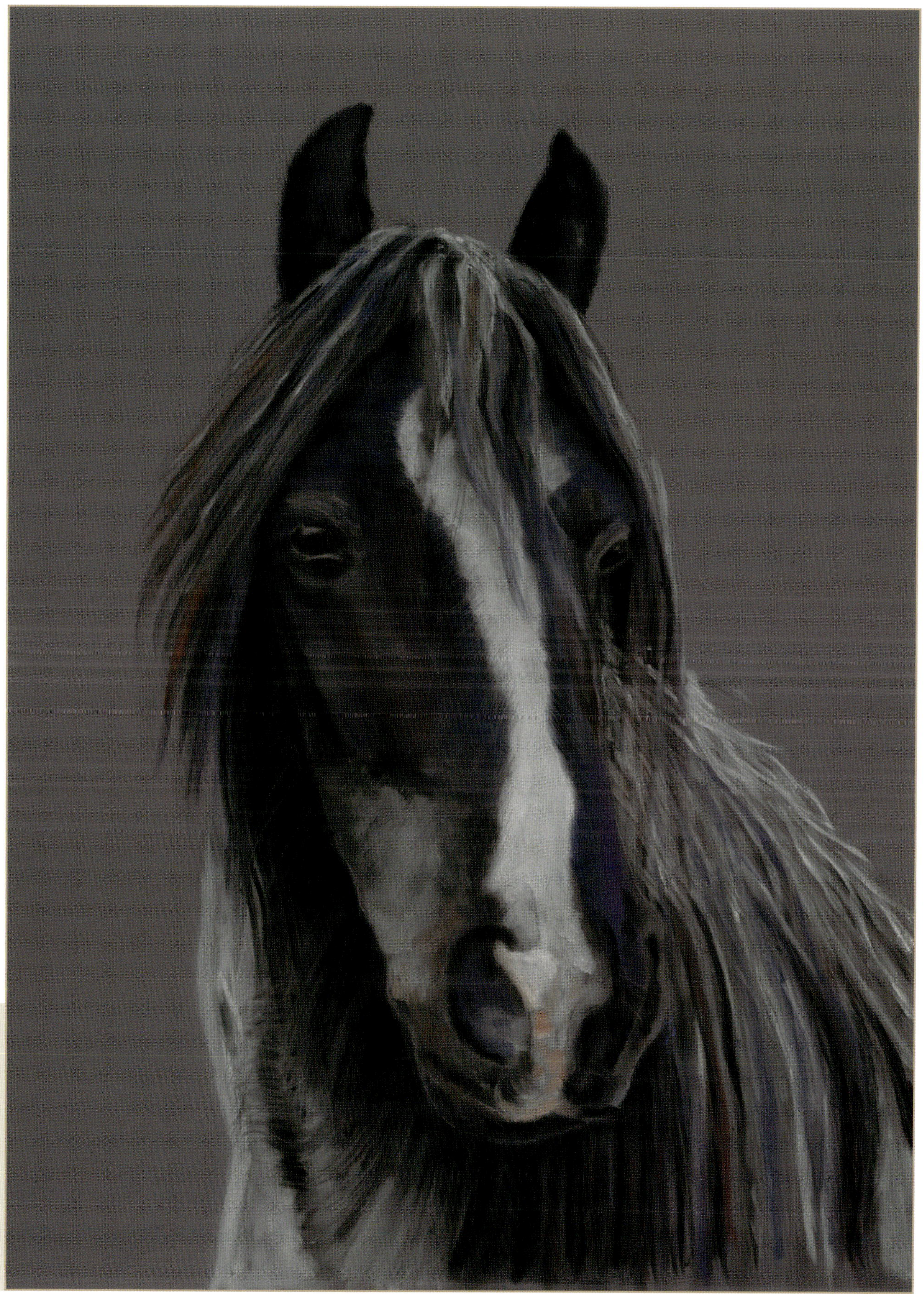

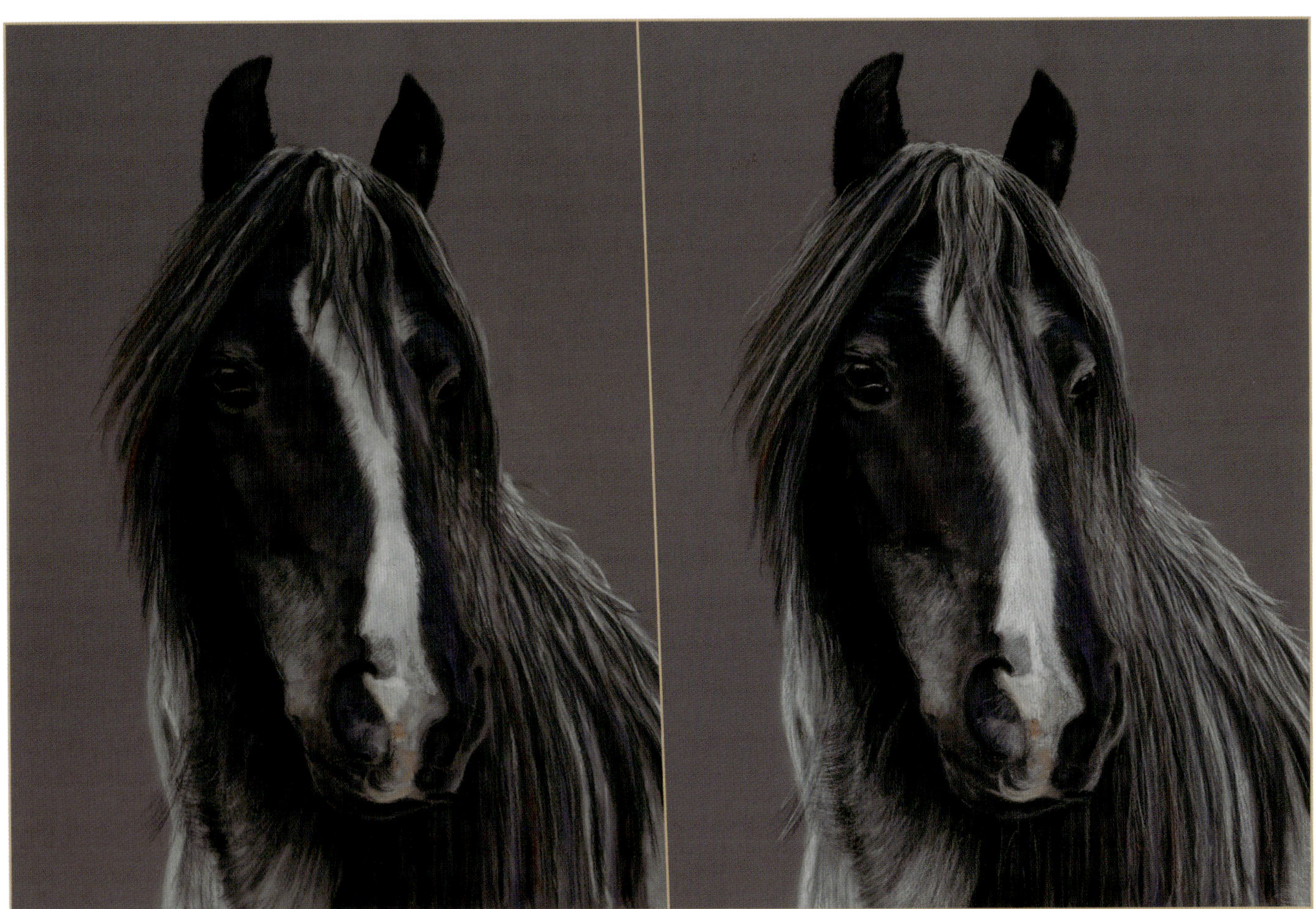

6 With the pastel base complete, it's time to move on to the pencil work. These initial layers are simply colour blocking, which presses the pastel down into the tooth of the support a little more. Each layer breaks down the previous bigger blocks of colour and tone into smaller ones, refining the image with each sweep. Start with black and then follow with the white in exactly the same order as the PanPastels were laid down. Use varying strokes appropriate to the area: long and tapered through the mane, short flicks across the face and stipple marks on the side of the muzzle.

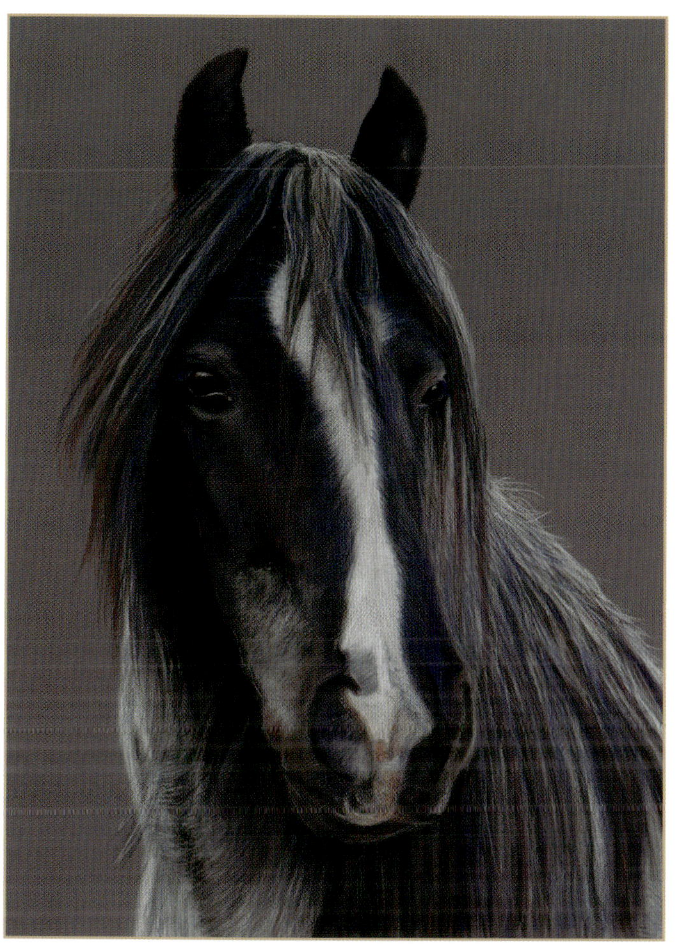 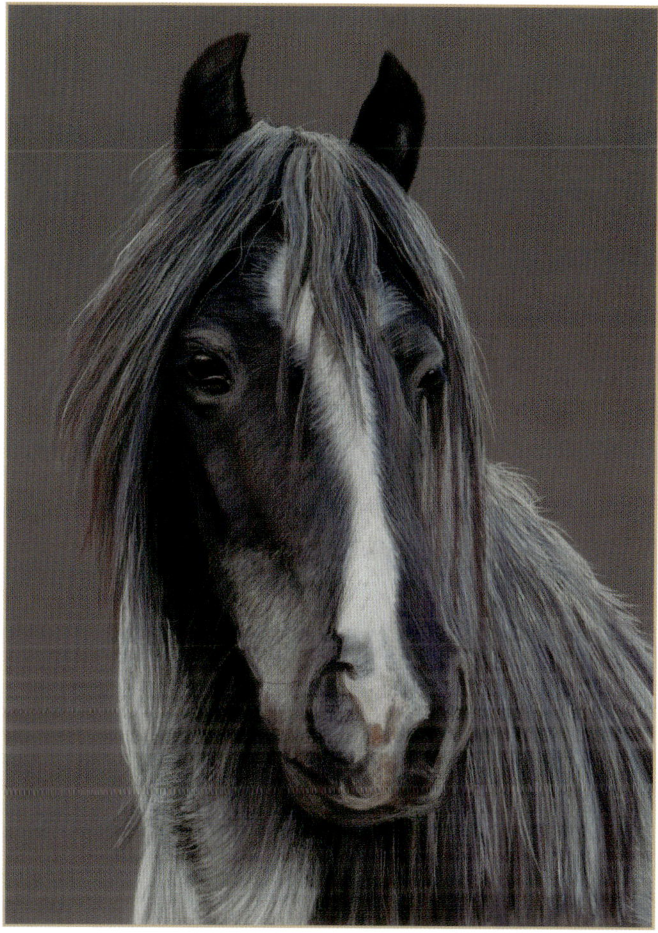

7 Move up through the mid-tones next, starting with indigo blue, Prussian blue and burnt sienna to pull out those blues and reds again. Greyish black and bistre will start to soften the bright highlights, creating some of the dirty-looking greys in the mane and hair.

8 Finally, move up to the lights. Use ash grey in the softer warmer grey areas. Work from mouse grey to silver grey then up to white in the cooler highlight areas. Pop in a touch of Mars violet into those soft light purplish areas.

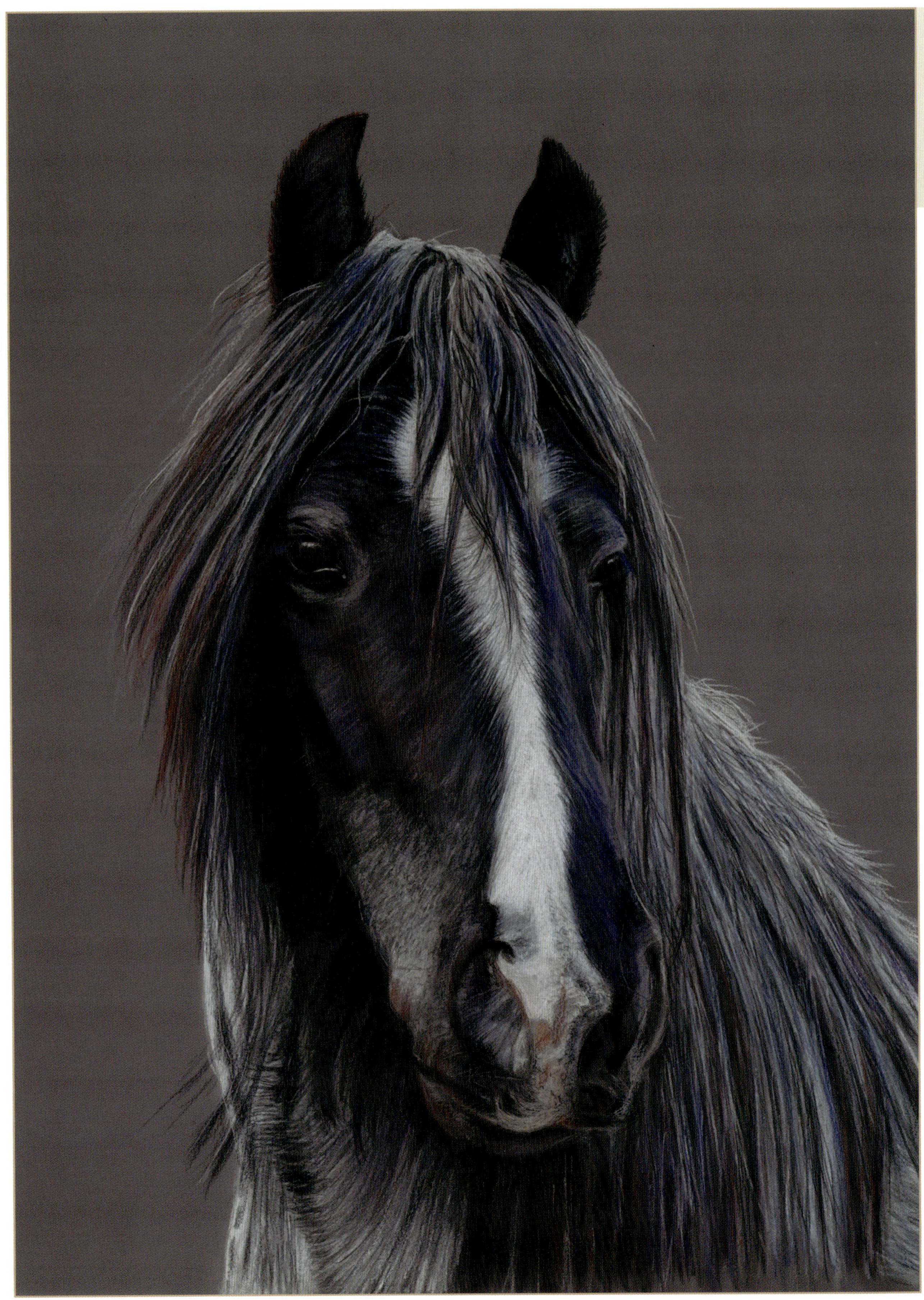

9 Repeat from step 6, working from darks up through the mid-tones using black, indigo blue, Prussian blue and burnt sienna.

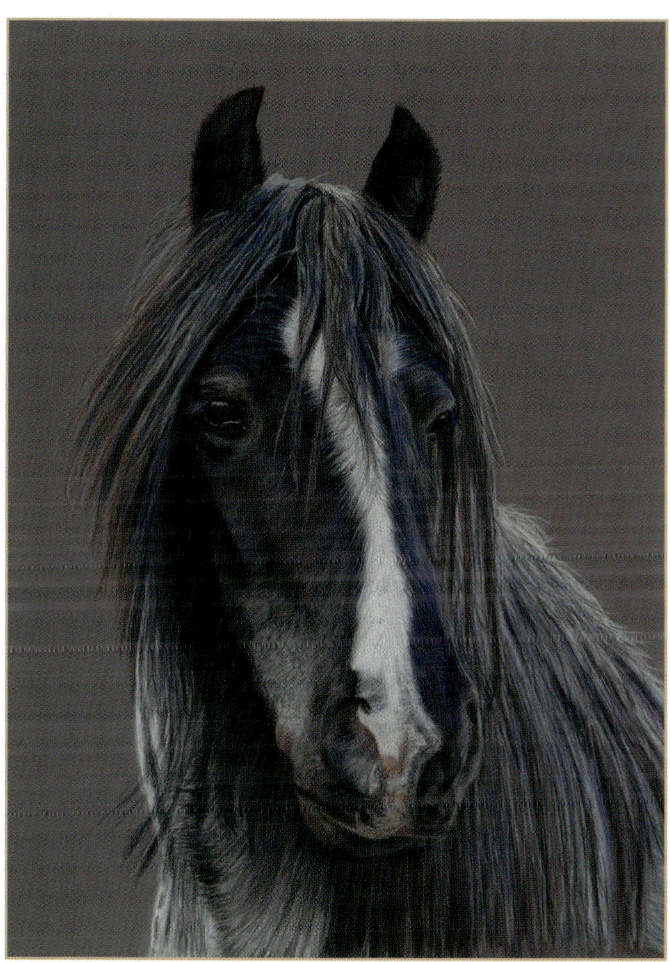

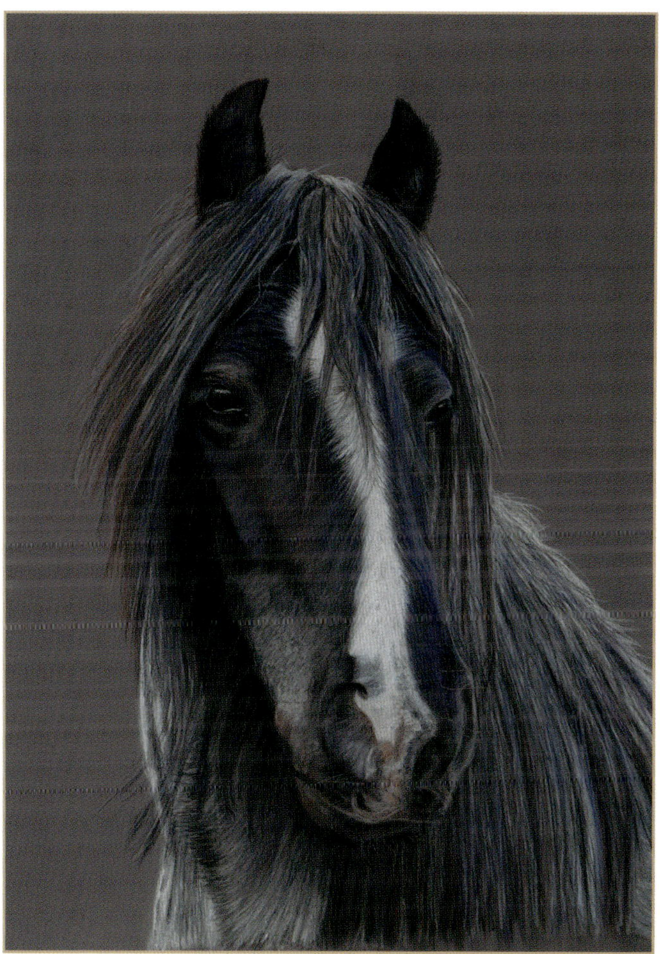

10 Continue to work up through the layers with greyish black, mouse grey, bistre, brownish orange and brownish beige. Keep looking at that reference photograph and remember to keep varying those different strokes!

11 Before going in with the lights, use the knife to subtract once again. This time, pay more attention to the direction and length of the strokes. As with the pencils, use long tapering strokes on the mane, short flicks over the face and stipple marks on the side of the muzzle.

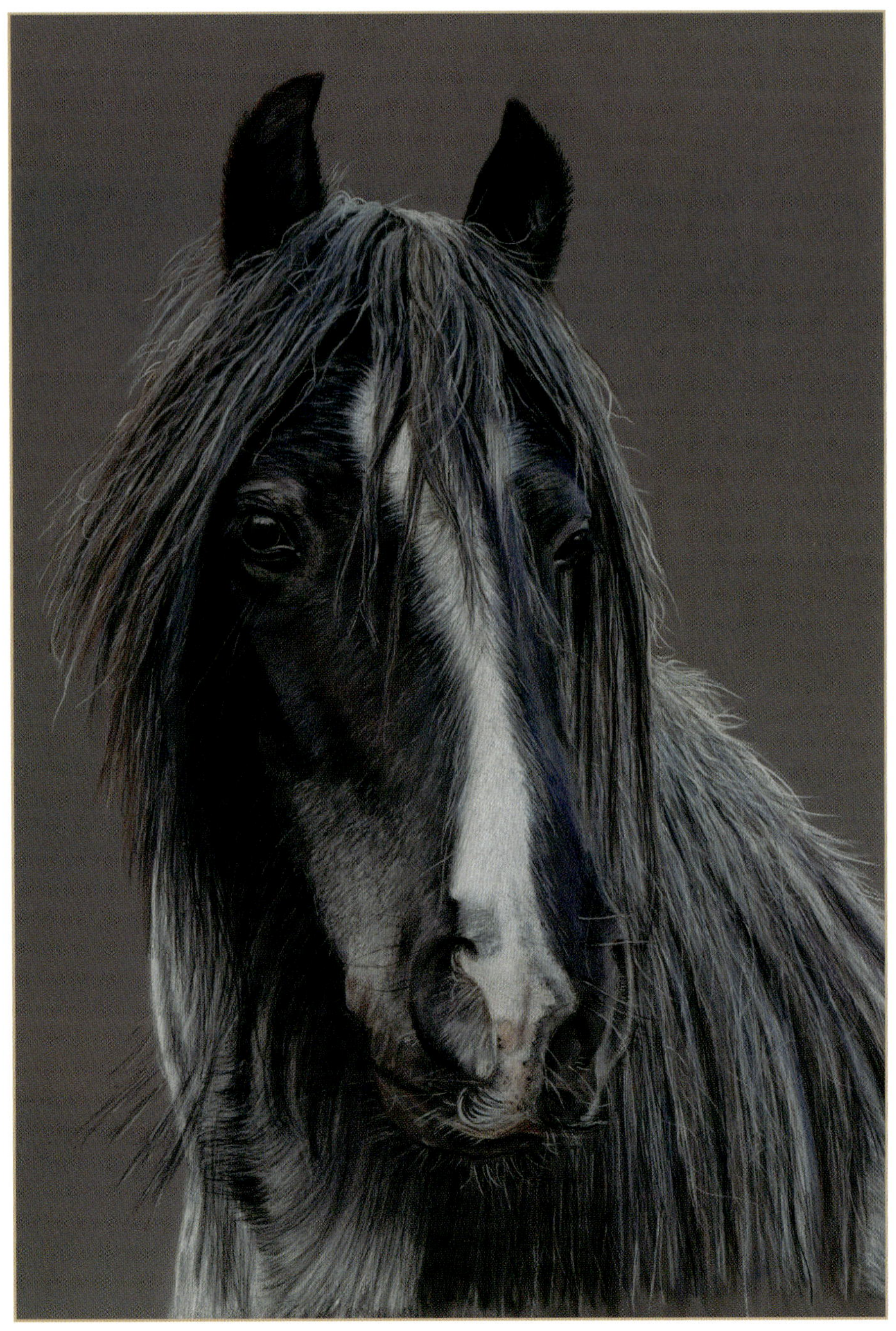

12 You need to keep sharpening your pencil after every few strokes with these final layers. Start with your lights: the greys, white and violet. Next, repeat any of the darks and colours if you feel you have lost them along the way. You can keep repeating the pencil layers, refining with each layer until you are happy with the look of the detail. Again, you must keep those pencils sharp! While those pencils are sharp, add in those little whiskers and loose hairs. Keep the pencil strokes over the mane loose and random in their direction, or the hair will look too uniform.

13 Tweak as much as you choose now. One last thing that I did was to go back in with my Sofft tool applicator to gently soften a few areas, mainly in the neck hair but also a small touch in the face.

The finished portrait

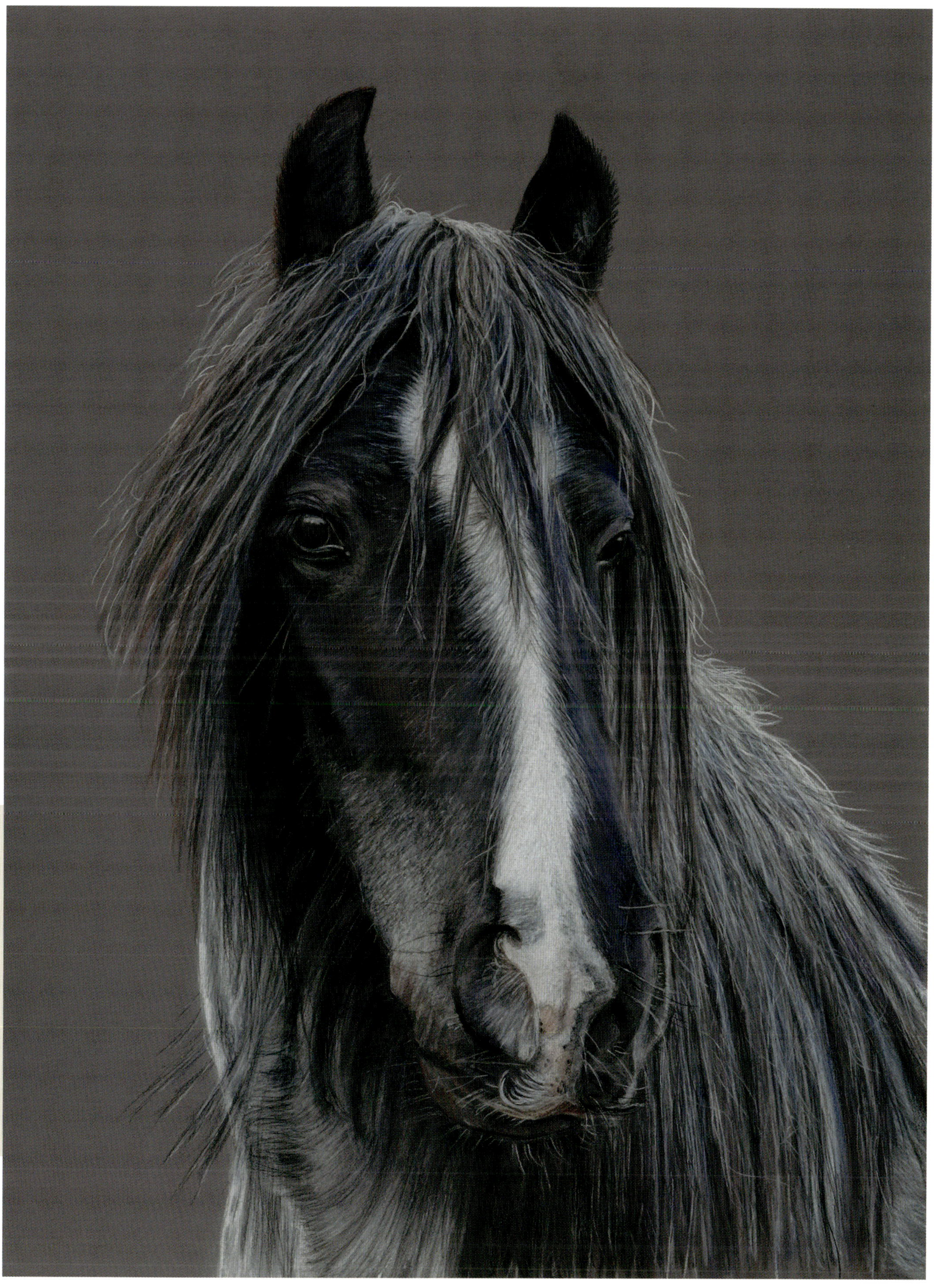

BRANDY

RED ANGUS COW

Brandy was another animal that I spotted from the roadside and felt compelled to track down with my camera. The sun caught the rich red colours of her body and I knew she had to be portrayed. I chose the suede mat board here as it helped with creating all that fluffy randomness to her coat. Be careful: the pigment soaks into the board and fades in between applications; so this project teaches yet another lesson of patience and repetition.

Remember, this is your rendition. It should have the look and feel of the reference but does not have to be an exact copy.

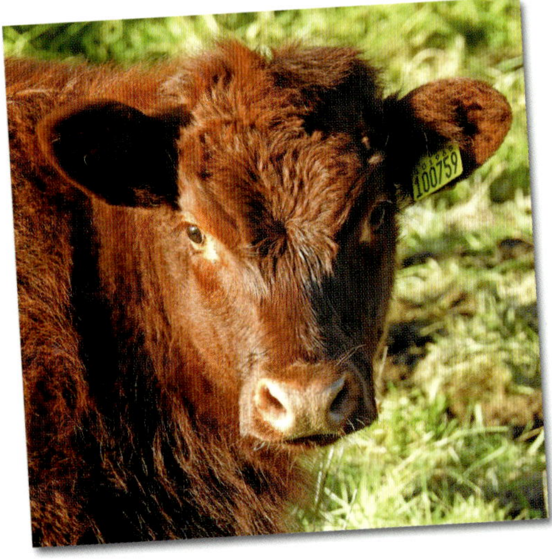

The reference photograph used for this project.

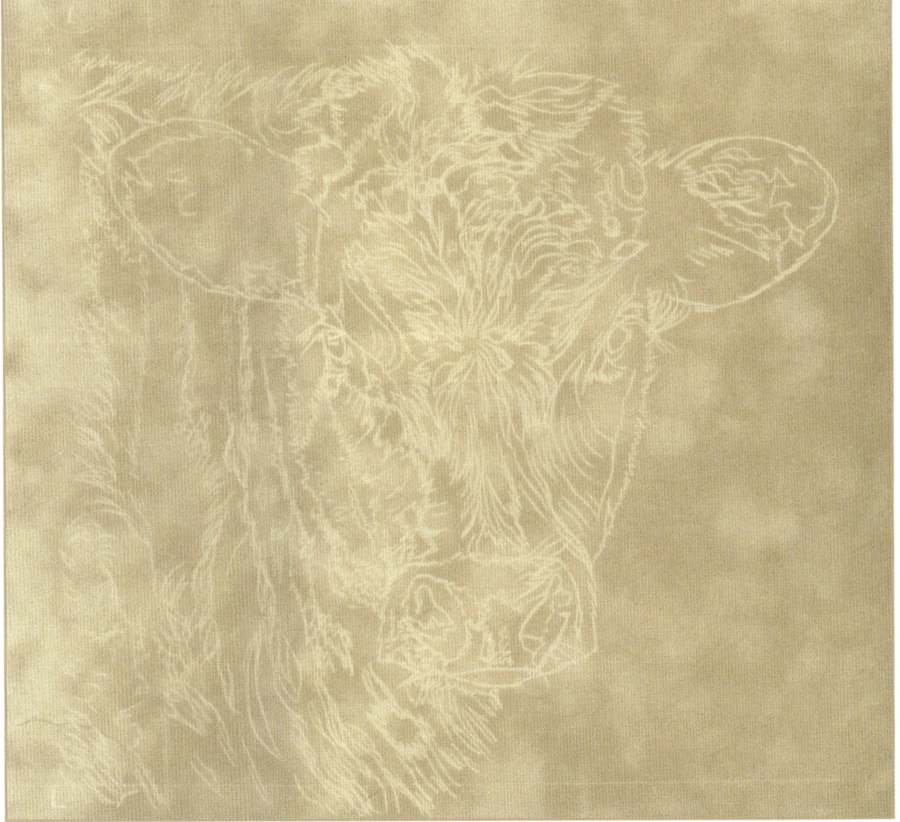

1 Transfer the line art using a stylus and the indenting method detailed on page 49.

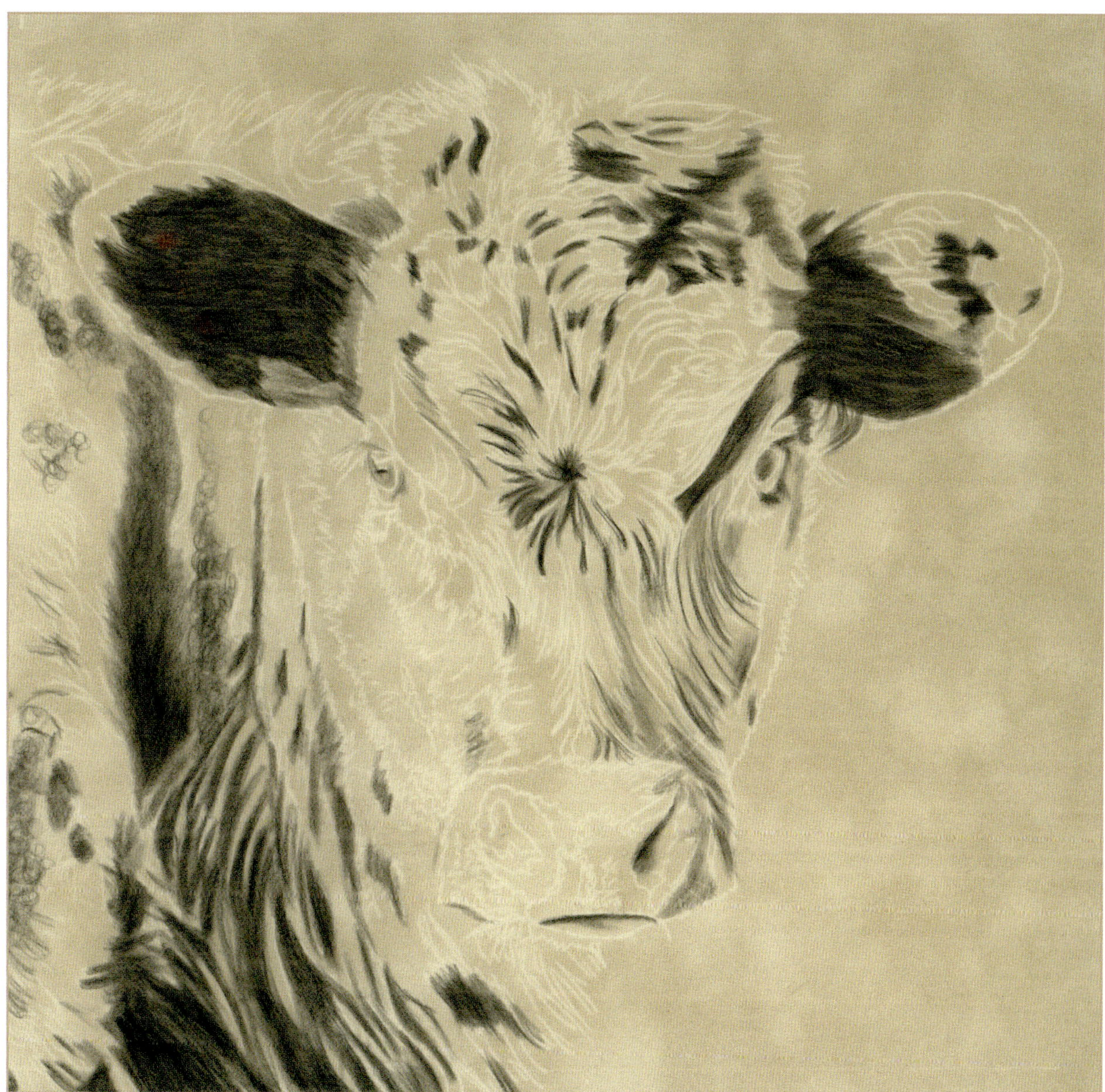

2 Use black to colour block in the darkest shapes from your reference. Depending on the type of hair texture, use a standard pressure and either a back-and-forth application or a loose circlular stroke. Inside the ears, for example, a back-and-forth stroke works best, while the neck and shoulder area is best approached with loose circles of varying size. In areas that need a deeper saturation of tone or colour, add more layers.

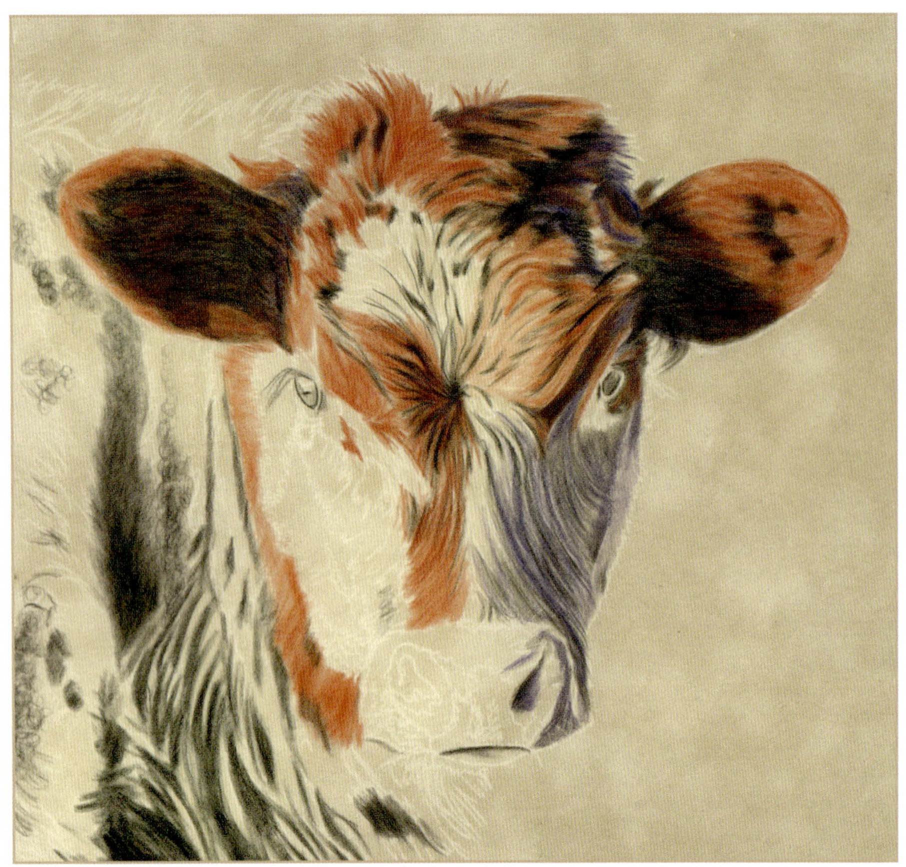

3 Next add in the brown and purplish coloured areas using the same method described in step 2 on the previous page. Use brown and indigo blue. Glaze some of this colour over the black shapes initially laid down. Note that the right-hand side of the face has a suprisingly large amount of the purple colour.

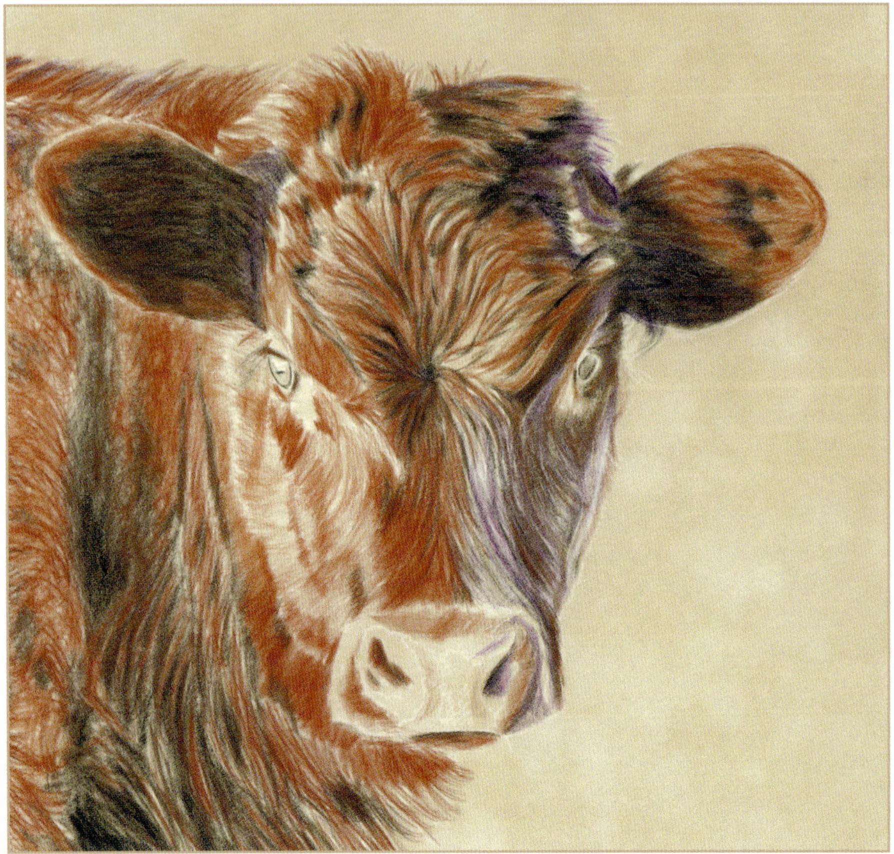

4 Glaze caput mortuum violet and more black into the ears and dark shadows.

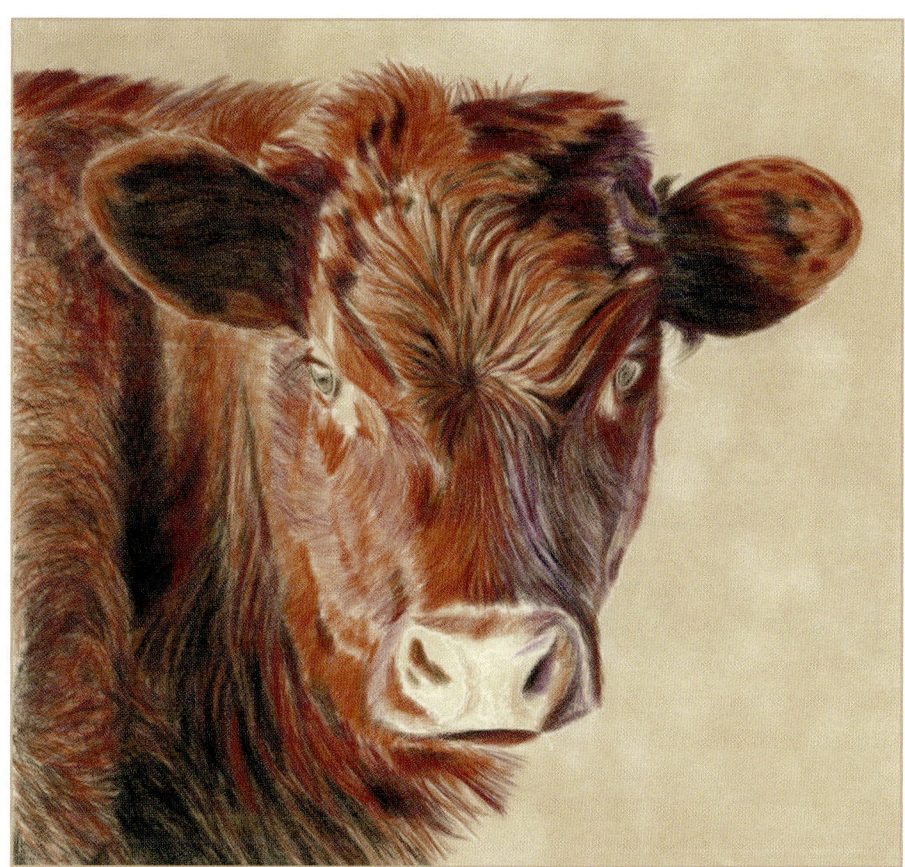

5 Glaze caput mortuum violet over the purplish right-hand side of the face to blend with the indigo blue.

6 Once happy with the tone and the saturation of colour all over, apply a light layer of solvent to sink the pigment down into the surface. Use a minimal amount of solvent to do this, taking off any excess from the brush with kitchen paper before applying it to the board. Work in a well-ventilated area and leave the artwork to dry overnight.

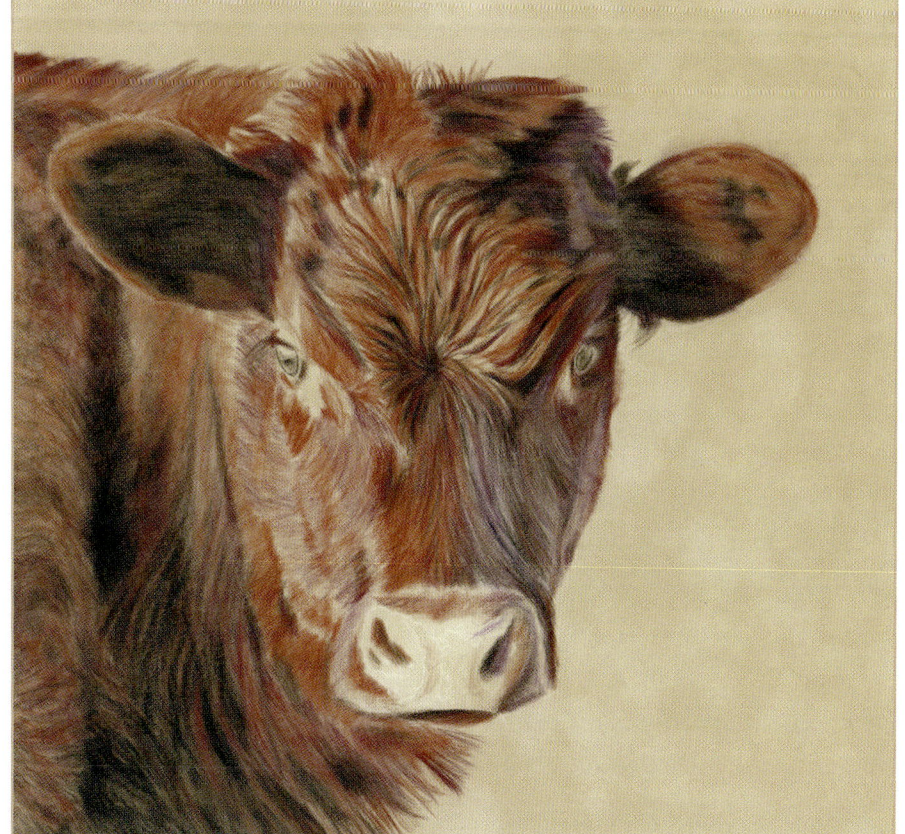

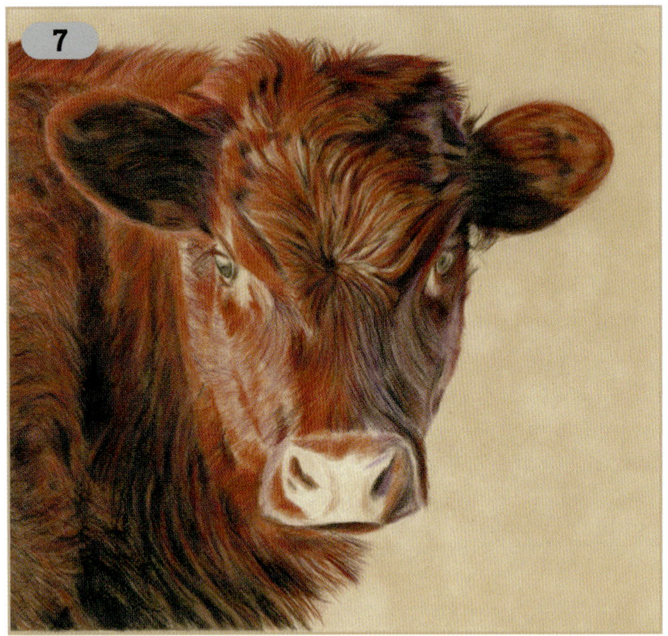

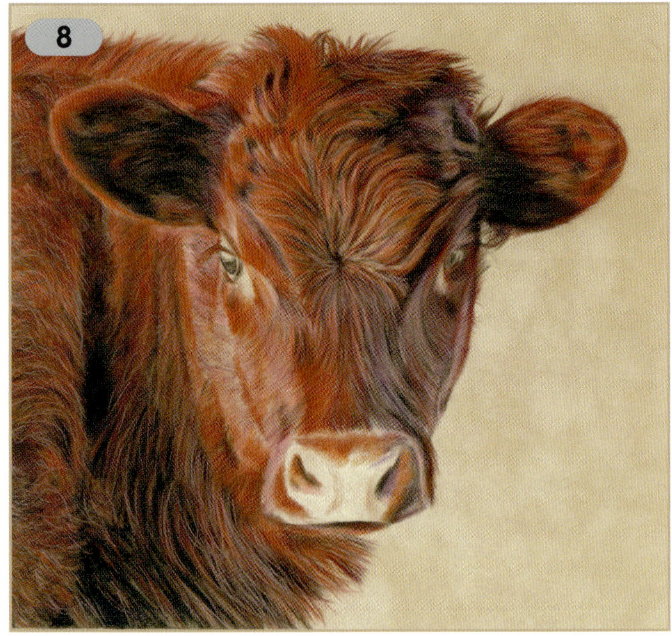

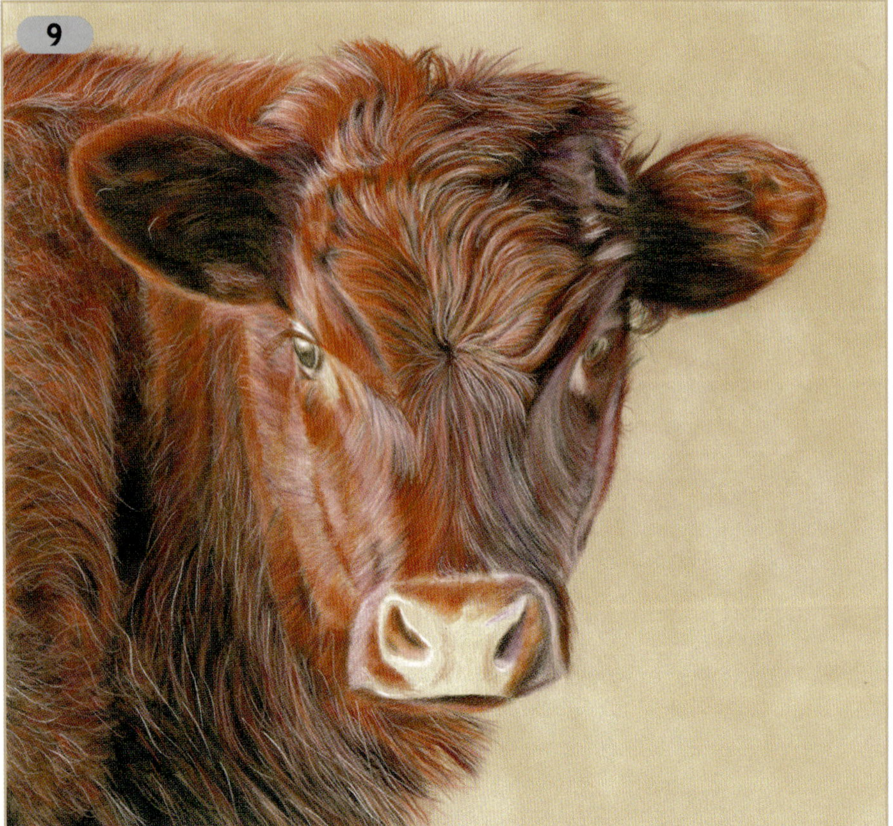

7 Intensify the darkest markings once more, using black and brown. Begin to use tapering flicks in your application of pigment, following the length and direction of the hairs. Keep a close eye on your reference photograph at all times!

8 Start to build some mid-tones next using the same method of application as the previous step. Use burnt sienna to soften some of the brownish hues. Add russet to the brightest orangey areas and then touches of cinnamon to the pinkish ones.

9 Time to add in the first layer of highlights with ash grey. Continue to use tapering flicks, and follow the length and direction of the hairs. Squint at your reference to help differentiate the highlights and shadows.

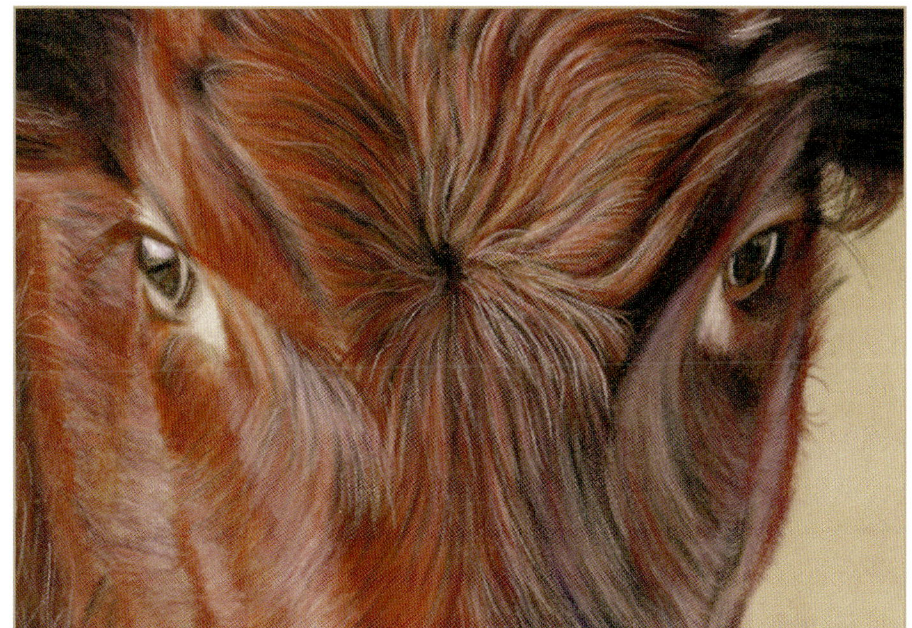

10 Now that we have a good initial foundation of the tones and colours all over, it is time to focus on the eyes and muzzle. The eyes should already have a touch of dark tone in there from the initial application layers. Pop in the highlight on both eyes using white, then add a touch of Prussian blue to the highlight in the left eye. Use black and a touch of russet to intensify the darks. Glaze over the iris with brownish beige. Finally, add cream to the skin surrounding the left eye. This will make the eye itself pop forwards.

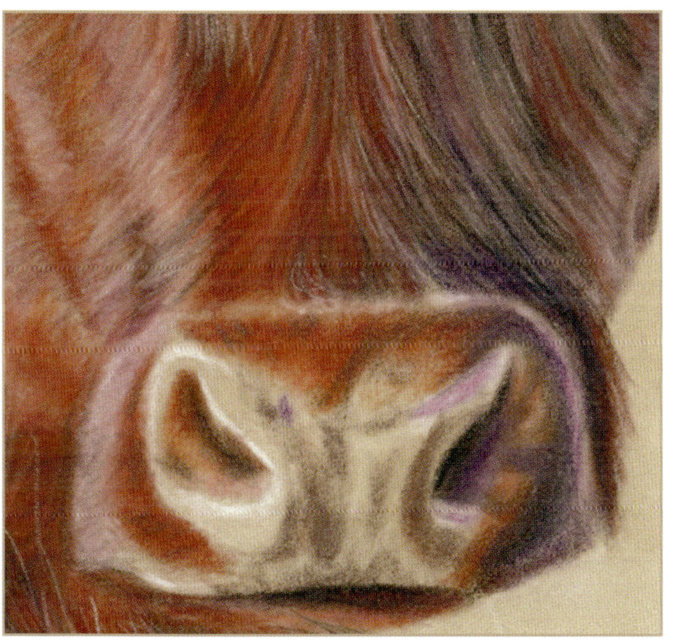

11 For the muzzle, begin by adding brown, bistre and a touch of indigo blue to create the initial dark markings.

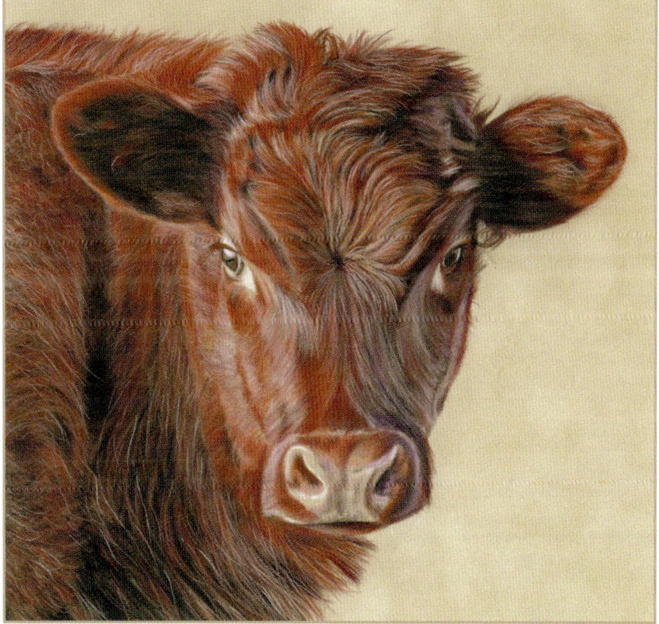

12 Scumble the mid-tones over the darks using burnt sienna in the brown areas, more bistre in the grey areas and cinnamon in the pinkish ones.

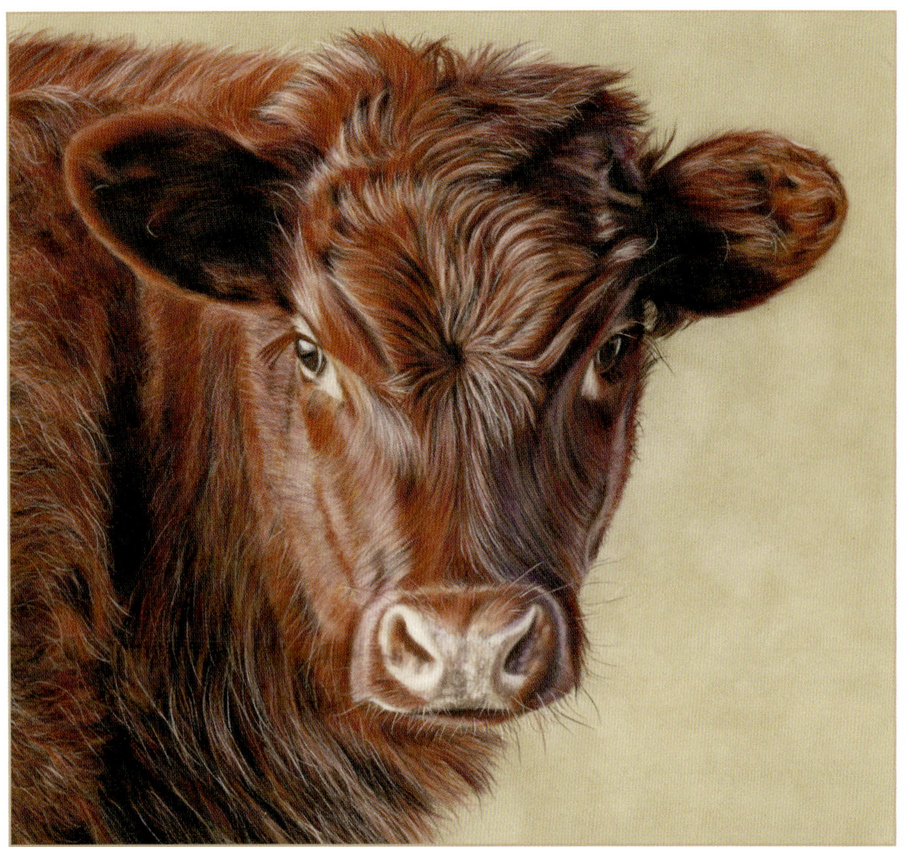

13 Add highlights and texture next. Let the ash grey create most of the highlight effect, and build extra layers where you need a brighter, more intense effect. Soften the transitions of the darks to lights using cinnamon and brown. Create the bobbly texture by stippling using cream, bistre and beige. Repeat if needed.

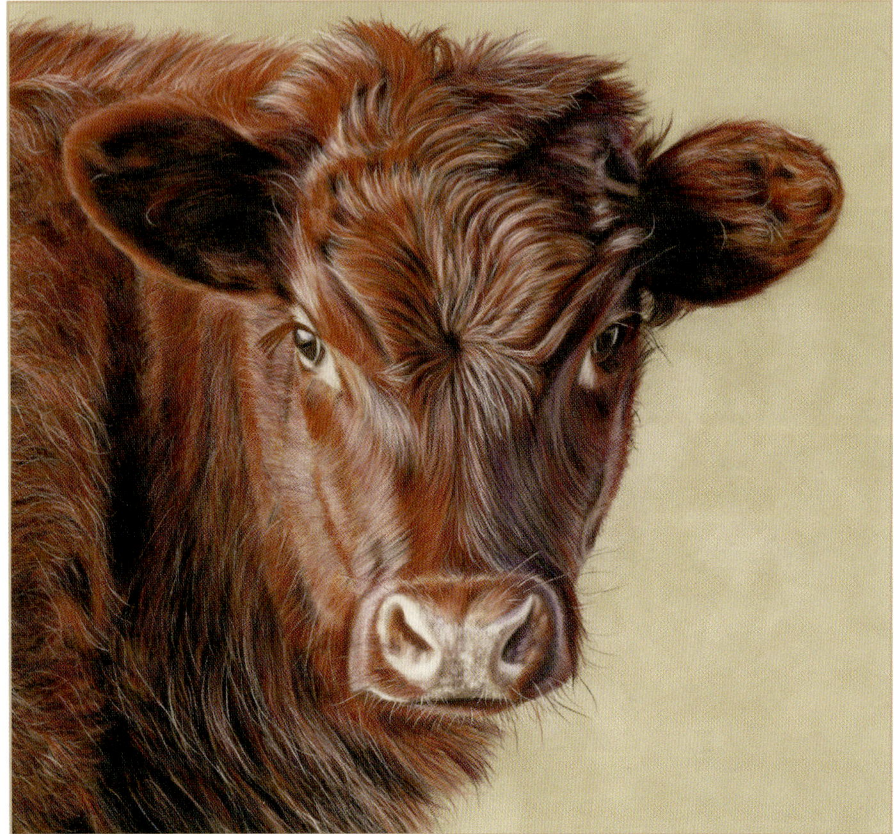

14 Repeat the process from step 7, working dark-to-light. Keep your pencils sharp now as you start to really build on top of the colour blocks to create the hair texture. Continue to work your pencils using strokes to match the length and direction of the cow's hair. Use black, brown, russet, indigo blue, caput mortuum violet, brownish orange, ash grey and ivory. Keep repeating this stage until you are happy with the result.

15 Step back, assess, then tweak any tones, colours and shapes you feel necessary.
For the final touches, use super sharp pencils to add in the fine hairs, whiskers and lashes.
Soften any transitions of these hairs so that they do not just sit on top of the surface. Your
cow should now be at the finishing point.

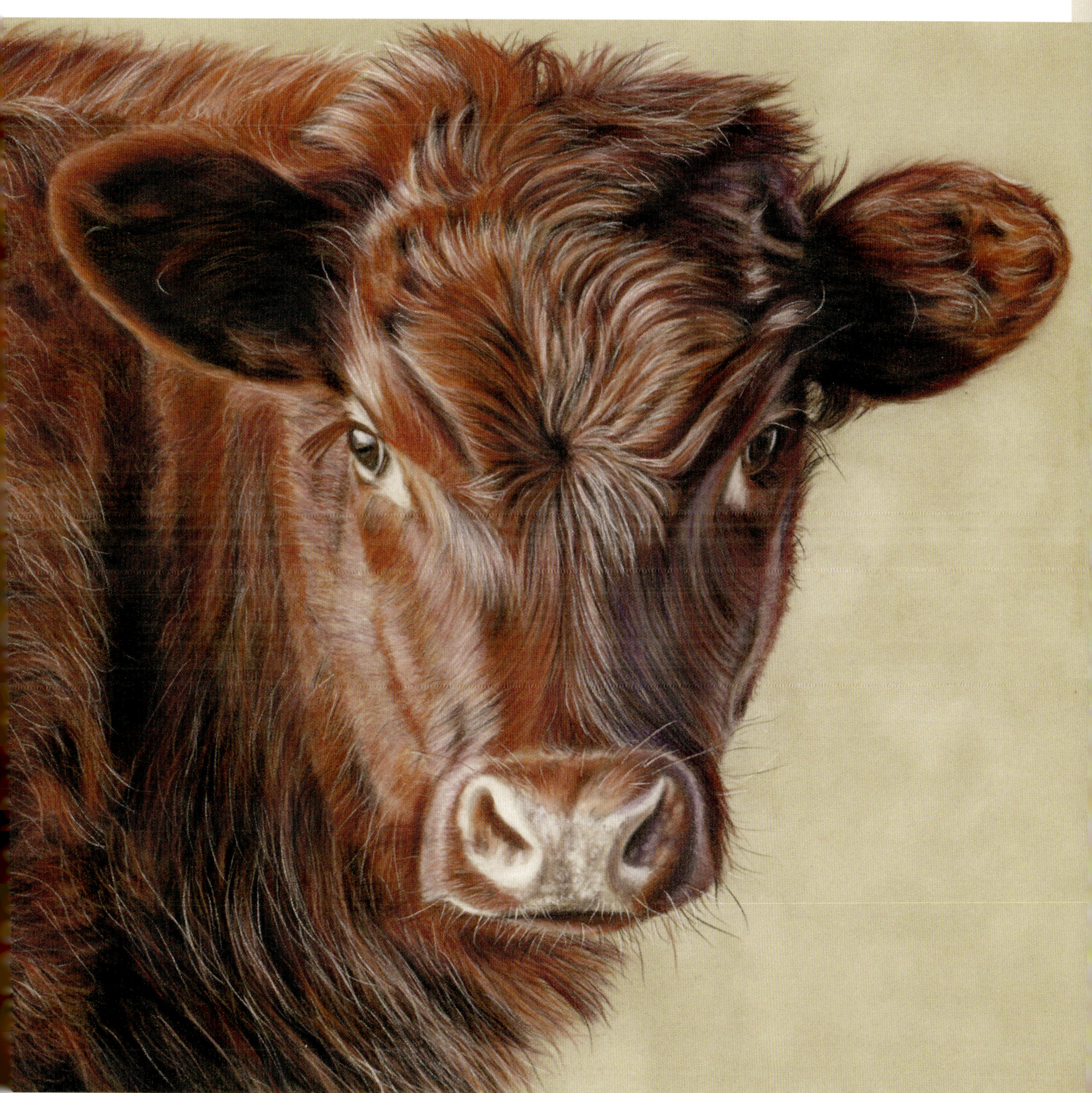

The finished portrait

INDEX

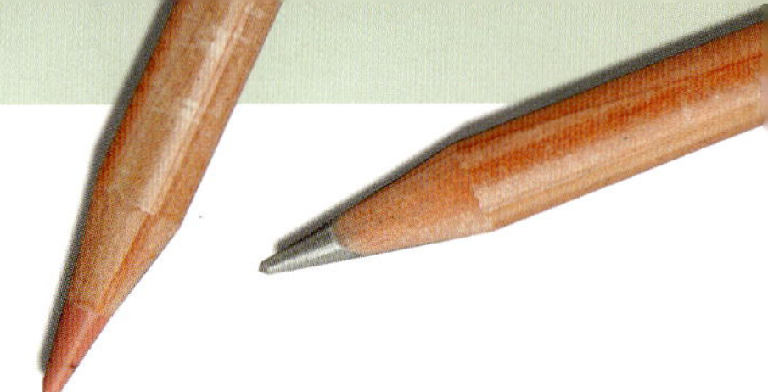